OCEAN PASSAGES

In the series *Critical Race, Indigeneity, and Relationality*,
edited by Antonio T. Tiongson Jr., Danika Medak-Saltzman, and Iyko Day

ALSO IN THIS SERIES:

Quynh Nhu Le, *Unsettled Solidarities: Asian and Indigenous Cross-Representations in the Américas*

Erin Suzuki

OCEAN PASSAGES

*Navigating Pacific Islander and
Asian American Literatures*

TEMPLE UNIVERSITY PRESS
Philadelphia / Rome / Tokyo

TEMPLE UNIVERSITY PRESS
Philadelphia, Pennsylvania 19122
tupress.temple.edu

Copyright © 2021 by Temple University—Of The Commonwealth System of Higher Education
All rights reserved
Published 2021

Library of Congress Cataloging-in-Publication Data

Names: Suzuki, Erin, 1978– author.
Title: Ocean passages : navigating Pacific Islander and Asian American literatures / Erin Suzuki.
Other titles: Critical race, indigeneity, and relationality.
Description: Philadelphia : Temple University Press, 2021. | Series: Critical race, indigeneity, and relationality | Includes bibliographical references and index. | Summary: "Ocean Passages explores how ocean space and the diverse experiences of transpacific passage operate as dynamic sites where Asian American and Indigenous Pacific subjectivities have been formed alongside, against, and in alliance with one another"— Provided by publisher.
Identifiers: LCCN 2020029882 (print) | LCCN 2020029883 (ebook) | ISBN 9781439920930 (cloth) | ISBN 9781439920947 (paperback) | ISBN 9781439920954 (pdf)
Subjects: LCSH: Pacific Island literature—History and criticism. | American literature—Asian American authors—History and criticism. | Ocean travel in literature. | Transnationalism in literature. | Decolonization in literature.
Classification: LCC PN849.O26 S89 2021 (print) | LCC PN849.O26 (ebook) | DDC 810.9/895073—dc23
LC record available at https://lccn.loc.gov/2020029882
LC ebook record available at https://lccn.loc.gov/2020029883

For my family

CONTENTS

Acknowledgments		ix
	Introduction	1
1	Militarized Passages: Securing the Sea	23
2	Refugee Passages: In the Wake of War	57
3	Commercial Passages: On Cycles and Circulations	91
4	Embodied Passages: "Local" Motions and the Settler Colonial Body Politic	127
5	Virtual Passages: Pacific Futures	161
	Conclusion	197
	Notes	203
	Works Cited	225
	Index	243

ACKNOWLEDGMENTS

It has been a true pleasure to write, think, and talk story with the many people who have shaped and inspired this book with their conversation, critiques, and generous support. I'm grateful to have the chance to thank some of them here.

This book been written on the lands and unceded territories of Kānaka Maoli (Hawaiʻi), the Muscogee Creek (Georgia), Te Āti Awara (Wellington, Aotearoa/New Zealand), the Tongva (Los Angeles), and the Kumeyaay (San Diego). I am grateful for their ongoing stewardship of these lands; this book is one way that I have sought to unpack the histories that have helped to bring me into these spaces.

I would not have started on this path if it were not for Daniel Kim, who encouraged me while I was an undergraduate at Brown University to follow my research interests into the literatures of the Pacific. At the University of California, Los Angeles (UCLA), Ali Behdad and Elizabeth DeLoughrey were the best advisers anyone could ask for, not only for bringing my attention to scholarship and perspectives that would inform my research in important ways, but also for being the kind of scholars and mentors that I aspire to be. Victor Bascara, Keith Camacho, King-Kok Cheung, and Rachel Lee were all important teachers and interlocutors for this project, while others—including Michael Colacurcio, Arthur Little, Chris Looby, Chris Mott, and Felicity Nussbaum—helped me to become a published writer and a more polished researcher, speaker, and teacher.

In many ways, the idea for this project first took shape in a conversation with the late Karen Peacock during a visit to the Hawaiian and Pacific Collection of the University of Hawai'i, Mānoa (UHM), library. Its subsequent directions have been inspired by other writers and scholars from UHM, especially Candace Fujikane, ku'ualoha ho'omanawanui, Brandy Nālani McDougall, and Craig Santos Perez. Research grants from the UC Pacific Rim Research Institute, the Ford Foundation, and the Stout Centre at the University of Victoria, Wellington, allowed me to complete my dissertation and pursue further research in Aotearoa/New Zealand. I express my profound gratitude to Joy Enomoto, Kathy Jetñil-Kijiner, Emelihter Kihleng, Brandy Nālani McDougall, Craig Santos Perez, Robert Sullivan, and Konai Helu Thaman for allowing me to engage with and reprint their work in this volume.

Far from the Pacific Ocean, my colleagues at Emory University created a lively and convivial intellectual community. Particular thanks go to Deepika Bahri, Geraldine Higgins, Lawrence Jackson, Abdul JanMohamed, Walter Kalaidjian, Valerie Loichot, Jim Morey, Laura Otis, Ben Reiss, Nathan and Mandy Suhr-Sytsma, and Craig Womack. I have likewise found myself among a truly wonderful community of scholars at the University of California, San Diego, and have found it a great pleasure and privilege to work with, think with, and learn from Jody Blanco, Keva Bui, Gloria Chacon, Yến Lê Espiritu, Amelia Glaser, Greg Pōmaika'i Gushiken, Jin Lee, Sang Eun Eunice Lee, Simeon Man, Wendy Matsumura, Andrea Mendoza, Daisuke Miyao, Jacobo Myerston, Hoang Nguyen, Sal Nicolazzo, Olivia Quintanilla, Shelley Streeby, Riley Taitingfong, Ameeth Vijay, Kamala Visweswaran, Katie Walkiewicz, and Meg Wesling, among others.

I thank the editors Sara Jo Cohen, Sarah Munroe, and Shaun Vigil at Temple University Press for their guidance through the many iterations of this project. I express particular thanks to Iyko Day, Danika Medak-Saltzman, and Antonio Tiongson for their suggestions and support for this project from its earliest stages to its present form. I am also grateful for the generous and very thorough feedback I received from my reviewers, as their suggestions for clarifying and amplifying the book's direction certainly changed this project for the better.

Over the years, this project has benefited from panels, meetings, and conversations across the intellectual communities created by the Association for Asian American Studies, the American Studies Association, and Verge: Studies in Global Asias. I am thankful to Santhosh Chandrasekhar, Jason Chang, Tina Chen, Yu-Fang Cho, Chris Fan, Jennifer Ho, Hi'ilei Hobart, Michelle Huang, Yi-Ting Huang, Sam Ikehara, Doug Ishii, Beenash

Jafri, Joe Jeon, Nhu Le, Andrew Leong, Anita Mannur, Josephine Park, Angela Robinson, David Roh, Iokepa Salazar, Aanchal Saraf, Dean Saranillio, Nitasha Sharma, and Chad Shomura, among many others, for initiating and hosting generative conversations in these spaces.

All along the way, I have been lucky to have had the many friends and colleagues whose encouragement, advice, collaborations, road trips, and impromptu house parties have made this journey a joyful one. At UCLA, Vivian Davis, Betsy Donaldson, Lana Finley, Dustin Friedman, Beth Goodhue, Adam Gordon, Aaron Gorelik, Georgina Guzmán, Laura Haupt, Renee Hudson, Lynn Itagaki, Kim Mack, Kate Marshall, Emily Morishima, Joe Rezek, Maureen Shay, Erin Templeton, Dennis Tyler, Marilu Utomi, Joyce Pualani Warren, and the late and deeply missed Sam See made graduate school a convivial and welcoming place. As a junior faculty member, I am particularly grateful to the writing group friends whose encouragement, advice, and unstinting generosity have inspired and sustained me through the writing of this book, several moves across the country, and the birth of my daughter: my thanks to Aimee Bahng, Munia Bhaumik, Anna Kim, and Jinah Kim.

This book is dedicated to my family: to my parents, Mabel and Tom Suzuki, and my late grandparents Elizabeth and Satoshi Suzuki, who have supported me in all of my endeavors and always emphasized the importance of giving back to the communities that supported and raised me. It is also for Sam and Adela Kullens and the family we have made together. You fill my life with joy.

OCEAN PASSAGES

INTRODUCTION

> If we listened attentively to stories of ocean passage to new lands, and of the voyages of yore, our minds would open up to much that is profound in our histories, to much of what we are and what we have in common.
> —EPELI HAUʻOFA, "The Ocean in Us"

While the focus of Ruth Ozeki's novel *A Tale for the Time Being* (2013) is the relationship between a Japanese teenager named Nao and a middle-aged Japanese North American author—also named Ruth Ozeki—who comes across Nao's journal and letters when they wash up on the shoreline of her island home in Canada, perhaps the most central "character" in the book is the Pacific Ocean that brings them together. The ocean, whose currents bring Nao's words to Ruth's attention, emerges in the novel as an entity that possesses its own, distinct modes of agency and temporality. Not only does it serve as a literal medium of communication between the novel's two protagonists, but its crowded waters, gyres, and tides gesture toward submerged and belated histories that have been ignored or occluded by the capital-driven structures of contemporary transpacific politics, economics, and policy. At various points within the novel, Nao and Ruth imagine the ocean as an animate entity that both exceeds and resists containment by human endeavor. By reflecting on how oceanic circulations highlight the limitations of anthropocentric perceptions of time, space, and self, *A Tale for the Time Being* engages the sea not as an object or metaphor but as an assemblage of material and epistemological complexity.

The tides and currents of the Pacific Ocean are likewise bound together with the violent remnants of transpacific history in Māori (Ngāpuhi) novelist James George's *Ocean Roads* (2006). As in *A Tale for the Time Being*, the trajectory of *Ocean Roads* moves through the Pacific wars of the twentieth century—this time through the complex genealogy of the Henare/Simeon family. Etta Henare is an award-winning war photographer, and her partner, Isaac Simeon, is a British nuclear scientist who developed the atomic bombs dropped on Hiroshima and Nagasaki; their children, Caleb and Troy, end up on opposite sides of the Vietnam War. While these characters' stories move through London, Antarctica, Hiroshima, Los Alamos, and Saigon, the novel remains centered on the family's coastal home at Rangimoana, just outside Auckland. Rangimoana—a place whose very name combines the heavens and the seas—is a space that invokes the ocean, its moods, and its tides. Throughout the novel, we can see Etta in particular filtering and interpreting the world through this oceanic perspective. For example, when she first photographs Isaac in the ocean near her home, she sees him as "a man of waves and troughs," reading his scientific accomplishments through his kinesthetic engagement with the ocean around him; near the novel's end, she turns to the sea and perceives it as an "immense book of ocean waves leafing down to the sand."[1] The novel's other characters and storylines—Isaac's work in nuclear physics, their son Troy's military achievement, their son Caleb's illness, and their daughter-in-law Akiko's choreography—are likewise mediated through an oceanic sensibility that illustrates their interconnectedness and the slow dispersion of their "nuclear" family through the ebb and flow of their lives. In George's novel, history is filtered through an oceanic lens rather than the other way around: instead of representing the sea as an object of study (or even a subjective assemblage, as *Tale* does), *Ocean Roads* posits that the sea operates as both an interpretive framework and a source, rather than subject, of knowledge.

This book attends to these narratives of ocean passage and explores their potential to engage in a deconstructive interrogation of race, subjectivity, and subject formation alongside the Indigenous-centered transnationalism that informs Epeli Hau'ofa's reconceptualization of the Pacific as an expansive, Oceanic "sea of islands."[2] In so doing, I seek to analyze how these ocean passages disrupt and revise hegemonic constructions of the region. If Ozeki's representation of oceanic space seeks to *de*construct hegemonic mappings of the Pacific to reveal the multiplicity of oceanic ontologies, George's novel *re*constructs these submerged or occluded connections through a place-based, Indigenous-centered aesthetic that begins at a specific site on the North Island of Aotearoa/New Zealand and radiates outward to engage with the fraught and violent transpacific histories of the twentieth and twenty-first centuries. While the ocean described by Ozeki breaks down and recombines human refuse and remains, returning them to the shore as so many fragments shorn of context—"fishing lines, floats, beer cans, plastic toys, tampons, Nike sneakers. A few years earlier it was severed feet"—the "ocean roads" described in George's novel extends the protagonists' trajectories from Aotearoa/New Zealand outward to the rest of the world. Yet both novels turn to material and metaphoric qualities of the Pacific Ocean not only to critique how the broader region has been made invisible and instrumental in the transpacific conflicts of the twentieth century, but also to construct ways of imagining otherwise.

In what follows I heed Hauʻofa's call to pay careful attention to these different "stories of ocean passage" as a way to read across the fields of transpacific Asian American and Indigenous Pacific studies for "what we are and what we have in common."[3] More specifically, I argue that these ocean passages operate as critical and dynamic sites from which to analyze how Asian American and Indigenous Pacific subjectivities have been constructed against and alongside one another in the wake of the colonial conflicts that shaped the emergence of the modern transpacific. While the sea has played a central role in Indigenous Pacific thought for centuries, and much of the work published by Indigenous Pacific scholars has repeatedly emphasized the importance of the oceans to Indigenous activism, art, and theories of globalization,[4] transnational Asian American studies—mapped across the same "sea of islands"—has been slower to address this body of Indigenous critique.[5] Yet as Asian American studies has begun to engage more substantively with Indigenous Pacific studies, particularly around the topics of militarization, nuclearization, and Asian settler colonialism, there has been an increasingly "oceanic" turn within the field of transpacific scholarship.[6] This project seeks to build on and extend this work by exploring what new ideas, alliances, and flash points might emerge when comparing and contrasting Asian and Pacific Islander passages across a shared sea. How might centering the Pacific in transpacific studies foreground points of intersection between Indigenous displacements and Asian migrations in the twentieth and twenty-first centuries? How can ocean passages disturb—or reinforce—settler colonial discourses *and* racialized fears of Asian "invasion" that linger as the discursive legacies of European, American, and Japanese imperial projects in the Pacific? How might a range of Indigenous Pacific and Asian American reflections on the meaning and materiality of ocean space serve to rethink and reshape a region that has been constructed largely on its abstraction? And how might a critical engagement with Indigenous studies and decolonial feminisms inform and contribute to theories of relationality emerging in transpacific scholarship in gender studies, science studies, and the environmental humanities?

The stories of ocean passage addressed in this volume highlight kinesthetic, experiential, and nonlinear modes of knowledge drawn from both Indigenous and Asian American histories and epistemologies; they both critique and assemble alternatives to the post–World War II geopolitical formations alternately known as the "Pacific Rim," "Asia/Pacific," and—by the turn of the twenty-first century—the "transpacific." Calling attention to the links between the discursive evacuation of Indigenous presence and anxieties about Asian ascendancy that served as the groundwork for these transpacific formations to emerge, I argue that attending to the ocean passages where Indigenous Pacific and Asian American cultures and communities have been intimately, although unevenly, intertwined is central to reimagining both "a new Oceania" and a "decolonial transpacific."[7] More specifically, I posit that as the term "transpacific" has become increasingly adopted as shorthand for an Asian American or Asian diasporic critique that seeks to move across national borders and boundaries, transpacific scholars must also be rigorous about insisting on its material and cultural entanglements within the Pacific itself—or risk repeating the colonial evacuation performed by earlier "Pacific Rim" formations.[8] Such evacuations of the Indigenous Pacific from the purview of transpacific scholarship illustrate the persistence of what Danika Medak-Saltzman has called the "specters of colonialism" that continue to haunt transnational studies paradigms that aspire to critique and move beyond the settler colonial stakes of the nation by taking for granted inherited scholarly methodologies that make it "arduous to work across disciplinary and temporal boundaries in attempts to call attention to subjects other than those privileged by conventional periodization."[9] In other words, scholarship that frames itself as "trans*pacific*" *must* engage with Indigenous Pacific histories, frameworks, and methodologies, or else the term loses its unique critical purchase. If the term "transpacific" is to meaningfully distinguish itself from the Pacific regional imaginaries that have directly preceded it, then scholars who pursue this line of study must address not only the sociopolitical dynamics and material and cultural objects that circulate between Asia and the Americas, but also how these circulations have been materially and imaginatively shaped by both colonial legacies *and* Indigenous Pacific epistemologies.

It is for these reasons that I return to the figure of passage to frame this study. By focusing on movement *through*, in addition to travel *across*, the ocean, these passages invoke and engage the dynamic potential that inheres in the prefix "trans-," speaking not only to the movements of peoples, objects, or ideas between fixed points, but also to how these very acts of circulation create their own epistemologies of passage with the potential to change and shape the worlds around them.[10] In contrast to neoliberal transpacific frameworks that rely on abstractive or extractive visions of the Pacific, a transpacific studies that remains critically attuned to Indigenous and Oceanic epistemologies can illuminate and emphasize an analytic of *relation*: a mode of comparison malleable enough to note the shifting and relative positionalities of different communities and cultures and the different ways that they continue to be entangled within and responsible to one another's histories. Such a comparative methodology indeed requires, as Hauʻofa observes, careful attentiveness to our varied "stories of ocean passage" in and across the sea, and here his specific focus on the role that *stories* have to play in this process highlights a second meaning of the word "passage": an extract from a book, poem, or other artistic work. Literary study often relies on the extraction of such passages to analyze how texts create and convey meaning, yet in doing so, it is important to preserve the sense of movement and connection that the term "passage" also implies. A text is not an isolated fragment to be explored as an object in and of itself; it also operates as a conceptual *passage*, connected to and emerging from a range of cultural, historical, and aesthetic contexts. Stories of ocean passage ask us to remain mindful of this fluidity and connectivity and to understand how position and context can shape both composition and interpretation. It is to these intersecting and overlapping passages, as articulated in contemporary Indigenous Pacific and Asian American literatures, that this study turns.

Navigating Ocean Passages

Within the mainstream of transpacific discourse, the Pacific Ocean is a site that is often rendered invisible through its very visibility. Often invoked as a site through which the region itself is imagined and brought into being, it is less frequently engaged in terms of its direct or material mediation of broader networks of trade, transportation, and cultural exchange.[11] This tendency to consider oceanic space as a metaphoric rather than material presence is by no means exclusive to transpacific scholarship. As Hester Blum observes, the ease with which oceanic fluidity gets taken up as a metaphor for cultural or historical fluidity means that the sea is often rendered "immaterial" in any number of transnational ocean-centered paradigms, such as Fernand Braudel's "Mediterranean World" and Paul Gilroy's "Black Atlantic."[12] Yet while this "oceanic turn," as Elizabeth DeLoughrey has termed it, has opened up important discussions of historical and cultural dynamics that move both through and beyond national and continental borders, its tendency to abstraction has often served to occlude the material impacts of these flows on both the ocean itself and the Indigenous communities whose relationship to the sea is not merely a metaphor but an important part of everyday life.

While ecocritical scholarship has sought to correct for this abstraction and dematerialization of ocean space by explicitly foregrounding the materiality, agency, and alternative ontologies offered by ocean environments and their inhabitants, these projects sometimes overcorrect, viewing the ocean as a "perspective- and self-dissolving" medium where national and cultural particularities are subordinated to the tides of a "universalizing sea."[13] An emphasis on oceanic materiality in this way can downplay the specific historical meanings of oceanic space to a range of Indigenous Pacific communities, particularly its role in maintaining and preserving a sense of cultural or linguistic community. As Jace Weaver, Alice Te Punga Somerville, Shona Jackson, Teresia Teaiwa, and others have noted, Indigenous histories and cultural productions—including their sustained engagement with oceanic environments—have been largely overlooked in the imagination and articulation of these broader social and environmental networks.[14] Such oversights have worked to implicitly render Indigenous contributions to these transoceanic networks as either absent or relegated to the historical past, bracketing their roles in the unfolding of transnational and ecological exchange and encounter.

These methodological oversights have created their own kind of temporal "drag" on the production of transpacific scholarship that engages the Pacific Islands. While scholars working in postcolonial and Indigenous studies have done important comparative work engaging the literatures of the Pacific Islands,[15] such work has come more belatedly to transpacific Asian American literary studies. This belatedness is in direct contrast to the ease and speed with which the category of "Pacific Islander" has been collapsed into "Asian American," especially in a U.S. academic context. Over the past two decades, the field of Asian American studies has increasingly taken the Pacific Islands into its purview, both domestically, where the demographic category of "Asian American" has increasingly come to include and absorb "Pacific Islander" communities, and abroad, where the field's "transpacific" turn has extended its geographic span through and across the region.[16] Yet even as the changing dynamics of the fields of Asian American and transpacific studies have opened up new ways for scholars and authors to think more critically and creatively about how the literatures, cultures, and histories of Asia and the Americas have mutually influenced one another, for the most part these fields continued to overlook or set aside the role that Pacific Island cultures and communities have played in that process of circulation and exchange, in this way replicating settler colonial erasures of Indigenous presence that form the groundwork for the very imperial mappings that transpacific scholarship challenges and contests.[17] For this reason, many Pacific scholars have expressed ambivalence about, if not outright objection to, the prospect of having their work included within the rubric of Asian American or transpacific studies. As J. Kēhaulani Kauanui, Lisa Kahaleole Hall, and others have pointed out, such inclusion tends to superficially invoke issues that are important to some Pacific Islander communities—particularly Indigenous rights and decolonization—only to subordinate them to critical frameworks that tend to be more hostile to postcolonial forms of nationalism.[18] And while other critics, including Candace Fujikane, Jonathan Okamura, and Dean Saranillio, have drawn attention to how Asian American studies' focus on experiences of diaspora and migration exhibits a tacit acceptance of national narratives, racialized categories, and global networks based on the erasure or appropriation of Indigenous lands, these important discussions of Asian settler colonialism in the Pacific have thus far been most robustly focused on the specific historical and cultural formation of Hawai'i and not directly linked to other sites or modes of transpacific passage where Asian and Pacific Island communities have been drawn together.[19]

As a consequence of these disciplinary omissions, the primary theoretical and intellectual interventions in these two fields—Pacific Islander and Asian American studies—have remained largely separate from each other. Important exceptions include the work on Asian settler colonialism in Hawai'i mentioned earlier and an emerging body of scholarship that explores comparative studies of Asian and Pacific Islander experiences of militarization, nuclearization, and colonial occupation.[20] However, Pacific Islands studies' investment in political and cultural decolonization for the most part has aligned the field more closely within the scholarly home of global Indigenous studies, while Asian American studies' focus on deconstructing racial formations in their historical, economic, and embodied human and nonhuman iterations tends to situate itself within the paradigm of a U.S.-based American studies. By and large, literary and critical works by Asian American and Pacific Island authors tend to reflect these different commitments and trajectories.

Given these disciplinary difficulties, trying to compile a comparative framework for studying Asian American and Pacific Island literatures necessarily struggles against a long history of how these fields (and communities) have been constructed beside, against, or on top of one another. This history, including the more recent history of Asian American and transpacific over-writings of Indigenous Pacific projects, bespeaks the need for care in attempting this comparative critique. As Eve Tuck and K. Wayne Yang have pointed out, there is a need to attend to the fundamental "incommensurabilities" between these positionings and to remain aware and critical of the "settler moves to innocence"—in particular, the "homogenizing of various experiences of oppression as colonization," a tendency that has been called out in debates around Asian settler colonialism.[21] Yet I argue that reading the transpacific in terms of both Indigenous Pacific and Asian Americanist frameworks not only has the potential to contribute to critical discussions in both fields but is a project that is both ethically and intellectually necessary for transpacific studies in particular. Such a move to critically engage Indigenous studies and histories in the emerging discipline of transpacific studies can be seen in recent scholarship on transpacific militarism and imperialism that have remained attentive to their effects on both Indigenous Pacific and Asian/American communities. This scholarship does not render these communities' experiences commensurate or equivalent but foregrounds how they may be *interrelated* through military, commercial, and communication networks.[22] *Ocean Passages* builds on and extends such work by turning to comparative literary and aesthetic representations as a way of reframing critical questions about the relationship of the local and the global as matters of perspective, as well as agency—a move that connects the critical work that has been done on formations of the transpacific with Indigenous critiques of empire and modes of ethical engagement with the region that have framed it as a deeply entangled and interconnected ecosystem that survives, adapts, and recalibrates in striking new ways. To do so, I trace out a literary theory of transpacific entanglement that places the deconstructive critiques foregrounded in Asian Americanist texts in dialogue with the intellectual, social, and aesthetic frameworks based on perspective and relationality that have been addressed in literary and scholarly works by Indigenous scholars and artists. As transpacific Asian Americanist scholarship turns to queer, feminist, and science studies frameworks to reconceptualize intimacies among differently situated human (and nonhuman) communities in ways that disturb the processes of subjectification and commodification responsible for producing a racialized Asian subject,[23] engaging more directly with Indigenous Pacific concepts of relationality is a necessary step in decolonizing transpacific critique.[24] It is to this end that I attempt my own scholarly passage among these incommensurate, yet interrelated, bodies of work.

In thus triangulating Indigenous Pacific, transpacific, and Asian American scholarship, *Ocean Passages* engages a reading practice that draws inspiration from Vicente Diaz and J. Kēhaulani Kauanui's invocation of *etak*—a Carolinian wayfinding technique that requires the navigator to triangulate one's position against known landmarks or phenomena—as a model or metaphor for a comparative Pacific studies that remains focused on local contexts and concepts while also using those terms to navigate and intervene within broader, more global discourses around colonialism, militarization, and late capitalism. The close attention to subtle shifts in context and relation so critical to *etak* and other open-sea navigational techniques operates not as a set of unchanging rules but, instead, as a framework within which different islands (and ideas) may be identified and evaluated in terms of their relationships to one another. Such a sense of place and positioning—in terms of navigating both the open oceans and the practices of everyday life—requires attentiveness to land and sea in equal measure, for just as ideas or concepts about island space cannot be fully imagined in isolation from the seas that surround them, so the oceangoing migrants or vessels also cannot be separated from the grounded histories that serve as their starting points, guidelines, or destinations. Such a "tidalectic" consciousness, as DeLoughrey (citing Kamau Brathwaite) calls it, provides a useful framework for "exploring the complex and shifting entanglement between sea and land, diaspora and indigeneity, routes and roots."[25] Yet in addition to the complex awareness of interconnection and interrelationality that *etak* and tidalectic perspectives engage, in reading these stories of ocean passage I seek also to call up critical moments of disconnection, disruption, and disunity, of passage as not only a mode of connection but also as *impasse* or *trespass*. Particularly in the context of modern Pacific histories of colonialism, conflict, and capital circulation, it is particularly important for transpacific partnerships and frameworks arrayed against hegemonic understandings of the region to remain critically aware of these moments of disjuncture and differentiation.[26]

On Passing, and Not Passing, through the Pacific

Spanning more than a third of the globe, the Pacific Ocean is one of the largest and most culturally and linguistically heterogeneous regions in the world. In addition to being home to a diverse range of Indigenous cultures and communities, the Pacific has also been claimed as a home or as a territory by migrants and settlers from Asia, the Americas, and Europe. The contemporary geopolitics of the Pacific Islands reflect this uneven modern history of settlement, colonial affiliation, and ongoing neocolonial entanglements. While some Pacific states, such as Sāmoa and Fiji, achieved official political independence in the second half of the twentieth century (or, in the case of Tonga, had always retained their political autonomy), other Indigenous Pacific communities—including Kānaka Maoli (Hawai'i), Māori (Aotearoa), Mā'ohi (Tahiti), and Chamorro (Guam)—continue to live under conditions of direct colonization. In addition, there are Pacific states that are politically independent but carry the status of "associated states," such as the Federated States of Micronesia and the Marshall Islands (in association with the United States) and the Cook Islands and Niue (in association with New Zealand). The difficulties that emerge in generalizing about "Pacific" cultures are often tied to the very different histories and cultures of these island communities, as well as to the legacies of colonialism that persist throughout the region.

Indigenous oral histories throughout the region indicate a long history of travel, settlement, and trade; even cultural communities whose origin stories focus on autochthonic creation in situ (rather than arrival from elsewhere and settlement) often indicate their position within broader Oceanic networks of trade, warfare, and alliances.[27] However, while these maritime networks long predate European contact, the tendency to categorize *all* such cultures and communities under the singular geopolitical category of the "Pacific" is, as Te Punga Somerville, Matt Matsuda, and others have observed, a "historically European" concept.[28] The name "Pacific" was first used by the Portuguese explorer Ferdinand Magellan during his circumnavigation of the globe; its eventual dominance—overshadowing other Indigenous names that referred to specific or local areas of the ocean, such as Te Moana-nui-a-Kiwa (Māori, North Island), Eon Woerr (Marshall Islands/Ailingalaplap), and Thakau Lala (Fiji)—paralleled the increasing influence of European and then American power in the region. Yet even as the "Pacific" came to both aggregate and eclipse these particular or localized sites, it also worked to create new networks and possibilities of exchange. In this context, even the name by which the region is called reenacts some of the same alliances and tensions among local, regional, and global commitments that continue to influence policy and practices in the contemporary Pacific Islands.

One way to reclaim these colonial namings and groupings emerged in the period of decolonization in the late 1960s and 1970s, when Indigenous activists and academics began to articulate the concept of a "Pacific Way." The Pacific Way—a term popularized by Fiji's Prime Minister Ratu Sir Kamisese Mara in 1970—highlighted the shared elements of a range of Pacific cultural practices and sought to engage and reclaim a historically grounded sense of coalition and commonality among diverse Pacific Island communities. Sina Va'ai points out that, at its best, the Pacific Way was a powerful force for anticolonial organizing and a "phenomenon that fostered institutions such as the University of the South Pacific and held together regional cooperation amongst former colonial territories . . . recognising the commonality in developmental problems that required a unity in cooperation by communality, collegiality, consensus and working together."[29] Yet it is also a term that became troubling for many of the region's writers and intellectuals, as they saw local elites take advantage of the Pacific Way concept to enrich themselves in a neocolonial global marketplace that increasingly viewed "authentic" traditions and cultural diversity as so many commodities to be "preserved," consumed, or traded. One of the sharpest critics of the Pacific Way ideology was the Tongan scholar and author Epeli Hauʻofa, whose short story "The Glorious Pacific Way" (1983) focused on the comic character "Ole Pasifikwei," a collector of oral histories and tales, to satirize the shift from celebrating and honoring one's cultural background to selling it out to Western development agencies. Yet today Hauʻofa is known less for his cynicism about the possibility for a trans- or pan-Pacific coalition than he is for his influential vision of the region as a networked "sea of islands," which he referred to not as the "Pacific Islands" but as "Oceania."[30] This deliberate renaming, Hauʻofa argues, is not incidental but in fact central to his (re)visioning of the region and its networks: while the term *Pacific Islands*, most commonly used in Anglophone political and economic discourse, foregrounds the geographic smallness and isolation of individual island nations, the Francophone *Oceania* imagines a mapping that "denotes a sea of islands with their inhabitants" and places those cultures and communities firmly at its conceptual center.[31] The "grand and somewhat romantic"[32] implications of the term *Oceania* also marks it out as a more literary or imaginative (as opposed to academic or social scientific) conceptualization of the region; something that Sāmoan novelist, playwright, and poet Albert Wendt also highlights in his essay "Towards a New Oceania":

> So vast, so fabulously varied a scatter of islands, nations, cultures, mythologies and myths, so dazzling a creature, Oceania deserves more than an attempt at mundane fact; only the imagination in free flight can hope—if not to contain her—to grasp some of her shape, plumage, and pain.[33]

For Hauʻofa and Wendt, "Oceania" invokes a dynamic, Indigenous worldview that exceeds the flattening epistemology of "the Pacific." If "the Pacific" served as an equalizing term, seeking to bridge differences and bring diverse people together through the homogenization of space, "Oceania" sought to restore a sense of depth and perspective to those new networks. The reemergence of the term "Oceania" in contemporary Pacific studies discourse speaks to this need to think about contemporary politics and policies in the region not only in terms of fiscal and statistical measurements, but also in terms of local and regional affiliations, habits, genealogies, and practices that long predate the modern nation-state. In other words, Oceania is a term that emphasizes the importance of communities and cultures in *relation*, as opposed to in *aggregation*.

This conceptual shift from thinking through the Pacific as an abstract geopolitical concept to a more multiply sited, relational space has likewise informed the transformation of contemporary Asia Pacific or "Pacific Rim" studies. If, as Rob Wilson and Arif Dirlik have argued, the very concept of the "Asia Pacific" was "dominantly a Euro-American formation" that, from the age of Magellan through the present day, has "shaped and integrated the peripheries and multiple cultures and polities of the region to serve Euro-American interests in the name of God, imperial glory, catapulting profit, and national (/transnational) management," it is a construction that has also seen a significant shift in the late twentieth and early twenty-first centuries.[34] In the second half of the twentieth century, as European colonial powers began to recede from the region, Asian nations such as Japan, Taiwan, Singapore, and South Korea began to emerge as major forces in the global marketplace. This shift in the global capital economy represented by these newly industrializing, non-Western nations led many Western academics, politicians, and policy makers to reconceptualize the "Pacific" as the "Pacific Rim." While imperialist imaginings of the Pacific had posited the region as a boundless expanse filled with territory to be claimed, Pacific Rim discourse, by its very naming, delimits the possibilities of territorial expansion. As Chris Connery points out, the focus on the idea of a "rim" rather than a region is theoretically more egalitarian, as it "presumes a kind of metonymic equivalence" among the nations in its circuit and calls into being "an interpenetrating complex of interrelationships with no center."[35] Yet even if Pacific Rim discourse made concessions to a model that rhetorically decentered Euro-American national interests to take into account the growing economic and political power of East Asian nations, it nevertheless adhered to a teleological framework that continued to promote a capital-driven universalism that focused more on maximizing financial and capital gains. Thus, it privileged the nations that developed a robust industrial or financial infrastructure while continuing to neglect the nations that lacked the means or opportunity to do so—particularly the island nations of the Pacific, which were located off the "Rim" entirely.

This market-driven elision and erasure of the Pacific "Basin" is a direct legacy of colonialism in the region. Paul Sharrad notes that, just as the Pacific had historically been represented as a "passive receptacle of observation, a space for European adventuring, an area of natural science, history, anthropology, and 'development studies,'" these habits of erasure persist in the contemporary juxtaposition of an active, economically vibrant Pacific Rim against a passive, economically dependent Pacific Basin.[36] Teresia Teaiwa highlights the gendered dynamics of this formation in her analysis of "militourism," which she defines as "a phenomenon by which military or paramilitary force ensures the smooth running of a tourist industry, and that same tourist industry masks the military force behind it."[37] In her analysis of this phenomenon, Teaiwa argues that the circulation of images of a "Polynesian body"—usually manifested as a light-skinned and scantily clad female body—operates as a legacy of the colonial, masculinist gaze that continues to be used to promote tourism industries throughout the region. This fetishized "body" not only eclipses and erases the living conditions and cultural and ethnic diversity of the different Indigenous Pacific Island communities throughout the region by homogenizing them as universally feminized and generically "Polynesian"; its seductiveness and promise of leisure also serve to mask the massive military force and military infrastructures required to sustain the hegemony of capital throughout the Pacific. By making the argument that both military projects and capital-driven developments hide in plain sight behind this historically fraught image of the desirable "Polynesian" body, Teaiwa addresses the multiple ways that these ongoing military and touristic projects draw from an explicitly gendered and racialized colonial legacy that continues to place the material cultures, histories, and concerns of Pacific Islands communities under erasure. In short, while "Pacific Rim" discourses intially encouraged a shift away from understanding the region in terms of Western territorial hegemony, by the end of the century they had in many cases been co-opted by the neocolonial dynamics of an emergent neoliberalism that arose as the Cold War era drew to a close, falling back into a rendering of the Pacific as absent or dependent in ways that reiterated and reified the gendered geopolitical assumptions of settler colonial hegemony.

In the years following the "Asian" financial crises of the late 1990s, scholars and policy makers alike shifted away from the capitalist teleology of Pacific Rim discourse and introduced a different term, the "transpacific," as an attempt to think through the region as being composed of a number of intersecting and overlapping relationships rather than as an aggregate of its parts. For scholars and intellectuals critical of U.S. hegemony in the region, this transpacific turn invoked a palimpsestic history of the region that drew attention to its multiple histories of colonization and migration.[38] Yet at the level of international policy making, "transpacific" became a term that attempted to *restore* the balance of powers articulated by "Pacific Rim" formations in ways that adjusted for political and economic changes after the Asian financial crises. Viet Nguyen and Janet Hoskins address these tensions between divergent "intellectual" and "corporate" interpretations of the transpacific, noting that while the latter—exemplified by the politics and policies of capital-driven multistate networks such as the Trans-Pacific Partnership—can be seen as the latest, finance- and trade-driven iteration of an unfolding teleological narrative of "exploration, exploitation, and expansion" in line with earlier colonial discourses, the former opens up to include "alternate narratives of translocalism" that have the potential to challenge and critique those capital-driven networks.[39] I stress the word "potential" here because the porous nature of these multiple transpacifics mean that they, like the many other geocultural constructions and formations discussed in this introduction, necessarily overlap and inform one another in ways that indicate the region's interrelationship and complexity. In other words, while some of these critical transpacific networks, texts, and travelers may challenge certain dominant assumptions about cultural borders and boundaries, they may at the same time become implicated in the creation of other hegemonic attitudes and formations. In particular, as the term "transpacific" has increasingly come to serve as shorthand for transnational Asian American or Asian diasporic cultural and political formations, we must attend to and be cautious about how the *elision* of Pacific history, theory, and scholarship from such frameworks might perform the same discursive evacuation of the "Pacific" in "transpacific" that pertains to "Pacific Rim" models of regional formations.

Given these rapid shifts and changes in Asian American and Pacific Islander alliances and cultural productions, what new transpacific networks, formations, and alliances might emerge when we attempt to view the Pacific through the Indigenous mappings and modes of knowledge production about the region rather than in terms of the top-down approaches favored by the economists and military strategists whose "Rim"-based visions have often resulted in both the erasure and exploitation of the Pacific Islands? How might we use an aesthetics of ocean passage to reflect on the ethics of alterity and assimilation that so often lies at the heart of Asian/Americanist work? How could engaging these Oceanic passages bring together these interrelated concerns around deconstruction and decolonization and aid us in imagining alternative futures for the region? These are some of the questions that push toward the methodological stakes of this work. In this context, my particular interest in *literary* representations of oceanic space in transpacific texts highlights how the intersections and friction points between Pacific Islander and transpacific Asian American literary and cultural praxes might work to complicate the apparent seamlessness of the "Pacific" central to dominant constructions of the region as a "geo-imaginary hallucination" of neoliberal capitalism.[40] As Wilson observes, it is literature that "can help us see . . . links and affects between ocean, self, and planet"; such an "ecopoetic" approach can serve to disrupt the binaristic, "taken-for-granted view of an Asia/Pacific imaginary with Asian cultures and sites cast as transnational capital forces of globalization and set relentlessly against the interior Pacific."[41] While Wilson's essay persuasively emphasizes the strong potential for transpacific ecopoetics to assert important transoceanic affinities and solidarities between Pacific Island and Asian and Asian American communities resistant to the normalization of neoliberal flows through the region, I also want to consider how articulations of difference, disruption, and incommensurability play an important role in the construction of these alternative transnational and transcultural networks. While literature works as a medium through which one encounters ideas, peoples, and situations with which we can empathize and forge new solidarities, it also—as David Palumbo-Liu argues—challenges us to confront our entanglement with forms of alterity that *cannot* be reduced or converted into the "systems and discourses of 'sameness'" that assign value to "others" insofar as their experiences can be understood as somehow commensurate with or related to our own.[42] Indeed, it is precisely the challenge of articulating or expressing different epistemologies and perspectives alongside more dominant viewpoints—and resisting attempts to collapse the former into the latter—that many artists and scholars in and around the Pacific have cited as being central to their aesthetic and activist projects. In contrast to the leveling forces of the policies and proposals that drive modern globalization, literature opens up a space for us to think through the way we establish relationships and affinities with people and entities that are not necessarily bound to the logics of liberal subjecthood.[43]

These interrogations of the liberal subject and its formation are likewise key to transpacific and Asian Americanist interrogations of how the project of liberal subjectification tends to place ethnic and cultural difference under erasure in ways that nevertheless affirm a racialized hierarchy where the Asian subject is always perceived as lacking. As the Indigenous Studies and Asian Americanist critics Aileen Moreton-Robinson, Jodi Byrd, and Iyko Day have argued, the possessive logics that laid the groundwork for settler colonialism and the erasure or overwriting of Indigenous bodies, histories, and epistemologies are also responsible for the racialization of Asian bodies and communities as an alien *threat* to that possession, aligning them with fears of dissolution, abstraction, and formlessness.[44] Kandice Chuh's observation that the very concept of the "Asian American" operates as "a term *in difference from itself*—at once making a claim of achieved subjectivity and referring to the impossibility of that achievement"—reclaims and reverses the critical potential of this racializing gesture, proposing to reconceptualize the field itself as a "*subjectless discourse*" that works to "prioritize difference" by critically analyzing the discursive mechanisms and "regulatory matrices" that make individuals legible (or illegible) as national subjects.[45] This centering of difference in Asian Americanist critique complements Yunte Huang's call for a "poetics of acknowledgement" as a venue for transpacific discourse that seeks to "recogni[ze] the ontological status of the Other and the epistemological gaps in our knowledge."[46] Huang's transpacific operates as a kind of spatial representation of subjectless discourse, described as a "deadly space between" diverse epistemologies and representations that "resist[s] narrative closure and historical teleology as enunciated and projected in transpacific space."[47] In this analysis, the space of the Pacific itself works to destabilize universalizing narratives and abstractions by confronting them with their own contingent and ambivalent constructions.

Yet while Chuh's and Huang's centering of alterity in discursive, spatial, and temporal modes is useful for an Asian Americanist and transpacific theory that thinks through the deconstructive and potentially radical applications of the Asian as a racialized figure of absolute difference, a "subjectless" transpacific critique nevertheless relies on some of the discursive premises that work to erase Indigenous presence in the region. For example, Huang's transpacific imagination represents the region primarily as a manifestation of discursive gaps or aporias, an "unfathomable chasm filled with perilous water."[48] Rendering place into space in this way problematically forecloses on Indigenous epistemologies that exhibit an entangled and intersubjective relationship to the lands and seas, where social constructions of Oceanic space are tied to its currents, tides, winds, and other phenomena: transforming this ecosystem into discourse renders such Indigenous epistemologies likewise "unfathomable." Similarly, Moreton-Robinson and Byrd have qualified Chuh's call for a subjectless discourse, noting that the very attempt to move away from the requirements of subjectivity inadvertently fixes or reifies those requirements as the domain of the possessive individual subject. By contrast, Moreton-Robinson argues that Indigenous subjectivity "is embodied, it is ontological (our being) and epistemological (our way of knowing), and it is grounded within complex relations derived from the intersubstantiation of ancestral beings, humans and land. In this sense, our sovereignty is carried by the body and differs from Western constructions of sovereignty, which are predicated on the social contract model, the idea of a unified supreme authority, territorial integrity, and individual rights."[49] Byrd points out that this entangled Indigenous subjectivity means that Indigenous peoples "cannot be made subjectless, because they are the site of difference from Western delineations of citizenship, rights, and inclusion that the settler state proffers as possession."[50] In an Indigenous context, then, the quest is not for subjectlessness but for an expanded conception of what subjectivity might entail.

While Asian Americanist and transpacific feminist criticism in particular have turned to new materialist and science studies frameworks to likewise think through what it might mean to expand the concept of subjectivity beyond the frame of the liberal individual,[51] Indigenous Pacific feminist and gender studies critics have long grounded their critiques of settler subjectivity in place-based epistemologies that decenter the assumptions and gaze of the male settler subject. Such practices are inextricable from the process of cultural and political decolonization and contain many of the formal and theoretical tools for articulating a worldview that considers human and nonhuman entities as always already in entangled relation. While such practices vary across different sites in the Pacific, there are a number of concepts that many Oceanic communities hold in common, including "spiralic" rather than linear conceptions of time; the use of genealogy as rhetorical praxis and strategy; the deployment of resonant metaphorical imagery that carries different meanings in different contexts; and the practice and art of weaving and/or cloth making as both literary trope and metaphor for community formation.[52] In terms of representing oceans, ocean passages, and terraqueous environments in particular, these Oceanic literary tropes and critical praxes emphasize an engagement with alterity, albeit one that is slightly different from the ethics of "otherness" addressed in Asian Americanist critique. Alterity in Oceanic discourse is engaged by the dynamic interactions of human and nonhuman agents in and around the ocean: a "seascape epistemology," as Karin Amimoto Ingersoll calls it, that speaks to a form of knowledge linked to a "visual, spiritual, intellectual, and embodied literacy of the ʻaina (land) and kai (sea): birds, the colors of the clouds, the flows of the currents, fish and seaweed, the timing of ocean swells, depths, tides, and celestial bodies all circulating and flowing with rhythms and pulsation."[53] The embodied quality of this knowledge means that it cannot be entirely abstracted from experience and practice and is less concerned with "knowing" (in a Foucauldian sense—that is, abstracting and claiming) the sea as with being able to *live within* and *alongside* it, a practice that includes being able to live with its vicissitudes and uncertainties. While the particular seascape epistemology that Ingersoll describes is connected to a Kanaka Maoli (Native Hawaiian) context and culture, its "approach to life and knowing through passageways" clearly resonates with a number of other Oceanic cultures and traditions.[54] As a number of Pacific scholars have observed, many Indigenous Pacific understandings of and relationships to the ocean similarly understand it as coextensive with—rather than separate from or opposed to—environments and peoples on the land, an expansive space that serves an important connective function between island cultures and communities.[55] As Hauʻofa puts it, "The sea is our pathway to each other and to everyone else, the sea is our endless saga, the sea is our most powerful metaphor, the ocean is in us."[56]

If transpacific Asian American literatures and scholarship have sought to assert the critical value of alterity or "otherness"—particularly by drawing attention to how the ocean's unknowability marks the limitations of contemporary colonial, postcolonial, and neoliberal discourses—Indigenous Pacific scholarship has addressed how a grounded engagement with otherness can work to produce decolonial forms of discourse by shifting the terms and frameworks for transnational (and transpacific) engagement. It is my hope that bringing these transpacific Asian and Indigenous Pacific literary and cultural texts into dialogue will help us to understand how a subject shaped by oceanic passage cannot be defined entirely through state-sanctioned forms of subjectification (such as citizenship status, ethnicity, or blood quantum); nor can it exist entirely independently of such forms (as in the idea of a "postnational," "postracial," or purely nomadic individual). Instead, the texts I explore in this book foreground the flexible and enduring nature of cultural practices, community formations, and legal regimes across periods of significant political and social change. Tracing these trajectories across space and time, these varied representations of oceanic passage index the many ways that these diverse forms and practices are not only deconstructed but also *re*constructed at moments of cultural crisis and creative transgression.

Such a comprehensive project could certainly span the length of several books, and it is my hope that the comparative frameworks and reading practices initiated here can serve as a starting point for future investigations and scholarly endeavors. My own limitations as a scholar have served to determine the limitations of this particular project. First and foremost, I do not have reading fluency in Indigenous Pacific or Asian languages, so my archive has been limited to English-language sources. Fortunately, a number of other scholars have already begun to address these important bodies of literature.[57] Even thus delimited to the English language, I still have an immense number of texts with which to work; in consequence, *Ocean Passages* focuses primarily on literature and texts produced after World War II, a historical period that, as discussed earlier, saw formal decolonization, heightened militarization, and the emergence and development of neoliberal networks of trade and finance throughout the region. This body of contemporary Indigenous Pacific and Asian American literature is, of course, vast and continually growing and is well beyond the scope of a single project. Earlier iterations of this project included analyses of a number of works and texts that, while certainly relevant to the governing concept of ocean passage, unfortunately could not be comfortably included within the frameworks that I set out here. I have excerpted and published, or plan to publish, some of this work elsewhere.[58] I also want to both acknowledge and regret the glaring absence of Pacific literature from western Pacific sites such as Fiji, Papua New Guinea, and the Solomon Islands from this project and refer readers to scholars who have discussed the literary and cultural dynamics of the western Pacific, as well as their role in the decolonization movements of the 1960s and 1970s, in greater detail.[59]

Each chapter of this book addresses a different, yet interrelated, form of oceanic passage. Chapter 1, "Militarized Passages: Securing the Sea," begins with an exploration of militarized oceanic passages, emphasizing how the (U.S.) occupation and militarization of ocean space and environments from the Cold War through the present connect racialized colonial power dynamics in Asia and the Pacific Islands. In the chapter I read George's *Ocean Roads* alongside James Michener's *Tales of the South Pacific* (1947) to analyze how the space of the ocean, and the experience of its crossing, might serve as a potential site of resistance against the militarized claims of nation-states that seek to reterritorialize and secure the space of the ocean for the interests of "liberty." The chapter interrogates how these writers use oceanic imagery to explore the connections that emerge among different communities affected by militarized violence in its various forms to foreground the range of new networks, communities, and alliances brought into being by the legacies of postwar militarization. Chapter 2, "Refugee Passages: In the Wake of War," builds on this analysis of militarized ocean space to focus on the specific trajectories and experiences of refugee passage across the ocean and to consider how they take shape in the "wake" of war. Here, I read Vietnamese American writer lê thi diễm thúy's novel *The Gangster We Are All Looking For* (2003) alongside Marshallese poet Kathy Jeñtil-Kijiner's work exploring the history and experiences of peoples displaced from the Pacific Islands by both nuclearization and climate change to explore how their representations of oceanic passage emphasize the entanglements and interconnections between environmental trauma and global migration. Together, these texts outline the occlusions and intersections of refugee experience in and across the Pacific—whether spurred by wartime atrocity or economic and environmental crisis—and amplify the necessity of placing these differently situated experiences into dialogue with one another.

Chapter 3, "Commercial Passages: On Cycles and Circulations," explores comparative representations of the passage of labor across and through the ocean—particularly the migratory circuits traced by remittance laborers, as described in the work of Chinese American fiction writers Ken Liu and Maxine Hong Kingston and Tongan authors Epeli Hauʻofa and Konai Helu Thaman—to analyze how these authors' focus on the *labor* required for the oceanic passage of peoples, communications, and commodities draws attention to the materiality of ocean space that often gets overwritten in more abstract discussions of transpacific trade. The chapter explores how both Asian and Pacific Island writers critique the neocolonial dynamics that emerge out of the capitalist deterritorialization of the Pacific in the late Cold War era, as hegemonic representations of the transpacific begin to shift from viewing the region as a theater of war to reimagining it as a space of capital. If, as Connery has observed, "water is capital's element," these texts emphasize how the ocean may *also* be understood as an integral conceptual and material medium that works to bridge heterogeneous cultures of circulation that run alongside or counter to dominant flows of transpacific capital.[60]

Moving from an analysis of these broadly transpacific movements across and through the Pacific to a specific site where these Indigenous and immigrant circulations intersect, Chapter 4, "Embodied Passages: 'Local' Motions and the Settler Colonial Body Politic," focuses on Hawaiʻi to analyze how discourses around state multiculturalism become enfigured (and commodified) as a multicultural "local" body that simultaneously invokes and evacuates Indigenous (Kanaka Maoli) presence. Turning to the work of Hawaiʻi-born Japanese American author Lois-Ann Yamanaka and Kanaka Maoli poet and scholar Brandy Nālani McDougall, the chapter explores the possibilities for communities that have been differently shaped by their experiences of settler colonialism to identify themselves with projects of Indigenous sovereignty that fundamentally reject the racialized assumptions of settler colonial nationalism. To this end, I focus on these authors' representations of the experience of moving through and with the ocean—of ocean passage as an embodied act—as a way of either opening up or closing down new possibilities of imagining a "local" or emplaced identity that meaningfully engages and supports, rather than simply gestures toward, Kanaka Maoli sovereignty.

Chapter 5, "Virtual Passages: Pacific Futures," analyzes how these varied forms of ocean passage, in tandem with a range of contemporary technologies, articulate different ways of imagining the future of the region as a whole. Although scientific, industrial, and communications technologies are often closely aligned with visions of transpacific futurities connected to a progressive temporality that aspires to increasing security, accumulation, and profit, in this section I return to *A Tale for the Time Being*, considered alongside texts by Pacific Island poets Robert Sullivan (Māori), Emelihter Kihleng (Pohnpei), and Craig Santos Perez (Chamorro), to articulate how these alternative speculations inspire, disrupt, and repurpose imaginations of economic futures bound to the securitizing of the Pacific as a region. In line with the cyclical nature of the oceanic aesthetics featured in these texts, and the methodology of this study as a whole, the chapter illustrates how perceptions of time itself are meaningfully shaped not only by the introduction of contemporary technologies, but also by Oceanic ecologies and epistemologies. By concluding with these explorations of oceanic temporalities, I hope to show how these varied aesthetics of oceanic passage might help us to situate our own varied passages through and across the Pacific in time as well as space. The ocean passages laid out in the twentieth and twenty-first centuries have been indelibly marked by our modern histories of colonialism, militarization, extraction, and pollution—yet they are also marked by a number of other histories and experiences of passage that have pushed back against the seeming inevitability of the present system. As seen through an Oceanic imaginary, these passages are not fixed lines on a map but operate as contingent passageways, navigated through a firm understanding of one's position and standpoint measured in a constantly changing relation to a fluid, dynamic world.[61] By remaining attentive to how their unfolding calls attention to context *as* trajectory—that is, understanding where we, and they, stand *in relation to* the past, the present, and one another—these ocean passages can help to chart the way forward to what, as Albert Wendt once declared, we might think of as a new Oceania.

1

MILITARIZED PASSAGES

Securing the Sea

Like the ocean from which the region draws its name, the Pacific serves as a deceptively peaceful moniker for a geopolitical space built on militarized conflict. From the colonial wars of the nineteenth century through the trade wars of the twenty-first, the "Pacific" has come to describe a diverse network of states whose peoples, politics, and environments have been shaped and reshaped by international struggles for global hegemony. Of these multiple and often overlapping conflicts, the battles between the United States and Japan during World War II—known as *the* "Pacific War" in Japan and the United States—have occupied a central and representative space in the construction of the contemporary Pacific. While the complex genealogy of the militarized Pacific both precedes and reverberates well beyond this particular era, the ideological and infrastructural legacies of the era served to both extend and occlude the ways that the ongoing presence of the U.S. military throughout the region operated as an extension of colonial projects in Asia and the Pacific, even through the period of formal decolonization in the 1950s–1980s.[1] The postwar narratives that reframed World War II as a "good" or just war positioned it as a war of liberation, in which the United States fought to free Asian and Pacific peoples from the illiberal fascism represented by Japanese imperialism.[2] Yet the freedoms that the United States won for the region were largely defined by, and dependent on, the establishment and maintenance of U.S. military infrastructures and institutions throughout the region. While a number of Asian and Pacific states declared formal independence in the second half of the twentieth century, many of them—such as South Korea and the Philippines—were nevertheless obliged to maintain established U.S. peacekeeping forces and military bases. Other states, such as the Marshall Islands and the Federated States of Micronesia, became "trust territories" subject to U.S. administration, while the island nations were supposedly being prepared to become self-governing states. In this way, the "decolonizing Pacific," as Simeon Man has called it, marked a "historical conjuncture when anticolonial movements in the United States, Asia, and the Pacific became intertwined with the U.S. militarization drive to secure the global capitalist economy,"[3] leading to the paradoxical and—in the cases of Korea and Vietnam—ultimately incendiary situations where decolonial and independence movements were curtailed by the promotion of *liberation* through *securitization*.[4]

This ambivalent synthesis of liberation and securitization would likewise influence postwar policies toward the administration of the oceans and high seas. The decision of the United States to take over active trusteeship of a number of Micronesian island nations—aggregated together as the Trust Territory of the Pacific Islands (TTPI) under an agreement struck with the United Nations in 1947—was influenced not only by lingering colonial attitudes that saw these island nations as *not yet* fit for self-rule, but also by significant changes in international policy toward marine and ocean space that ultimately led to a "radical territorial shift" that framed oceans as resources that could be claimed and administered by individual nation-states.[5] As Elizabeth DeLoughrey argues, the beginnings of this shift can be traced to a proclamation issued by President Harry S. Truman shortly after the end of the formal hostilities of World War II. As tensions between the United States and Russia began to ramp up near the war's end, military surveys discovered significant mineral and oil deposits on the sea floor. On September 28, 1945—less than a month after the surrender of Japan—President Truman issued an executive order that claimed exclusive rights to the "continental shelf" surrounding the United States, a space that included seabed resources extending far beyond the three miles that traditionally had marked a nation's territorial borders at sea. Ratified into international law by the United Nations Convention on the Laws of the Sea (UNCLOS) in 1982, Truman's proclamation ultimately resulted in the ability for coastal nations to claim up to two hundred miles of offshore resources as part of their exclusive economic zone (EEZ). This was, to be sure, a sweeping grab for (oceanic) territory: DeLoughrey points out that, following the annexation of the TTPI in 1947, the provisions of the proclamation effectively added "3.9 billion acres of submarine land and resources" to the United States, tripling the size of its jurisdiction.[6] Yet the proclamation itself repeatedly frames the United States' claim in terms of "conservation" and "prudent utilization," emphasizing the idea that such territorial oversight was necessary to permit the "orderly development" of extractive activities.[7] Indeed, the proclamation posits that "the exercise of jurisdiction over the natural resources of the subsoil and sea bed of the continental shelf by the contiguous nation is reasonable and just" precisely because "the effectiveness of measures to utilize or conserve these resources would be contingent upon cooperation and protection from the shore."[8] Here, the logics of securitization are clearly at work: to *conserve* the ocean's resources from the threat of overdevelopment, to *protect* against the danger of worldwide shortage, and to *preserve* the "free and unimpeded navigation of the seas" (which the proclamation notes "are in no way thus affected" by territorial claims to the seabed), these spaces must be surveilled, controlled, and patrolled.[9] Not unlike the U.S. military's postwar presence in the Pacific, where the United States likewise sought the "orderly development" of democratic nation-states in the face of the rising threat of communism, the government's intent to cultivate the Pacific Ocean itself as a militarily useful, and potentially profitable, site of extraction served to inaugurate the postwar Pacific as simultaneously a resource and a threat.

In this chapter, I read political, popular, and literary representations of these militarized oceanic passages through the Pacific against the transformation and extension of colonial power dynamics in the region during this period of formal decolonization. I argue that the legacies of both settler colonialism and Orientalism—which cast Asia and the Pacific Ocean as sites of subordination, subversion, and sacrifice—operate as racializing technologies that both anticipate and work alongside new undersea technologies to render the Pacific into a site of extraction. I begin by reading Indigenous critical theory against the post–World War II shift from the doctrine of the free seas (*mare liberum*) to the establishment of EEZs in order to draw out some of the ways that political and aesthetic representations of ocean space have been inextricably bound together with colonial discourses of race and racial hierarchy. As an example of how this racialized legacy came to be mapped onto postwar attitudes toward the Pacific Ocean, I read representations of Pacific and Asian peoples and environments in James Michener's best-selling *Tales of the South Pacific* (1947) alongside political discussions and debates around the status of the oceans and the incorporation of military bases and island territories in Asia and the Pacific during the early years of the Cold War. These texts celebrated the establishment of a militarized, infrastructural order over Pacific Island spaces—an order that discursively depended on rendering a wide range of Indigenous

Pacific peoples, Asian migrant laborers, and oceanic landscapes as interchangeable and synonymous entities. Yet by the turn of the twenty-first century, these romanticized narratives of oceanic "trusteeship" had begun to break down as the human and environmental costs of these attempts to territorialize the Pacific became more and more difficult to ignore. In the last section of this chapter, I return to Māori novelist James George's *Ocean Roads*—briefly discussed in the Introduction—to explore how its oceanic aesthetics usefully illustrate the entangled social and environmental effects of settler colonial dispossession, military campaigns waged in Asia, and nuclear testing in the Pacific Islands. George's novel provides a striking contrast to the heteropatriarchal fantasies established by U.S. narratives around environmental and social trusteeship of the Pacific Islands in the postwar era. While Michener's *Tales of the South Pacific* reimagines the region as a mixed-race family headed by a Western patriarch, George's *Ocean Roads* focuses on a family headed by an Indigenous matriarch—a family whose unresolved pasts highlight the continuities between the militarized postwar order and earlier colonial histories that framed both the Pacific Ocean and its peoples as resources to be exploited or threats to be mitigated. Although they are physically and psychologically marked by the effects of this history, the family at the heart of *Ocean Roads* shows that while the militarization of the Pacific was intended to expand the influence and interests of the United States in Asia, it also had the concomitant effect of creating a number of new and unexpected affinities, affiliations, and formations that would be shaped, but not confined, by the logics of securitization. In this context, *Ocean Roads* highlights how both oceans and peoples resisted these physical and conceptual modes of containment as their trajectories and travels moved them through and across the borders, boundaries, and territorial lines intended to keep them in check.

Whose Sea of Islands? From *Mare Liberum* to EEZs

In *The Transit of Empire*, Jodi Byrd places Indigenous critical theory at the center of contemporary debates around race, migration, and imperialism. Arguing that the "imperial planetarity" that gave rise to modern concepts of scientific rationality and liberal humanist beliefs in the freedom and equality of peoples was constructed around "discourses of savagery, Indianness, discovery, and mapping that served to survey a world into European possession by transforming indigenous peoples into the *homo nullius* inhabitants of lands emptied and awaiting arrival," Byrd cites passages from the Declaration of Independence and the U.S. Constitution to illustrate how this concept of "Indianness" has long been evoked to "evacuate sovereignty and international recognition from any nation or peoples the United States may one day seek to invade."[10] Framing non-Western peoples first as hostiles to be destroyed, then as "wards" to be assimilated into the U.S. imperium, this evocation of a "paradigmatic Indianness" operates as what Byrd calls a "transit"—a process in which the United States and other Western imperial powers expanded their influence and hegemony by repeating these foundational discourses of settlement as they appropriated territory across the North American continent and, by the turn of twentieth century, in and across the Pacific Ocean.

While Byrd's work focuses primarily on how the discursive transformation of Indigenous peoples into *homo nullius* corresponded to their political dispossession through the doctrine of *terra nullius* ("nobody's land," or land perceived by international law as empty or evacuated of sovereignty), Teresia Teaiwa has noted a similar dynamic at play in twentieth-century renderings of the Pacific as an invisible or empty space. This "objectification by rendering invisible" allows for the ongoing marginalization and erasure of Indigenous Pacific Island communities whose bodies suffer under conditions of colonial rule and environmental degradation.[11] The claims of Indigenous island and coastal communities to sovereignty over coastal waters and ocean space are similarly rendered invisible under the law, as their rights to traditional ocean resources and fisheries have been appropriated through a corresponding doctrine of *mare nullius*. For example, in the 1992 court case *Mabo v. Queensland* (no. 2), a ruling credited with overturning the doctrine of *terra nullius* in Australia by formally acknowledging prior land claims made by the Indigenous Meriam peoples of the Torres Straits, sovereignty over the sea spaces that also constituted the traditional territory of the Torres Straits Islanders was not, and still has not been, granted.[12] Even in cases where customary title has been granted to Indigenous people to use the oceans and waterways in accordance with traditional or customary practices, they are not allowed to prevent other actors from intervening in the space.[13] This is because the sea is still held—following the doctrine of *mare liberum*—to be a common property. Yet this "common property" model, as Sandra Pannell argues, not only has the potential to "deny the rights and interests" of the people who hold *customary* title to the ocean space, but it also serves to "deny the existence of the holders themselves. Not just a case of *mare nullius* but *homo nullius*."[14]

If, as Byrd posits, the transformation of Indigenous peoples into *homo nullii* operates as the transit through which modern empires have asserted their claims to territory around the globe, then by extension the discursive dispossession of Indigenous islanders and coastal tribes has likewise served to expand these empires' access to, and sovereignty over, the space of the sea. Yet what has allowed this maritime imperialism to hide in plain sight is precisely the way that the post-1945 territorialization of ocean space simultaneously champions and rejects the idea of the "free sea." The concept of *mare liberum*, first articulated by Dutch jurist Hugo Grotius in 1609, claimed the sea as a space whose "common use is destined for all men."[15] This declaration of the sea as an international commons, while broadly egalitarian in theory, in practice worked to benefit certain constituents over others. Grotius's doctrine of the free sea was primarily designed to arbitrate European trade in Asia and certainly did not take into account the extant rules and customs governing trade, fisheries, and waterways set down by Asian and Pacific Island peoples that had both predated European contact *and* provided the conditions for European trade in Asia to emerge.[16] Nor, as Renisa Mawani points out, did Grotius or subsequent interpretations of *mare liberum* "consider the *rights* of indigenous and/or Asian rulers to set their own course for maritime commerce, or to refuse European encroachment in their territorial waters."[17] As a result, the doctrine of *mare liberum* ultimately served to heighten territorial control and competition among different European colonial projects rather than to dismantle them.

While early modern concepts of *mare liberum* imagined the sea as a "free" space, they did not consider it an empty one. Mawani draws an instructive contrast between ocean space as imagined by Grotius's 1609 treatise and German theorist Carl Schmitt's interpretation of the oceans in *Land and Sea: A World-Historical Meditation* (1942) and *Nomos of the Earth* (1950): although both Grotius and Schmitt drew legal distinctions between land and sea space based on an understanding of ocean environments as fundamentally separate and distinct from terrestrial ones, Schmitt's work naturalized conflicts in world history by recasting them as battles between "land powers" and "sea powers," where "land powers"—states that derive their wealth from the earth—are pitted against the "sea powers" that derive their wealth from trade and technology. Like Grotius, Schmitt did not take into account non-Western cultural practices and attitudes toward their environments as he formulated his theory of elemental and unending conflict between land and sea, which he saw as repeating itself in a range of conflicts, from the battles between ancient Rome and Carthage through the developing Cold War rivalry between Russia and the Anglo-American world. Ultimately, Schmitt argued that the "unfettered technology" pioneered through the "maritime existence" of states such as Great Britain and the United States had allowed "sea power" to dominate the character of the current era and predicted that the state that "succeeds in *corralling* unfettered technology in order to dominate and insert it into a concrete order" would be the one that would dominate the next era of human history.[18]

At the time of Schmitt's writing, the state that appeared furthest along in the process of "corralling" technology toward the project of establishing a "concrete" global order was a resurgent United States, which had recently emerged victorious on the European and Pacific fronts of World War II. Technologies that had been developed for tracking submarines and scouting out underwater terrain during the war were transformed into tools used to survey and map the ocean floors, leading to discoveries of rich mineral and oil deposits. Such technologies effectively reterritorialized the sea, expanding a terracentric approach to land management—including the application of national boundaries and borderlands—to the sea floor. The Truman Proclamation's assertion of U.S. claims to the resources of this newly discovered undersea territory thus united the technological developments of Schmitt's conception of sea power with the territorial claims of land power while simultaneously claiming to uphold the doctrine of *mare liberum*, which it redefined as a right of "free and unimpeded *navigation*" through the high seas. In this sense, the proclamation combined elements of both Grotius's and Schmitt's thinking about the role of oceans in a modern global order into a paradoxical construction—one in which the space of the ocean must be secured as territory to become free to all.

The postwar reterritorialization of the sea was made possible not only through developments in sonar and other maritime technologies but also through the deployment of what Wendy Kui Hyong Chun has called "race and/as technology"—that is, how race has operated as a technology that mediates between biological/material and social/cultural worlds.[19] Chun argues that the ability of this racial technology to transform humanity into "standing-reserve" relies on a specific perspective (or "enframing," drawing on terms from Martin Heidegger) in which nature and humanity are seen as raw materials fit for exploitation or development. This racializing technology is part of the process Byrd highlights in her analysis of the figure of the *homo nullius*, or "paradigmatic Indian," in which the simultaneous threat and allure of the Indigenous "other" is used as the occasion for the expansion of imperial dominion over the resources of the land *and* the seas. Just as Schmitt viewed the sea as an elementally alien space that could be dominated only through the development of maritime technologies, postwar U.S. policy aimed at managing the Pacific relied on the racializing technologies of *homo nullius*, which reinscribed the seabed as frontier, making it legible as an exploitable resource.

To give just one example of the continuing impact of this frontierization of ocean space, I briefly turn to the ongoing controversy around the right of Māori iwi (tribes) to gain sovereignty over the foreshore and seabed territory adjoining or extending their titled lands in Aotearoa/New Zealand. While some scholars and community leaders have pointed out how the establishment of EEZs have helped to expand the political and economic influence of independent coastal and island states in the Pacific, the "foreshore and seabed" controversy speaks to the way that the reconceptualization of the seabed *as a national property* continues, under conditions of settler colonialism, to rely on the nullification of Indigenous concepts of land and sea as a continuous and coextensive space.[20] In 1963, Waata Tepania, a leader and elder of the Aupori and Rarawa iwi, applied for a freehold order (right to tenure) in respect to the foreshore of Ninety-Mile Beach. This foreshore was known to have been occupied and used by the Aupori and Rarawa before the 1840 Treaty of Waitangi, the document responsible for the establishment of the state of New Zealand. However, the resulting case—*In Re the Ninety Mile Beach*—established that the Crown held the rights to the foreshore, denying Māori title claims below the high-water mark. This ruling drew an explicit distinction between "land" and "sea" and argued that the investigation of Native title to lands *contiguous* to the foreshore paradoxically extinguished claims to the foreshore itself. While this decision would be overruled in the 2003 case *Ngati Apa v. Attorney General*, which upheld the right of the Māori Land Court to determine title to the foreshore as well as to contiguous lands, the subsequent passage of the Foreshore and Seabed Act of 2004 by the New Zealand Parliament vested full ownership of the foreshore and seabed in the Crown to provide for the "*recognition and protection* of ongoing customary rights to undertake or engage in activities, uses, or practices in areas of the public foreshore and seabed," as well as to "participate in the administration of a foreshore and seabed reserve."[21] As with the Truman Proclamation, the language of this law asserts that the *state* will provide the "recognition" and "protection" necessary for the free exercise of "customary rights" and will serve as the custodian or guardian of the ecosystem for future generations; yet in the year following the passage of the act, the state considered applications from international corporations interested in mining iron sands off the Raglan coast, and the Crown granted a private company the right to explore the seabed off the western coast of the South Island for gold deposits.[22] Although the act was subsequently overturned and replaced by the Marine and Coastal Area/Takutai Moana Act of 2011, which amended the previous act by vesting the foreshore within the public domain rather than the Crown, the law still frames the contested area as lying within the purview of common use, whose openness to all residents of Aotearoa/New Zealand is guaranteed by the state. In both acts, the state's position posits that tribal use rights are subject to a concept of free access that conceives of foreshore and seabed as both an alienable property *and* a public commons secured by the state. As with the case of the Torres Strait Islanders and other Indigenous coastal peoples living in settler colonial nations, this extension of a land-sea binary to the ocean—with premises to sovereignty based on a land-based model of property ownership—serves to further dispossess and displace Indigenous claims to place-based sovereignty, as those claims are often themselves built on the more fluid and relational premises of ocean-centered epistemologies.[23] In other words, just as a terracentric perspective—based on an understanding of land and sea environments as being not only materially but politically distinct spaces—has long served to frame the Pacific Islands as sites for exploitation due to their perceived status as remote "islands in a far sea," it is also consonant with the conceptual and legal transformation of ocean space *into* landed territory: territory from which the Indigenous community can be dispossessed. As marine technologies for exploring the sea floor have increasingly extended the undersea boundaries of coastal and island states—and improved the possibilities for its exploitation and extraction of mineral and other resources from that space—the ocean-centered vision of an interconnected "sea of islands" seems increasingly threatened by what DeLoughrey has termed a new "scramble for the seas," a twenty-first-century parallel to the colonial "race" for continental territory that characterized an earlier era of colonialism.[24]

Yet this technology-aided transformation of oceanic space into submarine territory comes with its own internal conflicts and contradictions. In contrast to Indigenous epistemologies that view land and sea as connected and coextensive, the Western cultural imagination has long represented oceans as an "alien" space—which, like Byrd's "paradigmatic Indian" (or, for that matter, the figure of the "subversive" Asian)—that appears as "a stranger who may be friend or foe."[25] Stefan Helmreich notes that this oceanic "alienness" not only enfigures the promises and perils that oceans pose for humankind; it also emerges at precisely the moments at which "uncertainty overtakes scientific confidence about how to fit newly described life forms into existing classifications or taxonomies, when the significance of these life forms for forms of life—and particularly, for secular, civic modes of governance—becomes difficult to determine or predict."[26] The potential *subversiveness* of oceans—exemplified by its simultaneous gifts of life and death and its resistance to externally imposed systems of control—is cautiously addressed through the language of oceanic stewardship and conservation, particularly as it emerges in the second half of the twentieth century. At the same time, this perceived "alienness" of oceans can also serve, as Stacey Alaimo notes, to encourage not only resource extraction but also its conceptual *evacuation*: one material result of thinking about oceans as "alien" space is that the damage done to them can be easily dismissed or forgotten, since they seem so "radically disconnected" from the land.²⁷ Both of these attitudes toward an "alien" ocean can be seen in attitudes and policies toward the Pacific Ocean in the decade immediately following World War II. The Pacific was seen as a necessary resource to be plumbed, a potential site of subversion, *and* an "empty" dumping ground for toxic wastes and fallout. Against the ocean's alienating unpredictability, mid-twentieth-century policies toward the governance of ocean space—particularly those initiated by the United States—approached the Pacific as a space requiring both *management* and *infrastructure* through a mode of conceptual enclosure that paralleled the militarized strategy of containment during these opening years of the Cold War. These territorial approaches to managing ocean space were profoundly intertwined with U.S. attitudes toward Asian and Pacific Islander populations during this period. These communities were seen as potential allies and resources in the United States' fight against communism; yet at the same time, their racialized bodies marked them out as potential sites of subversion or sacrifice.²⁸ Ultimately, however, both oceans and peoples could not be contained or constrained by these militarized infrastructures, as their transpacific trajectories highlighted both the limitations of—and the collateral damage caused by—the U.S.-led project of "securing" the seas.

"You've Got to Be Carefully Taught": Gender, Race, and Space in the Postwar Pacific

On September 2, 1945, a Japanese delegation surrendered to the United States aboard the *USS Missouri*, officially ending the hostilities of World War II. On September 28, President Truman issued an executive order laying claim to an unspecified area of seabed territory beyond the continental borders of the United States. While these two events do not, on the surface, appear to have much to do with each other, they were both foundational to the expansion of U.S. power in the region. In contrast to the celebration and regular rehearsal of the end of the war with Japan, the Truman Proclamation—and its unilateral appropriation of a vast seabed territory—goes largely unremarked within mainstream public discourse. Yet it was the Truman

Proclamation that allowed the United States to lay claim not only to the Marshall Islands and Federated States of Micronesia, island states formerly occupied by the Japanese, which the United Nations designated as "trust territories" of the United States following Japan's surrender, but also to the ocean space and resources surrounding them, providing the conditions for the Crossroads tests at Bikini Atoll in 1946.

The visibility of Japan's surrender and rehabilitation forms an instructive counterpoint to the *invisibility* of U.S. imperialism via the Truman Proclamation. These two moves formed the conceptual foundation of the Pacific Rim–Pacific Basin dyad that became the dominant geopolitical imaginary of the "Pacific Rim discourse" that emerged from these militarized passages.[29] If the justification behind the U.S. reconstruction of the region depended on the *visible* defeat of a hostile enemy and that enemy's reeducation and assimilation into a democratic world order, the transformation of oceanic space under the Truman Proclamation from *mare liberum* to *mare nullius* depended on rendering both oceanic ecologies and Oceanic communities *invisible* against a backdrop of increasing global militarization.[30] Together, these contrasting lenses—one highlighting Asian bodies, the other erasing Pacific Island ones—served to bolster Cold War narratives that sought to distinguish U.S. imperial designs from the colonial projects of an earlier era.

To give one example of the role that racial visibility played in the construction of this postwar narrative of transpacific benevolence, we might consider the "Hiroshima Maidens," twenty-five young Japanese women who were horribly scarred as children by the dropping of the atomic bomb. In 1955, Norman Cousins, the editor of the popular *Saturday Review*, raised money to bring them to the United States for plastic surgery, and in his editorials following their progress, he emphasized how the women's surgery operated as a metaphor for their country's reconstruction. As Christina Klein notes, the Maidens "marked the shift away from the terms of wartime propaganda and toward new terms that fit with Japan's postwar status as an ally and subordinate partner. . . . Their wounds marked them as human beings with whom Americans could identify and feel sympathy, and their femininity distanced them from the masculinity of the Japanese military."[31] The episode also cast the United States in the role of benefactor and savior. The public rehabilitation of the Hiroshima Maidens provided a model of transpacific amity and healing that reflected favorably on American economic abundance, scientific prowess, and personal generosity.

By contrast, the horrific effects of the ongoing nuclear tests in the Pacific on the Indigenous peoples of the Marshall Islands were not publicized and remained, for the most part, classified information. As cancers and other disorders manifested themselves in the bodies of the Marshallese people exposed to the extraordinarily high levels of radiation caused by nuclear fallout, U.S. government agencies represented them as test subjects rather than victims to whom Americans might relate. When the residents of Rongerik and Rongelap atolls were exposed to nuclear fallout following the Castle Bravo nuclear test in 1954—the same test that exposed a group of twenty-three Japanese fishermen to nuclear radiation, causing an international incident and providing the inspiration for the Japanese *kaiju* (monster) film *Godzilla*—they were initially evacuated from the islands. However, they were allowed to return two years later, even though the islands still exhibited evidence of radioactive contamination. While repatriation posed a clear hazard to the indigenous population's health, it was also seen by scientists at the Atomic Energy Commission (AEC) as an opportunity, as one scientist observed, to "go back and get good environmental data . . . so as to get a good measure of the human uptake when people live in a contaminated environment." The scientist's relative indifference to the suffering of the Marshallese people doubled down on the colonial trope of "savagery" versus civilization as he went on to note that, "while it is true that these people do not live . . . the way Westerners do, civilized people, it is nevertheless also true that these people are more like us than mice."[32] This framing of Indigenous Pacific bodies as death-bound test subjects ("more like us than mice") served to further erase their voices—and the evidence of colonial violence enacted on their bodies—from emerging discourses around global nuclear power. These discourses framed the dangers of nuclear fallout as the fatal effects of a generalized human hubris rather than holding the U.S. government accountable for the explicit damages to people and environments caused by the military technologies they had designed and tested on properties they supposedly were holding "in trust" for the benefit of its inhabitants. This "nuclear universalism" also worked to frame Japan and the Japanese as paradigmatic victims, eliding their role as a wartime aggressor and imperial power.[33] While such reflections on the dangers and damage of nuclear warfare thus allowed for the recuperation of U.S.-Japan relations in the Cold War era, it was nevertheless a transpacific partnership whose premises relied on the implicit and continued erasure of both nations' imperial legacies in the Pacific Islands.

These implicit tensions in post–Cold War narratives about Asia and the Pacific furthered the conflation of Asians and Pacific Islanders in the popular transpacific imagination, with the latter largely disappearing into the former. The Cold War Orientalism that sought to contain, recuperate, and assimilate Asian bodies as visible signs of U.S. benevolence depended on the repression and conceptual evacuation of Pacific Island communities precisely because they bore witness to the ways that U.S. militarism extended colonial legacies in the region.[34] Indeed, the deliberate conflation of Indigenous Pacific bodies with Asian ones in this era expresses a variation and extension of the colonial project that Maile Arvin has called "possession through whiteness," which she defines as the processes through which the production of social-science knowledge in the early twentieth-century sought to naturalize Western possession of the Pacific by positioning Polynesians as an essentially mixed yet also predominantly white race.[35] Arvin argues that by racializing Polynesians as "almost white," Euro-American colonialism was reframed as a *restorative* project that allowed "white settlers to claim, in various ways, rightful and natural ownership of various parts of Polynesia."[36] In a similar vein, J. Kēhaulani Kauanui points out that laws around "blood quantum" in Hawai'i—which specified the percentage of documented Indigenous "blood" required to be recognized as such—sought to frame Polynesians, particularly Kānaka Maoli, as a discrete racial group to limit their ability to lay claim to contested territory. White settlers who moved to the islands and intermarried with Kanaka Maoli women could thus deploy these "blood logics" to secure their claims to Hawaiian territory as *property* while simultaneously excluding nonquantifiable modes of relating to space and place, such as genealogy and descent lines, from serving as legitimate claims to living on the land.[37] In short, while the hybridization of whiteness provided Anglo-American settlers with the ability to exert increasing colonial control over the Asia-Pacific region, the hybridization of Polynesian Pacific Islanders served to further dispossess them of their rights and sovereign claims to lands and seas.

These colonial attitudes toward race and territory, in which the assimilation of peoples and lands was a project intended to operate more or less unidirectionally, continued even through the more liberal turn of transpacific discourse in the postwar era. Although Asians were frequently contrasted with Polynesians in the years leading up to World War II—with Polynesians often standing in as a proxy for an "Indigenized" whiteness against a rapacious Asian threat—in the years following the war, both Asian and Polynesian bodies circulated, sometimes interchangeably, in ways that emphasized their perceived assimilability to whiteness or American citizenship. As Lisa Kahaleole Hall and others have observed, over this period, Asians came to stand in for Polynesians (and, especially when it came to questions of U.S. statehood, for Hawaiians), and Polynesians/Hawaiians also came to stand in for non–Polynesian Pacific Islanders, particularly the

Micronesians and Melanesians who tended to vanish from public discourse at the very same time that they were seeking to establish national independence.[38] The cultural work enacted by popular circulations of these "almost white" (and usually female) bodies served to shift the biological destiny of the United States from a narrative of racial homogeneity to one of multicultural hegemony.[39] While opposed to expressions of explicit racism, these narratives and celebrations of multiculturalism nevertheless continued to rely on an implicit racial hierarchy. These stories' multiculturalist emphasis on intermarriage and cross-cultural romance ostensibly sought to combat race prejudice, yet nevertheless preserved a colonial attitude that imagined genetic hybridity as a solution to perceived racial failings and to once again naturalize, through the medium of intermarriage, Western claims to Pacific (and Asian) territory.[40] Likewise, it was made clear that the Asians and Pacific Islanders who were adopted into this system were subordinate partners who had to leave behind their old ways and become *educated* into the ways of Western modernity.[41] Like their homelands and territories, which were being reconstructed or held "in trust" by the United States, both Asians and Pacific Islanders were seen as potential resources in need of protection, conservation, and development.

This emergent narrative of liberal expansionism took on concrete literary expression with Michener's *Tales of the South Pacific*. His fictionalized version of his experiences serving in the Pacific theater of World War II received widespread acclaim: the book was a national best seller, won the Pulitzer Prize in 1948, and was adapted as the popular Rodgers and Hammerstein Broadway musical *South Pacific* in 1949. It also served as explicit propaganda for the expansion of U.S. power and ongoing militarization of Asia and the Pacific. This work was certainly on Michener's mind when he began to collect and draft the material that would make up the narrative of *Tales*: he noted that if "America was committed to the retention of bases in the Pacific, then many Americans would have to live in the region, and living there would not be as bad if silly preconceptions were not allowed to prejudice first judgments."[42] The "silly preconceptions" that Michener sought to unseat with his writings were, first and foremost, American racial prejudice against the Asians and Pacific Islanders who occupied the islands and oceans of the South Pacific. The stories in the collection most directly concerned with performing this kind of racial liberalism are the collection's tales of romance, including "Our Heroine," which follows a working-class southerner, Nellie Forbush, in her (successful) attempt to overcome race prejudice by marrying Emile DeBecque, a French plantation owner with mixed-race children; "Fo' Dolla," which follows an upper-middle-class northerner, Lieutenant Joe Cable, in his (unsuccessful) attempt to overcome both race and class prejudice through his romance with a young Tonkinese (Vietnamese) girl; and "Those Who Fraternize," which details a love triangle among two naval officers and Latouche Barzan, DeBecque's eldest mixed-race daughter. Particularly in "Our Heroine" and "Fo' Dolla"—the two short stories from the collection that would eventually be adapted into the musical *South Pacific*—Michener emphasized the important role that romantic and domestic intimacy had to play in the establishment of the American presence in the Pacific and how racial prejudice would have to be overcome for that future-oriented mission to succeed. While Nellie Forbush rejects her Arkansas fiancé and the idea of returning to Little Rock, choosing instead to embrace DeBecque's mixed-race family and the challenges of life in the South Pacific, Lieutenant Cable rejects his love for the Tonkinese girl Liat because he is unable to imagine a future for himself beyond his prescripted life as the son of an upper-middle-class, mainline Philadelphia family. Nellie lives on and presumably prospers as a new settler on the emergent Pacific "frontier," while Cable, with little left to live for, dies heroically on a beachhead. Both Americans, portrayed as having been profoundly changed through their experiences with interracial intimacy, operate as agents who help to develop the material and cultural infrastructures of U.S. hegemony in the region. Cable's sacrifice helps to establish a key airstrip that proves pivotal to the war effort, and Nellie is destined to raise her biological and adoptive children to guide and intermarry with the "fine American young men" who will eventually be stationed at military bases on the island.[43] In this way, the results of their romantic adventures provide the bases for the indefinite extension of U.S. presence in the region.

While "Our Heroine" and "Fo' Dolla" (and later the musical and film *South Pacific*) emphasized the *intimate* infrastructures of U.S. militarization in the region, the other stories in Michener's collection address the development of its *material* infrastructures, along with the bureaucratic and informational apparatuses necessary to the waging of war. The entire collection is loosely set up around a series of events leading to a pivotal battle on the fictional island of Kuralei, which serves as the background connecting the various short stories and vignettes. The stories "Alligator," "The Airstrip at Konora," and "The Strike," in particular, operate as odes to military logistics. "Alligator," which details the extensive planning that went into the siege at Kuralei, emphasizes the hierarchy of central planning over local conditions. As the unnamed narrator notes, the campaign, codenamed Alligator, "was a triumph of mind, first, and then of muscle. It was a rousing victory of the spirit, consummated in the flesh."[44] Unlike the Allied victory at the battle of the Coral Sea, which is depicted in *Tales* as only a contingent success, Michener depicts the fictional Kuralei campaign as a battle that was won before it was even begun. "Alligator" details the sheer amount of planning and knowledge production that went into the campaign: the entire plan was hatched by military strategists in Washington, DC; distilled down to a single book; and brought by the narrator from Pearl Harbor to the fleet admiral at Noumea in a "medium-sized briefcase, unusually heavy."[45] This book contained information regarding all environmental elements that might bear on the execution of the campaign, including the weather ("At this time of year no hurricanes are to be expected. There is, however, record of one that struck three hundred and eighty miles southwest of Kuralei in 1897"), the local flora ("If something looks good, smells good and tastes good, eat it!"), and the Indigenous people ("The natives on Kuralei should be presumed to be unfriendly. Long and brutal administration under the German was not modified by the Japanese. . . . Under no circumstances should they be used as runners, messengers, or watchers").[46]

The parallels between local environments and the people who live within them, as described by the campaign book, illustrate the extent to which the U.S.-based military viewed Indigenous people as an extension of the local environment: they were viewed as an elemental factor—like the hurricanes—that could be predicted and planned for from the distance of the U.S. mainland. This conflation of local peoples and local landscapes continues throughout the collection. In "Fo' Dolla," when Lieutenant Cable returns to Bali Ha'i after being told that his Tonkinese lover Liat has gone to marry another, he sees the island for the first time with the cold eye of a military strategist rather than an eager lover. In this context, he sees a "useless little island with a few coconut trees and a mysterious wartime family of women. The channel was sometimes blue, but no important craft could ever find harbor there, and those little black children, if left alone, would soon revert to savagery."[47] In parallel to the landscape itself, Cable sees the Indigenous inhabitants of the island as needing consistent and responsible management, lest they "revert" to their "savage" ways—or, like the natives of Kuralei, be otherwise bent to subterfuge and sabotage through cruel treatment.

Indeed, throughout the collection Melanesians are consistently portrayed as being the most alien and least assimilable of the Pacific races, the farthest removed from a shared or common humanity. Even in stories that explicitly sought to disturb the color line in the American imagination, the apparently inassimilable blackness of the Melanesians illustrated the limits of Michener's racial liberalism. The successful interracial, transpacific family unit modeled by the conclusion of "Our Heroine" stops short of incorporating Melanesians into the scene of domestic intimacy: the deceased mother of two of DeBecque's children is repeatedly referred to as "Polynesian"; and while she is clearly intended to stand in for all nonwhite Pacific Island races to Nellie's prejudiced mind, the substitution of a lighter-skinned Polynesian woman for the more local (and logical) choice of a Melanesian woman speaks to the writer's and audience's potential discomfort with the transgressiveness of a relationship between a white man and a dark-skinned Melanesian woman. Such discomfort illustrates the implicit antiblackness at the heart of the project of settler colonial discourses in the Pacific, as Pacific Islanders' proximity to blackness comes to symbolize discourses of indigeneity that remain at odds with white settlers' attempts to naturalize their own claims to the region.[48] The novel's (and later the film's) persistent erasure and exceptionalization of Melanesian peoples from the very islands to which they have genealogical and historical claims is a direct outgrowth of the project of settler colonialism, which itself is rooted in the racial project of white possession.

The short story "Fo' Dolla" lays out a different aspect of white possession in a scene in which the Tonkinese Bloody Mary is shown exerting her own "endowed rights over the inferior Melanesians," as she "clear[s] the way for the greater nobility, a white lieutenant, to step ashore" on the islands.[49] This satirical aside not only works to establish the figure of the Asian indentured laborer in terms of its proximity to whiteness; it also shifts the labor of maintaining this racial hierarchy to Bloody Mary herself. If Michener positions the Indigenous body as aligned with the raw materials and environments of the Pacific while white Americans represent the strategic planning needed to construct the material infrastructures supporting the U.S. military presence in the region, the Asian (and particularly the mixed-race Asian) body is made to serve as the affective or libidinal infrastructure that binds the former to the latter. The short story "Those Who Fraternize" describes how DeBecque's four grown mixed-race daughters acquired American husbands, and they come to embody both the means to and justification for a continued U.S. presence in the Pacific. The DeBecques apparently desire the protection and affluence represented by the American soldiers, while the bonds of marriage and kinship give the soldiers an excuse for remaining. Racially mixed individuals of Asian, Polynesian, and European descent, the DeBecques operate as biopolitically valuable subjects who serve to conflate *race* and *indigeneity* in ways that ignore the colonial violence inflicted on Indigenous communities, preemptively framing the land as a "white possession" through a "discourse of security."[50] The DeBecques are the only island-born people in the novel who are able to clearly express and pursue their wishes; their desires thus come to stand in for the desires of all the peoples of the islands—even though they themselves are not indigenous to this space. Their desiring and desirable bodies are used to serve as the biopolitical vector through which the United States naturalizes its militarization of the region.

The domestic bonds forged by the DeBecques and the Americans ultimately work to shape a militarized future in which, as the American officer Tony Fry, the eldest DeBecque daughter's lover and a major recurring character in *Tales*, predicts, "We'll all be out here again. We'll be fighting China or India or Malaysia. Asia's never going to let Australia stay white.... This is the crossroads of the world from now on."[51] Against Fry's vision of an inevitably militarized transpacific future, all other possibilities—however briefly addressed in the novel—are explicitly foreclosed. Such alternative futurities include, for example, the more subversive model of interracial intimacy modeled by the mysterious Remittance Man (in the short story "The Cave") who marries a local Melanesian woman, integrates himself into the local society, and is not only the sole Westerner in the book to establish a robust relationship with the Indigenous Melanesian communities, but also the only one to refer to Indigenous people by their given names and the places they are from ("Basil and Lenato from Malaita. Jerome from Choiseul. Morris and his wife Ngana from Bougainville").[52] Yet Fry—like the Remittance Man and Joe Cable—dies during the war, leaving his legacy and future vision of imperial liberalism incomplete. In the collection's final story, the book's unnamed narrator visits the graves of these three men and contemplates the potential future directions of the region: a strong and expansive U.S. presence fueled by Fry's attitude of racial liberalism or a weak imperialism corroded by race prejudice. At the end of Michener's novel, the future of American empire is left uncertain: while the book's largely sympathetic portrait of Fry and others like him suggest that both Michener and his narrator remain convinced that the Pacific will be secured as a "white" space, that optimism is balanced against the ongoing threat of regression, dissolution, and decay. If Michener's *Tales* sets the blueprint for the progressive narratives that allowed the postwar American occupation of the Pacific to be framed as a just cause, it also hints at the *contingency* of these narratives and speaks to the need for regular maintenance and reinforcement at both physical and psychological levels.

Although Fry is presented as the most racially liberal character in the collection, his prediction that "Asia's never going to let Australia stay white" illustrates how white possession continues to lie at the heart of the temporal logic of American expansion, as this projected use of force to defend "white"

Australia explicitly relegates Indigeneity/Aboriginality to the past and renders Asian aggression inevitable. In Fry's (and Michener's) analysis, military infrastructures in the Pacific required consistent maintenance against this future threat, which—at the time *Tales* was published—was shaping up to be the worldwide battle against communism, which in the Pacific arena was already emerging as a conflict with China. Just as the physical infrastructures of the military and communications installations required regular maintenance and construction to stand against the degradation caused by the environmental effects of the ocean and seascape, the affective infrastructures that governed relationships among Pacific Islanders, Asians, and Americans required regular maintenance through the development of a racial liberalism that rejected racial *prejudice* while maintaining racial *hierarchy*. This rejection of racial prejudice is made explicit in Richard Rodgers and Oscar Hammerstein II's musical adaptation, particularly in the song "You've Got to Be Carefully Taught," in which Lieutenant Joe Cable bitterly explains to Emile DeBecque that Americans like he and Nellie are not *born* with racial prejudice but, rather, instructed into it. The implication of the song, of course, is that if one can be "carefully taught" racial prejudice, one can also be educated *out* of it. Yet in the musical and film version, Nellie's education is considered complete when she is able to shed her personal racial prejudices to take her place within an undisturbed racial hierarchy—as a parent to DeBecque's two young mixed-race children. As Klein notes, Nellie's maternal love for DeBecque's children "offers a sustainable model of interracial relations" that maintains the colonial conceit of adult white Westerners supervising children coded as ambiguously Asian or Indigenous.[53] (The casting of the children in the film, identified as Polynesian but played by Asian actors, further performs the disappearance of Indigenous identity into Asian visibility in ways that extend and disguise the film's colonial context.) These ambiguously raced children are viewed as figures who must also be "carefully taught" to participate—albeit as proxies and subordinates—within the transpacific modernity that U.S. militarization has brought into being.

This concept of *wardship* as a way to establish a liberalized racial hierarchy supporting the ongoing U.S. military occupation of the region mirrors how discourses of sustainability and custodianship were being deployed, on political and environmental fronts, to justify the United States' territorial expansion into the Pacific. In this sense, Nellie's adoption of the two DeBecque children, which concludes the stage and film versions of *South Pacific*, parallels the U.S. acquisition of the real-life Micronesian and Melanesian islands as a "trust territory" in 1947. Like the Japanese imperial forces that preceded it, the United States was able to acquire trusteeship over these Pacific Islands largely by virtue of already having established a military presence there.[54] The mandate or terms of this trusteeship, as outlined in the United Nations Security Council's Resolution 21 (1947), required that the "Administering Authority"—in this case, the United States—work to "promote the *development of the inhabitants* of the Trust Territory toward self-government or independence."[55] This "development" included the encouragement of "economic advancement and *self-sufficiency* of the inhabitants," to which end the United States was granted the authority to "regulate natural resources, encourage the development of fisheries, agriculture, and industries; protect the inhabitants against the loss of their lands and natural resources; and improve the means of transportation and communication."[56] Ironically, the developmentalist rhetoric of the resolution that established the TTPI—which framed the trustee states as currently incapable of self-government and assigned the United States to educate them toward the goal of self-sufficiency and eventual "independence"—was complicated by the same resolution's designation of the territory as a "strategic area" that "shall play its part . . . in the maintenance of international peace and security." To this end, the United States was given authority to "establish naval, military, and air bases and to erect fortifications in the Trust Territory"; to "station and employ armed forces in the Territory"; and "to make use of volunteer forces, facilities and assistance from the Trust Territory in carrying out the obligations toward the Security Council undertaken in this regard by the Administering Authority." In moments when different parts of the mandate came into open and obvious conflict—for example, when the injunctions to "protect the inhabitants against the loss of their lands and resources" and to "protect the health of the inhabitants" came up against the "requirements of security," which the United States took to include the nuclear tests that caused catastrophic damage to the lands, resources, and health conditions in the territory—the needs of *security* always won, exposing the colonial logic served by both the developmentalist bent of the resolution and the sentimental liberalism featured in cultural texts such as *Tales from the South Pacific*. Indeed, Fry's observation that the Pacific might be seen as the "*crossroads* of the world from now on" takes on a hard double meaning when read against the events surrounding the novel's publication: as Michener was writing his novel in 1946, the United States inaugurated the Operation Crossroads nuclear test to great fanfare and publicity. The highly destructive but photogenic explosions created a worldwide sensation, even as the effects on the displaced Marshallese population were largely overlooked or forgotten. In this process, the very island that bore the brunt of the bomb's destructive power, Bikini, became eclipsed by the skimpy two-piece swimsuit that came to take its name—a conceptual displacement that, as Teresia Teaiwa points out, *reveals* to *conceal* the traces of gendered, racial, and colonial violence responsible for its production.[57]

In the decades that followed, the social and ecological effects of the United States' trusteeship of its Pacific Island and oceanic territories began to manifest in increasingly visible and violent ways. Narratives addressing these political and environmental legacies of World War II were better able to accommodate the voices and perspectives suppressed by the ideological constructions of a postwar transpacific order expressed in popular fictions such as *South Pacific*. While Rob Wilson, Paul Lyons, and Vernadette Gonzalez have pointed out that the musical's sustained popularity reveals how the Pacific Islands continue to be subjected to "militouristic" or "histouricist" discourses that depend on a "fantasy of Pacific space imposed upon Hawai'i" and other U.S.-occupied Pacific sites,[58] new narratives around the legacies of the postwar Pacific sought to highlight the damaging consequences such fantasies had on people and environments across the region. If the interracial intimacies of Michener's *Tales* and the expansion of territorial control achieved under the aegis of "security" in the early years of the Cold War had sought to both reinforce and sustain the inevitability of an "American" Pacific, by the end of the century the growing ecological and social costs of ongoing warfare in Asia and the Pacific began to draw critical attention to the contingencies and contradictions on which these militarized networks were constructed.

Through a Different Lens: Rewriting the Militarized Pacific in the Post–Cold War Era

Even as Michener's *Tales* mapped out a progressive romance of democratic expansion in the "American" Pacific during the 1940s and 1950s, conflicts attending the decolonization of Asia and the Pacific Islands indicated that the project of securing Asia and the Pacific could never be quite so clear-cut or simple. While Michener's fictional hero Tony Fry predicted that ongoing U.S. military presence would be necessary because "Asia's never going to let Australia stay white," the Cold War militarization of the Pacific served instead to illustrate Western nations' reluctance to allow Asian and Pacific nations to fully decolonize. Although these decolonization movements did not all *begin* in the postwar era, the stark contrast between U.S. rhetorics of liberation and the realities of ongoing militarization, colonial administration, and economic dependence certainly contributed to their increasing sense of urgency. As European colonial rule began to give way to U.S.-led hegemony, principles of self-determination increasingly came into conflict with the imperial logics of securitization as government opposition to Asian and Pacific independence movements were frequently framed in the name of state or global security. Indigenous sovereignty activists, such as those involved in the Maʻasina Rule movement in the Solomon Islands in the 1940s, were prosecuted by British colonial governments as subversive actors who posed the threat of "organized terrorism and robbery of the native people."[59] During the same period, U.S. military actions in Asia found justification through the idea of "containing" the global communist threat emerging in the newly decolonized nations of Korea and Vietnam. Far from providing a stable structure for a newly decolonial Asia-Pacific to assimilate peacefully into a new, democratic world order, U.S. military infrastructures sought to contain and control the rising tide of anticolonial sentiment throughout the region.

This gradual shift away from midcentury optimism about the liberatory potentials of transpacific military infrastructures to a growing awareness of the complex realities of decolonization and democratization coincided with increasing scientific attention to the dynamism and complexity of the oceanic and atmospheric environment. While advancements in technology increasingly allowed nation-states to survey and exploit the ocean's undersea resources, the ability to collect and assess more detailed information about the ocean, its currents, and the surrounding atmosphere also led to a greater understanding of how military and industrial technologies were affecting the environment as a whole. To take one example, information gleaned in radiation studies carried out by the AEC in the wake of nuclear tests in the Pacific were central to shaping the emergent field of ecosystems ecology.[60] In a study performed in 1954 in the wake of the nuclear testing at Enewetak Atoll in the Marshall Islands, the ecologists Eugene and Howard Odum pioneered the field of "radiation ecology," which explored how radioactive materials dispersed through their interactions with both biotic and abiotic elements of the surrounding environment. While the Odums' research method was based on an assumption that island and ocean environments could operate as a relatively independent or closed ecosystem, the classified research program Project SUNSHINE (1955–1958) drew samples—sometimes illegally and without consent—from a broad range of subjects from around the world to illustrate that the dangers of nuclear fallout could not be contained to a single area but were, through atmospheric and oceanic dispersal, spread across the globe.[61] Oceanographic studies from this time period likewise illustrated how not only nuclear but also *carbon* wastes created by fossil fuel–based technologies carried the potential for global environmental impact. Roger Revelle of the Scripps Institute—initially commissioned by the AEC to track the diffusion of radiation through open ocean currents—became intrigued instead by variations in the ocean's temperature at different depths, which he connected to the ocean's limited ability to absorb atmospheric CO_2. In 1957, Revelle and the chemist Hans Suess posited that the oceans were able to absorb only about a quarter of the anthropogenic CO_2 circulating in the atmosphere; this meant that most of it either remained in or would return to the atmosphere, where its overall rise had the potential to lead to global climate change.[62] Taken together, these landmark studies of environmental science not only highlighted the profound entanglement of human and nonhuman actors within a given ecosystem, but also emphasized how the environmental consequences of militarization and industrialization resisted local containment to become truly global in scope and effect. While such studies were, in many ways, shaped by the assumptions and constraints of the military structures and technologies that provided their funding and research opportunities, they nevertheless reached conclusions that challenged the territorial logics of securitization that governed the ongoing U.S. military occupation of Asia and the Pacific.

Just as these new developments in the fields of oceanography and ecosystem ecology highlighted how local environments were materially connected to other spaces and places around the globe, the mass displacement, migration, and circulation of people through and across the Pacific during the second half of the twentieth century were bringing people across Asia and the Pacific together in new and unexpected ways—sometimes creating new networks and alliances while at other times creating bitter conflicts. The interracial intimacies that emerged from this period did not clearly or consistently follow the progressively assimilationist model illustrated by the DeBecque family from Michener's *Tales*. Indeed, while *Tales* naturalized U.S. claims to Pacific territory by way of romantic or domestic relationships with Asian and Polynesian bodies, representations of other kinds of transpacific intimacies—and the difficulties of sustaining them—highlighted the lingering trauma from the physical and psychological damage inflicted by the ongoing militarization of the Pacific. These militarized infrastructures not only upheld U.S. hegemony; they also supported the ongoing regional influence of Australia and New Zealand, two settler colonial nations whose "whiteness"—as Tony Fry would have it—indicated their colonial and imperial affinities with the emerging U.S. nation-state. Yet if a commitment to helping Australia and New Zealand "stay white" helped to motivate the militarization of the region in the second half of the twentieth century, alternative coalitional dynamics also emerged through the interconnections and unexpected interactions created through these militarized networks.

One such coalition lies at the center of Māori novelist James George's *Ocean Roads*. While George's earlier novels *Wooden Horses* (2000) and *Hummingbird* (2003) largely centered on the Northland region of Aotearoa/ New Zealand, *Ocean Roads* takes place in and around Auckland, following a loose-knit, multiply uprooted family whose uneasy circulation mirrors the militarized currents of the twentieth-century Pacific. The dispersal and estrangement of the Henare/Simeon family at the beginning of the novel illustrate the extent to which the long legacies of British colonialism and U.S. militarization have disrupted and fragmented the bonds forged among the people and the communities who have resisted or been erased from a progressive vision of the postwar transpacific. Etta Henare, an acclaimed photojournalist, is a Māori woman originally from the Northland of Aotearoa/ New Zealand. While the novel does not go into great detail about her background before the war, the weight of her ancestral and personal histories of displacement reverberates through her decision to travel the world without returning home for years at a time. The father of Etta's first son, a serviceman named Joaquin Alvarez who died in the battle for Tinian, likewise had a family history marked by migration: he was a third-generation Mexican American whose family worked on a cattle ranch in New Mexico. Isaac Simeon, Etta's husband and the father of her second son, was also an emigrant—an Anglo-Jewish man whose "people had dispersed from North Africa, among the numberless wandering Hebrews criss-crossing the desert."[63] Isaac emigrated first to America to work on the nuclear program, and then to Aotearoa/New Zealand after meeting Etta. Troy, Etta's eldest son, enlists to fight in the Vietnam War and becomes estranged from his mother when she takes a photograph of him as he saves two young Vietnamese children after a firebombing, then publishes it and wins a Pulitzer Prize. Troy's brother, Caleb, a promising physicist like his father, is afflicted with terminal cancer; he has also been aiding an antiwar terrorist group responsible for setting out a number of increasingly destructive explosions around Auckland. Akiko, a Japanese woman involved with Troy and Caleb, is a *hibakusha* (atomic bomb victim) from Nagasaki—the same bomb that Isaac helped to develop. All of these characters are indelibly marked, physically and psychologically, by the violence of the wars that connect them. Yet rather than coming together to create an assimilationist, progressive nuclear family unit like the DeBecques, the Henare/Simeon family is slowly pulled apart by the same tides of war that had brought them together. In 1959, after witnessing the destructive capabilities of the thermonuclear bombs being tested at Bikini Atoll, Isaac travels to Antarctica, where he has a dissociative episode connected to his feelings of guilt over his role in the creation of such destructive technology and is committed to a mental institution; a decade later, Troy and Caleb, who find themselves on opposite sides of a protest over New Zealand's involvement in the Vietnam War, end up killing each other, and Etta, who can no longer bear to be around her home and its memories, takes to the road. The dispersal and diminishment of the family as they navigate the physical and psychological wounds of these cold war(s) represent the lasting trauma and incommensurable damages of transpacific militarization that have been largely suppressed by the progressive narratives of interracial alliance and romance promoted in the popular fictions and films of the era.[64]

While *Ocean Roads* does not flinch from highlighting the fragility of these transpacific relationships, neither does it posit their dispersal or fracturing as an inevitable *end* to the Henare/Simeons' story and genealogy. Instead, the family story moves onward through the processes of survival, renewal, and reconfiguration. As opposed to the colonialist genealogy of *Tales of the South Pacific*, the genealogical dynamic of *Ocean Roads* is framed around *whakapapa*, a Māori epistemological framework that—as Alice Te Punga Somerville notes—emphasizes the "layered" nature of genealogy in which "verticality is less important than multidirectional relationships."[65] It is the reconnection to these multidirectional relationships that forms the crux of George's novel: as it draws to a close, the family draws together once more, reunited through the different ways they have come to terms with their entangled histories, environments, and relationships. This survivance—defined, following Gerald Vizenor, as "an active sense of presence" that continues to unfold, denying narratives of "dominance and victimry" that would relegate Indigenous presence to the past—is rendered most vividly in the storylines of the women Etta, Akiko, and Rai.[66] The lives of these women, who represent three generations of the same family, are drawn together by, and narratively parallel, the relentless ebb and flow of the "ocean roads" of the novel's title.

Rai, the youngest member of the Henare family, is a medical student whose chosen profession indicates her interests in the processes of healing and recuperation. Her character is shown to be steady, grounded, and responsible; she is the person who, through her actions, works hardest to hold the remaining fragments of her family together. She makes a point of regularly checking in on her mother and her grandfather and is later made responsible for maintaining and opening the house at Rangimoana for Etta's homecoming. Rai is also a character whose actions most directly gesture toward the debate over the Foreshore and Seabed Act, which had been written into law only two years before the publication of *Ocean Roads*. After receiving a phone call from Etta, who mentions her intention to return, Rai goes to her family's oceanfront home and finds a flier stuck in the doorway offering to buy the house, which she discards:

> No. No sale here. Not today.
> In the morning she goes down to the beach and walks in the surf, looks along the sand to where the old man, Koroheke Rock, crouches staring out to sea. She moves up the beach, up above the high tide line, sits among the shells and driftwood and burrows her feet into the soft sand. She pushes her hands beneath the surface, the sand cool away from the day's touch. She sits for a long time, watching the dark clouds cast shadows on the water like huge schools of fish. She takes a deep breath, glances down at the first raindrops freckling the beach's face.
> She burrows her hands and feet further in.[67]

After immediately rejecting the offer to give up her family land for sale, the actions that Rai takes to refamiliarize herself with her childhood home speaks to her ability to think and feel beyond the binary distinctions of land and sea, human and nonhuman, and animate and nonanimate entities. Not only does she observe "the old man, Koroheke Rock... staring out to sea," attributing an animacy to the geologic landmark that belies its status as a common territory or property, she likewise watches "the dark clouds cast shadows on the water like huge schools of fish," drawing attention to the consonance between the pelagic migrations of the sea creatures and the shapes of clouds formed and reformed through atmospheric drift. She interprets the first fall of rain around her as "freckling the beach's face," using anthropomorphic metaphor to again emphasize the sense of kinship she feels with the place. Rai makes all of these observations from the liminal space of the beach, where she carefully situates herself "up above the high tide line"—the demarcation of space determined, in the Foreshore and Seabed Act, to distinguish what could be determined as "foreshore" and thus property subject to the Crown. Sitting at the edge of her titled land, Rai "pushes her hands beneath the surface" to the cooler sand below, then "burrows her hands and feet further in"—grounding and situating herself in a place that resists permanence and settlement.

By situating Rai as both the family caretaker and the figure most directly attuned to a sense of place, George reverses the expected progressive narrative relationship of grandmother and grandchild: Rai is the one who remains at home and attuned to the nuances of the changing relationships between land and sea, while grandmother Etta is the one seeking respite and reconnection after a long journey abroad. This role reversal is briefly prefaced by the novel's introduction of the "twins paradox," a physics problem in which one twin, traveling at the speed of light for eight years, returns home two years younger than the one who has remained on Earth. In a textbook Rai consults, this discrepancy is explained as the result of *"time dilation at great speed, predicted in Einstein's theory of special relativity. Time on the spacecraft passes twenty percent slower than on earth. Time is not constant for everyone."*[68] While the textbook description of the twins paradox emphasizes the way that the speed of *light* works to reveal time as a relative construct, in the context of the book's engagement with oceanic space, it is also useful to think about the way that, as Anna Ryan has observed, time is also "integrally bound up with the physicality of the *sea*."[69] This oceanic understanding of time—not as a standard linear progression but as a fluctuating assemblage composed of a number of atmospheric and oceanic elements—invokes a temporality based on the cyclical rhythms of the oceans rather than a terrestrially based framework that tends to abstract time from its physical or natural surroundings. If the very concept of progressive time is based on terracentric concepts that imagine a "material world of stable ontologies that persists in spite of transformations within either the geophysical or social domain,"[70] a thallocentric approach frames time as emerging from and profoundly entangled with the material, social, historical, and atmospheric currents of the ocean. Such an approach to time is inherently *circular* rather than progressive; it takes its cues from the cyclical motion of tides, currents, and weather patterns instead of the presumptive stability of geological time.

Although twenty-first-century scholarship around the concept of the Anthropocene—which frames the impact of human activity on Earth as the start of a new geological epoch—has likewise drawn attention to these entanglements of "human" and "natural" history, such theories often remain wedded to an understanding of time as inexorably progressive in ways that lend themselves to universalizing discourses based on a shared sense of threat or crisis around a looming (and seemingly inevitable) apocalypse.[71] Postcolonial and Indigenous studies critics have objected to the universalizing tendency of this discourse, pointing out that the causes and effects of human-induced climate change have never been experienced in the same ways or at the same time, and, indeed, for many communities—particularly Indigenous and minoritized communities and people living in the global South—such apocalyptic and genocidal events, in the form of colonial projects, have already occurred.[72] A more nuanced accounting of the interactions between global and local elements of the Anthropocene thus requires, as DeLoughrey suggests, a "multiscalar method of telescoping between space (planet) and place (island) in a dialectic or 'tidalectic' way"—in other words, an oceanic mode of understanding time and space.[73] Such an approach works to further decenter the assumptions of human exceptionalism that remain embedded in many discourses of the Anthropocene, which—in popular renderings of climate change discourse especially—can rely on an apocalyptic teleology that engenders apathy or pessimism rather than hope. Indeed, Oceanic texts' principled resistance to fatal-impact theories of environmental trauma emerges from their grounding in cultural practices and epistemologies that foreground the entanglement and interrelationship of human and nonhuman entities.[74] By shifting away from the construct of the individual human as a privileged subject moving through empty and homogeneous time and space, an ocean-centered approach to space/time opens new venues for revitalization and resurgence.

Ocean Roads invokes this cyclical, tidalectic temporality—not only by reversing Rai's and Etta's expected positions at the novel's beginning, but also by cycling through different time periods and points of view and refusing to privilege a single perspective or (progressive) trajectory. Instead, the novel's subject is the entire Henare genealogy. As Rai's mother and Etta's daughter-in-law, Akiko operates as an intermediary figure in this *whakapapa*. While Akiko embodies the connection between Etta and Rai, her Asian-identified body is not simply a procreative vessel or vector through which a "new" transpacific futurity might be birthed. Akiko's body is both marked by and makes its mark on the transpacific histories that have brought her into this family. The scarred body of Akiko, as a *hibakusha*, has been rendered into a spectacle, subjected not only to an erotic but also to a scientific gaze. Unlike the well-chronicled journeys of the Hiroshima Maidens, Akiko's experience with medical treatment served to indicate not so much as her recuperation within a national or transnational body politic as her alienation from it. As she tells Caleb,

> Every two years . . . the week of my birthday, I had to go for medical tests. I had to take all my clothes off and get into a white robe. They took my blood, did X-rays, an electrocardiogram. Everyone had to. They tested my heart rate, the oxygenation of my blood, made me exercise in a room with white walls to match my white robe. The

white of my bones in the X-rays. They did everything but treat me. Treat us.[75]

While the erotic gaze that Michener's novel deploys renders Asian female bodies hypervisible by emphasizing their sexual desirability and proximity to whiteness, Akiko's experience with the medical gaze emphasizes the alienating qualities of this visibility: she disrobes and is made into an exceptional spectacle, one that may be studied but is never meaningfully "treated" or reincorporated into a community. Like those of the Hiroshima Maidens, Akiko's body serves as a visible trace of the damages done by nuclear war, yet like that of the Marshallese subjects of the classified "Project 4.1," Akiko's proximity to the whiteness emphasized by the "white walls," "white robe," and "white . . . bones" does *not* bear the promise of regeneration. Rather, it threatens her with exclusion, invisibility, and death. Yet Akiko is able to push back against the sterility of this medicalized and militarized gaze by reclaiming her body as an artistic medium through which she actively and creatively processes the traumas of her past through dance. Her movements as a choreographer take their cues from the ocean's "ebb and flow," mimicking "sea foam," breaking and reforming in new patterns.[76] Such choreography imagines the separate dancers together as a single entity. While they are in constant motion across the stage, either independently or together, they are united kinesthetically through the movement that "seeps back from the floorboards, back through their feet, and they realise the parts of the creature that they are." As the author of their movements, Akiko watches them as her "bones feel the current as if she dances with them," a sensibility that she developed by recalling the rhythms of life growing up in a fishing village where "everyone took their breath from the sea."[77] Dance is the way that Akiko uses her body to remember, reconfigure, and knit back together the different pieces of her fragmented life. As she dances, she sees

> her mother's face, her father's face, neither of which she has a memory of beyond photographs. They're with her now. The pigeons from the peace park in Nagasaki swirl around her also, are part of her dance. As is the kiwi soft toy with the broken eye at Auckland Airport. She swoops and rises on the wind currents, currents she wishes could flow against history, wear it down like the sea wears away stone cliff.[78]

Drawing together images from her childhood, her adolescence, and her first arrival in Aotearoa/New Zealand, Akiko weaves these partial and incomplete fragments of her own human history, memory, and pain together into an oceanic composition built on the nonhuman timescale and movements of the restless sea.

Akiko's recuperative visions as a dancer and choreographer rely on *movement*, particularly the body in motion. As a result, she "cannot draw portraiture—her eye loses touch with figure and features if they remain still."[79] By contrast, Etta, a photographer, has a unique talent for capturing the quicksilver essence of a person or event in a still image. This is the skill that brings her success in her career as a photojournalist and estranges her from Troy when he becomes her subject rather than her son. Etta's war photography, like Akiko's choreography, seeks to collect and document moments or memories that otherwise would be lost to time, a rendering that George replicates in the text with short descriptive captions whose formatting sets them apart from the flow of the narrative:

> A SINGLE FLOWER SITTING IN THE MUD, BETWEEN A DISCARDED ARMY BOOT AND A STEAMING SHELL CASING.
>
> A SOLDIER WITH THE DARK SMUDGES OF BOOT-BLACK ON HIS CHEEKS FOR CAMOUFLAGE, WEARING A BADGE THAT SAYS I LOVE LUCY.
>
> A SAFFRON-ROBED MONK PRAYING AMONG SHELLFIRE AND FALLING MASONRY.[80]

The fragmentation and juxtaposition of imagery here invokes the particular history of photography and its entanglement with the technologies of militarization. The technologies that produce and improve photography and the technologies that enable the increasingly destructive abstractions of modern warfare collapse space into time in a visual field, turning spatial distance into *time-distance*.[81] In a military context, such technologies are used to visualize space to render them as potential subjects for domination: read against this history, Rey Chow notes, the dropping of the atomic bombs on Hiroshima and Nagasaki becomes an "epistemic event in a global culture in which everything has become (or is mediated by) visual representation and virtual reality," ushering in an era that, following Heidegger, she terms the "age of the world target."[82] Yet if, according to Chow, the very act of seeing in a postatomic world becomes entangled with a militarized "means of destruction"—where "destruction" refers to the nuclear or military obliteration of a target space—the longer history of this destructive "sight" can be traced back through the colonial history the Pacific.[83] The Pacific Islands have long been framed by a "visual economy of colonialism" that has presented its people and environments for the purposes of extraction, circulation, and consumption.[84] In this sense, the shift from colonial mapping to military targeting indicated not so much a change in *perspective* as a change in the *speed* with which such destructive sighting both isolates and wreaks its havoc on targeted populations.

Certainly, Etta's photography bears visible traces of the medium's entanglement with its militarized and colonial histories. Her prizewinning photograph of Troy rescuing two Vietnamese children resonates as betrayal precisely because she put the camera between herself and her son, viewing him as a soldier/subject before recognizing him as her flesh and blood. Her subsequent publication of the photograph transforms this vulnerable moment into a prizewinning, globally circulating image—one that participates in a colonial aesthetic that has long conditioned the fetishization and commodification of Native men's bodies in the West.[85] While Etta's picture of Troy serves as an example of how the photographer's sight operates as both a mode of appropriation *and* a "means of destruction" (where the thing that is "destroyed" here is not a city or landscape but a family bond), in other contexts she uses her lens to focalize images and details that go largely unnoticed by other documentary narratives. Etta's attention to incongruous images such as a flower sitting next to a shell casing and the "I Love Lucy" badge on a soldier's uniform provides a different perspective on war and its costs; such images honor moments that simultaneously evoke the destructiveness of war and the resilience of everyday life. In so doing, Etta's photographs contribute to an alternative documentary archive. If, as Susan Sontag notes, photographs teach us a "new visual code" that "alter[s] and enlarge[s] our notions of what is worth looking at and what we have a right to observe,"[86] Etta's photography expands the "visual code" of photography to foreground the medium's entanglement with the destructive violence of military and colonial science, as well as its ability to create lasting images that serve to document and archive the moments and experiences that might otherwise be swept away or overlooked by grand narratives of history. Thus, even as Etta's Pulitzer Prize–winning photograph of Troy carrying two Vietnamese children out of danger presents an (apparently) uncomplicated image of Western martial heroism—one that further naturalizes or normalizes ongoing U.S./Western military presence in Asia by foregrounding Troy's racially marked body—her photographs of the more quotidian elements of war speak to both the destructiveness and the incongruity of that presence, as well as to the resilience of the people and landscapes that bear the brunt of that violence. It is this element of everyday transformation and resilience that is largely missing from extant transpacific narratives of the war, and it is these images, rather than the award-winning photograph of Troy and the children, that Etta chooses to display in her retrospective exhibit.

Like Etta's photography (and Akiko's choreography), the novel as a whole operates as an alternative archive of the modern transpacific. By presenting the complex histories of a family displaced and dispersed by multiple layers of colonialism and war, George provides a new perspective on mainstream narratives—such as Michener's and Rodgers and Hammerstein's *South Pacifics*—that supported Cold War logics of securitization through the portrayal of progressively assimilative interracial families. Indeed, George's decision to begin and end the novel in 1989, the same year that saw the fall of the Berlin Wall, marking the beginning of the Cold War's end, explicitly periodizes the novel's events as a reflection on (or, perhaps more accurately, a *refraction* of) this era of militarized imperialism. This intention is made clear in the opening lines of the novel, as Etta goes on assignment to take photographs of the Trinity nuclear testing site in New Mexico. As she "looks up over her light meter," she observes that above her "the clouds drift like icebergs, as if the sand and burnt grass of the plain and even the distant mountain tops lie beneath water."[87] This momentary shift in perspective, which reimagines the desert landscape as seabed territory, is the very first image in the novel, both setting up and serving as a frame for the connections that George draws throughout between oceanic and terrestrial environments. It also highlights the refractive properties of water—specifically, the deflection or bending of light waves as they pass from one medium into another. Refraction is likewise central to our own eyes' ability to focus light so we can make out visual images; a process that is emphasized as Etta "blinks hard, wipes her eyes," and "adjusts the focal length" of her camera before turning her gaze and lenses back on the deserted site before her.[88] Yet the novel's opening invocation of a landscape viewed through a watery medium likewise suggests that there are at least two ways of seeing a single event. Just as the refractive properties of water can appear to bend an object placed within it, George's text calls into focus the histories and legacies of World War II and the Cold War that lie askew from the narratives of expansionist progressivism that have shaped our understandings of the contemporary transpacific. If militarized infrastructures—developed around visualizing technologies that work to transform *space* into *time*—reframe the increasing territorialization of ocean space as a narrative of inexorable progress, the ocean-based "seascape epistemology" invoked by the cyclical narrative structure of *Ocean Roads* exposes and pushes back against these assumptions by emphasizing the entanglement of time with *space* and *place*.⁸⁹ In this way, an oceanic approach brings into focus the many stories, images, and experiences that have been left outside the purview of progressive racial and imperial narratives of a militarized transpacific, and these stories explicitly address how its project of *securing liberty*—particularly through militarized and technological means—has, through its own essential contradiction in terms, always harbored the possibilities of its own unmaking.

As I have argued here, U.S. military projects in the Pacific and Asia have been premised on a model of transpacific securitization that applies terracentric spatial and temporal logics to oceanic environments. Such securitization goes hand in hand with the submarine expansionism posited by the application of U.S. and other nation-states' technologically aided claims to the resources of the ocean floor, first articulated through the Truman Doctrine and confirmed as international law by the UNCLOS. Yet such a model is—as Dean Saranillio has noted of U.S. imperial and capitalist projects in the Pacific—ultimately an "unsustainable" enterprise.⁹⁰ While Michener envisioned the second half of the twentieth century as a progressive unfolding of a liberal democratic hegemony across the Pacific and into Asia, by the century's end, writers such as George were grappling with the significant environmental, emotional, and biopolitical legacies of the militarized logics, infrastructures, and technologies deployed to "secure" the way for these so-called freedoms. As an alternative to abstractive models that reframe ocean space as a commons while denying Indigenous people sovereignty over waters considered coextensive with heritage lands, George's characters position themselves at the liminal site of the beach or foreshore, where the land operates by the logics of the sea rather than the other way around. The foreshore operates as land that can be *claimed* but not permanently *secured*, as it is continually shaped and reshaped by a shifting assemblage of land, sea, and atmospheric conditions. While the foreshore is intended to represent the divide between the ocean and "cultivated or developed land," it also vividly illustrates how this division is constantly in flux. Not only can "cultivated" land be reclaimed by the oceans, new lands can also be *created* by the tide's ebb or another geological event. By occupying the space of the foreshore, *Ocean Roads* posits that it is not just the sea that resists a terrestrial concept of fixity. The land itself can be thought of as fluid and dynamic, as well.

The mass migrations of Asian and Pacific Island communities in the twentieth and twenty-first centuries have likewise brought these oceanic sensibilities to bear on *landed* territory, destabilizing assumptions about terrestrial fixity that give coherence not only to the modern nation-state but also to the bodies of global governance built on a system of international relations premised on the elemental differences between land and sea. In particular, the experiences and trajectories of Asian and Pacific Island refugees—borne by the tides of war and global climate change—have worked to disrupt a range of institutional and social spaces that have been designed to alternatively isolate and assimilate them into the national bodies of their "host" nations. Although refugees have been discursively framed in legal, literary, and popular terms as victims or contaminants requiring quarantine or absorption into the main "stream" of the nation, their stories of ocean passage highlight how their transpacific trajectories have been differently entangled within the broader settler colonial and capitalist structures that have contributed to their displacement. By tracing out affinities and resonances between these experiences of Asian American displacement and Pacific Island dispossession, such stories offer substantive critiques of (and alternatives to) global initiatives around refugee resettlements *and* environmental stewardship. To this end, the next chapter turns to stories of refugee passage and considers what it might mean to think of refugee aesthetic production as an oceanic form.

2

REFUGEE PASSAGES

In the Wake of War

Refugee communities have long been pejoratively associated with oceanic phenomena—tides, floods, waves, surges—that threaten to overwhelm and dissolve the social structures and political hierarchies of the terrestrially bounded nation-state. These thalassic metaphors, whether deployed in explicitly nativist terms or in more sympathetic ones, often work to dehumanize refugee communities by comparing them to forces of nature.[1] Yet these metaphors also gesture to the specific challenge that the figure of the refugee presents to the very concept of the "human" that operates as the basis and justification of the nation-state. As Hannah Arendt and Giorgio Agamben have observed, the refugee serves as a figure of "bare life" whose treatment reveals how the universal human rights on which the sovereignty of the modern democratic nation-state is premised are in practice limited to citizens alone.[2] The refugee must be transformed into a citizen or else remain a figure of bare life existing beyond the scope of human rights—a glaring contradiction in terms that draws attention to how the humanity of the citizen has been constructed both on and against the stateless refugee.[3]

While Arendt and Agamben do not directly address the role of race in their discussion of how the refugee challenges received ideas around the "human," the refugee as a figure of violent exclusion clearly resonates with the function of other, differently racialized bodies that have been marginalized against the project of American definitions of "freedom."[4] Writing against the desire to "explain or resolve the question" of Black exclusion from citizenship through discourses focused on "assimilation, inclusion, or civil or human rights," Christina Sharpe turns to the image of the "wake"—a word with multiple meanings, including "the track left on the water's surface by a ship" and "the disturbance caused by a body swimming or moved, in water"—as a critical approach to progressive narratives around race and liberation, articulating instead "the impossibility of such resolutions by representing the paradoxes of blackness within and after the legacies of slavery's denial of Black humanity."[5] Sharpe's exploration and examination of this "wake work" emphasizes the ongoing nature of these histories and legacies of violence, as the image of a wake that continues to move outward long after the disturbance or disruption has passed gestures to a nonlinear temporality in which "the past that is not past reappears, always, to rupture the present."[6] The narratives of assimilation and progress that lie at the heart of the rights-based discourses that Sharpe, among others, have found inadequate to addressing the complex histories of Black and other racially marked bodies in the modern world similarly fall short in the representation of refugee experience, where—as in the temporality of the wake—events unfold in ways that are neither linear nor immediately apparent. In this sense, refugee narratives can likewise be seen as occupying a kind of fugitive space/time, cast as not only a political but also a racial and temporal "other" to the homogeneous, progressive time of the nation-state.

The metaphoric associations of refugees with tides, currents, and floods indicate how the challenge that the figure of the refugee poses to the nation-state is not only an existential and racial but also an explicitly *territorial* one. Just as floods and rising tides have the ability to literally remake the topography of the earth, mass migrations across national boundaries unsettle states' sovereign fictions of a stable and natural alignment among "state/nation/territory"—particularly the implied consonance between one's place of birth and one's nation that forms the basis of the sovereign territorial claims of the settler colonial nation-state.[7] While Agamben and Arendt focus primarily on how the figure of the refugee reveals increasing levels of dissociation between nativity and nationality in the context of intra-European mass migrations and population displacements, Evyn Lê Espiritu extends this critique to show how, in settler colonial states, the refugee can "activate a particular politics of deterritorialization" that might productively align with Indigenous claims to the land—since such claims likewise work to "unsettle" the nation-state's claims to sovereign rule by asserting prior claims to nativity.[8] This potential for alliance between refugee and Indigenous communities highlights the complexity of what Espiritu terms the "refugee settler condition"—a condition that attends to the complex triangulation among refugee communities, Indigenous communities, and the settler state. In some cases, the settler state may present itself as aligned with, or the protector of, Indigenous or indigenized communities against a perceived threat of immigrant or refugee populations, who are framed as invasives, contaminants, or a security risk.[9] (Such a tendency aligns with what I discussed in Chapter 1 as a discourse of *securitization*.) In other cases, refugees are encouraged to become naturalized citizens and thereby work to strengthen and legitimize the claims of the state over the prior claims of Indigenous peoples. This operates as a discourse of *domestication*.[10] These discourses around securitization and domestication are, as I argued in Chapter 1, meaningfully connected to the reterritorialization of the seas in the years following World War II: they align with a political, technological, and conceptual shift that reconfigured oceanic space from a "free," non-national commons to an exploitable (or renewable) resource. In extending territorial logics from land to seas, these discourses of securitization and domestication—whether attached to human or nonhuman entities—leave the sovereignty of the settler colonial state unchallenged. However, the work that I turn to in this chapter focuses on "unsettling" these territory-based assumptions about citizenship and rights, opening the floodgates (so to speak) for connections between Indigenous and refugee communities to emerge. By highlighting and disrupting the anthropocentric worldview that grounds settler concepts of *territoriality* and *temporality*, these refugee passages expose the settler colonial logics that extend beyond the state to govern the international projects of resettlement and climate change.

This chapter juxtaposes work by Southeast Asian and Pacific Island authors and artists, highlighting these moments of emergence and resonance in texts that directly address the twentieth- and twenty-first-century displacements of Southeast Asian and Pacific Island communities. While many within these communities have been portrayed as paradigmatic figures of a universalized "refugee condition"—as victims or abject figures who must alternately be rejected and recuperated into a national body politic—they also serve as harbingers of a future that demands new ways of thinking beyond the territorial assumptions and ambitions of the modern nation-state that serve as the living legacies of our colonial and imperial history.[11] Following Yến Lê Espiritu's call for a "critical refugee studies" that reimagines the figure of the refugee "not as an object of investigation but a *paradigm* [that] . . . radically calls into question the established principles of the nation-state and the idealized goal of inclusion and recognition within it," the texts featured in this chapter illustrate how both Southeast Asian and Pacific Islander refugees foreground the disjunctures between their experiences of displacement and how their displacement has been represented in hegemonic discourses around human rights, legal regimes, and remediation.[12] In particular, I turn to the work of Vietnamese American novelist lê thi diễm thúy and Marshallese poet Kathy Jetñil-Kijiner to illustrate how artists from these various communities have sought to "unsettle" these discourses by embracing the disruptive and deterritorializing, yet also place-making, potentialities of the oceanic ecologies with which they have been aligned—whether as "boat people" (in the case of lê) or as victims of sea level rise (in the case of Jetñil-Kijiner). After addressing the different ways that diasporic Southeast Asian and Pacific Islander communities have been popularly represented and politically incorporated as "war refugees" and "climate refugees," respectively, I argue that what these artists share is a commitment to making their experiences register at an *affective* level that demands recognition of the ongoing, uneven dynamics of the relationships between land and sea, human and nonhuman environments, "host" nation-states and homelands. Against the idea of a temporally and territorially bounded nation-state empowered to decide whether or not refugees are ready for incorporation into the national body, these refugee artists and authors articulate oceanic sensibilities that show how our shared experiences of modernity have led to a global community that is already profoundly affected by and implicated in the fates of the dispossessed. Just as the rising temperatures of the ocean reflect the centuries of waste that has been poured into the land, ocean, and atmosphere, so do the trajectories of refugee and migrant communities reflect the ongoing histories of colonialism, occupation, and environmental exploitation that continue to produce them. Thus, they appear as both a model for survival/survivance in diaspora *and* a warning of the potential for dispossession in a world that continues to reverberate with the material and environmental costs of its making.

Reclaiming the "Refugee"

Refugee movements—understood most broadly as large-scale community migrations of people seeking refuge from war or economic or environmental crises—certainly did not begin in, and have not been limited to, the twentieth century. Yet following Lisa Malkki's argument that "'the refugee' as a specific social category and legal problem of global dimensions" first emerged within formalized institutions and administrative procedures for refugee resettlements near the end of World War II, I focus in this section on the articulations and contestations of the figure of the modern "refugee" figure as it has been produced through these twentieth-century (and twenty-first-century) legal regimes and technologies of power.[13] In particular, I am interested in how this figure gets produced by and within the legal constructions and distinctions drawn among political, economic, and (more recently) environmental, or "climate," refugees.

The working definition of peoples eligible for "refugee status" under international law was established by the Geneva Convention Relating to the Status of Refugees of 1951 in response to the need for refugee resettlements following World War II in Europe. The convention defines the refugee as a person who, due to "events occurring before January 1, 1951," experiences a "well-founded fear of *being persecuted* for reasons of race, religion, nationality, [or] membership of a particular social group or political opinion."[14] The subsequent United Nations Convention and Protocol Relating to the Status of Refugees (1967) extended this definition of peoples eligible for refugee status by overriding the Geneva Conventions' stipulation limiting refugee status to those displaced by events that occurred in Europe before 1951. The internationalization of refugee status allowed for displaced peoples from Asia, Africa, and the Americas to be recognized as refugees and eligible for resettlement; however, the experience of political or social persecution remained central to the ability to claim refugee status. Host nations such as the United States were thus able to position themselves as sites of "refuge" and a space of "freedom"—even when, in the case of the Vietnamese diaspora in particular, military interventions by the United States and other Western nations played a significant role in creating the political and social conditions for refugee flight in the first place.[15]

Since the 1970s, the United States has sought to frame refugees—particularly refugees from Southeast Asia—as beneficiaries of American largesse in order to recuperate and overwrite not only memories of failed U.S. military projects but also to further its ongoing imperial ambitions in the region.[16] Mimi Thi Nguyen observes that these transpacific refugee passages are recast as a "move from subjection to subjectivity" that naturalizes the United States as the site of the liberal subjecthood to which refugee communities must aspire, while simultaneously obscuring the disruptive "violence of liberalism's powers."[17] The resulting "'good refugee' narrative" has not only served to reframe U.S. interventions in Vietnam as a "good war" undertaken on behalf of the Vietnamese people—what Espiritu has called the "we-win-even-when-we-lose syndrome"—but it has also worked to reposition refugees within the broader contours of an immigrant narrative.[18] When reimagined as an immigrant, the refugee is transformed from a deterritorializing figure into an assimilable one; a figure that requires and desires rehabilitation to become legible as a proper subject of the nation-state. As Viet Nguyen observes, the progressive logic of the refugee-as-immigrant narrative ultimately works to "affir[m] the nation-states the immigrant comes from and settles into" while subverting the radical potential of the refugee to "question the viability of the nation-state" as a form altogether.[19] This renarration of the refugee's passage as a teleological as well as a spatial journey leaves the role of Western imperialist violence and aggression largely out of the picture, erasing or avoiding the question of the host nations' ethical or moral responsibilities while emphasizing their generosity and largesse.

Debates around the status of "environmental" or "climate change" refugees illustrate a similar tendency to emphasize mechanisms of accommodation and adaptation rather than addressing and targeting the broader context of environmental damage that was, and continues to be, perpetrated by large industrial economies.[20] While there is certainly a demonstrated need to develop international political and legal strategies that can address both environmental refugee resettlement *and* the anthropogenic climate change that has driven them from their homes, the slower pace and uneven effects of climate change often mean that discourses around climate change refugees tend to represent them as victims in need of immediate aid rather than as actors whose choices speak directly to the critical need for global policy reforms around carbon emissions and other environmental pollutants. Like the migration of Southeast Asian refugees into the nations that invested most heavily in the wars that displaced them, the resettlement of climate change refugees in industrialized nation-states both reflects and deflects observations of the global power imbalances that exist between heavily industrialized, carbon-polluting states and the (often) environmentally exploited, less industrialized states from which climate change refugees emerge.

The term "environmental refugee" first appeared in a 1985 publication by the United Nations Environmental Program (UNEP) that defined such refugees as "those people who have been forced to leave their traditional habitat, temporarily or permanently, because of a marked environmental disruption (natural and/or triggered by people) that jeopardized their existence and/or seriously affected the quality of their life."[21] Yet this working definition of what constitutes an environmental refugee has been criticized for being too broad or vague to be effective.[22] The difficulty of reckoning with the varying temporal scales of environmental crisis makes it difficult to distinguish which communities might qualify for refugee status. While there are some environmental crises, such as earthquakes, floods, and volcanic eruptions, that can be clearly accounted for as a specific event requiring either temporary or long-term resettlement, there are others—such as declining soil quality and sea level rise—that take place over a much longer period of time and have a broader range of causes and effects. Precisely because the legal mechanisms for refugee resettlement—still largely governed by the concepts set forth by the 1951 Geneva Convention framework—focus on political refugees fleeing "persecution," they are less able to account adequately for the multiscalar issues facing climate change refugees. In consequence, the question of climate change or environmental refugee resettlements requires a new and radically different approach, one that is fundamentally *decolonial* in outlook.

The reframing of climate-displaced peoples as "refugees" extends and perpetuates some of the oversights within emergent scholarly and political debates around the state of the environment more broadly. In this context, Indigenous scholars have emphasized the importance not only of reckoning with the legacies of our colonial past but also of taking meaningful steps to actively decolonize how we think about the environment and humans' place within it.[23] Such a decolonial approach considers the earth not as a collective resource that can be plundered or protected by man, but as a complex series of relationships whose balance can be disrupted and rectified in a number of different ways.[24] From this perspective, sustainability and mitigation practices must combine a strict and rigorous international accounting for the unevenness of global carbon and waste production—holding the largest polluters responsible for their actions—with localized, community-driven actions led by people with the most specific knowledge, informed by daily and even generational observation, about the environments around them. However, this shift from a top-down to bottom-up approach would require a profoundly radical rethinking of settler colonial capitalism and the global power structures it supports by *decentering* the liberal "human" subject, which finds political expression in the idea of the modern citizen.

Just as discourses around climate "crisis" can oversimplify the multifaceted and multiscalar elements of global environmental change, resettlement discourses that identify both political and climate "refugee" populations as problems to be solved address only one part of a complex relationship among the territorial ambitions of industrial nation-states, global capitalism, and environmental exploitation. The positioning of the climate or war refugee as a victim—or, in more xenophobic contexts, as a racial or cultural threat— isolates the figure of the refugee and metonymically identifies it with the very concept of global or environmental distress that has driven them from their countries and places of origin. While the problematic nature of this mode of identification is clear when used in explicitly xenophobic discourses, it is similarly deployed in more liberal policies that focus on the resettlement of refugee populations rather than addressing the events driving refugee flight. Against this universalizing narrative of refugee as victim (or refugee as threat), contemporary scholars and artists working in critical refugee studies have highlighted the diversity and complexity of refugees' experiences. In the context of Southeast Asian studies, this critical work expands on the potential for refugee narratives to "unsettle" or decenter the claims of the bounded nation-state (and the United States in particular), reclaiming the refugee's radical, deterritorializing potential. Yet the "deterritorializing" focus of critical refugee studies directs us not only toward the deconstruction of the nation-state, as Agamben envisioned, but also toward the articulation of a "refugee form" or "refugee epistemology" that, as Yến Lê Espiritu and Lan Duong have argued, foregrounds and contributes to modes of "social reproduction and innovation" that occur and emerge in practices of everyday life.[25] These refugee epistemologies and forms emphasize how refugee art and writing foreground refugees' creative *agency* in imagining a decolonial future beyond resettlement. For example, Ma Vang and Quynh Nhu Le have pointed out how Hmong and Vietnamese diasporic writers frame their experiences of refugee flight in the context of longer histories of Southeast Asian imperialism and dispossession that can be traced to a period *before* Western interventions in the region. By reflecting on the ebb and flow of these overlapping invasions and displacements, writers draw from a "deterritorialized subjectivity" (Vang) or "karmic worldview" (Le) whose complex relationships to territory and temporality challenge the progressive tendency of ethnic/immigrant American literature to aspire to or assert a "claim" of belonging to the nation-state. By breaking from the progressive logics that promise "freedom" through affinity and affiliation with the colonial nation-state, these alternative epistemologies open up space for other intimacies among differently dispossessed communities to emerge.[26]

Scholars working in Pacific studies have likewise sought to redefine the "refugee" label by seeking to challenge and problematize current discourses around climate-vulnerable populations. While—as Carol Farbotko and Heather Lazrus argue—dominant narratives of resettlement that focus on the inevitability of climate change and the inability of climate-vulnerable populations to reverse it can serve to "entrench vulnerable communities in inequitable power relations, further redirecting their fate from their hands," Pacific Island communities in climate-threatened areas contest this representation, instead focusing on their communities' strategies for survival and resilience in the context of Indigenous concepts of mobility, migration, and environmental stewardship.[27] Many Indigenous Pacific communities have long viewed the land and seas as being interrelated and coextensive; however, as Jetñil-Kijiner points out, these localized epistemologies, knowledges, and observations—developed over the course of many generations—still tend to get dismissed as irrelevant or superstitious until ratified by the measurements of climate scientists.[28] Yet as this scientific evidence increasingly points to what Pacific Islanders have already observed and known for quite some time about the damaging effects of climate change, Indigenous Pacific communities are already leading the way in terms of incorporating sustainability practices into government policies and practices of everyday life, not only because their lands and livelihoods are immediately (and disproportionately) affected by rising sea levels caused by climate change, but also because in many cases such practices were central to the very forms of local culture and governance that were often radically disrupted, in the past century, by the introduction of Western forms of land tenure.[29] In this context, the actions that Pacific Island communities are taking to address climate change also operate as decolonial actions that reclaim and reassert Indigenous ways of living with(in) the environment.

In the case of both war and climate refugees, the insistence on an epistemological shift that prioritizes refugee *agency* over *victimhood* not only serves to provide a critical perspective on the relations and technologies of power between "host" nations and states of origin, but also foregrounds and emphasizes the material and affective sense of interconnectedness, entanglement, and mutual responsibility that lie between peoples and places in a globalizing world. Yet it remains important to keep in mind that a sense of mutual implication and entanglement does not (and should not) operate as a universalizing gesture that renders all differences equivalent.[30] Given their different positioning vis-à-vis one another and the militarized presence and infrastructures of the U.S. nation-state, it may be premature to make unified claims to a solidarity that would be able to clearly and explicitly conjoin the political and social goals and aims of Asian refugee and Indigenous Pacific communities. Instead, this chapter turns to narrative, literature, and performance to sound out moments of intimacy or affinity between the two— connections that have been placed under erasure, or made otherwise unthinkable, by the territorial claims of the nation-state.[31] To this end, I find it useful to return to the metaphoric association of refugee communities with oceanic phenomena and consider how such a metaphor simultaneously refuses the stability of *solidarity* while engaging the currents of *affinity*. The fluidity implied by a "refugee tide" or "wave" can emphasize the entangled and palimpsestic histories of both "home" and "host" nations and how all parties have been mutually—though unevenly—affected by and implicated in the crises that have provoked these large-scale migrations. The artists, authors, and advocates whose work is explored in this chapter have sought to communicate the effects of these upheavals to the broader global community in immediate, visceral, and affective ways. Drawing inspiration from the ebb and flow of the ocean and its tides, these representations of refugee experience reverberate simultaneously as both hope and threat. They are cautionary tales of a present and future shaped by competing imperial ambitions, extractive economies, fear, and greed. But they are also a celebration of survival and survivance through and beyond the politics, technologies, and infrastructures of what all too many of us have come to accept as the governing conditions of modern life.

"I'm Taking You with Me": Rethinking Vulnerability in Climate Change Discourse

> The Prime Minister of Tuvalu was quoted as saying
> if we save Tuvalu
> we save the world
>
> But what if we don't save Tuvalu
> what if bees and butterflies become extinct
> what if our/my islands don't survive
>
> just who
>
> do you think
>
> will be next?
>
> I'm taking you with me
>
> I'm taking you with me
>
> I'm taking you with me
>
> —KATHY JETÑIL-KIJINER, "The Butterfly Thief"

In October 2018, the Intergovernmental Panel on Climate Change (IPCC), a scientific panel convened by the United Nations, released a report announcing that at current rates of greenhouse gas emissions, global temperatures would rise by as much as 1.5 degrees Celsius by 2040.[32] This rise in global temperatures would result in a number of environmental changes with damaging results, giving a significantly smaller window for mitigating action on climate change than previous estimates had delivered. While the IPCC's announcement made headlines for how it undercut the conventional wisdom of the "two-degree threshold"—the idea that a rise in global temperatures of 2 degrees Celsius over preindustrial levels will be the point at which we will see a sharp increase in risk for potentially catastrophic climate events, a benchmark that has been used as a target for setting global policies around greenhouse gas reduction programs—the leaders of island states in the Pacific and Atlantic had been calling for a lower policy threshold of 1.5 degrees Celsius since the issue emerged during the negotiation of the Copenhagen Accords in 2009.[33] The IPCC's report simply brought the urgency that such island states were already experiencing as a day-to-day reality to the attention of a global audience writ large.

Despite a broad scientific consensus on the inevitability of climate change—and even the potential for its catastrophic effects to manifest themselves globally within the span of decades rather than centuries—climate change is a problem whose urgency has largely remained theoretical for many who live in First World industrial nations. For those whose everyday lives have been largely sheltered from the material effects of rising tides and global temperatures, the connections between the habits of everyday life and the problems of climate change remain relatively abstract. In such conditions, the political will and energy to agitate for meaningful actions on climate change on the part of major industrial nations are often subordinated to issues that have more immediately visible effects, such as economic growth, domestic health care, and immigration reform. This, in turn, offloads the burden of environmental stewardship to smaller, less wealthy, and less industrialized nations that are more directly and immediately threatened by the environmental changes already occurring due to climate change. As is the case with many Pacific Island states, these are often nations that play a negligible role in creating greenhouse gas emissions and that generally lack the financial resources needed to respond to dramatic environmental changes. Moreover, their personal and political efforts to curb climate change are frequently disregarded or canceled out by the actions of major industrial states such as Australia and the United States.

The uneven distribution of the long-term damage caused by environmental pollution, waste, and climate change—which includes the melting of polar ice caps, warming of the seas, drought events, toxic drift, and extreme weather conditions—illustrates what Rob Nixon has called the "slow violence" of climate change, defined as "a violence that occurs gradually and out of sight, a violence of delayed destruction that is dispersed across time and space, an attritional violence that is typically not viewed as violence at all."³⁴ Yet while Nixon aligns the invisibility of slow violence with the equal invisibility, on a representational and political scale, of the communities that most suffer from it, an exception might be made for the case of Pacific Island communities—particularly those living on the island states of Tuvalu, Kiribati, the Federated States of Micronesia, and the Marshall Islands. Due to the immediate threat that rising tides and ocean acidification have posed to their communities, Pacific Islanders have come to play an important role in representing the pressing issue of global climate change. Sea level rise in Tuvalu and Kiribati, in particular, has drawn a number of journalists, scientists, and development specialists to document the environmental and cultural effects of climate change on the islands; it has also given rise to productions and performances showcasing how local and regional beliefs, trends, politics, and cultural practices in the affected islands have shaped a range of responses to changing environmental conditions.³⁵ Yet the overall visibility of these Pacific Island states in the context of a growing international interest in climate change policy has had mixed consequences.

On the one hand, visibility has provided Pacific Island states—including Tuvalu, Kiribati, Fiji, and the Marshall Islands—with a public platform from which they can use their experience and testimony to lead the way in both regional and global efforts to curb greenhouse gas emissions. As members of the Alliance of Small Island States (AOSIS), Pacific Island states have been instrumental in helping to shape goals and policies governed by the United Nations Framework on Climate Change (UNFCC) and exerted significant "moral leadership" in the shaping of the 2009 Copenhagen Accords.³⁶ While AOSIS's efforts to make the temperature rise of 1.5 degrees Celsius above preindustrial levels the target for determining emissions policy for signatories ultimately failed—2 degrees Celsius prevailed—its efforts nevertheless "opened doors for a larger consideration of 1.5 degrees Celsius in scientific research and future negotiations."³⁷ Indeed, AOSIS took up discussion of the 1.5 degree threshold again during the negotiations of the 2015 Paris Agreement, a move that led directly to the commissioning of the 2018 IPCC report.³⁸

Yet even the 1.5 degree threshold—like 2 degrees Celsius—is still merely a heuristic, an abstraction intended to make the threat of climate change legible to policy makers rather than a magic number at which, or beyond which, the problem of climate change will be "solved."³⁹ Above and beyond the debate over threshold numbers, the problem of climate change requires a broad range of reforms to the very structures of industrial and extractive capitalism central to both First World nations and global forms of governance. Thus, while Pacific Island states have continued to take on leadership roles within the context of international and intergovernmental climate change, material changes in climate policy have been slow to follow.[40] Financial commitments to clean-energy and climate-resilience programs from industrial nations have not been forthcoming or easily accessible,[41] and in 2017, U.S. President Donald Trump announced the withdrawal of the United States, a country responsible for the second-largest percentage of global greenhouse gas emissions, from the emission reduction goals set by the Paris Agreement.[42]

The reluctance of industrialized nations to take meaningful action on climate change has found expression in mainstream representations of Pacific Islanders from climate-threatened states as paradigmatic *victims*, largely due to their territorially and demographically small sizes and limited political power. Although many island-threatened states have been required to repeatedly perform, narrate, and give measurable evidence of their "vulnerability" to secure funding for mitigation/resilience efforts and renewable energy and emissions reductions projects,[43] most resist or outright reject the label of "climate refugees" because of how the term naturalizes their displacement by making it seem both irreversible and inevitable.[44] While the depiction of Pacific Island communities as victims to be "saved" is certainly consistent with the narrative contours of the refugee discourses discussed in the previous section, the naturalization of Indigenous dispossession *through* highly visible and even sympathetic representation is also clearly a continuation of settler colonial tropes of the "disappearing" or time-bound Native and the conceptual "smallness" and remoteness of islands in the global context.[45] Discourses around aid for renewable energy projects and environmental resilience projects in Tuvalu, for example, tend to represent or construct the island nation as a "laboratory and litmus test for the effects of climate change on the planet" in ways that problematically echo similar assumptions about islands' "smallness" and isolation used to justify the project of nuclear testing—and subsequent studies on the effects of radiation exposure on human subjects—in the Marshall Islands half a decade earlier.[46] Moreover, mainstream representations and receptions of environmental refugees in sites such as the United States, Aotearoa/NZ, and Australia have tended to view them not as people making informed choices around cultural survival but have instead fallen back into colonial stereotypes around these communities' perceived "backwardness."[47] The stereotyping and scapegoating of climate refugees—which aligns the larger problem of global climate migration with the communities most directly affected by them—are illustrative of a kind of climate denialism that allows the citizens of industrial states to avoid thinking about the many ways that their daily habits directly contribute to the ongoing production and emissions of carbon, industrial, and nonindustrial waste that have worked to displace climate refugees in the first place. Similarly, by focusing on the *refugee* communities as ones that are in need of acculturation and assimilation to industrial modernity, such views also implicitly take on the progressive assumptions that have formed the groundwork for settler colonial, military, and extractive projects in the Pacific Islands: the very systems that have materially contributed to the current climate crisis and potential need for resettlement.

The intimate entanglement of these global and international systems with the environmental crises they seek to mitigate makes it increasingly clear that the "climate refugee" crisis cannot be solved through legal instruments only—for example, by clarifying and making specific rules for defining who qualify as refugees and determining the conditions under which they will be accommodated. Instead, it requires a much more ambitious agenda, including a profound rethinking of resource management in ways that emphasize entirely different ways to approach the relationship between land and sea, the human and nonhuman worlds. Thus, while Sophie Webber and Inés de Agueda Corneloup and Arthur Mol have argued that small island states use performances of vulnerability to deploy a form of "moral leadership" that allows them to exert political influence within international climate talks and agreements that appear disproportionate to their limited structural and economic power within these systems,[48] arguments set forth by Epeli Hau'ofa, Vicente Diaz and J. Kēhaulani Kauanui, and Teresia Teaiwa suggest instead that the Native Pacific Islanders' moral leadership in global climate discourse springs *not* from their positions as victims facing the loss of their land but, rather, from the depth of their generational knowledges gathered from centuries of living with and on the seas.[49] I want to suggest here that these knowledges and Indigenous epistemologies meaningfully rethink and repurpose the very concept of "vulnerability" at the core of climate refugee discourse, shifting its implications from narratives of victimhood and powerlessness to a discourse shaped by (1) an approach to territory that views land and sea as coextensive rather than as ontologically distinct categories; (2) an understanding of time that thinks in terms of generational cycles rather than speed and progress; and (3) ways of living in the world that emphasize the intimacies, rather than estrangement, between human and nonhuman entities. As Margaret Jolly notes, the most critical and valuable concepts that Indigenous knowledges have to contribute to current climate discourses—and what is most frequently ignored by climate scientists—are not so much the "'traditional ecological knowledge' of environment and climate, such as the capacity to deal with those natural disasters (earthquakes, cyclones, tsunamis, floods, and droughts) that regularly affect the region, but the ability to grapple with the broader epistemological, political, moral, and metaphysical relations between human beings and the nonhuman world."[50] In other words, the problem of climate change cannot be tackled through scientific discourse and international law alone. Rather, it requires a significant shift in the way we think about our relationships with the world around us, and a radical openness to the *vulnerability* of shared or distributed agency. Such vulnerability is not weakness but wisdom, a way of navigating the complex and profoundly interconnected world that we live in. It is in their recognition and articulation of this ethics of vulnerability that Pacific Island states have been able to take up a sense of meaningful moral leadership on the international stage.

This (re)turn to local knowledges has included a resurgence of interest in local practices of resource management—including the Polynesian *rahui*, or a "restriction placed on a resource (for instance, plantations or a species of fish) or a territory (a valley, a river, a lagoon, or an ocean) for a given time."[51] Yet precisely because this and other Pacific practices are based on a worldview that presumes an intimate and complex entanglement of political, aesthetic, and spiritual systems, such practices are not always immediately legible to the legal languages and scientific methodologies central to the construction and operations of international policy. Indeed, as Linda Tuhiwai Smith has argued, such languages and methodologies historically have worked to silence and subordinate Indigenous ways of knowing by insisting on the division and isolation of these categories.[52] In consequence, some of the most effective ways that Pacific Island states have demonstrated leadership in the call to recognize our *mutual* and *global* vulnerability has been through oratory, debate, performance, and poetry—fields that are not considered "scientific" testimony yet incorporate complex analytic methodologies that transgress Western academic disciplinary boundaries. As Cresantia Vakaʻuta, Lingikoni Vakaʻuta, and Rosiana Lagi have argued, "Indigenous Pacific conceptions of custodianship and the role of humans within the known universe, in communion with land, sea, and sky," see these arts as "critical to a meaningful discourse about sustainability."[53] Skill at oratory and debate and the use of engaged give-and-take dialogues have been a central element of leadership in a number of Pacific Island communities; they are also skills that have been deployed to significant effect within the circuits of international policy, as former President Anote Tong of Kiribati and Prime Minister Enele Sopoanga of Tuvalu, among others, have emerged as powerful and effective speakers who have used their voices to keep the very specific and immediate challenges faced by island states in the conversations on climate change at United Nations and international conferences. Along similar lines, under Fiji's presidency, the United Nations Climate Change Conference introduced a "Talanoa Dialogue" in 2017, loosely based on the Fijian practice of "multi-level and multi-layered critical discussions and free conversations," which invited a range of proposals from different global constituencies for mapping out creative ideas on approaching climate change.[54] The opening up of these dialogues at least nominally represents an attempt to shift power away from a top-down model, where policy is set by a handful of powerful global stakeholders, and toward a model inspired by a localized practice of dialogue and discussion driven by "mutual respect" where all who are affected may participate.[55]

Yet perhaps some of the most sharply effective calls for climate change reform have come from artists and activists whose work demonstrates these connections between Pacific politics and Pacific storytelling aesthetics, and the particular power that such epistemologies have for thinking through the pressing problems of climate change. The Marshallese poet Kathy Jetñil-Kijiner is one such artist/activist whose poems, short films, and impassioned testimony reveal a powerful model for approaching climate change through a historically informed, empowered, and profoundly entangled sense of vulnerability. Jetñil-Kijiner gained international recognition when she presented her poem "Dear Matafele Peinem" at the opening of the UN Climate Summer in 2014. Imagined as an open letter addressed to Jetñil-Kijiner's infant daughter, "Dear Matafele Peinem" is a powerful piece that outlines the threat climate change and rising sea levels pose to the Marshall Islands and calls on the rest of the world to take action. Jetñil-Kijiner is celebrated for her ability to bring the voices of people most directly and dramatically affected by climate change to the forefront of the debate; her poetry and activism also contextualize the current climate change "crisis" as embedded within the long history of dispossession, displacement, and environmental exploitation experienced by the peoples of the Marshall Islands. Jetñil-Kijiner's work highlights how the modern world that many in the West have come to take for granted has been built on a series of violent dispossessions, from the copra industries pioneered during the years of German colonization through the U.S. nuclear testing programs of the twentieth century, that now threaten to displace us all.

In 2016, the British renewable energy company Good Energy asked Jetñil-Kijiner to create a new poem inspired by crowdsourced ideas about the potential damage and effects of climate change. Writing about the process, Jetñil-Kijiner notes:

Interestingly enough, I noticed quite a few responses indicated concerns with the loss of bees and butterflies. There really aren't that many bees and butterflies back home in the Marshalls, so this caught my attention. I did some basic online research, and found out that actually populations of both bees and butterflies are facing extinction—one of the reasons contributing to this threat is climate change. . . . I decided to connect this impending loss with the impending loss of our islands.[56]

The poem that resulted from this project, "The Butterfly Thief," borrows and revises a phrase from an image that Jetñil-Kijiner encountered during the course of her research. As she describes it in the poem:

> I came across a cartoon
> that showed a bumble bee
> cute tubby and smiling
> with a message in a little cartoon bubble
>
> If we die
>
> we're taking you with us.[57]

The bumblebee's threat—"we're taking you with us"—is given a "Marshallese face," realigned with the individual speaker's voice (*"I'm* taking you with *me"*), then recurs as a refrain throughout the poem that plays with the multiple implications of the phrase, which can be interpreted as a promise of both (local) survivance and a threat of (global) extinction.

Emphasizing the global effects of the climate change that threatens her islands' shores, the speaker in "The Butterfly Thief" warns that industrial nations neglect the islands' fate at their own peril: "If our islands drown out / due to the rising sea level / just who do you think / will be next? / I'm taking you with me."[58] That refrain, "I'm taking you with me," punctuates the end of each stanza as a sharp reminder of how climate change reveals the profoundly entangled and interconnected nature of life on this planet. Like the "butterfly effect," a model drawn from chaos theory that posits that a small change or atmospheric disturbance (such as the flap of a butterfly's wing) can have a significant impact on the system as a whole, "The Butterfly Thief" points out that the actions taken by people and industries in one part of the globe can result in widespread damage to the environments and communities in another. Yet the speaker's repetition of "I'm taking you with me" emphasizes the *mutuality* of this damage and potential for species extinction within a longer time frame that shifts our perspective beyond the immediate future ("just who do you think / will be next?").

Shifting the poem into this broader timescale gesturing to periods both before and beyond the human, the speaker reflects on a story of origins:

> Some stories say our ancestors came from volcano stone
> Lidrepdrepju—a basalt rock goddess rooted in reef
> Today I keep a basalt rock on my bookshelf
> What tokens of our land shall we/will we
> store in our selves
> inside our honeycomb of chest bones
> the buzzing of a shore long gone
>
> I'm taking you with me.[59]

In this context, the refrain "I'm taking you with me" takes on a different sensibility, registering not as a threat of global extinction but as a promise to the speaker's ancestors/the land itself that they will not be forgotten or left behind, even if the worst comes to pass. Stored "in our selves" even when the shore itself may be "long gone," these stories, these memories, this culture, the speaker promises, will continue to survive and thrive through the lives of a community in diaspora. The speaker's promise for the island's survivance moves the poem's vision for the climate-threatened Pacific *beyond* the immediate necessities of survival or even resilience, terms that can sometimes delimit the extent of one's agency to a restoration of the status quo. Instead, it resonates with the speaker's demand that survivance requires a future that is not merely restorative but *revolutionary*—one that will operate on dramatically different premises than the dominant discourses around climate change, where mitigation, resettlement, and adaptation remain the only foreseeable outcome.

These options, as Jetñil-Kijiner points out, are defined and maintained by the nation-states and corporations that most benefit from the profoundly uneven global power dynamics that have both precipitated and work to extend the ongoing climate crisis. Noting President Trump's appointment in 2017 of Rex Tillerson, the former chief executive of ExxonMobil, as U.S. secretary of state, the poem's speaker calls out how wealthy and powerful nations and corporations *continue* to exploit the resources of the world for their own gain, extending a pattern of territorial extraction and exploitation that dates at least back to eighteenth- and nineteenth-century colonial projects:

So whose colony is it collapsing today?
Is it just the bees?
Or is it also the human race
funding the world to be washed into the sea?
Trust—
I'm taking you with me.⁶⁰

Jetñil-Kijiner's deployment of the image of an endangered "colony" of bees gestures to this longer history of environmental damage and how today's powerful industrial nations have profited from a centuries-long history of managing and exploiting human and nonhuman bodies through colonial and imperial projects executed throughout Asia, Africa, the Americas, and the Pacific Islands. Read against Jetñil-Kijiner's other poems, which directly address how the Marshall Islands and its people have suffered under U.S. administration, the profoundly interconnected histories of colonial and environmental exploitation at this particular site are made even more explicit.⁶¹ In this context, the refrain "I'm taking you with me"—which repeats three times to end the poem—recurs as a threat of retribution, not only at a personal or political but a *planetary* scale, pointing out the dangerous unsustainability of empire that has come to threaten us all.⁶²

While "Dear Matafele Peinem" uses direct address to reach out to a beloved daughter, the "you" from whom "The Butterfly Thief" demands recognition is the complacent class of Western/First World peoples, perhaps more familiar with bees and butterflies than oceans and beaches, who have not yet been directly affected by the impacts of their consumption. The emotional impact of this address is magnified when the poem is performed—something that Jetñil-Kijiner, with her background in performance poetry and video production, well knows. The piece appears as a "video poem," a multimedia art piece that features Jetñil-Kijiner reciting the poem to the camera, with her back to a tree-lined shore. "The Butterfly Thief" is deliberately simple in its effects: unlike some of her other, more highly produced video poems, this video appears to be taken in a single take. As she speaks, Jetñil-Kijiner slowly advances on the camera, her relentless forward movement telegraphing the intense urgency of her mission and the demand she is posing to her viewers. Her movement also mimics the slow yet relentless advance of the very processes she describes, the encroachment of water from the shores onto the land. By the time the poem ends, with the last three repetitions of "I'm taking you with me," Jetñil-Kijiner stands several feet inland from where she began, on a grassy field. The distance she has traveled parallels the slow yet devastating effects of sea level rise; read against a central anecdote in the poem in which an elder describes the desertification of Ellekan Island ("He says only 10 years ago / that island was lush. Full of coconut and pandanus trees. Now / just a pile of sand and stone"), the implication is that this field, barring meaningful actions or change, will soon become the new shoreline.

Jetñil-Kijiner's performance emphasizes the strategy of communicating not only through information but through emotion. The anger, anguish, and determination that Jetñil-Kijiner expresses throughout the video poem, from sorrow for the loss of land to the determination that punctuates the repeated "I'm taking you with me" refrain, connect the precarity of the islands' existence with the vulnerability of the globe writ large. In this context, the apparent helplessness or vulnerability of the speaker to fight back individually against climate change is tied back to the conceptual division between the "I" and the "we," where it is only the global "we" that might be capable of saving "Tuvalu" and therefore "the world." The threat that recurs in the refrain—and concludes the poem—is that, stripped of this sense of global responsibility, only the "I" remains, and the "I" alone lacks the agency to do anything but "take you with me." Yet as the poem is being recited, "you" and "me" are brought together through the speaker's direct address, with the performance *itself* serving to draw both speaker and audience into the position of a temporary "we." The question that Jetñil-Kijiner thus leaves open for her audience in the poem is whether or not they will take up their end of the dialogue; whether or not they will be able to set aside their *own* perceptions of individual agency ("I") in order to enter into the "we" of mutual entanglement and mutual responsibility.

In this way, "The Butterfly Thief"—in line with Jetñil-Kijiner's other work, and the performances of other Pacific Island artists and activists—makes a strategic use of *performance* as a mode of taking action and articulating an agency that moves beyond the individual.[63] As individuals, we are all vulnerable to the effects of climate change, yet at the same time, coming to terms with and expressing that vulnerability can be a powerful way of asserting agency. As Karen Barad notes:

> Agency is about response-ability, about the possibilities of mutual response, which is not to deny, but to attend to power imbalances. Agency is about possibilities for worldly re-configurings. So agency is not something possessed by humans, or non-humans for that matter. *It is an enactment.*[64]

This idea of agency as "enactment"—that is, a "possibility for worldly re-configurings" that must be dynamically created *between* people, as well as between humans and nonhumans—is not only described but itself performed and executed in "The Butterfly Thief," which (as a "YouTube poem") engages a complex assemblage that includes not only Jetñil-Kijiner and her viewers/listeners but also the crowdsourced contributors who inspired the poem, the videographer, the technologies for producing the video, and the screens that receive them; the physical cabling and undersea networks that provide the infrastructure for its dissemination and distribution; and the island itself that appears in silent eloquence behind Jetñil-Kijiner as she speaks. Upon viewing, all of these forces come together to "enact" an agency that is not invested in the speaker or audience member alone but that draws them together, through the medium of these nonhuman elements, into a state of shared vulnerability. Such an enactment of vulnerability, understood as entanglement or as having a distributed agency, is diametrically opposed to what Sophie Webber describes as the "compelled" performances of vulnerability (read as victimhood or *lack* of agency) that serve to maintain the unevenness of power structures in the field of climate-change mitigation and development.[65] Rather, by emphasizing these moments of entanglement not merely as a threat of mutual destruction but as an opportunity to think beyond the logic of mitigation, Jetñil-Kijiner's activist performance fits in with a genealogy of Pacific political and aesthetic thought that considers lands and seas, human and nonhuman worlds as coextensive and coresponsible. Such reframing encourages us to think about climate change not simply as an abstract problem to be solved but as a force that is bringing all of us together into new and sometimes discomforting relationships and intimacies with one another and with the nonhuman world. What we make of these new intimacies will determine how we will survive, or not, in a changing world.

Time and Tide: Refugee Passages

> In Vietnamese, the word for *water* and the word for *a nation*,
> *a country*, and *a homeland* are one and the same: *nu'óc*.
> —LÊ THI DIỄM THÚY, *The Gangster We Are All Looking For*

While the work of Kathy Jetñil-Kijiner and other Pacific Island artists and activists emphasizes our shared vulnerability to climate change, the ocean passages of Southeast Asian communities collectively visualized, stigmatized, and memorialized as boat people highlight the global implications of the mass migrations and displacements caused by war. If the nation-state is premised on a terrestrially based understanding of identity, statehood, and citizenship, how might we interpret the specific case of refugees from Vietnam, a nation that asserts a sense of national identity not based on claims to rootedness in the *land* but, rather, through the constant ebb and flow of *water*? How might this reinterpretation of national identity or belonging through a cyclical, oceanic space shift our understandings of the nation's orientation to both time and space in ways that denaturalize the contingencies and vulnerabilities of its construction? How might reconfiguring the concept of a "refugee tide" not as a threat of dissolution but, instead, as an opportunity to reconceptualize subject formation on a different temporal scale reshape discourses around migration to be more in tune with contemporary patterns of global movements and diaspora?

In this section, I outline how Southeast Asian experiences of ocean passage inform a "refugee epistemology" in which experience unfolds along alternative modes of temporality, complicating what Benedict Anderson, following Walter Benjamin, has called the "homogeneous, empty time" crucial to the imagining of the nation-state.[66] Whereas the "empty time" of the nation-state presumes that time's passage is experienced in a uniform or "universal" way, the experiences of refugee passage puncture and disrupt this presumption of temporal homogeneity by emphasizing how temporality—much like one's personal or bodily vulnerability to the violence of war—is differentially experienced in ways that largely depend on one's position and ability, or inability, to move through space. For people who have been left to languish in the liminal space and time of the refugee camps, or who continue to live out cycles of poverty in First World "hyperghettos," an experience of time as *static* or *cyclical* marks what Eric Tang has termed "refugee temporality"—a perception of time that complicates the positioning of refugee resettlement and assimilation as part of a progressive narrative from abjection to full liberal subjecthood.[67] These refugee temporalities foreground how capital-driven systems of oppression continue to work against refugee communities even when they are "resettled" in a new space; thus, they challenge the progressive, assimilationist rhetorics that seek to incorporate refugee communities into the settler colonial project of naturalizing the territorial nation-state. By turning to the space of the ocean, I hope to reimagine or reengage the status of the refugee figure *at sea*, focusing on how these refugee figures' personal and political vulnerability—in ways that resonate with the entangled vulnerability addressed by Pacific Island artists and activists—can operate both as a call to action *and* an epistemological framework through which we might think otherwise about the temporal and territorial assumptions grounding the logics and logistics of refugee resettlement.

Reflecting on her mother's refugee passage across the ocean, the performance artist Patricia Nguyên posits that water is central to "the performance and theorization of Vietnamese subjectivity and subjection" precisely because it gets at the intense vulnerability inherent in the refugees' experience of "statelessness at sea."[68] On the open seas, and adrift in international waters, refugees are not only left to the mercy of the elements but are unprotected by the government or legal system of any one nation.[69] In the case of Vietnamese refugees, thousands of people who fled the country by boat never arrived at their intended destinations, due to shipwreck or kidnap and murder by pirates. Yet refugees' experience of enforced statelessness is also directly linked to territorial states' border policies, including not only the increasing refusal on the part of first-asylum nations such as Malaysia and Singapore to accept them, but also the selectively uneven "processing" of refugees already at the camps for resettlement in the United States and other nations. Criteria for resettlement in these nations grew more and more stringent in the 1970s and 1980s, and, as Yến Lê Espiritu points out, they were also "not neutral": they privileged "men . . . over women, South Vietnamese over North Vietnamese applicants, and nuclear over non-normative families" and required applicants to persuasively demonstrate their opposition to and persecution by communism.[70] Thus, while "boat people" became popularized as an image of abject collectivity synonymous with humanitarian crisis, the border politics that continued to render these refugees as stateless (and, implicitly, subjectless) entities remained largely unremarked and unseen. Instead, boat people became metaphorically and figuratively aligned with the oceanic environment that surrounded them, constituted as naturalized problems or threats, rather than as a response to the actions of First World nations.

For Nguyên, however, this "statelessness at sea" is central to the articulation of a Vietnamese diasporic subjectivity centered on absence and displacement rather than reclamation or recovery. In her performance work, Nguyên illustrates how this absence is not simply a *lack* of presence or subjectivity. It can also be an *excess* or plenitude that likewise serves to overwhelm and create vulnerability. As Nguyên notes, displacement—understood as "excess or overflow"—is "at the crux of the oral histories of Vietnamese boat refugees, wherein the possibilities of life and death at sea are overdetermined by an excess of water."[71] In her work *salt | water*, performed in 2015, on the fortieth anniversary of the end of the Vietnam/American war, Nguyên demonstrates this excess as she steps into a bucket filled with water and salt and begins to drown herself in it:

I begin to drown myself in the water, submerging my head in the bucket, inhaling and swallowing gulps of salt water, lifting my head up as I gasp for air and then dunking my head into the water again, while my lungs fill with a burning sensation. It is as though my insides are going to rupture from the pangs of salty water ingested. Gasping for air, every crevice of my body is burning from the irritation of the salt.[72]

More than an "absent presence," where the pointed absence or lack of an object or event calls attention to its erasure within mainstream discourses, Nguyên's performance, by foregrounding the pain of becoming one with water, focuses on the ways that the *excessiveness* and *transgressiveness* of water can emphasize its status not as an empty space for projection but as a material presence with immediate and visceral effect.[73] The violent displacement of water (by her body as she moves into the tub) and air (by water as it enters her lungs) reimagines the term not only as loss but as an overflow or plenitude that chokes out life. In ways that resonate with the discourse around climate change in the Pacific Islands, salt | water emphasizes the undeniable materiality of ocean space and environments in ways that cut across the abstractions of political debate and policy positions that structure and shape international human rights law. By foregrounding the visceral effects of oceanic excess on bodies, as well as the land, Nguyên's work complements the work of Jetñil-Kijiner and other climate activists who insist on foregrounding the materiality of ocean environments as a counterpoint to the abstractions addressed by policy and climate science.

Reconstituting a sense of oceanic subjectivity around the experience of oceanic passage and the ebb and flow of water likewise pushes back against a progressive narrative of healing, restoration, and recuperation that has tended to position Vietnamese refugees as subjects and beneficiaries of the "gift of freedom," moving from abject collectivity to individual liberty.[74] Mainstream representations of Southeast Asian refugees as initially abject yet progressively assimilated and upwardly mobile communities—particularly but not exclusively in the United States—have both aided in the rehistoricization of the Vietnam War as a "good war" *and* worked to recategorize refugees as a subset of voluntary "immigrant" communities, who have become aligned with the goals and the ideologies of the settler nation-state.[75] In these ways, mainstream refugee discourses around resettled Southeast Asian communities serve a dual temporal function: first, they relegate the events of the Vietnam War to a fixed historical *past*; and second, they naturalize a progressive temporality in which assimilation to and (incorporation within) the settler nation-state is presumed to be the end goal or completion of the refugee's trajectory.

Yet as many scholars, artists, and critics have pointed out, this neat timeline of refugee resettlement does not reflect the fuller and more complex experiences of refugee communities in the United States and the West. First, the periodization of the Vietnam War as a temporally bounded event— beginning in 1955, with the start of U.S. intervention in the region, and ending in 1975, with the fall of Saigon—does not include the many conflicts that led up to its beginning, the *longue durée* of its legacies, and the ongoing cycles of migration and return or repatriation that continue to this day.[76] Second, the experience of refugee migration and flight from war—often accompanied by repressed memories of trauma, feelings of nostalgia for a lost homeland, and grief over the absent presence of loved ones either left behind or passed away—is not experienced or always processed as a straightforward story of abjection to assimilation. Instead, as scholars working in the field of trauma studies and around the issue of post-traumatic stress disorder (PTSD) have amply shown, memories of the past can often emerge in recursive, circular, and disruptive ways, puncturing the perceptual divide between past and present.[77] Following Marianne Hirsch, such memories can manifest in material and psychological consequences well into the next generation, as refugee "postmemory" (which Hirsch defines as "the relationship of the second generation to powerful, often traumatic, experiences that preceded their births but that were nevertheless transmitted to them so deeply as to seem to constitute memories in their own right") comes to shape the identities and trajectories of even the generations who have little, if any, direct memory of the experience of displacement and refugee flight from their home countries.[78] For many who fled the war, as well as their descendants, the war cannot be neatly categorized and periodized. Instead, it continues to make its presence felt through personal and family memories and the practices of everyday life.[79]

The disruptive temporality of trauma and postmemory, as reflected through and around a central trope of oceanic passage, is vividly depicted in the Vietnamese American author lê thi diễm thúy's novel *The Gangster We Are All Looking For* (2003). Lyrical and episodic, lê's novel moves fluidly between past and present, focusing on the life of a young Vietnamese girl who has resettled in the United States. Interweaving the narrative of her family's resettlement in San Diego with their recollections of their life and flight from Vietnam, the novel combines one family's disparate experiences of wartime displacement into a work that does not fall into the pattern of a traditional *bildungsroman* so much as it provides a reflection of how one family was repeatedly torn apart and knitted itself back together, again and again. *Gangster* is not a story of resolution and recovery from trauma. It is an archive of the cycles of debility created by war, displacement, and their aftermath, as well as the acts of care and material needs necessary to live with these legacies rather than the closure needed to heal and move-beyond.[80] Indeed, the very idea of closure can operate as a form of epistemic violence against those who are always already marked by war's passage, a concept vividly explained by the narrator's mother:

> When I was born, [Ma] cried to know that it was war I was breathing in, and she could never shake it out of me. Ma says war makes it dangerous to breathe, though she knows you die if you don't. She says she could have thrown me against the wall, until I broke or coughed up this war that is killing us all. She could have stomped on it in the dark, and danced on it like a madwoman dancing on gravestones. She could have ground it down to powder and spat on it, but didn't I know? War has no beginning and no end. It crosses oceans like a splintered boat filled with people singing a sad song.[81]

Ma's lyrical depiction of war rejects the idea that it can be separated or exorcised from the family and its history. She imagines it as a toxic entity embedded in the very air that they breathe, yet "you die if you don't" breathe it in; it has become so intimately entangled with their bodies that any attempt to isolate and stamp out the war that is "killing us all" would also possibly break or kill them, as well, in the process. The very idea that one could stomp or grind out the war's effects was itself a pointless task, for—as she concludes—"war has no beginning and no end" and "crosses oceans like a splintered boat filled with people singing a sad song." Ma's analysis of war's effects thus not only traces out the entangled intimacies between human bodies and nonhuman environments, but also how they initiate similarly entangled relationships across the space of oceans.

Per Ma's metaphor, it is *war itself* that is the "splintered boat filled with people singing a sad song"—where the boat and its people are represented not as objects or victims of war but as a conduit through which war's effects pass back and forth across the space of the Pacific. War is therefore reconfigured as an endless *condition* that continues to reverberate through individuals and families rather than a stage that can passed through or beyond. In configuring war this way, Ma revises the more mainstream or stereotypical images of boat people that the narrator encounters earlier in the novel, which attempt to insert the refugees into more palatable and teleological narratives of healing and repair. Yet these stereotypical narratives have also played an important role in shaping the family's transpacific trajectory, as it also moved the family's American sponsor, Mr. Russell, to host her family after imagining them as "nameless, faceless bodies lying in small boats, floating on the open water."[82] To Mr. Russell, a U.S. Navy veteran who had been stationed in the Pacific, "The Vietnamese boat people merged with his memories of the Okinawans and the Samoans and even the Hawaiians."[83] For the well-meaning Mr. Russell, the narrative of Vietnamese victimhood is inextricably interconnected with a longer history of U.S. imperialism in the region, marked by his inability to distinguish Vietnamese from other Pacific and Asian peoples displaced by, and subsequently appropriated or subsumed into, twentieth-century U.S. military projects.[84] As with those earlier displacements, the imagining of Vietnamese as victims to be saved, assimilated, and incorporated into the United States indicates the profound entanglement of this progressive teleology with disavowals of the imperial violence that rendered Vietnamese, Okinawans, Sāmoans, and Hawaiians homeless, "faceless," and ultimately interchangeable in the mainstream U.S. imagination.

A different, yet related, image of boat people—this time represented by a photograph of the boat on which the narrator, her father, and her uncles escaped—depicts people who are not "blank slates," or potentially assimilable or educable individuals. Rather, they are an abject collectivity diminished and objectified in time and space. The narrator tells us that the picture

> was taken by someone standing on the deck of the ship that had picked us up. I don't know who took the picture or how one of the uncles came to have it. In the picture, our boat looks like a toy boat floating in a big bowl of water. There are little people standing in the boat. We are among the people in the picture but I can't tell who is who because we are so small. Small faces, small heads, small arms reaching out to touch small hands.[85]

While Mr. Russell's vision of boat people rendered them anonymous by imagining them as "faceless" figures, in this passage the figures on the boat are rendered indistinguishable not through erasure or substitution but through diminishment and distance. Viewing the image, the narrator understands in the abstract that she, her father, and her uncles are depicted in the photograph, but she feels absent from this representation. Instead, she dissociates from the image by placing herself in the position of the viewer, the person "standing on the deck of the ship that had picked us up," looking down on all of the "small faces, small heads, small arms reaching out to touch small hands." She imagines that those Americans on the rescue ship were all "laughing at us," which is why it "took them so long to lower the ladder."[86] By noting the hesitance on the part of the rescue ship to "lower the ladder," the narrator imagines that the Americans on the rescue ship must have

> laughed so hard at the sight of us so small, they started to roll around the deck like spilled marbles and they had to help one another to their feet and recall their own names—Emmett, Mike, Ron—and where they were from—Oakland, California; Youngstown, Ohio; Shinston, West Virginia—before they could let us climb up and say our names—Lan, Cuong, Hoang—and where we were from—Phan Thiet, Binh Thuan.[87]

In taking on the subject *position* of the Americans on the ship, the narrator also imagines the Americans as briefly subject*less*, transforming them from an observing subject ("*someone* standing on the deck of the ship that had picked us up") to a nonhuman collectivity ("they started to roll around the deck like spilled marbles"). In consequence, before proceeding with the rescue mission they have to pause to reconstruct and renarrate themselves back into subjectivity—starting with their names ("Emmett, Mike, Ron") and the places that they have, within the context of the settler colonial state, claimed as their homes ("Oakland, California; Youngstown, Ohio; Shinston, West Virginia")—*against* the un-settling potential represented by the spectacle of the boat people. Similarly, the rescuees are required to articulate themselves as individual subjects with specific names ("Lan, Cuong, Hoang") and homelands ("Phan Thiet, Binh Thuan") as they move from the collective space represented by the boat and onto the individuated space of the ship. In this way, the narrator speaks to how representation—in this case, photographic representation—can serve to override a sense of individual subjectivity, not only on the part of those who are being represented, but also for those who have positioned themselves as viewing subjects.[88] In both cases, it is the act of representation itself—the taking of the photograph—that creates a brief moment of intersubjectivity between the people on the boat and the people on the ship, providing the catalyst for this momentary unsettling (and subsequent resettlement) of "American" subjecthood.

If the highly visible spectacle of the Vietnamese as a collective entity left the narrator briefly "unsettled" by the feeling that she was lacking in individual agency, then her brother—who, as we discover later in the novel, died from drowning while the family was still in Vietnam—reverses this dynamic, being most vividly present through his absence. The brother's fate is slowly revealed over the course of the novel; the narrator pointedly avoids mentioning him in the novel's first chapter ("suh-top!"), encounters a sudden sensation of the brother's immaterial yet immediate sense of presence in the second chapter ("palms"), and finally describes the event of his death in the last chapter ("nu'ó'c"). The revelation of the brother's story—which moves the time frame of the narrative from the present back into the past—is juxtaposed against the narrator's progressive development as she comes of age in the United States. She arrives in the United States as a six-year-old refugee in the first section of the novel; by the novel's last section, she has gone away to college and left her family home behind. Yet these parallel timelines—one moving forward in time; the other moving backward—speak to how the brother's absence has remained intimately entangled with the narrator's trajectory.

While the brother's death is a personal matter for the narrator and her family, it also operates in the context of the novel as a whole in a more broadly allegorical register, coming to stand in for the many hundreds of thousands lost in passage.[89] His death by drowning parallels the *excess of water* that, as Nguyên's performance vividly demonstrates, contributed to the deaths of so many thousands of Vietnamese fleeing the country by boat. Even the neighboring women's superstitious reaction to the narrator's brother's death—blaming their grandfather for carrying the brother's body and the "bad water" it held into the home—recalls the suspicions and fears that caused neighboring countries to close their borders to refugee communities.[90] In this context, the brother's death serves as a remembrance of the personal *and* collective trauma that continues to draw the narrator further back into the past, even as she appears to follow a progressive trajectory into the future; it operates as an undercurrent that moves backward and away from the surface-level appearance of her constant forward motion, suggesting an alternative, cyclical temporality that escapes or exceeds dominant narratives that presuppose refugees' progressive assimilation into the national body or that seeks to contain them in a state of permanent stasis.

The connections between this alternative "refugee temporality" and the currents and undercurrents of oceanic passage emerge most strongly in the novel's final scene. Returning to a time not long after their arrival in the United States, the narrator recalls:

Ba drove us to the beach. We got out of the car and he led us toward the sea. At first, there seemed to be nothing but that long familiar expanse of darkness. We'd seen it before; it was the open sea, late at night, with no one around.

As we walked toward the water, I noticed that in the silence following each wave's crash scattered sparks of light appeared across the sand.

The beach was covered with small silver fish whose bodies gave off a strange light. The fish made their way toward us, turning their backs and baring their bellies to the full moon. They writhed in the wet sand and it seemed the more they writhed, the brighter they became. Up close, their little mouths moved busily, as if they could not get enough of the cool salt night air.

Out from the darkness of the sea, wave after wave of small, luminous bodies washed to shore.[91]

The narrator ends the novel by taking us back to where we were at the beginning, but this time, the family is reunited. While the novel begins with the family *divided* by water, with Ma "standing on a beach in Vietnam while Ba and I were in California," in this memory they are all together, standing on the same Southern California shoreline.[92] As they head toward the "open sea," that "long familiar expanse of darkness," the narrator suddenly notices the "sparks of light" across the sand—in truth, thousands of tiny silver fish who have beached themselves on the shore. The vivid image of these fish gasping and writhing on the shoreline reflects Huỳnh Sang Thông's observation, "To say in English that a man has 'lost his country' is not the same as to say in Vietnamese that he has 'lost the *nu'óc*' (*mât nu'óc*). If the English phrase sounds almost abstract, the Vietnamese expression evokes an ordeal by thirst, the despair of fish out of water."[93] Yet the implied parallel between the "small, luminous bodies" of the fish washing ashore and the lost and unmourned Vietnamese evokes not a sense of pity (as in Mr. Russell's imagination of the "faceless" boat people) or repulsion/hilarity (as in the photograph of the refugee boat). Rather, it evokes a sense of *recognition*: the narrator notes, "My father turned to my mother and me and, smiling broadly, pointed at the fish, as if we knew them."[94] In this scene, the fish washed ashore are regarded with neither pity nor disgust; instead, they are regarded with a feeling like kinship as the family recognizes their shared precarity as beings who have likewise found themselves washed ashore on unfamiliar land. As the novel ends with a final image of the narrator's younger self running toward the shining bodies of the beached fish—metaphorically transformed from individualized, "luminous" bodies into a collective "light"—it concludes not by moving us toward a transcendence that seeks to heal and move on from past pain and trauma but, instead, attempts to describe a *return to* this sense of collective precarity and vulnerability shared across oceanic, geographic, human/nonhuman, and temporal divides.

In lê's novel, the oceanic currents that brought the narrator and her family to American shores at the beginning of the novel draw them back together at the novel's end in ways that subvert the progressive narrative expectations that attach to the genres of the *bildungsroman* and the immigrant novel.[95] It likewise emphasizes the joy and beauty that can be found in a sense of transpacific kinship and connection in which the relationships broken and severed by war and oceanic passage can—through an oceanic perspective that considers the recursive circulation of matter, memory, and time—be reconstructed and remade. This reconstruction of family bonds, however, should not be confused with a simple narrative of repair or moving beyond: by ending the novel at a moment of epiphany set *before* the temporal end point of the narrative, lê shows us that these moments of epiphany mark not the ending of a story but important points of convergence. By the end of the novel, we already know that the family will break apart again and again after this shared moment. We also know that they will also come back together, albeit in different permutations and configurations.

In this sense, the "refugee temporality" that the novel maps out through this recursive narrative style—a worldview that remains *critical* of dominant narratives that position refugees as abject victims while articulating an alternative epistemology that emphasizes the significance of connections drawn across the conceptual divides of time, space, and human/nonhuman entities—echoes and emphasizes the entanglement of materiality and temporality illustrated by the ebb and flow of the ocean itself, drawing out significant resonances to the "seascape epistemology" that Epeli Hauʻofa and Karen Amimoto Ingersoll, respectively, have identified as central to Oceanian and Kanaka Maoli ways of knowing.[96] Indeed, it is through these differently situated orientations to the space/time of the ocean that we can see some of the potential resonances and cross-currents between a Southeast Asian "refugee epistemology" and Oceanic epistemologies and praxes begin to emerge. Both take up a cyclical, oceanic worldview that unsettles universalist assumptions premised on an anthropocentric, progressively unfolding temporality—manifesting in both nationalist narratives of assimilation *and* the universalizing concept of the Anthropocene— that does not always account or allow for human and nonhuman forms of resurgence.

There are, however, critical positional differences to keep in mind while engaging in a comparative analysis of war and "climate" refugees. First, while there are clearly philosophical similarities between Vietnamese and Oceanic attitudes toward the interrelationship and coextensiveness of land and sea, given the divergent development of these cultures over a period of thousands of years, such attitudes certainly cannot and should not be read as equivalent or interchangeable.[97] Second, the different histories of colonial interventions in Southeast Asia and the Pacific Islands mean that, while the marginalization of climate change "refugees" from the Marshall Islands, Tuvalu, Tokelau, and other small island nations are based on narratives of erasure or extinction that have informed the histories of colonial appropriation in the region, suspicions about the resettlement and integration of Southeast Asian war refugees tend to refer to a binary logic of alienation and assimilation that accompany the anxieties and contradictions of the Cold War.[98] These disparate histories have also contributed to sites of *conflict* between "refugee" and Indigenous populations, as in some cases refugee communities have become incorporated or enlisted into the projects of settler colonialism, while in others Pacific Island peoples have been made complicit in the detention and sustained "statelessness" of refugee populations.[99]

Yet a politics of affinity that takes into account the resonances *across* these divergent histories and epistemologies speaks to a potential for coalition building through and beyond the historical and disciplinary divisions that have separated these discourses or set them against one another. These opportunities for convergence and coalition have the potential to open up alternatives to assimilation and identification with the settler colonial nation-state, whose possessive logics contribute to divisions and competitions among differently articulated "refugee" populations.[100] While legal debates over the status of climate and war refugees have been focused largely on parsing out the differences between their conditions to improve or refine their (distinctive) categorization, comparative literary and cultural expressions can articulate some of the epistemological resonances that operate as an undercurrent to these different historical events and conditions, drawing out important moments of convergence, as well as difference.[101] Literary texts do not have to base themselves in the epistemological framework of human rights laws, which generally tend to focus on the rights of the individualized subject and the potential for redressability of their harms within the context of a progressive (or "developmental") temporal frame. Instead, they can express the experiences of displacement and statelessness *outside* a rights-based discourse that seeks primarily to reintegrate them into those more normative forms and trajectories of individual subjectivity.

It is in this spirit that I have sought to juxtapose the resonant connections between Jetñil-Kijiner's poem addressing global vulnerability to climate change and lê's novel about shared precarity in the face of endless global warfare. Jetñil-Kijiner's poem is delivered from a Marshallese shoreline in danger of being rendered lifeless through an excess of water, while lê's novel ends with the image of a school of fish slowly dying in water's absence. Yet both emphasize the ways that the *ocean itself* mediates and responds to the entangled interrelationship among humans, animals, and environments thrown into new configurations and new forms of intimacy by the forces of climate change and endless global war. Focused on the fluid and flexible space/time of the ocean, both works demand that we revise and reconsider what it means to embrace one's vulnerability to natural and historical forces in ways that mark the material and conceptual limitations of individual agency and subjectivity. These works illustrate that vulnerability is not exceptional, inhering only in the bodies and habits of those whose lives have been most directly affected. Rather, it is a condition that we all share in, although its effects have been differentially and unevenly distributed. In this context, the lessons to be drawn from the experiences, art, and activism of climate and war refugees are not isolated stories of individual triumph over adversity but, rather, collective strategies for survival—strategies to which we should all pay heed. For just as we may agree that our *oceans are endangered*, we must recognize that we are equally *endangered by oceans*: a global problem against which the individual alone cannot stand. It is this recognition of our mutual and collective vulnerability that becomes particularly critical for taking meaningful actions on climate change and other global crises. As the oceans continue to warm and rise, they will most certainly take us with them.

While the transpacific refugee passages outlined in this chapter have addressed the decolonial potential of deterritorialization, the next chapter explores how settler colonial *capital* likewise seeks to move through and across national borders, often obscuring the militarized state power that continues to determine the direction and provide the conduits through which such capital is allowed to flow. The abstraction of the material conditions and historical contexts that have conditioned contemporary transpacific capitalism into celebratory narratives of East Asian "miracle" economies and "transpacific partnerships" also serves to conceal the experiences of colonialism and postcoloniality that connect Asian and Pacific Islander migrants in their different trajectories through and across the Pacific. In the next chapter, I turn to works that highlight the travels of migrant laborers from Asian and Pacific Island nations as they circulate through and challenge the economic infrastructures that have framed the Pacific as an abstract space of capital. By reading these texts alongside one another, I highlight the complex networks of relation that have the potential to draw these differently situated communities together, and to help break down the reified and racialized distinctions that often keep them apart.

3

COMMERCIAL PASSAGES

On Cycles and Circulations

In the short story "A Brief History of the Trans-Pacific Tunnel," Chinese American author Ken Liu imagines an alternative history in which a Shōwa-era imperial Japan joins forces with a Depression-weakened United States to construct an undersea tunnel between Asia and the Americas as a solution to the global economic crisis threatening both nations. Hailed as a miracle of engineering, the transpacific tunnel, in the novel, serves as "the first real Keynesian stimulus project, which shortened the Great Depression," and the engineering demands of the complex infrastructure project drives "many technological advances," including the invention of the modern computer.[1] In this alternative timeline, World War II never takes place: the struggles over resources and capital that provided the most material rationale for warfare are apparently resolved through economic and diplomatic, rather than strictly militarized, means.

Yet the absence of outright war in this scenario leads to a peace built on a system of enslavement and suffering to which the world is all too eager to turn a blind eye. As the Japanese Empire continues to expand, conscripted prison labor from China and comfort women from Korea are brought in to aid in the construction of the tunnel, while the paid laborers—like the story's narrator, "Charlie," who identifies himself as a Formosan (Taiwanese) subject of the Japanese Empire—suffer under brutal working conditions and second-class citizenship, even as they identify and are made complicit with the Japanese imperial project. In the story's final revelation, we learn that

Charlie himself was responsible for the deaths of a number of the laboring prisoners, including a fellow Formosan, when he was forced at gunpoint to wall off a section of the tunnel occupied by a work gang to prevent the tunnel from flooding. The memory of this act haunts Charlie, and at the story's conclusion he strikes his own name from the commemorative plaque celebrating the tunnel's completion. In its place he carves the symbol of three interlinked ovals: "The links that bound two continents and three great cities together . . . these are the shackles that bound men whose voices were forever silenced, whose names were forgotten."[2] While profoundly belated, Charlie's recognition of the role he has played in other men's deaths—and his small act of resistance at the story's end—speaks to how such a reckoning must occur to imagine beyond the oppressive hierarchies that have shaped the status quo. That is, for transpacific subjects to have the potential to think beyond the mere *maintenance* of the global balance of power between the powerful and powerless, they must recognize the ways in which they have been entangled with, and responsible for silencing, the people who otherwise have been "forgotten" by the grand narratives of history.

As East Asian nations began to emerge as significant economic and industrial powers in the 1970s and 1980s, Evelyn Hu-DeHart notes that a new narrative around "Asian Americans as transnationals and bridge builders on the Pacific Rim" meant that Asian Americans came to be seen as a "primary instrument of this linkage and connection" across the space of the Pacific.[3] Although some Americans of Asian ancestry embraced this role of international go-between, Hu-DeHart cautions, individuals engaged in this kind of cross-cultural work need to consider whether they are truly building meaningful and transformative cultural networks or serving as "*compradores* for non Asian-American global capitalists, who merely use Asian Americans, with their cultural capital, as conduits and instruments to penetrate the Asian market or as subcontractors to manage production and labor relations at the floor level."[4] The concern about Asian American participation in a transpacific economy likewise begged the question of whether Asian Americans were "door openers or financiers"—that is, people with the agency and (financial/political) capital to shape the global economy—or merely the "bridges, links, and compromisers" that allow capital to flow through them.[5] In either case, the implicit connection between Asian mobility and the free flow of capital was assumed and taken for granted as Asian bodies and communities became aligned in the transpacific imagination, not only with the promises and potential of the globalizing economy, but also with its worst excesses and its most negative effects.[6]

"A Brief History of the Trans-Pacific Tunnel" literalizes this metaphoric conceit of diasporic Asians as bridge builders—or, in this case, tunnel diggers—across a transpacific region that has been powerfully and persistently reimagined as an abstract space of capital.[7] Liu's story emphasizes how these infrastructural and economic networks can both liberate and enslave as the systems that allow for increased mobility and circulations of capital serve to profit certain transpacific populations at the cost of others. For example, if elite Asians began to be reimagined as bridges for human and financial capital to traverse the space of the Pacific in the mid-1970s, the unskilled or "low-skilled" Asian laborers who were simultaneously migrating through and across the region were rendered invisible as "excludable populations in transit," ineligible for many of the basic protections and privileges that accrued to diasporic elites.[8] As Aimee Bahng points out, this occlusion of the "precipitous divide between the cosmopolitan elites and the continually displaced migrant workers of the world" prevents a true reckoning with the massive levels of inequality created through and sustained by these transpacific circulations, preventing or subverting alternative possibilities for transpacific connections and alliances.[9]

Just as Asian labor recedes within dominant articulations of this "new Pacific century," the Pacific Ocean and the Pacific Islands are likewise reduced to a metaphor for liquid capital or dismissed altogether from discourses about capital circulations and modernity. The emergence of "Pacific Rim Discourse"—which pointedly excludes the Pacific Islands in its articulation of a regional identity—marked a departure from the more spatially grounded, state-centered regional strategies that formed the logic for the policies of containment that resulted in military stalemates in Korea and Vietnam. Instead of attempting to "contain" communist influence by intervening militarily in postcolonial conflicts, the United States turned to an ocean-centered regional model that used economic power to leverage their influence in both the region and the world. Here, the "Pacific Rim" operates as a geopolitical expression of the postnational construct that Michael Hardt and Antonio Negri termed "empire," which "establishes no *territorial* center of power and does not rely on fixed boundaries or barriers."[10] This capital-driven empire is imagined as a "*decentered* and *deterritorializing* apparatus of rule that progressively incorporates the entire global realm within its open, expanding frontiers," drawing important symbolic parallels to the medium of the ocean itself.[11]

In contrast to the U.S. attitudes toward the Pacific in the early Cold War period (1945–1962) that—as I argued in Chapter 1—drew from racialized legacies of settler colonialism and Orientalist rhetoric to *reterritorialize* ocean space, the post–Vietnam War era in which this "Pacific Rim Discourse" emerged (1975–1997) saw an increasing *deterritorialization* of the Pacific, which increasingly framed the region in terms of the flows of abstract and speculative forms of capital. This shift toward deterritorialization can be seen as a response in part to the challenges that a series of global crises had posed to the fictions of boundedness central to the sovereignty of the territorial nation-state.[12] Rather than directly confronting the complex and meaningful entanglements among people, places, and objects revealed by the contingencies of state power, this deterritorializing discourse indicates, as Benjamin Lee and Edward LiPuma argue, a "planetary shift in power away from national state political systems, or perhaps political systems of any kind, and toward the global financial markets."[13] Yet by drawing attention away from how state power continues to provide the infrastructures for these markets, this capitalist abstraction also works to occlude and subvert potential sites of connection and coalition between Asian diasporic and Native Pacific communities. Abstract capital's discursive erasure of material conditions of colonial exploitation across Asia and the Pacific encourages Asian migrants and settlers to participate in the settler colonial premises of global capitalism without acknowledging how they infringe upon the sovereignty of Native Pacific communities. This erasure likewise encourages Native Pacific populations to view Asian migrants and settlers as racialized figures aligned with capital. By reifying these racialized *distinctions* between these two groups while largely erasing the complex networks of *relation* that have brought them together, abstract capital has worked to create a political, cultural, and even epistemological disconnection between these communities that makes it difficult to think beyond the premises laid out by global capitalism. It is the bridging of *this* particular "gap" that this chapter seeks to engage.

Key to the discursive shift from colonization to what Hardt and Negri have termed a capital-driven "empire" was the emergence of *speculative capital* as the primary driver of the global economy—a moment that Lee and LiPuma date to the early 1970s, coinciding with the rise of East Asian industrial economies and the emergence of Pacific Rim discourse.[14] Speculative capital is money invested not in the direct production of manufactured *goods* but in the production of value over a determined period of time. Since both value and time are intangible concepts, traders use instruments called derivatives to objectify value and quantify risk, then trade those instruments on a derivatives market. Yet just because derivatives themselves are immaterial does not mean, as Lee and LiPuma argue, that they do not have significant material consequences. Indeed, they posit that speculative capital produces "what people on [the economic] periphery experience as *abstract symbolic violence*."[15] Such violence can "engender the conditions (such as impoverishment) that precipitate violent crime and warfare" while remaining abstract "in the sense that it never appears directly; rather it mediates and stands behind local realities—such as interest rates, food costs, and the price of petroleum."[16]

While Lee and LiPuma attempt to distinguish abstract symbolic violence from other kinds of global violence by arguing that it is "not accomplished physically by means of military force or colonialism," in the case of the Pacific Ocean and Pacific Islands, the "abstract" violence that accrues to nations on the economic periphery is enabled by and layered on top of the very colonial and military projects that have been instrumental to the material development, construction, and ongoing maintenance of transpacific economic infrastructures. The Pacific Islands and their communities have provided not only the physical harbors, airstrips, and cable stations necessary for transpacific travel and communication, but also the militarized labor that supports the production and circulation of capital both within the Pacific and on its "rim." In this sense, the erasure of the Pacific Islands and Pacific peoples through these financialized abstractions not only glosses over the historical violence of the colonial projects that sought to refashion them into the way stations of empire; it also conceals the ongoing military force required to maintain the "freedom" of the seas and their openness to the circulations of capital.[17] In this way, we can see how the apparent transformation of the Pacific from a theater of war to a zone of economic opportunity in the years after the Vietnam War ended is enabled by, and profoundly intertwined with, this shift in perceptions of the Pacific as a material space to a more metaphoric one.

Pushing back against the abstractive tendencies inherent in both Hardt and Negri's and Lee and LiPuma's analyses of the financialized mappings of the Pacific, I focus on Pacific Island and Asian American texts that foreground the presence of migrant labor *on* and *across* the ocean—works that directly address the migratory circuits traced by sailors, scholars, and overseas workers, figures central both to the articulation of Asian diasporic identities and to Epeli Hauʻofa's reconceptualization of the region as a "sea of islands." This focus on migrant labor not only challenges its erasure within finance-driven narratives of a Pacific Ocean rendered seamless and immaterial by capital; it also allows us to explore other meanings and interpretations that accrue around ocean space in ways that often get overwritten by a more singular focus on discussions of transpacific political, economic, and cultural networks. While reimaginations of the Pacific as a space of capital have tended to reify a binary of complicity and resistance that echoes through both Asian American studies and Pacific studies, I turn to Chinese American author Maxine Hong Kingston's *China Men* (1980) and the work of Tongan poet and scholar Konai Helu Thaman to analyze how their focus on the *labor* involved in the oceanic passage of peoples, communications, and commodities illuminates how such work defies the resistance-complicity binary by navigating "*between* and *within* imperial systems and migratory routes."[18] Far from being excluded from, or exclusively defined by, their position within these global cultural flows, these authors articulate creative modes of circulation that not only negotiate questions of national and diasporic identities, but also disentangle local and global systems of value by thinking through the way that stories of ocean passage might illustrate alternative modes of circulation that do not necessarily align with the relentless futurity of finance capitalism's aims. In so doing, these works critically interrogate how regional and national identities have come to align themselves with different transpacific political and economic networks and articulate alternative modes of transnational affiliation and engagement.

Cultures (and Countercultures) of Circulation

Whether celebrated as "bridges" opening up new economic opportunities or condemned as compradors profiting from the exploitation of local labor, diasporic Asians have often been portrayed as being *complicit* with a capitalist system of circulation that channels local resources into a global market. By contrast, Pacific Islanders have been metonymically aligned with the very local sites and resources that are being exploited by capitalism, yet their *resistance* to this form of exploitation has often been ironically romanticized and appropriated by these same capitalist circulations that position them as the disappearing trace of the "real." In this section, I argue that the forms of racialization that result from these "Pacific Rim" discourses—which use Asian figures to stand in for the abstractions of finance and commerce, and Pacific Islander figures to represent an always receding sense of cultural purity, nature, or authenticity—are embedded in settler colonial logics of elimination and exclusion. These racial forms also conceptually sustain the framing of the transpacific as a deterritorialized space of capital. The implied distinction between intangible (circulation-based) and concrete (production-based) forms of capitalism, and the reification of that binary through the form of racial stereotype, obscures how *both* positions contribute to the growth of an expansionist form of capitalism that increasingly renders all forms of racialized labor both surplus and abstract. In this context, the dynamics of complicity and resistance to capitalism's spread are largely overdetermined by the universalizing and homogenizing tendencies of contemporary capitalist circulation itself. Those who seek to challenge the seeming inevitability of capitalism's expansion—like Charlie from "A Brief History of the Trans-Pacific Tunnel"—must be able to envision, acknowledge, and grapple with the other kinds of experiences, archives, and histories that have been excluded from its universalizing narrative. It is through the recovery and attention to these heterogeneous modes of circulation that we can begin to imagine something other than a world always already shaped in the image of an ever-expanding frontier.

Colleen Lye posits that, as the effects of modern capitalist circulations began to manifest themselves in the late nineteenth and early twentieth centuries, capitalism's *negative* consequences were displaced onto an "Asiatic racial form" that circulated as the sign or symbol of the unseen or immaterial forces of finance capital.[19] Because this "new stage of world capitalism" emerged around the same time that U.S. and European interventions into Asia spurred the mass migration of Asians seeking labor to other parts of the globe, the racialization of Asians became "freighted with an abiding tension between U.S. national interests and capital's transnational movement," indexing the way that Asian bodies and communities came to operate as a "sign of globalization" symbolizing capital's threat to national sovereignty rather than appearing as one of the many groups that bore the brunt of its effects.[20] Iyko Day develops and extends this concept of Asian racial form to highlight the trope of "romantic anticapitalism" on which it is based—a trope that asserts and reifies a binary distinction between the concrete and abstract dimensions of capital, recast as a distinction between a romanticized "nature" (which "personifies concrete, perfected human relations") and an alienating, abstract capitalism.[21] This distinction between authentic *nature* and artificial *capital* maps this form of Asian racialization onto a settler colonial mode of identification that seeks to appropriate indigeneity through the "erasure of the alien and the romantic identification with the Native."[22] Through this process, the figure of the (white) settler comes to appropriate the position of the Indigenous precisely through their resistance to the alienating abstraction represented by the "Asian" other. These combined logics of "elimination" (of Indigenous peoples through settler colonial genocide) and "exclusion" (of Asian bodies at the borders of the nation-state) thus allowed for the extraction of both land and labor that informed U.S. expansionism at home and overseas while the settler colonial myth of romantic anticapitalism allowed the nation to continue to position itself as a so-called empire without colonies.[23]

As capitalism expanded through and across the Pacific, however, the conditions of both Asian and Pacific Islander circulations became inflected by a different set of dynamics, particularly in the contexts of *non*-settler and postcolonial states marked by other types of colonial histories, political regimes, and regional alliances. In particular, the dynamics of *elimination* and *exclusion* that define the racialization of Indigenous and Asian figures in the context of the United States and other settler colonial states shift, in a transpacific context, to emphasize processes of *appropriation* and *incorporation*. If the processes of elimination and exclusion emphasize the settler state's investment in clearing out and claiming space or territory, the processes of appropriation and incorporation focus on transnational capitalism's need to lay claim to time and temporality. As Lisa Lowe points out, both settler colonialism's appropriation of *space* and transnational capitalism's colonization of *time* are part of liberalism's broader project to articulate and define a trajectory of human freedom whose "others" are marked by the ongoing persistence and circulations of racial forms—forms that themselves change over time as they trace the shifting limit of what or who is (or is *not*) considered part of this genealogy of the "human."[24] Against the presumed universality, homogeneity, and inevitability of this capitalist time and settler colonial space, Indigenous aesthetics and epistemological practices get abridged, objectified, and transformed into commodities that can circulate within a market system, as Indigenous *thought* and Indigenous *concepts*—in addition to Indigenous bodies, artifacts, and land—become reframed as alienable, if intangible, properties. Take, for example, the commercial circulations of the Hawaiian terms *aloha* (love/respect/connectedness) and *'ohana* (family, kinship), or the controversies over the appropriation of Polynesian myths and culture by the Walt Disney Company in its feature film *Moana*.[25] The global popularity of these "Pacific" concepts is not only distorted to symbolize vaguely nebulous concepts of "connection," "empowerment," and "authenticity"; their commodification and circulation also illustrate how capitalism makes these ideas and aesthetics yield concrete profits. While this selective appropriation of decontextualized Indigenous Pacific concepts may yield some small material benefits to the groups whose cultures are being circulated—either with, but more often without, their consent—it comes at the cost of meaningful alternatives to the dominant cultures of capitalist circulation whose universalizing and homogenizing tendencies continue to position the Pacific Islands as marginal and belated.

By way of illustrating this dynamic of appropriation—as well as the potential for moving away from or beyond its logics—I turn to two works by the Tongan scholar and author Epeli Hauʻofa: his short story "The Glorious Pacific Way" (1983) and his celebrated essay "Our Sea of Islands" (1993). Born in Port Moresby in 1939, the child of two Tongan missionaries, Hauʻofa lived and worked in Papua New Guinea, Tonga, Australia, Canada, and Fiji, where he taught for many years at the University of the South Pacific and was the founder and director of the Oceania Center for Arts and Culture until he passed away in 2009. Hauʻofa was a careful, critical, and irreverent observer of the postindependence dynamics that shaped the region in his lifetime—Fiji and Papua New Guinea gained independence in 1970 and 1975, respectively, while the Kingdom of Tonga was never formally colonized—and his work explored how development economics operated to extend colonial dynamics by other means, especially through the commodification and cooptation of Pacific Islanders themselves. His satirical short story "The Glorious Pacific Way," first published in 1983, focuses on the transformation of Ole Pasifikiwei, a modest functionary (the "Chief Eradicator of Pests and Weeds") in the fictional Pacific Island nation of "Tiko" who spends his free time seeking out and collecting family genealogies and local oral traditions, which he writes down and compiles in an ever-growing stack of exercise books piled in the corner of his home. While it is his greatest wish to have a "machine for typing his material and some filing cabinets for their proper storage," he has "no money for these luxuries" until his work gets noticed by the local Ministry of Culture, which introduces him to a visiting Western diplomat.[26] The diplomat, Mr. Minte, promises Pasifikiwei an undisclosed amount of financial assistance but stipulates that Pasifikiwei must write to ask his agency for help first. At first, this encounter leaves Pasifikiwei "disturbed and feeling reduced"; filing such a claim feels a bit too much like begging, and his pride makes him reluctant to "ask from a stranger." However, he rationalizes that he needs the typewriter and filing cabinets "not for himself but for the important work he ha[s] set out to do," swallows his pride, and goes to ask Mr. Minte for them.[27]

When Pasifikiwei formally makes the request, however, Mr. Minte responds that he cannot give him the materials outright. Instead, he offers Pasifikiwei a grant of $2,000 a year to form an undisclosed cultural committee. Although Pasifikiwei again hesitates to accept Minte's offer—and an acquaintance, Manu, warns him about the irreparable damage that can come from "shelving" his self-respect—Pasifikiwei is ultimately convinced of the greater good of entering into the circuits of development finance. Thus convinced, Pasifikiwei gladly receives his first $2,000 check from Minte and an invitation to a six-week training course in Manila. He asks an elderly aunt to watch over his house while he is gone, but when he returns, he learns that his aunt has taken his books of oral traditions and genealogies and used them for toilet paper. Pasifikiwei's despair at seeing his years of work literally gone to shit soon transforms into opportunism, as he realizes that since his "books had gone down the drain, [he] would henceforth go after the whales of the ocean."[28] The story ends with Pasifikiwei becoming an expert in international development whose "name had become well known in certain influential circles in Brussels, The Hague, Bonn, Geneva, Paris, London, New York, Washington, Wellington, Canberra, Tokyo, Peking, and Moscow, as well as in such regional laundry centers as Bangkok, Kuala Lumpur, Manila, and Noumea."[29] As the narrator concludes, Pasifikiwei has "since shelved his original sense of self-respect and has assumed another, more attuned to his new, permanent role as a first-rate, expert beggar."[30]

Hauʻofa's story satirizes the seductions of capitalist "development" by juxtaposing the absurdity of its abstractive and speculative logics against the daily needs of the people it is intended to serve. While Mr. Minte's agency and others like it are willing to give out thousands of dollars not for direct aid to communities but, instead, to individuals who form cultural committees that will, in turn, write *proposals* for aid projects, the costs of basics such as food (and toilet paper) have risen beyond the means of the average Tikoan. The story similarly takes aim at how this entry into capitalist circulation depends on cultural commodification—beginning with Pasifikiwei's seemingly harmless hobby of collecting oral histories and genealogies and transcribing them into exercise books. By transcribing these stories and histories into the books that he keeps stacked up in his home, he takes them *out* of circulation—that is, out of the social and environmental contexts in which such stories are handed down, shared, and exchanged—and transforms them into collector's objects, which he has no real plan to share. Ultimately, such decontextualized knowledge is, as the story memorably demonstrates, worth less than the paper used to wipe one's ass. Yet it is this abstracted cultural "knowledge," which can be circulated in the absence of local context, that forms the basis for Pasifikiwei's success within the circuits of development finance.

Both the story's title—"The Glorious Pacific Way"—and its main character, Ole Pasifikiwei, directly reference the "Pacific Way" rhetoric deployed by postindependence Pacific Island leaders, clearly indicating the target of Hauʻofa's satire. While the concept of the Pacific Way was intended to invoke a history of regional identity and affinity that predated Western colonialism in the region, in practice it came to signal what Hauʻofa identified as an "elitist" alliance that profited the political, intellectual, and business elite of its constituent countries while failing to foster meaningful cultural exchange and dialogue throughout the region, or to offer a unified vision or plan for the region's future.[31] Yet as a member of this intellectual elite, Hau'ofa himself confessed to the difficulties of thinking beyond the "belittling" frameworks established by the century-long legacies of Western colonial policies and his own academic training as a social scientist. In his essay on "Our Sea of Islands" (1993), Hau'ofa writes that these political and academic frameworks represent Pacific Island states as "too small, too poorly endowed with resources, and too isolated from the centres of economic growth for their inhabitants ever to be able to rise above their present condition of dependence on the largesse of wealthy nations," a perspective that Hau'ofa says he initially not only "agreed wholeheartedly with" but also "participated actively" in propagating.[32] Yet, as he came to realize, "In propagating a view of hopelessness, I was actively participating in our own belittlement." Hau'ofa came to understand that the "reality" presented by these representations of the Pacific Islands' marginality is an

> economistic and geographic deterministic view of a very narrow kind that overlooks culture history and the contemporary process of what may be called world enlargement that is carried out by tens of thousands of ordinary Pacific Islanders right across the ocean— from east to west and north to south, under the very noses of academic and consultancy experts, regional and international development agencies, bureaucratic planners and their advisers, and customs and immigration officials—making nonsense of all national and economic boundaries, borders that have been defined only recently, crisscrossing an ocean that had been boundless for ages before Captain Cook's apotheosis.[33]

While Hau'ofa's often-cited reconceptualization of Oceania as a "sea of islands" rather than "islands in a far sea" emphasizes the same qualities of mobility, expansiveness, and border-crossing transgressiveness that characterize capitalism's cultures of circulation, it nevertheless resists capitalism's drive to universalism and the rendering of experience as abstract and interchangeable.[34] Instead, it focuses on the ways that Oceania invokes a more "holistic perspective" that considers such circulations "in the totality of their relationships," which include not only the top-down, "deterministic" viewpoint held by regional planners, but also the perspectives of the "ordinary people" who circulate through the region "completely undaunted by the deadly serious discourses . . . on the nature of the Pacific Century, the Asia-Pacific coprosperity sphere, and the dispositions of the post-cold war Pacific Rim, cultivating their ever-growing universe *in their own ways*, which is as it should be, for therein lies their independence."[35]

Central to Hauʻofa's vision of Oceania as an alternative to homogenizing capitalist "cultures of circulation" is its attention to the contours and dynamics of migrant labor in particular as expressive of what we might call a "*counter*culture of circulation." While the focus on migrant laborers may seem to emphasize concrete elements of their work, this vision of Oceania does *not* seek to reproduce or rearticulate the concrete-abstract binary characteristic of romantic anticapitalism. Rather, these circulations of labor are firmly contextualized within the abstract dimensions of the "myths, legends, and oral traditions, indeed the cosmologies of the peoples of Oceania."[36] The power of Hauʻofa's "sea of islands" as a counterculture of circulation lies in its very ability to *reclaim Pacific knowledge and epistemology* as an important part of Pacific heritage, moving against its abstraction and commodification under capitalist forms of circulation. The reimagination of Oceania as a sea of islands in fact emphasizes how objects that may not be considered "valuable" in a capitalist sense accrue meaning and worth as they circulate within and across different cultures of circulation. As an example, Hauʻofa describes the migratory circuits of his friend, a Tongan man who works as a gardener and groundskeeper in Berkeley, California. Every few months he flies to Fiji, bringing T-shirts to give as gifts to friends and relatives; he purchases kava to take back to Berkeley, where he sells it to other diasporic Pacific Islanders. All of these exchanges are negligible within a money economy, but the money economy is only *one* of the cultures of circulation through which Hauʻofa's friend moves: the goods he carries back and forth between Fiji and the United States accrue their worth and meaning through different Pacific cultures of circulation rather than through their pure global market value. While this is a deliberately modest and "everyday" example, the heterogeneity and plurality of the Pacific cultures of circulation it illustrates run counter to the homogenizing and totalizing scope of capitalist circulation's expansive aims.

While Oceanian countercultures of circulation push back against an understanding of capitalist circulation as a universal and universalizing process, figurations of "Asianness" continue to symbolize the passageway or point of transit *into* this capital-driven remapping of the Pacific. In "The Glorious Pacific Way," for example, Ole Pasifikiwei must pass through Manila to enter into the world of development finance. The invocation of Manila as the site of passage between an extracted resource (in this case, local oral histories) and its circulation within a global marketplace references both its past history as a crucial port in the Spanish "Manila Galleon" trade and its contemporary position as a state that occupies a crucial, yet still subordinated, position within Pacific Rim discourse—a point emphasized by Hauʻofa's description of the city as a "regional laundry center" alongside the cities of Bangkok and Noumea. By metonymically aligning these Southeast Asian cities with the New Caledonian capital of Noumea—home of the South Pacific Commission, a regional development organization—Hauʻofa satirically emphasizes how these sites' incorporation as equivalently belated or secondary partners in a culture of circulation anticipates and prefigures Tiko's own uneven incorporation into this realm. Even Pasifikiwei's aunt's casual prejudice against Filipinos as cannibal "heathens"—a stereotype that historically has attached to Pacific Islanders, as well—speaks to the mutuality of their fates as potential converts to the culture of capitalist circulation.

Indeed, the twentieth-century history of the Philippines both illustrates and prefigures the changing dynamics of incorporation that confronted postcolonial Pacific Island states as they navigated their shift from formal to informal empire in the years following independence. Along with Guam and Hawaiʻi, the Philippines had first been incorporated as a formal colony of America's archipelagic empire in 1898; occupied by Japan during World War II, it was "liberated" by the United States and granted independence following Japan's defeat in 1946. However, the Philippines' formal political independence came at a steep economic cost. Under the terms of the Bell Trade Act, signed in 1946, the United States lent the Philippines $800 million toward rebuilding its war-devastated economy; in return, the Philippines agreed to engage in free trade with the United States for eight years. This agreement allowed inexpensive American goods to flood the Philippine market, driving out competition and increasing demand by making U.S. products cheaper to purchase than domestically produced goods; it also included a "parity" clause that gave U.S. citizens and corporations the right to purchase and use Philippine land and resources. Together, these elements of the Bell Trade Act reinforced the logics of colonialism through the mechanisms of debt. When the terms of the Bell Trade Act and the subsequent Laurel-Langley Trade Act of 1955 expired in 1975, almost thirty years of enforced dependence had taken its toll on the Philippine economy. By the 1970s, the neocolonial dynamic created by this highly unequal postwar debt structure was superseded by neoliberal economic reforms undertaken by President Ferdinand Marcos that placed the nation in debt not to the United States but to the International Monetary Fund (IMF) and the World Bank.[37] By 1981, the Philippines were more than $20 billion in debt and had to agree to stringent new conditions set by the IMF that resulted in the dramatic devaluation of the nation's currency.[38] As a way to service this debt, the Philippine government was increasingly transforming itself into what Robyn Rodriguez calls a "labor brokerage state," or a state defined by "institutional and discursive practices through which the Philippine state mobilizes its citizens and sends them abroad to work for employers throughout the world while generating a 'profit' from the remittances that migrants send back to their families and loved ones remaining in the Philippines."[39] By the time Hauʻofa was publishing "The Glorious Pacific Way," in 1983, the Philippines' debt burden had moved from a colonial/neocolonial model to a global/neoliberal one. This shift and the state's turn to "labor brokerage"—which was discursively framed as being a part of Filipinos' migratory history and culture—paralleled a similar set of problems and choices that were coming to face independent Pacific Island nations during this time.[40]

Just as the "Asiatic" racial form that emerged from an earlier era of imperialism had served, as Lye has argued, to "disclos[e] the ways in which U.S. colonial and race relations are marked by power's more totalizing reach and increasing abstraction," by the end of the century, it had moved beyond a U.S.-specific context to come to stand in for abstract capital's general unrepresentability in sites around the globe.[41] While such an "Asiatic" racial form continues to carry with it the same connotation of "economic efficiency" that made Asians a scapegoat for progressive reform in the early twentieth century, this efficiency by the century's end also came to symbolize a successful example of non-Western modernity to which other formerly colonized nations might aspire.[42] Yet this reification of "Asianness" as a metaphor for or gateway to economic progress overlooks how such progress has—as in the example of the Philippines—been profoundly entangled with neoliberal policies that tend to maintain colonial power structures. Teresia Teaiwa notes that, while many scholars from the Pacific Islands have been encouraged to study Asia "in the hopes that we would learn how to emulate the macroeconomic successes of the 'tigers' . . . or simply absorb the good work ethics and business acumen of 'Asians,'" she also wonders what it means when "Asia" is "reduced to signifying wealth" and speculates about the potential for Asian and Pacific Island studies to relate to one another beyond narratives of economic coprosperity.[43] If Asians continue to be imagined—and to imagine themselves—as "bridges" or conduits through which capital circulates through and beyond the formal boundaries of the colonial nation-state, it is also important to question whom these circulations benefit and whether or not they represent a meaningful change from older, colonial power dynamics. What would it mean to imagine diasporic

Asian communities operating as bridges or conduits not for the circulation of global wealth, but for other forms of cultural exchange and systems of value? How might we rethink their ocean passages as circulating through transpacific networks shaped by Indigenous epistemologies and histories, as well as capitalist infrastructures?

To address these questions, I turn in the next section to work by Maxine Hong Kingston to highlight the different—and highly gendered—ways that she draws attention to *labor* as a mode of rethinking this conceit of Asians as transnational bridge builders. Here I am interested in exploring how trajectories of transpacific Asian labor not only have shaped and been shaped by the circulations of transpacific capital, but also open up opportunities to establish "countercultures of circulation" along the lines of Hau'ofa's sea of islands. If we can think of Asian bodies and Asian labor as being associated not only with the *devaluation* of labor into "abstract" commodities for circulation but also with how the process or act of circulation itself shapes, channels, or lends value to these commodity flows, we may be able to consider the role that Asian migrant labor might have to play in the context of an Oceanic sea of islands that acknowledges and adjusts for cultural and temporal difference, rather than operating only within a discourse of incorporation into "transpacific partnership" that seeks to harness these differences toward a progressively expansionist end.

Building Bridges, Digging Tunnels: The Labor of Circulation in Maxine Hong Kingston's *China Men*

The twenty-first-century ideal of Asian Americans as highly visible bridge builders crossing and connecting transpacific space operates as both an inversion and an extension of narratives around Asian American infrastructural labor from the late nineteenth and early twentieth centuries. In this earlier period Asians, and particularly the Chinese, were notably involved in the construction of the first U.S. transcontinental railroad; they labored under extreme conditions yet were deliberately rendered invisible within the dominant narratives and representations of technological and economic "progress." (To take one infamous example, the official photograph of the "Golden Spike Ceremony" taken to commemorate the completion of the Transcontinental Railroad in 1869 deliberately excluded Chinese laborers, erasing their contributions from the official archive.) By the turn of the twenty-first century, Asian labor was certainly more recognized, but it was, at the same time, more abstract; it was less connected to the kind of manual labor that had characterized an earlier generation of Asian Americans and increasingly associated with the abstractions of high finance and globalization. In this context, Asian Americans were viewed not as literal bridge builders but, rather, as mediums or intermediaries. As Day and Lye have observed, Asian Americans became increasingly aligned with neoliberal financial cultures of circulation that privileged market forms of value over other reckonings of worth.[44] Representations of Asian Americans as infrastructural figures have similarly toggled between a focus on the *material* labor of bridge (or railroad) building and the more *metaphorical* labor of individuals who serve in the function of cultural or economic intermediaries. While the two are clearly interconnected, the discursive tensions between the material and metaphorical work of "bridging"—and its implicit privileging of manual labor as the site of either "Americanness" or resistance to the same—extend the fetishization of concrete labor that racializes Asian bodies into what Day has called "alien capital."[45]

The emphasis on representations of manual/concrete labor has been especially pronounced in the work of Asian American scholars and artists who sought to restore their ancestors' stories and experiences to the narratives of mainstream American history by emphasizing the glaring contradictions between popular American narratives of democratic inclusion and the actual practices of exclusion that disenfranchised the racialized labor force constructing the material infrastructure for American expansion. Yet while the recovery of this particular (masculine) laboring history has operated as a way to assert an American identity that deviates from and critiques the racist assumptions around who does and does not belong to the nation, the continued insistence on "claiming America" means that such representations remain entangled with the settler colonial and capitalist logics of the very concept of Manifest Destiny that demanded both the erasure of Indigenous peoples *and* the exclusion of Asian ones. As David Eng notes, while the Chinese were not themselves intended to be—and were in fact legally excluded from becoming—settlers themselves, their alienated labor was nevertheless key to the project of settler colonialism insofar as it worked to "build the national economic infrastructure supporting westward expansion."[46] Further, these workers' labor on the Transcontinental Railroad aided the shipping trade on the West Coast—a trade that served as the impetus for American overseas projects in the late nineteenth and early twentieth centuries, including the overthrow of the Hawaiian Kingdom in 1893; the acquisition of Hawai'i, Guam, and the Philippines in 1898; the Philippine-American War in 1899; and the quelling of the Boxer Rebellion and the establishment of the Open Door Policy with China in that same year. In this broader historical context, David Leiwei Li notes that these laborers unwittingly "became accomplices in the exploitation of their ancient empire."[47] In this sense, Chinese migrant laborers operated not only as a sign but also as a symptom of a broader system of capitalist circulation that would shape, condition, and transform their families' lives in China, just as surely as they worked to shape the laborers' lives in the United States.

More immediately, an overemphasis on (concrete) labor as a site of resistance also worked to reinscribe settler colonial norms by using labor as a vector to lay claim to land. As an example, I turn to Kingston's *China Men*, a text widely cited for its representation of Asian labor in both the making of America and the claiming and remaking of an "American" identity. In the story "Great-Grandfather of the Sandalwood Mountains," Kingston's ancestor Bak Goong signs up to work for a company whose representative has promised his family riches. However, after traveling to Hawai'i as a crewman on a merchant ship, he finds out that the working conditions are harsh and his overseers are miserly and cruel. He and the other workers are not allowed to speak while they work and are punished if they do; as a form of resistance, they dig a large pit in the earth and shout all of their words and secrets into it, hoping that the words and secrets will be seeded in the ground and carry their stories on the wind. This moment, when Bak Goong and the others declare themselves the "founding ancestors" of this place, resonates in the novel as an act of resistance designed to push back against their silenced history. Scholars have interpreted the China Men's gesture as an "alternative means of claiming America, one which has not been co-opted by American economic interests."[48] Yet the very idea that one might "claim America" by asserting a stake in what was, at this time, land under the jurisdiction of the Hawaiian Kingdom is very much in keeping with U.S. settler colonial practices and economic interests.[49] The China Men's presence as disenfranchised laborers on Hawaiian land positions them as simultaneously resistant to and complicit with the project of settler colonial capitalism, a duality that Kingston highlights through her use of metaphor:

> One day, like a knight rescuing a princess, Bak Goong broke clear through the thicket. The demons bought bullocks; they had longer horns than water buffaloes. He yoked them to the stumps, which they yanked out. But the Hawaiians quit rather than help pull the boulders out of the earth. The remaining workers plowed around groups of big rocks in the middle of the fields. They were the first human beings to dig into this part of the island and see the meat and bones of the red earth. After rain, the mud ran like blood.

Although Bak Goong frames his work in heroic, highly gendered terms ("like a knight rescuing a princess"), this heroism is immediately juxtaposed with the violent results of his labor. After noting—but not explaining—the Hawaiians' refusal to move the boulders from the earth, the narrator describes the labor of clearing the land in terms of vivisection and physical dismemberment, exposing the "meat and bones" of the earth, causing the mud to run "like blood." While remaining at odds with the white "demons" throughout the novel, here we see both China Men and the white men working in tandem and partaking in the elation of discovery ("They were the first human beings to dig into this part of the island"), for which it is necessary to silence and sideline the "Hawaiians" who refuse to participate in this act of desecration. In this moment, the positioning of Chinese labor as complicit with the silencing project of settler colonial capitalism extends, even as it desires to either avoid or overcome, the tensions that lie in the triangulation of Indigenous land, Asian labor, and white possessive logics.

By contrast, Bak Goong's son, Ah Goong ("The Grandfather of the Sierra Nevadas"), offers a different way of interpreting his relationship to the land. Hired to lay tracks for the Transcontinental Railroad, Ah Goong—like Bak Goong—labors under extreme conditions to reshape the landscape itself for the purpose of profit. Yet rather than viewing his labor as heroic, the experience of digging and tunneling through rock leads Ah Goong to confront the ontological disparity between the speed demanded by his white overseers ("'Faster,' they said. 'Faster. Chinamen too slow'") and the timeless "immovability of the earth":

> This mountain would have taken no new shape for centuries, ten thousand centuries, the world a still, still place, time unmoving.... When he stumbled out, he tried to talk about time. "I felt time," he said. "I saw time. I saw world." He tried again, "I saw what's real. I saw time, and it doesn't move. If we break through the mountain, hollow it, time won't have moved anyway. You translators ought to tell the foreigners that."[50]

Here, Kingston emphasizes the intersection of two different ways of experiencing time that refuse incorporation into a single, universal or homogeneous temporality. In Ah Goong's experience, "Labor time and natural time are presented as frustratingly out of sync with each other," resulting in a profoundly divided sense of temporality that ultimately remains unresolved.[51] This divided perspective on time allows Ah Goong, unlike Bak Goong, to vividly imagine possibilities for identifying with the land outside the dominant paradigm of settler colonialism: after witnessing how the mountain refuses to submit to settler norms of "labor time," Ah Goong can no longer view it as alienable property that can be shaped and molded to accommodate human actions and desires. Instead, he struggles to articulate how he sees it operating on a timeline and temporality of its own.

Just as Ah Goong rejects the progressive (capitalist) temporality of his American overseers, he also rejects the racist and patriarchal laws that have dictated the circumscribed conditions of his labor, repeatedly questioning his *own* relationship to masculinity and heteropatriarchy by taking out his penis and "wondering what it was that it was for, what a man was for, what he had to have a penis for."[52] This questioning of his own masculinity within the framework of a patriarchal settler colonial system is immediately followed by his reflections on a story he had heard of an "Injun woman called Woman Chief, who led a nomadic fighting tribe from the eastern plains as far as these mountains. She was so powerful that she had four wives and many horses."[53] The juxtaposition of Ah Goong's limp penis and the powerful Woman Chief speaks to an alternative "Americanness" defined not by a heteropatriarchal, settler colonial penetration of the land but an explicitly feminine, queer, and Indigenous-centered protection of it. While in an earlier generation Bak Goong struggled against but ultimately submitted to the masculinist settler logics governing the conditions of his labor, it is Ah Goong—often mocked and humiliated by his friends and family for his eccentricities—who is able to most radically subvert his settler colonial positioning by *refusing* to stake a permanent claim on the land. Like the Formosan laborer Charlie, who in "A Brief History of the Trans-Pacific Tunnel" strikes his name from the commemorative plaque and replaces it with a symbol that could be read alternately as a sign of connection and a sign of bondage, after the 1906 earthquake and fire in San Francisco, Ah Goong deliberately erases himself from the historical record, disappearing from official archives. Although it is speculated that he did not die in the fire and in fact left with a "child in his arms," potentially living on to be incorporated into a new, non-heteronormative genealogy, his further history—like that of the Woman Chief—continues to circulate outside official history as rumor unconfirmed by the archive.

While representations of Asian labor on the land thus grapple with the legacies of U.S. settler colonialism, representations of Asian *maritime* labor emphasize the simultaneously incorporative and subversive potentialities of work that often get rendered as mediative, ephemeral, and immaterial—labor that is not so much territorializing as it is deterritorializing. Indeed, while many canonical Asian American texts address or depict the working conditions of immigrant labor on the land, the conditions of labor at sea are often overlooked or rendered metaphorical and abstract. To return to *China Men*, while Bak Goong's work on the plantations of Hawaiʻi is rendered in agonizing detail, the labor he performs during the ship's passage is not depicted in the text. Instead, we get a description of his first opium trip, which he experiences as an epiphanic manifestation of profound interconnectedness:

> His thoughts branched and flowed and branched again and connected like rivers, veins, roads, ships' lanes. New ideas sparked, and he caught his breath when he saw their connections to old ideas. Circles wheeled by, whirled concentrically, and stilled into a simple light. The bald heads of monks, who sit in circles, bowed toward the center like a hand, a lotus flower, or wood sorrel closing. The world's people arranged themselves in parades, palaces, windows, roads, stadiums, attempting to form this bond. These men in the hold were trying to circumnavigate the world. Men build bridges and streets when there is already an amazing gold electric ring connecting every living being as surely as if we held hands, flippers and paws, feelers and wings.

While this ocean-spanning, Whitmanesque vision of interconnection provides, as King-Kok Cheung notes, a powerful "counterpoint to the laws of the white ruling fathers" and a "utopian vision that decries brute reality and jibes with the author's own pacifist world view,"[54] it also operates as a profoundly universalizing epiphany that collapses the world's peoples, animals, and environment into one conjoined circle. Bak Goong's maritime labors are discursively replaced by the metaphorical labor he performs by drawing connections among people, places, and old and new ideas: he becomes a bridge builder of the most abstract, albeit philosophical, kind—indeed, he *is* the bridge. Yet Bak Goong's description of this connective tissue among all living creatures as an "amazing gold electric ring" speaks not only to the ethical ideal of interconnection but the *gold*—the fixed value—that binds them together. In this context, his rhapsodic vision of a profound connection between the world's peoples and animals seems to more closely resemble Karl Marx's description of the "mystical" workings of commodity fetishism, or the process through which social relations between people assume the "fantastic form of a relation between things," a state of affairs that is affected by the "magic of money." This "magic" allows money, in the form of gold taken from the earth, to stand in as "the direct incarnation of all human labor."[55] Like the "money form" that works to establish the equivalence and exchangeability of all people and things, Bak Goong views this global interconnectedness from a holistic, rather than relational, perspective. Moreover, he himself does not appear in this vision beyond serving as the pathway for connection, his thoughts drawing these different elements together "like rivers, veins, roads, ships' lanes." In this sense, Bak Goong's vision situates him as a mediative figure, taking on the mystical (and leveling) quality not only of religious epiphany, but of monetary exchange.

While Bak Goong's visions are most directly attributed to his first experience with smoking opium, they are also narratively linked to his experience of being with and on the ocean. Later in the story, he experiences a brief flashback to this feeling of holistic interconnection while staring out to sea and resolves that "he mustn't sit so long looking at the ocean."[56] Although he blames these flashbacks on the lingering effects of the opiates, he later discovers that he does not have any visions when he is away from the water, even after eating a number of psilocybin mushrooms in the canefields. The mushrooms, which taste of "earth and must," remind Bak Goong of his provisional belonging on the land; however, the ocean's fluidity reflects Bak Goong's mediative capacity. If water, as Chris Connery has observed, is "capital's element," then in his first ocean-crossing vision Bak Goong affiliates himself with capital's liquidity, which "has struggled to free itself from the earth just as the bourgeoisie"—or, in this particular case, Bak Goong— "struggled to free [itself] from tilling the soil."[57] Yet while Bak Goong *begins* his journey as such a seeker of profit, his experience of the stringent working conditions of indentured labor begins to change his outlook. Indeed, while Bak Goong's first vision of a unifying "gold circle" operated as a capitalist fantasy of a world mapped and interconnected through a series of multicultural exchanges and equivalences, his second vision, which he experiences *after* his labors, is significantly less rhapsodic:

Two people were standing in the black water halfway between him and the horizon, halfway between the sky and earth. A yellow light shown from them; their random movements repeated in series, a dance. They revolved in the only brightness, and stopped, hands and feet held like Balinese temple dancers. Time moved at their rate of motion. It was either two people or one Hindoo with four arms. He heard music draw out into one long note. The waves going in and out forever was the same as no motion at all. The ocean remains the same basic water. Flesh does not evolve into the necessary iron. He yearned for the sun to blast out of the ocean. He sat for hours in the exact center of eternity.[58]

Unlike his earlier vision of incessant circulation, here Bak Goong specifically locates himself and others within a fixed landscape: he is sitting on the shore while the two people he is watching are "halfway between him and the horizon, halfway between the sky and earth." While there is still a movement toward unity and union—he is uncertain whether he is looking at two people or one "Hindoo" and hears "music draw out into one long note"—this unity is not confused with transcendence, as he observes that "the ocean remains the same basic water" and "flesh does not evolve into the necessary iron." He then experiences a vision of "rows of shining people" coming up to him, before having that vision broken by the interjection of the (real-life) man and woman who had been night fishing on the reef, who offer him one of their fish and move on.

Bak Goong's second ocean-inflected vision is not transcendental so much as it is relational: rather than assuming a kind of profound interconnectedness or metaphoric interchangeability among everything he sees, he sees himself and everything around him in terms of their relationships to one another. The ocean, the people on the horizon, and the "rows of shining people" that Bak Goong sees remain distinct and separate entities, if not necessarily from one another, then certainly from him. After coming to understand his own profound alienness, he is interrupted by the couple who offer him a fish for no other reason than that he is there and they have more than enough; their generosity comes in direct contrast to the plantation owners and overseers who are constantly seeking to reduce his share of wages. In this context, we are briefly given an alternative vision of oceanic interconnection, a vision that is not based on the leveling of differences so much as on the willingness to acknowledge those differences in position and navigate relationships across and through them.

While intrigued by these ways of imagining otherwise, both Bak Goong (and his in-law Bak Sook Goong) ultimately return to their roles within the system of global capitalist circulation that brought them to Hawai'i in the first place. Yet Kingston notes how the profit, experience, and expanded sense of agency that the "China Men" bring back from their journey also come explicitly at the cost of the Hawaiian people and land. Just as Bak Goong returned to his family, turning away from the economy of abundance demonstrated by the night-fishing Hawaiians in order to bring the slender (monetary) profits of his labor back to his village, Bak Sook Goong also chooses to take his "Hawaiian" wife to China rather than remain with her in Hawai'i, even though the king and queen had ruled that "a China Man who married a Hawaiian would be called Hawaiian."[59] This decision results in the silencing of his wife, who is taken far from her home and has no one who understands, or cares to understand, her language. Given the novel's overall alignment of silence with unfreedom, it is clear that Bak Sook Goong's wife *loses* agency and mobility in direct proportion to how Bak Sook Goong *gains* it.[60] In other words, if Bak Goong's act of "claiming" Hawaiian land through the "shout party" and Bak Sook Goong's relationship with his Hawaiian wife offered them a brief sense of freedom from the demoralizing conditions of their labor in the islands, then Kingston concludes the chapter by illustrating how their exercise of agency in this limited context ultimately worked to diminish and devalue the Hawaiian environment and its people.

Taken together, the "bridging" work of Asian labor in these tales illustrates the tensions between the individual-centered "freedoms" aligned with liberal humanism and capitalism and the desire to push back against the materially damaging effects that these ideologies have had on transpacific environments and communities. In the cases of Kingston's Chinese great-grandfathers (as well as in the case of Charlie, the Formosan laborer from "A Brief History of the Trans-Pacific Tunnel"), we can see how the individual gains a degree of agency within a capitalist culture of circulation, at the cost of alternative ways of articulating or situating themselves in relation to the people or environments that they encounter. This is because capitalist circulations rely on the *homogenization* of temporal and spatial relationships as a backdrop against which individual agency can be read and recognized—as opposed to alternative economies of exchange, such as gift economies, that do not presume this kind of epistemological equivalence.[61] If the former more closely resembled Bak Goong's first, ocean-inspired vision of his thoughts reaching out to draw all the world together into a transcendent "golden ring," the latter is exemplified by his second hallucination, where he locates himself in the "exact center of eternity" yet still notes his relation to others from this position and does not collapse his surroundings into himself ("time moved at *their* rate of motion ... the ocean remains the same basic water"). By focusing on the practices and conceptualizations of affinity that similarly keep them "centered" while accounting for different and conflicting perceptions of place, space, and time, the marginal and marginalized figures of *China Men* and "A Brief History of the Trans-Pacific Tunnel" illustrate the potential for Asian migrant labor to serve not as the conduit for an expanding flow of transpacific capitalism, but as complex figures that can hold these competing temporalities and spaces in tension without reducing them to a single, homogeneous whole. In this context, the mediating, bridge-building role taken on by the Asian migrant laborer might be usefully juxtaposed with the experiences of diasporic Pacific Islanders, particularly those hailing from independent or newly independent nations, who are similarly engaged in navigating the shift from colonial to post- and neocolonial networks of trade and empire.⁶² While (as Hauʻofa notes) the circulation of Pacific Islanders through and across the Pacific draws from a history of Oceanic trade and travel that long predates the establishment of modern shipping lanes and trade infrastructures through the region, their mobilizations in the twentieth and twenty-first centuries must likewise navigate and engage with the currents of capitalist circulation that seek to collapse these diverse histories into their own. In the next section, I briefly return to Hauʻofa's writings and turn to the poetry of Konai Helu Thaman to explore some of the resonances and divergences in these differing Asian and Pacific Island experiences of oceanic passages.

Spanning a "Sea of Islands": Decolonizing Transpacific Cultures of Circulation

As Hauʻofa notes in "Our Sea of Islands," remittances—money sent back to the home country by citizens working abroad—make up a substantial part of the Tongan economy. Although China, India, and the Philippines account for the largest *numbers* of remittance laborers sent worldwide, as of 2017, remittances accounted for more than 37.1 percent of Tonga's gross domestic product.⁶³ The importance of remittances to Tonga's economy means that large numbers of Tongans migrate overseas for labor and engage in practices of "circular migration" that, as Murray Chapman notes, fit into the category of neither "migration," which denotes a population shift that is "permanent or quasi-permanent," nor "circulation," which denotes a move that is "intentionally impermanent."⁶⁴ Thus, Tongan workers, like the Asian workers discussed earlier in this chapter, operate as bridging figures who constantly draw together and blur the lines between the worlds of home and abroad. However, as Hauʻofa argues, an analysis of remittance labor in a Tongan/Oceanian context needs to account for specific histories and cultural practices that can frame such practices not as "dependence but interdependence."⁶⁵

Hauʻofa's concept of a sea of islands has been successfully used to articulate a broadly Oceanic framework of "interdependence." It is useful to note how this remapping draws from Tongan regional histories of transoceanic trade, exchange, and migration. From approximately the seventh century through the eighteenth century, Tonga was the center of the Tuʻi Tonga, a maritime trade network that at its height extended from parts of the Solomon Islands and Fiji to Niue. Historians have debated the propriety of equating Tonga's widespread influence with the forms of hegemony we have come to understand as "empire" and "imperialism," as it was largely maintained and legislated through genealogical, rather than strictly military or commerical, systems. Yet all agree that "there can be little doubt about the significant array of evidence, derived from archaeological research, oral traditions, and ethnohistorical sources, that substantiates the existence of a large, thriving, and complex network of exchange activities and relations among the island groups of Western Polynesia and Fiji, with Tonga playing a central role."[66] While the Tuʻi Tonga began to decline from its height in the fifteenth century,[67] the transoceanic circuits that it had developed through genealogical and cultural links continued to sustain its influence for generations to come.

The precedent set by the Tuʻi Tonga speaks to how contemporary Oceanic practices of interdependence through "bridging" have been informed by the *genealogical* structures that supported this ocean-spanning network, albeit in ways that have been adapted for the exigencies of modern life. Tongan scholars—including ʻOkusitino Māhina, Konai Helu Thaman, and Tēvita Kaʻili—have emphasized the concept of *vā*, a term that Kaʻili defines as indicating the materiality and mediative capacity of a "space in-between" two or more points—an idea that is the exact opposite of contemporary capitalist mappings that render such spaces as emptied sites for the circulation of people, goods, and capital.[68] Thaman emphasizes the social and interpersonal aspect of *vā*, which she transliterates as *vaa*, and the "high regard people place on rules governing different kinds of interpersonal relationships and social interaction." In this sense, *vā* refers not only to a material or physical space between individuals but also to the immaterial kinship and social relationships that link them together.[69] More broadly, *vā* operates as a term that indicates "sociospatial" connection, an idea of *space* that gets articulated in terms of familial or other social connection.[70] In direct contrast to capitalist cultures of circulation, which presume a flattened and standardized spacetime through which goods and people are largely stripped of their sociospatial contexts as they move through a global marketplace, *vā* imagines a transnational network that depends on precisely these kinship and cultural contexts as the conditions of circulation.

In a contemporary context, the practice of *tauhi vā* (protection/nurturing of *vā*) and the relationships and values they represent operate alongside and sometimes within the circuits of transpacific flows of capital. Because *vā* possesses both interpersonal *and* spatial qualities, *tauhi vā* also serves to maintain diasporic Tongans' relationship to their home islands, villages, and family lands.[71] The value of maintaining these connections exceeds capitalist reckonings of value; Hauʻofa gets at this dynamic when he observes that specialists analyzing contemporary Tonga's "remittance" economy "overlook the fact that for everything homeland relatives receive, they reciprocate with goods that they themselves produce, by maintaining ancestral roots and lands for everyone, homes with warmed hearths for travelers to return to permanently or strengthen their bonds, their souls, and their identities before they move on again."[72] While the monetary value of the goods and funds remitted to the Pacific states is easily quantifiable, the reciprocal value represented by the "homeland" is not as easily measured within a strictly economic framework. What Hauʻofa seems to be suggesting is that this practice of reciprocity comes to serve an important intermediary function between a global capitalist economy and a Pacific-centered network where one's connections to land and ancestry circulate as important signifiers of cultural identity independent of their monetary value. In this context, money ceases to operate as the exclusive grounds of exchange and is instead revealed to be only one strand within a heterogeneous set of circulations that link Pacific Island nations to diasporic communities in "Pacific Rim" states. To gain a more holistic or balanced view of the social and cultural impact of globalization on twentieth-century remittance economies in the Pacific, as Hauʻofa suggests, one cannot allow the presumably transparent or universal exchange system represented by the money economy to occlude the value of the land and all that it has come to represent.

At the same time, however, these homelands and cultural values are themselves also being shaped and reshaped by capitalist circulations. While tourist and industrial development has not encroached as heavily on Tonga as it has on other Pacific Island nations, Tonga's lands and seas are similarly susceptible to runoff pollution, ocean warming and acidification, and other environmental effects of a global industrial economy. And a liberalizing consumer culture, as in many other places around the world, has had significant effects on the articulation of local practices and relationships, though there are many different opinions regarding the degree of impact that "Western" cultural practices have had on Tongan society.[73] As a concept centered on both the ocean spaces and cultural systems that connect the island archipelagoes of Oceania to one another, *vā* can speak to the way that both physical environments and social formations in Tonga and other Pacific Islands respond to these dynamically shifting and changing crosscurrents. In this way, a methodological framework that places *vā* as its center resists the tendency to obscure the materiality of ocean space and Pacific social networks in dominant academic and policy discourses.

In her literary and scholarly work, Konai Helu Thaman foregrounds this principle in her representations of the changing contours of sociospatial connection in both Tonga and the broader Pacific region. Widely considered one of the pioneers of Pacific Islands literature in English, Thaman gained regional recognition through her publication in regional literary magazines including the *Pacific Islands Forum* and *Mana* magazine and is perhaps best known for her five volumes of poetry: *You, The Choice of My Parents* (1974), *Langakali* (1981), *Hingano* (1987), *Kakala* (1993), and *Songs of Love* (1999).[74] Born and raised in Nukuʻalofa, Tonga, Thaman attended high school and college in New Zealand and received postgraduate degrees from the University of California, Santa Barbara, and the University of the South Pacific in Fiji, where she currently teaches. Like Hauʻofa, Thaman has traveled extensively throughout the region and has been steeped in both Tongan and Western knowledges from a young age.[75] Attentive to both circulations abroad and changes at home, Thaman's skillful weaving of Tongan and Western cultural influences and literary techniques reflects her interests in addressing the deeply personal desires and needs of the individual alongside broader social critique of how capitalist cultures of circulation have eroded and reshaped those individuals' cultural and familial networks.[76] It is not only the speakers or subjects of Thaman's poems that serve as "bridges" between capitalist/individualist and Oceanic circulations; the poems themselves mediate between these alternately intersecting and diverging worldviews. In this way, Thaman connects her literary aesthetic to ongoing projects of national and regional in(ter)dependence, modeling her own vision of a dynamic "new Oceania" that draws both Tongan and Western traditions into a connected fabric that highlights, rather than erases or belittles, the potential for both systems to contribute to the well-being of all of the human and nonhuman inhabitants of the Pacific, instead of serving only the wealthy few.

Thaman's combination of English and Tongan literary forms shows that engaging a counterculture of circulation is not so much a matter of simply resisting or rejecting the secular or abstract epistemologies represented by capitalism and the "West" as being able to perceive their potential and limitations from a perspective that remains centered in one's local culture and community. In this sense, Thaman's poems are illustrative of what Aotearoa/New Zealand–based Sāmoan poet Selina Tusitala Marsh has called a *"mana tamaʻitaʻi"* critique: a Pacific-centered feminist framework open to incorporating new ideas and possibilities that have emerged from the Western academy—particularly women of color feminisms—yet remains grounded in local cultural values. While remaining critical of the way that Western culture and science have ignored or degraded Indigenous knowledges, Marsh notes that it would be equally disastrous to "dismiss theory because of its strong Western implications." Marsh argues that, although "the construction of the framework [of these theories] may have largely been dominated by Western thought, it is a construction we can also define for ourselves."[77] In this context, Marsh argues for the productivity of Western thought and theory insofar as they can operate as useful tools for the furtherance of philosophies and politics centered on the experiences of Pacific Islands women—a politics that often includes critiques of and principled opposition to both local and colonial patriarchal structures and systems. As Marsh, Sina Va'ai, and Briar Wood point out, Thaman's poetry skillfully blends these two strains of critique together, particularly in her sensitive treatment of Pacific Island women's status.[78] While Thaman has hesitated to label her work "feminist"—most notably, because of the hegemony of Western ideology in contemporary articulations of feminist theory—she has embraced the idea that her interest in portraying women's lives, knowledge, and status is explicitly decolonial in nature. In a keynote speech at the conference "Decolonizing Pacific Studies" in 2003, Thaman noted that the work of decolonization requires both "acknowledging and recognizing the dominance of western philosophy, content, and pedagogy in the lives and education of Pacific people" and "valuing alternative ways of thinking about our world, particularly those rooted in the indigenous cultures of Oceanic peoples."[79] It is from this perspective, which requires scholars to acknowledge their positionings vis-à-vis Western academic and local knowledges, that new Pacific-centered ideas and philosophies can emerge, concepts that can be both "culturally inclusive and gender sensitive."[80]

Thaman illustrates this situated perspective in her short poem "Women's Lib," which appears in *You, The Choice of My Parents*, her first published collection of poems. While the first three lines of Thaman's poem appear to celebrate the speaker's adventurousness, freedom, and mobility ("If we always knew / Where we were going / We'll never take a step"), the poem takes a turn in the fourth and fifth line: "So come with me sister / Let's take a chance and make the break."[81] When read alongside the first three lines, this idea of the "break" appears to be purely liberatory, defying popular representational practices that naturalize Indigenous peoples'—and particularly Indigenous women's—relationship to the land.[82] However, the poem's last two lines ("After all, we cannot all go back / to the land") qualify the speaker's initial exuberance. With these lines, Thaman reveals that the speaker's decision to "take a step" has been determined largely by her *lack* of choice regarding the possibility of return. The poem concludes by situating the speaker's desire for liberation in the context of the apparent incompatibility between the personal freedoms represented by her privileged mobility and the more traditional social and family relationships represented by "the land." But why, the poem seems to suggest, must this be the case? Why must the goals of "women's lib"—here articulated as women's agency and mobility—be set at odds with the concepts of community and stewardship represented by the "land"?

One possible answer—and a topic that Thaman directly addresses in her other poems—is that the expanding capitalist culture of circulation exacerbates this divide between individual and communal identity and agency. The liberal individualism that informed the emergent movement for "women's lib" during the period of the early 1970s is also profoundly entangled with the rise of neoliberalism, an economic philosophy that David Harvey succinctly defines as "a theory of political economic practices that proposes that human well-being can best be advanced by liberating individual entrepreneurial freedoms and skills within an institutional framework characterized by strong private property rights, free markets, and free trade."[83] Such a philosophy contrasts starkly with the *vā*-based, Oceanian ideal of social networks based on reciprocity and the maintenance of "ancestral roots and lands for everyone."[84] The expanding hegemony of neoliberal circulations over Oceanian circulations is reflected by the plight of Tongan migrant workers in Thaman's poems "They Won't Leave" and "A Working Relative," which depict the hand-to-mouth existence of remittance workers abroad. Unlike the women who are ambivalently liberated by their mobility in "Women's Lib," the itinerant laborers of "They Won't Leave" are at once "on the run" and hemmed in, "packed like sardines / into a one-room apartment / eating fish heads / and left-overs from plush hotels / where they wash dishes / in their spare time."[85] The "relatives" who have been in the country for a longer period of time still live on the fringes of society: they are "second-class citizens" who are "ready to marry anybody / before their visas expire," then immediately divorce their wives "for incompatibility."[86] In this poem, the itinerancy of the speaker's "fellow countrymen" parallels what appears to be their permanently provisional status in the new land. Unable or unwilling to return home, yet foreign to, subaltern within, and ultimately "incompatible" with the new country, they are paradoxically caught up in a constant state of movement that has come to efface the original sense of purpose with which they set out on their journey. Their tragedy is not so much that they—like the women of "Women's Lib"—*cannot* return to the land, but that "they *won't* leave": it is not only their inability but their stated refusal to embark on the return voyage home that becomes a marker of their physical and mental incarceration. In Thaman's poem, the apparently universal logic of capitalist accumulation has overwhelmed the practice of reciprocity. There is no glimmer of generosity or exchange between the "fellow countrymen" and their "relatives," and even marriage is dictated by the logic of economic necessity rather than the desire for a romantic or social union.

In addition to addressing the fates of the remittance workers who have gone abroad, Thaman's poems explore the changing local landscape that the people who remain at home in Tonga must negotiate. The men and women who remain "at home" are geographically fixed, yet they, too, are conceptually or culturally on the move. As Hau'ofa argues, Tongans at home are just as involved in the global circulation of goods, labor, culture, and ideas as their relatives abroad, yet their participation not only counters but can, in fact, mirror or reflect those capitalist circulations.[87] Thaman's poem "A Working Relative" chides a friend or family member who appears to remain "calm and unaffected" when she knows that her "husband is sleeping / At the back of my friend's car / Every night" in the United States, working endlessly "for treasured bills / To build you that new *fale palangi* (Western-style home)."[88] In fact, the "working relative" is so busy and kept on the run that he "forgets to remember that his time is up," yet even as he is being deported for overstaying his visa, "he will remember / That new dress you had asked for; / The other women will have new overseas dresses too." In contrast to the migrant workers of "They Won't Leave," the "Working Relative" of this poem is portrayed as being entrapped not by his own desires but by his *family's* hunger for Western-style status symbols such as the *fale palangi* and "overseas dresses." In this context, it is the family's (and particularly the wife's) materialism that distorts the practice of reciprocity required for the cultivation and protection of the sociospatial ties (*tauhi vā*) connecting the Tongan family to the diaspora overseas.

The practice of *tauhi vā* speaks to the material force and maintenance of both Tongan social networks *and* the spaces and environments to which they are linked. Indeed, while the previous two poems address how Western-style consumer culture has had negative influences on interpersonal social practices home and abroad, Thaman's other poems more closely analyze how the local environment itself has been reshaped and remade through these influences. In "Langakali," the title poem from the collection of the same name, Thaman uses this central image of the endangered yet culturally significant flower and some of the conventions of Tongan poetry and poetics—in particular, *fakatangi* (lament) and *laumatanga* (nature poetry)—to emphasize or foreground the physical and ecological effects of Westernization and global capitalism on Tonga.[89] Structured as a series of vignettes woven together around the theme of ecological destruction, the poem begins with a direct address to the langakali, an indigenous flower that is becoming increasingly endangered: "Langakali! / Have you heard the latest? / The jellyfish at Fanga'uta swim freely in the wastes / Of Vaiola, refuge of our ailing brothers / From the north."[90] This opening image of pollution and infection—ironically, on the site of a local hospital—sets up the political urgency and practical difficulties of cultural and economic decolonization that the poem will address, while the named places and environmental features work to ground and locate the poem's critique within a geographically specific context. As Briar Wood notes, the identification of the hospital as a site of pollution operates as a "metaphor for the way in which the disruption of cultural boundaries involves a disordering of the natural world."[91] Indeed, "Fanga'uta" is the lagoon that lies at the center of Tongatapu, the "cradle" of Tongan culture.[92] Its pollution by the runoff from the hospital at Vaiola, therefore, is a dilemma that illustrates how the health and sustainability of the local environment is ironically endangered by the very medical technologies that provide a "refuge" for "our ailing brothers / From the north."

In a similar vein, the poem contains several references to locally significant plants and flowers that have become endangered by overdevelopment or overuse. In addition to the increasingly rare langakali, the speaker laments the loss of the hangale flowers ("Government houses have killed them all") and the use of traditional medicines:

> Must you throw this medicinal branch
> Out the door?
> It will put out roots
> And one day the tree will destroy
> Your brick house,
> You, and your sick son.[93]

Here, however, the lament is double-edged: the speaker cautions that the rejection of the natural environment can come back to "destroy" those who neglect its powers. The rejected Indigenous knowledges represented by the medicinal branch have the potential to disrupt and uproot the Western knowledges represented by the "brick house," gesturing to the way that abandoning these ecologically centered traditional practices threatens to displace us all. Like the speaker of "Women's Lib," the speaker of "Langakali" can no longer return to the land of her birth, since the land itself has been reshaped and reformed almost out of recognition. Upon the speaker's return from her journeys abroad, she is greeted by the weeping langakali and the "darkness and the soot / Of our burnt-out fale."[94] The speaker encounters others who have also lost their land, including an old man whose land was seized by the government to build an airstrip, and his son, whose home was repossessed by the bank. Bereft of his ancestors' land, the old man "only had the rain and the surf," and it is to this watery element that he apparently returns. The last mention of him in the poem notes that "it was a stormy day / When he paddled away / In a borrowed canoe."[95] Eventually, the speaker follows the old man's lead. Perhaps responding to the "song of the sea" that suggested "I could still find a place," she urges the langakali in the final lines of the poem to "give me now a fast canoe" to head out to sea and take up a pelagic identity alongside the "fish of the ocean / And together we will weep / For the works of the night." In this sense, the speaker joins her individual identity to an Oceanic one: mourning the damage that has already been done, she turns to the sea to find both personal and cultural revitalization.

The poem's conclusion is mournful and elegiac, which is largely in keeping with the conventions of *fakatangi*, an emotionally nuanced, melancholic form that Futa Helu describes as "a sense of submissive, universal sadness often expressed in a language of hopelessness and rejection which is in reality an assertion of power and joy."[96] This articulation of simultaneous hopelessness and strength can be seen in the speaker's shift from a land-bound to a pelagic existence at the conclusion of the poem. While this shift has been impelled by the destruction of the speaker's home environment, it also opens up new possibilities for the speaker to engage in a mode of circulation that honors, rather than diminishes, her sense of social and genealogical connection to their ancestors and their environment. Unlike her earlier travels, which had taken the speaker out of her element and sent her alone into the sky "to bathe in the stormclouds" (l. 42), the journey that the speaker sets out on at the conclusion of the poem is not only one in which she is accompanied by, and follows along the path of, the "fish of the ocean" (l. 108); it is also a journey that mirrors the paths taken by her ancestors, those "warriors and conversationalists" who, like the speaker herself, had traveled far beyond their own islands to create a new form of overseas or transnational Tongan diaspora.[97] In this context, the speaker's decision to go to the sea represents not so much an abandonment of the land or a capitulation to a global marketplace as a reclamation of a heritage that, as Hau'ofa has noted, considers both land and sea together as a "sea of islands" rather than distinct and separate "islands in a far sea."[98] It is by tapping into this diasporic history, these cross-currents of *vā*, that the poem's speaker attempts to revivify the Tongan (and broader Oceanian) cultures she sees as being diminished by the encroachment of colonial attitudes toward the land and the region, as well as the capitalist cultures of circulation that seek to standardize these heterogeneous sociospatial relationships to fit within the abstractions of the global marketplace. Like the "medicinal branch" dismissed and abandoned by Western science, these Indigenous knowledges—while currently discarded or thrown aside—continue to have the potential to "put down roots" and rise up, disrupting the homogenizing and apparently impenetrable forces of Western/capitalist cultures of circulation.

Conclusion

The work of countering capitalist cultures of circulation is, at its heart, a decolonial project. As Thaman's and Hau'ofa's writings show, the intellectual and critical work of decolonization does not rely solely on the achievement of political independence or sovereignty. It also requires disinvestment from colonial attitudes toward space and time that allow commodity cultures and commodity fetishism to flourish. Such decolonization does not entail a wholesale rejection of Western and capitalist cultures of circulation so much as the reclamation and centering of an Indigenous worldview that uses local knowledges and practices to navigate the structures and systems of colonial modernity. Strengthening the status of these Indigenous knowledges, Thaman persuasively argues, would not only redound to the benefit of local communities. It would also contribute to the "future of university studies" more broadly, as it invites

> an inclusive and holistic way of thinking [that] champions stewarding nature, participating in community, and valuing interpersonal relationships. It complements beliefs in rational objective thinking, suspicion of emotions and feelings, material productivity, and personal autonomy.... Today, while modern global technology allows us to be detached from the earth and from people, indigenous wisdom is about the connectedness and interrelatedness of all things and all people.[99]

By foregrounding the potential of "indigenous wisdom" to articulate new forms of "interrelatedness"—a term that invokes an understanding of not only one's connections with but one's *relations* and *responsibilities to* the others that are brought within our circuits—Thaman pushes back against the adoption of capitalist cultures of circulation, a process that she compares to "the spread of monocultures in agriculture where imported, hybridized, fertilizer-dependent seeds, produced at a profit for multinational corporations, crowd out indigenous local varieties."[100] As she cautions in "Langakali," the privileging of short-term profit over the long-historical legacies of the local "medicinal branch" carries with it the harm of losing that knowledge forever—a loss that has long-lasting effects on the local and the global community.

The Asian laborers of *China Men* are similarly confronted with these tensions between local and global cultures of circulation. While the narrative of Bak Goong—the Great-Grandfather of the Sandalwood Mountains—focuses on his suffering in a capital-driven plantation system that seeks to extract the maximum amount of labor from his body for a minimal return, brief glimpses of an alternative economy of abundance circulate at the fringes of the tale.[101] Fleeting references to these local economies appear in Bak Goong's initial reflection on the islands' overwhelming natural bounty to the generosity that marks the local peoples' interactions with both Bak Goong and Bak Sook Goong, sharing their food and opening up their homes to them, respectively. As plantation workers, the great-grandfathers labor under harsh and parsimonious conditions in a space that is so naturally abundant that "with a handful of rice, [Bak Goong] could live without working": an irony that emphasizes the unnatural violence and labor required to clear the land for sugarcane, a crop that provides profit but not human sustenance. Indeed, this irony highlights how the profits from the cane that redound to the plantation's owners produce scarcity for the Chinese laborers and Kānaka Maoli alike, who are subjected to reduced resources as the plantation's profits grow. While Bak Goong and Bak Sook Goong ultimately reject a lasting affiliation with Hawai'i and its people, Kingston, in briefly introducing the reader to the road not taken by these ancestors, also invites us to speculate about what might have happened had Bak Goong and Bak Sook Goong rejected the financial and filial obligations drawing them back to China and, instead—like "many another Paké grandfather"—become "*Hawaiian*" (as opposed to "American") forefathers, committing themselves to the structure of hospitality and abundance with which they had been welcomed rather than to the circulation of settler colonial capitalism that had rendered them abject.[102]

A commitment to "bridging" the rich and varied cultures of circulation that move through the Pacific requires both an acknowledgment of and a commitment to preserving these Indigenous and local epistemological and social frameworks. Whether rejecting a singularly progressive capitalist temporality (like Ah Goong, the "Grandfather of the Sierra Nevadas" from

China Men), refusing to remain complicit with a celebratory narrative of expansively commercial globalization (like the laborer Charlie from "A Brief History of the Trans-Pacific Tunnel"), or resisting the subordination of local knowledges to dominant economic and cultural regimes (like the speakers of Thaman's poems or Manu from "The Glorious Pacific Way"), the protagonists of the stories and poems explored in this chapter illustrate how the labor of keeping these cross-cultural bridges open often means suffering from economic, social, and cultural marginalization in a world dominated by capitalist cultures of circulation. Yet in the *absence* of these commitments to decolonial praxes, both Asian and Pacific Islander migrants can become enmeshed in an expanding and continuous cycle of capitalist appropriation and incorporation, where expressions of individual freedom and agency are articulated against a homogeneous spatiotemporal field under which both Asian labor and Pacific Island cultures have been conceptualized as so many commodities to be leveraged and exchanged. Under this regime, both Asian and Indigenous Pacific bodies are rendered not only relatively interchangeable but endlessly exploitable. By contrast, in attending to how Asian and Pacific Islanders' transpacific circulations can be interpreted not in terms of the accumulation of cultural and material capital but in terms of the shifting, specific, locally inflected relationships created through their respective ocean passages, these texts by Kingston, Hauʻofa, and Thaman gesture to the emergence of new possibilities for alliance beyond the logics of assimilation and incorporation. These stories of ocean passage likewise highlight the potential for these differently situated bodies to move through the world in ways that run counter to the cacophonic racial logics of settler colonial capitalism, which uses a framework of scarcity to coerce different Asian and Pacific Islander communities into subscribing to hegemonic projects or stereotypes that serve to either erase or render the "other" into the abject.

The next chapter turns to the unpacking and disentangling of these racial logics, whose roots in the optics of difference speak to how such systems work to privilege the visual over other sensory modes engaged by the act of oceanic passage. The importance of the visual—not only to cultures of capitalism, but also (as discussed in Chapter 1) to discourses of war, violence, and scientific inquiry—has long been bound up with the colonial project of understanding and ordering the world by being able to *see* it in a particular way, an aesthetic practice that helps to determine whose bodies and lands might be made more or less available to exploitation and extraction. Ways of knowing based on other sensory inputs—auditory, olfactory, gustatory, kinesthetic—are often subordinated to the visual, even though all of these senses are crucial to understanding how bodies move through and interpret the world. In the next chapter, I examine Hawai'i and its unique settler colonial dynamics to explore how different histories of ocean passage can come to inhere differently in the body and its gestures. In particular, I focus on how discourses of state multiculturalism work to shape and form the "local" body, as well as how alternative understandings of living with and in the ocean might reimagine and revalue those bodies that are abject to or remain unrecognized by the state. Through close readings of poems by Japanese American author Lois-Ann Yamanaka and Kanaka Maoli poet Brandy Nālani McDougall, I explore the different ways in which bodies can be trained (or forced) to move with transpacific flows of colonialism and capitalism, even when they run counter to one's own bodily integrity, as well as how they can learn to move instead with the tides of the ocean and use its strength to counter the pull of transpacific capital.

4

EMBODIED PASSAGES

"Local" Motions and the Settler Colonial Body Politic

Nicknamed the "Aloha State," Hawai'i has figured over the past half-century in both the U.S. and the global imaginary as a space of racial harmony and hospitality. Indeed, Hawai'i is often represented—and frequently represents itself—as an explicitly multicultural state, a "melting pot" uniquely capable of incorporating and assimilating racial, ethnic, and cultural differences. While the emergence of cross-cultural affinities that reach across racial and ethnic lines has been effective historically in mobilizing resistance to both U.S. racism and global capitalism, the transformation of this specific coalitional history into a more abstract multicultural "local" identity can also be made to serve the very structures of U.S. settler colonialism and transnational capitalism against which the concept of the local was constructed. A key to this transformation is the settler appropriation of *aloha*, which—as Lani Teves argues—not only defines a set of ethics and practices that have been mobilized toward "a Hawaiian cultural and political resurgence," but also has been used as an "ideological discourse" that seeks to encompass and suppress such resurgence when it threatens the settler colonial logics of the state.[1] The ways that local identity and local belonging get dispersed and diffracted through these differing practices of *aloha* mark a range of responses to changing conditions of local life in Hawai'i that simultaneously center and erase Kanaka Maoli (Native Hawaiian) epistemologies and cultural practices.[2] Such changes include the state's shift from an economy based on agriculture to one based on tourism and the military, as well as its enhanced role in establishing American soft power around the globe by serving as a multicultural "bridge to Asia."

Under these influences, these "local" motions, styles, and bodies—and the *"aloha* spirit" that animates them—began to circulate independently of, and sometimes in opposition to, the grassroots coalitions and communities that created them. Yet while these embodied, gestural, and affective expressions of local identity may work to individuate or *disperse* the relational affinities and interpersonal obligations expressed by the Kanaka Maoli value of *aloha*, they also possess the potential to *diffract* these concepts in ways that emphasize their embeddedness within and responsibilities to Kanaka Maoli epistemologies, cultural practices, and communities. It is to this end that this chapter traces the figure and aesthetics of ocean passage through the contemporary literatures and cultures of Hawai'i, exploring the problems and possibilities that emerge when the practice of subject making shifts from a historically situated series of events to an identity that can be embodied by different individuals through gesture, movement through space, and interpersonal behavior. In particular, I argue that engaging ethically and respectfully with Kanaka Maoli aesthetics and cultural practices can serve not to *restore* this local body to a desired individual "wholeness" but, rather, to *reconstruct* it in ways that account and adjust for their component parts' shifting positions within the changing tides of history.

As a construction that emerged out of conditions of settler colonial capitalism, "local" identity operates as a heuristic that unites and divides Native and non-Native communities in Hawai'i. Initially deployed as a coalitional identity based on shared experiences of racialized oppression and capitalist dispossession, the idea of the "local"—much like the Kanaka Maoli concept of *aloha*, discussed earlier—had been repurposed by the late twentieth century to support the project of settler colonialism by expanding its claims to nominally include people of all ethnicities.[3] Yet because the underlying structures and discourses of settler colonial inequality have remained largely unchanged, constructions of local identity and local belonging have transformed from a site of coalition into a zero-sum game that has positioned the interests of locals against one another, primarily by framing Kanaka Maoli claims to sovereignty as operating in conflict with discourses of progressive racial inclusivity as represented by the multicultural state.[4]

It is in the interests of interrogating and teasing apart this contradictory construction that this chapter turns to the questions of what it means for a range of local bodies and communities that have been differently marked by these violent histories of racism and colonialism to seek redress from a framework that promises restoration through enhanced participation in the settler state. What might be appropriate *alternatives* for racialized communities that aspire to dignity, healing, and wholeness if not through association and identification with the progressive and individualist narratives of the (U.S.) nation? And is it possible for local communities to identify themselves not with narratives of state multiculturalism but, instead, with projects of Kanaka Maoli sovereignty that fundamentally reject the racialized assumptions of settler colonial nationalism? In exploring these questions, I turn to the kinesthetic as a space that opens up the *possibility* of imagining an alternative to settler colonial identity that engages rather than simply gestures toward Kanaka Maoli histories and cultures. If the global circulation of "Hawaiian" identity as a set of behaviors or embodied practices operates as a reflection of a community set on the move by the ebbs and flows of neoliberal capitalism, I seek to explore how these practices have the potential to not only replicate, but also to resist, the logics of possession, consumption, and "deracination" that have worked to interpellate modern Hawai'i as both colony and commodity. While many kinesthetic and embodied elements of local identification undoubtedly have been shaped by neoliberal forces, they also have important roots in Kanaka Maoli practice and philosophy. It is toward this end that I explore a range of representations of what it means to articulate an embodied local identity in the hope of reconnecting the desire for local belonging to the project of Indigenous resurgence.

I begin with a brief analysis of popular contemporary representations of the local/"Hawaiian" body as it circulates in global politics and popular culture, attending to how it facilitates the settler state's vested interests in maintaining a heteropatriarchal order premised on the normativity of the traditionally masculine body—particularly as represented by one of the world's most powerful men, former U.S. President Barack Obama, and one of its most famous movie stars, Dwayne "The Rock" Johnson. Turning to the feminized, non-normative, and otherwise abjected bodies that are left out of such celebratory narratives, the next section turns to the poetry and prose of Japanese American author Lois-Ann Yamanaka and its representations of local bodies that do not exhibit this kind of camera-ready perfection but, instead, reveal the physical and psychic trauma of the systemic and ongoing racialized violence of the plantation system. Yet while Yamanaka's work still seeks recognition for this fragmented "local" body, the poetry of Kanaka Maoli poet and literary scholar Brandy Nālani McDougall argues that such forms of recognition, framed by the settler colonial gaze, continue to enact violence on the Native body. In particular, McDougall's poems draw attention to how, under settler colonial discourse, the Native body is *always already* dismembered and rendered in pieces, both legally and conceptually severed from the lands and environments that are both genealogy and inheritance. McDougall's poems reject recognition by the settler colonial state altogether, finding an alternative route to wholeness and interconnection by focusing on processes of reconnecting and giving life back to the Native community and the land. Such practices are based in both linguistic and kinesthetic modes of engaging with the environment and moving through space, forms of ocean passage that operate not as a discursive or metaphoric trope for navigating/mastering space but as embodied practices of learning to move and live with the dynamic currents of the land and sea.

Barack, "The Rock," and the Embodiment of U.S. Multiculturalism

In the summer of 2008, Senator Barack Obama of Illinois—who had recently, in a stunning upset, beat out his better-known challenger Hillary Clinton to become the Democratic nominee for president—made a brief trip to Honolulu, the city where he was born and raised. The U.S. media breathlessly covered Obama's first trip "home" as the presumptive party nominee, resulting in widely circulated images of a shirtless Obama bodysurfing at Sandy Beach. Echoing the liberal exuberance that attended the creation and circulation of the photographs that only seemed to enhance the idea of Obama as possessing a kind of island-inflected "cool," news reports of his two-week visit sought to link the political power of Obama's multicultural appeal to his upbringing in Hawaiʻi. Stories that speculated about the influences of Hawaiʻi's multicultural population and "Hawaiian" cultural norms on Obama's political philosophy and worldviews proliferated, yet such speculations rarely, if ever, addressed the militarized settler colonial practices that had created this multicultural community in the first place or the role of those practices in the ongoing displacement and dispossession of Native Hawaiian communities. Indeed, such practices were both functionally extended and discursively elided by reportage that remained blithely unconcerned about distinctions between Native and non-Native residents of the state, often referring to Obama simply as "Hawaiian."[5] One such report from *Time* magazine went as far as to frame the visit in terms of a reversed narrative of imperial conquest, noting that in spite of Obama's desire to keep fuss to a minimum, there would be "little chance of the trip not looking like victorious Caesar returning from the front: not only did Obama win the Aloha State's primary and the Democratic nomination, he is arguably already the best-known Hawaiian native ever."[6]

Although both Native and non-Native residents of Hawai'i certainly knew better than to classify Obama as either "Hawaiian" or a "native," he was certainly welcomed back as a "local boy," as many were eager to see the specific legacy of multiculturalism emerging from Hawai'i's post-statehood history reflected through the lens of his national success. Hawai'i's admission to U.S. statehood in 1959 coincided with not only the emergence of the civil rights movement at home but also the ongoing prosecution of the Cold War abroad, and in this context, Hawai'i's admission as the fiftieth state was explicitly framed around the argument that its multiracial, multiethnic population served as a model for what America, as a truly global nation, could become.[7] In a counterpoint to the racialized fears expressed by South Carolina's Senator Strom Thurmond, who opposed the admission of Hawai'i as a state because of its nonwhite majority population, progressive congressmen such as Representative George Rhodes of Pennsylvania argued that Hawai'i had the potential to serve as a "test tube of democracy in the Pacific" that "proved that people of varied racial, cultural, economic and political backgrounds can live and work together to build a truly American society."[8] Such rhetoric, which simultaneously celebrates the idea of the multicultural "melting pot" *and* evacuates Native claims to Hawai'i by configuring the islands as the sterile space of a laboratory or a "test tube," served to align both the national movement for civil rights and the more localized politics of Asian American economic and social mobility with the ongoing projects of American settler colonialism and the expansion of U.S. interests around the globe. This realignment of the militarized settler state with the politics of racial liberalism resulted in what Jodi Byrd has called a "cacophony" of "discordant and competing representations of diasporic arrivals and native lived experiences . . . that vie for hegemony within the discursive, cultural, and political processes of representation and identity."[9] In other words, under the settler colonial context of Hawai'i's admission to statehood, the recuperation and revaluation of certain types of (Asian and mixed-race) bodies were achieved at the cost of the desecration and devaluation of other types of (Indigenous) bodies—not only human bodies, but also animal bodies, terrestrial bodies, and bodies of water.

While narratives that celebrated Hawai'i's multiculturalism as demonstrating "a truly *American* society" took shape during the Cold War era in which statehood took place, the idea of Hawai'i as a racial and ethnic paradise has persisted throughout the twentieth and twenty-first centuries, featuring prominently not only within ongoing narratives of U.S. exceptionalism but also as an attractive simulacrum of consumable cultural diversity that circulates freely in an increasingly transnational, global capitalist economy.[10] The aspirational multiculturalism at the heart of this "rhetoric of anti-conquest," as Houston Wood has called it, was certainly part of the appeal that helped to nominate and then elect Barack Obama as the forty-fourth President of the United States.[11] Obama's mixed-race heritage, immigrant parentage, and childhood experiences in Indonesia and Hawai'i placed him at a remove from fraught histories of Black-white relations in the continental United States while also burnishing his image as a global citizen and living symbol of the success of liberal multiculturalism. When Obama was elected to the presidency, his tenure seemed to signal the ascendance of the United States as a truly multicultural superpower. Yet this was not a vision that was welcomed by all Americans, particularly those who combined toxic racial grievance with a sense that they were being "left behind" by a globalizing economy. For these Americans, Obama's blackness, as well as his apparent *foreignness*—signaled by his father's nationality (Kenyan), the Arabic middle name that they shared (Hussein), and his "exotic" childhood in Indonesia and Hawai'i—inspired a rash of conspiracy theories speculating about Obama's birthplace and religious beliefs. (Indeed, the most famous proponent of these profoundly racist speculations, Donald J. Trump, would go on to win the presidency in 2016.) On both the left *and* the right, Obama's support of unpopular trade policies—most notably, the Trans-Pacific Partnership—and other elements of a broadly neoliberal agenda was framed as a threat to American supremacy and sovereignty in the interests of foreign investors and multinationals.

Largely absent from the debates over what Obama (and Hawai'i) might represent to the United States, however, is what Obama (and the United States) represented to Hawai'i. For the most part, the predominantly positive feelings for Obama in Hawai'i index the alignment of contemporary local identity with the soft power of U.S. imperialism, as Obama's vision of a progressive, multicultural America fit in with many Hawai'i locals' celebration of their own diverse community. Such a vision certainly glosses over extant antiblack attitudes in Hawai'i, as well as the resistance of blackness to dominant local narratives of the so-called racial melting pot.[12] This resistance is referenced in Obama's own memoirs when he reflects on his sense of unbelonging as a young Black man growing up in a place that did not have a sizeable Black community.[13] Yet as a successful national figure, Obama was embraced by most Hawai'i residents as a "local," despite the relative brevity of his family history on the island. Writing in the *New York Times*, Lois-Ann Yamanaka pointed out this discrepancy, saying that while at first she did not consider Obama a true "local"—which she defined as "those of us who have been here for a few generations and plan to stay"—she changed her mind when she saw the picture of him bodysurfing at Sandy's, one of the images produced during his first official visit to Hawai'i as a national figure. She observed that he had "that local-boy reach of the arm as he glided down a huge summer swell, the grace of his relaxed face, proud, turned into the tidal force of current, the way only a local boy can take a real wave and make it his very own ride, sleek and easy. A natural local boy."[14]

In the context of Hawai'i, the designation "local" is neither neutral nor uncontested. The earliest articulations of a unified local identity emerged out of political coalitions created in response to racist and oppressive treatment of Kānaka Maoli and other nonwhite ethnic groups by white American military officers and plantation owners, particularly around events such as the Massie Trial of 1932, in which five local men were falsely accused of the rape of a white U.S. Navy officer's wife, and the sugar strike of 1946.[15] However, Jonathan Okamura points out that by the 1970s, the idea of local identity was not so much predicated against a *haole* (white) ruling class as it was against the "nonlocal"—a category that had expanded to included Asian businessmen, land developers, and multinational corporations, all of which could no longer "be equated only with whiteness or the West."[16] In this context, Kānaka Maoli and non-Native settlers again joined in unified struggle, this time against the encroachments of capitalist development. These tactics were exemplified by the Kalama Valley protests in 1971, in which Native and non-Native locals came together to protest the eviction of farm tenants living on land that was slated for development. While protestors from the mainland were also present, Peggy Myo-Young Choy notes, "There was the awareness that Hawaiians and 'local' youth and community members—those born and raised in Hawai'i—were taking a stand on a local issue."[17] The protest was eventually dispersed and the tenants were evicted; however, the events of Kalama Valley led to the formation of Kōkua Hawai'i, an organization that advocated for the independence of Hawai'i from the United States.[18] Although Kōkua Hawai'i's main focus was Hawaiian sovereignty, Choy notes, it "supported struggles in other communities" and highlighted the connections and commonalities between the struggle of Kānaka Maoli for sovereignty and the labor struggles of Asian immigrants and their descendants.[19] The coalition of Native and non-Native residents brought together by Kalama Valley and Kōkua Hawai'i would go on to organize and support other movements that sought to defend Hawaiian land from military and capitalist incursion, including successful protests against development in Waiāhole-Waikāne in 1973, the extended campaign against the military bombing of Kaho'olawe island from 1976 to 1993, and many others.[20]

Yet these claims to belonging in and on the land—so central to both Native and non-Native "local" communities—would later become an important point of distinction between those two cultural identifications. Kānaka Maoli conceive of their relationship to the land as a *genealogical* one: in this context, land is not merely property but a sustaining ancestral and/or familial figure. By contrast, many non-Native locals whose roots go back several generations mediate their sense of relationship or belonging to the land through a history of *labor*—specifically, how the experience of plantation and other agricultural labor worked to forge a unified coalition in the early part of the twentieth century.[21] While this shared labor struggle emerged out of a specific set of responses to adverse socioeconomic conditions, the persistence of its legacy across several generations has served to transform this concept of belonging to the land through labor as a genealogical inheritance in its own right, over time transforming the idea of local identity from a tactical political maneuver into a narrative of cultural inheritance. Yet this local genealogy differs from Kanaka Maoli *moʻokūʻauhau* (genealogical narratives) in a number of ways, most specifically around the question of land. Local genealogies implicitly accept the concept of land as property that grounds a progressive multicultural narrative that reflects locals' increased political and economic mobility over time. However, *moʻokūʻauhau* narrates a sense of familial and communal attachment to the land (*aloha ʻāina*) that understands the land not as an instrument or as property but as an active, agentive entity with which one enters into relation.[22] This shift from an intimate and sacred relationship with the nonhuman world to a more secular focus on the land as a property or "environment" exemplifies the investment of the "local" in the modes of possession that inform both settler colonial frameworks and the circuits of transnational capital.[23]

Indeed, even as local communities organized themselves in response to U.S. national and transnational encroachments on the space of Hawaiʻi during the 1970s, 1980s, and 1990s, both Native and non-Native local communities were being set on the move by the ebbs and flows of global capital in a period marked by increasing market deregulation and globalization. Rob Wilson notes how the articulation of "localist strategies" that increasingly emphasized local identification as a distinct or "bounded possession" in the 1980s and 1990s emerged in dialogue with the "(uneven) global/local dialectics" engendered by the neoliberalizing economy during this time period.[24] The 1980s saw a boom in Hawaiʻi's economy—largely driven by overseas investment and the tourist industry—that significantly drove up the cost of living in the islands. Yet the state's dependence on Japanese investment in particular led to a sharp decline in the 1990s, when economic growth slowed. As the cost of living rose and economic opportunities grew more scarce, Hawaiian-born locals (Native and non-Native) began moving to the continental United States in significant numbers—nearly 100,000 of them in that decade alone.[25] The substantial number of locals out-migrating to the continental United States, combined with the increasing number of immigrants from abroad and "in-migrants" from the continental United States, meant that by the early 2000s residents born in Hawai'i represented a *minority* of the state's population for the first time in more than a century. As Okamura notes, in the present day the majority of Hawai'i's current residents "lack the long-standing social and cultural ties to and appreciation of the land, peoples, and cultures of the islands that are such distinctive features of Hawai'i's people."[26]

These historical changes and demographic shifts have affected the articulation of post-1970s local identity in three ways. First, the concept of local identity in the space of Hawai'i itself has become less overtly politicized and more individualized in the sense that it focuses more on interpersonal interactions than on broad structural or institutional change.[27] Second—especially for self-identified locals who no longer live in Hawai'i—local identity becomes problematically aligned with *consumption*. As Lisa Kahaleole Hall notes, for Natives and non-Natives alike, the "shared loss of ongoing connection to the land is manifested in the marketplace," resulting in the increasing popularity of Hawaiian-branded goods, festivals, and restaurants on the continent that reconstruct local communities through shared consumer habits.[28] Finally, local identity set on the move gets expressed through *performance*, particularly how one expresses "authentic" local belonging through appearance, gesture, speech, and other performative modes. All three articulations of contemporary local identity speak to how the "local" circulates in both national and transnational contexts as a mode of embodied experience situated uneasily between Indigenous and settler ontologies and epistemologies.

A number of Kanaka Maoli scholars, including Hall, Haunani-Kay Trask, and J. Kēhaulani Kauanui, have pointed out how these modes of local identification are problematically linked to settler colonial logics that seek the erasure of Hawai'i's Indigenous people. As Kauanui notes, the idea that "Hawaiianness" can be performed (or, as Hall argues, can be consumed) contributes to a form of "diasporic deracination" that recasts local belonging as purely a matter of nostalgia, culture, taste, or habit, thereby contributing to and complicit within the genocidal logics whose end result is the "erasure of Hawaiians *as a people*."[29] From this perspective, Yamanaka's interpretation of Obama's "local" status—as intuited through her reading of an image

Figure 4.1. *Barack Obama bodysurfing in Hawai'i, August 2008.* (AP Photo/Alex Brandon)

of the future president moving with assurance through a local surf spot—operates as a perfect example of this kind of erasure. Yamanaka notes a slight shift in her determination of who counts as "local," moving from a focus on genealogy and community ("those of us who have been here a few generations and plan to stay") to a more broadly experiential and kinesthetic mode of relation ("that local-boy reach of the arm" [see Figure 4.1]). The concept of a local identity that expands to embrace Obama manifests itself not so much in terms of the depths of one's roots as in how one navigates through the world, and it is ironically in this way that the concept of the "local"—a formation that historically has been articulated in response to, or against, both the "national" and the "global"—could extend to include the man most literally representative of the U.S. nation-state and its role as a global hegemon.

Yet Yamanaka's interpretation of this kinesthetic mode of local belonging also speaks to another set of complex desires for and investments in local identity and authenticity. Her interest in how Obama moves through space speaks to her own understanding that local identity cannot and should not be objectified and reduced to a set of easily purchasable and portable signifiers (T-shirts, foods, slogans, and so on). Local identity is, instead, something that must be practiced, experienced, and lived. The local body, to Yamanaka, is a body that has been formed *in relation to* the environments and cultures of a particular place, an embodied sense of place that expresses itself through gestures that are developed through everyday practices of engagement and interaction within a specific local community. In this sense, local identity is interpreted as a quality that simultaneously *inheres* in the body and extends *beyond* it. It signifies not a personalized or individualized set of gestures but, rather, a set of social and environmental interactions that, through regular practice and habit, have become written on the body. In this context, Yamanaka's analysis of local identity as coproduced through a sense of affinity and association with community and place attempts to move toward a mode of local identification that focuses on how people live with or relate to their environments rather than how they purchase or develop them.

When taken beyond the space of the local, however, such movements can often lose their cultural and place- or community-based specificity through their subsequent decontexualization and translation into more broadly universal principle or gesture. Much like the nebulous idea of the "*aloha* spirit"—which, as Teves has pointed out, has often served to appropriate Kanaka Maoli discourse to support a settler colonial agenda—the concept of an embodied sense of belonging, when taken out of its context, can be repurposed to bolster the idea of an individualist Western subjectivity rather than mitigate it.[30] For example, while the kinesthetic trace of these practices illustrates how Obama's character and personality may have indeed been meaningfully influenced and inscribed by his upbringing in Hawai'i, they also become enfolded into a broader mythology of local exceptionalism that fetishizes the fragment or the trace of authenticity or Indigeneity in the context of settler colonial capitalist practices. As Kauanui points out, the adoption of a "Hawaiian" identity by off-island, non-Native locals is "inextricably bound to the commodification of Hawaiian culture within a multinational tourist complex that thrives in a place where Hawaiians are outnumbered and do not hold self-governance over Hawaiian trust lands"; thus, "Off-island permutations of this form of cultural appropriation need careful interrogation."[31] While Kauanui, Hall, and others have already analyzed how this fetishization of local identity often expresses itself through nostalgic or strategic modes of consumption, the reclaiming of Obama through his "local-boy" affects illustrates how such fetishization can also be expressed through a mode of aspirational interpellation or identification.[32] Obama's Hawai'i connections have not been deployed to hold him directly accountable to the local or Native communities who continue to live there. Rather, the traces of local identity that Obama exhibits in his movements and mannerisms serve as a model not so much for *resisting* the imperial pull of "mainland" United States and the global economy as for successfully *navigating* those same forces. By insisting on the foundational and, indeed, embodied nature of Obama's experiences in Hawai'i, locals' claims to Obama as one of their own illustrate an ongoing fascination with how a historically marginalized body like his—and theirs—might be recuperated and transformed into an ideal national subject, the ultimate "local boy made good."

If the image of Obama bodysurfing at Sandy's (see Figure 4.1) gestures toward a kinesthetic mode of local identification, its circulation as a photograph—a static visual object—speaks to how the radical potentials of the kinesthetic get contained through their capture within a primarily *visual* regime. Such visual regimes are not only connected (as Edward Said and Mary Louise Pratt, among others, have noted) to the colonial "gaze" that embeds a "fantasy of dominance and appropriation that is built into [an] otherwise passive, open stance," it is also explicitly a regime that naturalizes the alienation and exploitation of the environment in much the same way that it naturalizes violence visited on bodies racialized as "other."[33] As discussed in Chapter 1, the physical and material violence inflicted by this visual regime is clearly evident in the long history of scientific racism in the Pacific, from the eighteenth- and nineteenth-century wars of colonization to the late twentieth-century examples of what Elizabeth DeLoughrey has called the nuclear "wars of light."[34] All of these experiments, launched on both human bodies and bodies of water in the Pacific, were premised on the conflation of knowledge and mastery with *sight*, heralding the emergence of the current condition of global militarization that Rey Chow has termed the "age of the world target."[35]

Key to the expansion of this visual regime in the twentieth and twenty-first centuries have been not only improvements in photographic and filmic technology, but also their deployment in the creation and circulation of an increasingly global form of popular culture. The emergence of the U.S. film and television industry during this time illustrates how the kinesthetic elements of movement or passage through space have continued to be transformed into *spectacles* that circulate as both commercial products and cultural propaganda. It is in this context that I turn to another globally famous figure whose body spectacularly circulates as simultaneously "local," "Hawaiian," and "American": the former wrestler and current film star Dwayne "The Rock" Johnson. Like Obama, Johnson is a global icon who frequently has been identified with Hawai'i. Most recently, he has been controversially cast as the legendary Hawaiian monarch King Kamehameha in an upcoming project directed by Robert Zemeckis (known for films such as *Back to the Future, Forrest Gump,* and *Contact*) and written by Randall Wallace (*Braveheart, Pearl Harbor*). While several Kanaka Maoli critics and scholars have objected to the casting of Johnson and, more particularly, how the film industry "works hand in hand with U.S. imperialism and has historically created racist portrayals of Hawaiians and other Pacific Islanders to support U.S. hegemony and justify military control of the entire region," the movie is, as of this writing, still planned for a future release.[36]

While Johnson has spent even less time as a resident in Hawai'i than Obama, his mixed-race Sāmoan heritage and his genealogical connections to the region through his mother's family have made it easy for many locals to embrace him as one of their own. Johnson likewise welcomes the Hawai'i connection and has often discussed his time growing up in the islands, as well as his fellow feeling for other famous former local residents, including Obama and the singer Bruno Mars, who is of Filipino and Puerto Rican heritage: "He looks like he could be my uncle, Obama. I look like I could be Bruno Mars's big brother. That's the way it is here in Hawaii!"[37] Besides establishing a sense of affinity among these three different men through their shared experience of growing up in Hawai'i, Johnson's comment indicates how their personal appearance operates as a significant marker of their local status. Johnson's observation draws attention to the fact that one of the things that allows all three men to circulate as both local and global icons is how they not only perform but appear to *embody* a particular kind of idealized multicultural masculinity. This construction emerged from the optimistic discourses of liberal multiculturalism that ushered in Hawai'i's statehood and created a template for state-sanctioned forms of local identification in the late 1950s and early 1960s.

While many Hawai'i locals are indeed of mixed-race heritage, the idea that "local" identity is something that may be located in, or circulate as, a racially ambiguous *body* merges with ideologies of U.S. liberal multiculturalism in ways that serve to gloss over unresolved questions of Native sovereignty and settler colonialism, as well as the glaring structural and economic inequalities that persist among different racial and ethnic groups within the state.[38] The subsequent reduction of Hawai'i's complex social history to the figure of a racially hybrid local body does not simply celebrate the ways that Kānaka Maoli and a range of immigrant groups have strategically negotiated race relations in the context of the global changes of the past century. It also forces them to fit within the broadly universalizing category of "manhood" that allows them to be recognized as individual rights-bearing subjects. James Michener's "Golden Men," featured at the conclusion of his bestselling novel *Hawaii* (1959), served as the midcentury model of this type. Described as a type of man "influenced by both the west and the east, a man at home in either the business councils of New York or the philosophical retreats of Kyoto, a man wholly modern and American yet in tune with the ancient and the Oriental," the "Golden Man" nevertheless "did not depend for his genesis upon racial intermarriage," as "his was a way of thought, and not of birth."[39] Yet as Stephen Sumida observes, the apparent cultural and intellectual diversity of Michener's "Golden Men" ultimately render into a sameness that is not only cultural but *biological*, as the narrator's regular references to the ancient shared kinship between his differently raced characters indicate that "what is ultimately important . . . is that men's blood origins are said to be the same."[40] In this context, the "Golden" local body ironically serves as a vehicle for a form of universal humanism that aspires to transcend the concept of racialized embodiment by rendering all bloodlines "the same"—a gesture that, Kauanui argues, operates as a way of "vanishing, dissolving, and diluting Hawaiians" by "rely[ing] on the presumption of both cultural and biological assimilation that lies at the core of blood racialization."[41]

The gendering of the empowered multicultural local body as an explicitly masculine "Golden *Man*" speaks to the way these changing attitudes toward mixed-race or "multicultural" individuals continue to rely on heteropatriarchal structures and systems necessary to the assertion of the settler state. Although early twentieth-century U.S. representations of nonwhite "local" Native and non-Native men did emphasize criminality and sexual threat—particularly around the 1932 Massie Trial—by the twenty-first century, these racially marked local bodies were being recuperated into the body politic through the prism of a postmodern or late-capitalist mode of multiculturalism that sought to transform cultural and racial difference into a commodity for circulation. As bell hooks has argued, this serves as an appropriative strategy that distracts or diverts from the broader economic, social, and political conditions creating the "postmodern malaise of alienation" that informs the West's (ongoing) "crises of identity."[42] While hooks cautions that "no sense of grounding, no redemptive identity, can be manipulated by cultural strategies that offer Otherness as appeasement, particularly through commodification," she nevertheless notes that "diverse ethnic/racial groups can also embrace this sense of specialness, that histories and experience once seen as worthy only of disdain can be looked upon with awe."[43] Certainly, many Native and non-Native local men—particularly those aligned with hegemonic signifiers of American masculine power, including the armed forces, the government, business, and sports—have benefited from this desirous "awe," gaining social mobility or currency through their circulation through systems that remain firmly enmeshed within the project of U.S. settler colonialism. Yet these models of masculinity are often based on assimilation into a settler ideology that—as Ty Kāwika Tengan has argued—works in practice to disempower and disenfranchise Kanaka Maoli men who do *not* participate in or subscribe to these state formations by representing them as inept, invisible, or hopelessly stuck in patterns of criminality and neglect.[44] In this sense, the most dominant or hegemonic models of masculinity available to local men tend to work within and uphold a heteropatriarchal system that diminishes and erodes alternative modes of gender expression.

Johnson's career has benefited from the more positive affiliations and associations with multicultural masculinity, as his embodiment of this ideal—along with his cheerful charisma and grueling work ethic—has fueled the rise of his global celebrity. Johnson started out as a professional wrestler, following in the footsteps of both his father, the Afro-Canadian wrestler Rocky Johnson, and his Sāmoan grandfather, Peter Maivia. Initially appearing under the name "Rocky Maivia," he soon gained widespread celebrity in his own right as "The Rock." While he initially became famous as a "heel" (villain) character, he soon transformed into a "face" (hero) who would go by the nickname "The People's Champion." He branched out into film and other media in the early 2000s, and by 2013 Johnson had become the world's top-grossing actor, with his films bringing in $1.3 billion worldwide.[45] A recent article in *GQ* magazine noted that in studies commissioned by the film industry, he has been shown to test well with men and women of all ages, from all backgrounds—a level of popularity so widespread that he has even considered following in the footsteps of fellow "local boy" Obama and pursuing a presidential run.[46] Johnson's appeal, as both a wrestler and a movie star, is unavoidably attached to the spectacle of his body. In addition to being heavily muscled and appearing almost larger than life, Johnson's body is also quite unmistakably *nonwhite*, something that his pride in, and performance of, his Pacific Island heritage serves to bring to the fore. Building on long-held Western constructions of Pacific Island men as representing a particular kind of authentic or (as Māori scholar Brendan Hokowhitu has noted) a "pre-modern" and therefore static and enduring form of patriarchal masculinity, the spectacle of Johnson's body promises both exoticism and stability, an "otherness" that reads as universally relatable.[47]

While Johnson's body operates as a visual signifier of strength that recuperates a sense of neo-"primitivist" authenticity against the abstract and alienating forces of global capitalism, his celebrity is also largely produced within and circulated through an entertainment industry that relies on those same neoliberal infrastructures. Johnson's image circulates as a valuable commodity on the global market—a mode of commodification highlighted by the controversy that arose over the marketing of Disney's animated feature *Moana*. In the film, Johnson serves as the voice of the demigod Maui, depicted as an insecure braggart and trickster who begrudgingly assists the heroine on her journey. While *Moana*'s Maui is based on a Polynesian sacred figure, in the film the character is also refracted through the lens of Johnson's global celebrity. He sports Johnson's larger-than-life physique, and in his introductory song, "You're Welcome," he brags about the fame of "the hair—the bod!" that establishes him as a celebrity within the world of Disney's imagined pre-contact Pacific.[48] Disney's marketing push for the film made this objectification literal by including in its merchandise a Maui "costume" that consisted exclusively of "the hair" and "the bod": a wig and a bodysuit made to resemble Maui's curly hair, brown skin, muscular physique, and tattoos. Although Disney quickly pulled the costume following an outcry across social media about its disrespectful appropriation of Pacific Island bodies, the marketing and circulation of the costume in the first place certainly speaks to the ease with which such bodies are objectified and commodified on a global scale.

While the costume controversy spoke primarily to dynamics of cultural or racial appropriation, another part of Johnson's visual appeal to mass audiences is his physical strength, which suggests his potential to engage in violence, to dominate, to reduce other bodies to fragments. Johnson's roots in pro wrestling and his current widespread popularity as an action movie superhero speak to how the particular masculinity that he embodies, even in its most family-friendly versions, is bound up with both the promise and performance of violence. While Johnson himself is an advocate and ambassador of both Oceanic cultures and women's rights, several of the roles that have made him famous have been deeply invested in patriarchal and nationalist forms of masculinity. In his films he is often cast *as* a patriarch, albeit one who can sail through tsunamis or blow up helicopters to save his family. This protective violence is most often deployed against an "other," often constructed as a foreign agent, a natural force, or—in the case of Johnson's role as the lifeguard Mitch Buchannon in the action comedy *Baywatch* (2017)— both. In the movie's climactic sequence, Johnson's character confronts the film's villainess, played by Indian actress Priyanka Chopra, and delivers a mock-heroic monologue before literally blowing her into bits:

> I was born of the sea. I eat fire coral, and I piss saltwater. I scratch my back with a whale's dick, and I loofah my chest with his ball sack.

I'll die when the tide stops and the moon drowns. (pause) I'm Oceanic, motherfucker!⁴⁹

While the monologue begins and ends with statements affiliating Johnson's body with his Oceanic/Pacific Island heritage, the rest of the speech renders the natural world into fragments for comic effect. Rather than expressing affinity with the ocean and its creatures, Buchannon's speech deconstructs and instrumentalizes them—in particular, the "whale's dick" and "ball sack," signifiers of an outsize masculinity, are dismembered and recontextualized as grooming tools. This rhetorical dismemberment likewise foreshadows the fate of Chopra's villainess, whose body is blown into fragments that rain down on Buchannon's cringing associates. In contrast to the spectacle of Johnson's recuperated multicultural masculinity, the dismembered female and oceanic bodies represented both visually and rhetorically in this scene reflect their objectification, instrumentalization within, and abjection from a national body politic. It is to the fate of these feminized bodies rendered abject and in parts, and how they circulate within the United States and around the globe, that I now turn.

A Body in "Parts": The Impasse of the Local

In the poem cycle "Parts," published in her 1993 poetry collection, *Saturday Night at the Pahala Theater*, Lois-Ann Yamanaka articulates the experience of life as a "Girl in Parts." The cycle expresses the speaker's verbal and implied physical abuse of an unnamed "girl," refracted through a series of poems named for different body parts (e.g., "The Eye," "The Foot," "The Nostril," "The Ass"). Each poem in the cycle addresses how the speaker—who, it is implied, is the girl's mother—considers each part in isolation from the girl's body and renders it objectionable, unworthy, or otherwise abject. "The Brain" gives the speaker a "headache"; "The Foot" is accused of harboring "toe jams" that create a disgusting smell; "The Ass," "The Crack One," and "The Crack Two" simultaneously reduce the girl's value to her sexual organs and then render them shameful.⁵⁰ In "The Crack Two," the speaker's angry response to the girl's confession to having been raped not only configures the girl as an abject figure in relation to her society; it also uses that shame to estrange her from her own body. Stripping the girl of a sense of agency over her own body, which circulates as an objectified commodity ("Everybody / going use you"), the intense shame that the speaker attaches to the girl's "parts" renders pleasure itself abject ("Dirty girl / Dirty / girl").⁵¹ As a result, the final poem in the cycle ("What the Hands Do about All of These Parts") reveals the girl's introduction to cutting, an act that performs the extremes of both bodily alienation and inhabitation. The speaker of this final poem is not the girl's mother but one of her peers, a friend who has done this before and is teaching the speaker about how to derive pleasure through the act of self-harm. On the one hand, the act of cutting renders one's own body as separate from oneself, an instrument or object that can be observed in a relatively detached or clinical manner. Yet, on the other, it engages a heightened sense of embodied sensation that gestures toward the fundamental entanglement of the body and the speaking subject: the speaker explains the "gray" and "numb" feeling that takes over one's body with the pain of cutting and even describes the "taste" of her own blood, "'cause that's me coming out of myself."[52] The act of cutting extends rather than mitigates the logic of objectification and dismemberment that informs the girl's (and both speakers') *lack* of agency over how their bodies circulate. Yet at the same time, the girl's wounded body refuses to hide or mitigate the violence of that logic, and she ends up leaving the name of her abusive mother written on the sidewalk in blood so that "she going know / you was here / and she going know / how much you love her."[53]

While it is the mother's critical words and unsympathetic attitude that fragment the girl's body—and it is her love and recognition that the girl still painfully desires—Rachel Lee points out the implicit correlation between the "divisive social structuring of Hawai'i's plantation economy" and the speaker's "language of command" that "performatively instantiate[s] this daughter or 'you' as a divisible corporeality."[54] Like the harsh parent of the poem, the plantation system in Hawai'i brought the modern multiethnic local community into being, yet it also deliberately conceptualized that community as an objectified and fragmented body, relying on linguistic and cultural differences among the Japanese, Chinese, Filipino, Korean, Portuguese, and Hawaiian laborers to keep them from joining forces and organizing for better conditions. While the development of a local "pidgin" English and cross-ethnic activism were able to bridge these ethnic divides for key moments of coordinated activism—notably in the sugar strike of 1946, which wrested important concessions for plantation workers—ethnic divisions within that "local" body, generally along social and economic lines, continue to the present day. Indeed, Yamanaka's work became a focal point for these divisions, as widespread controversy over her representations of Filipino men as sexual predators in *Saturday Night at the Pahala Theater* and her 1997 novel *Blu's Hanging* spoke to the ongoing inequities among the ethnic groups that have generally prospered under statehood (particularly Japanese Americans—a group to which Yamanaka belongs) and those whose mobility has been more constrained.⁵⁵ The controversy served to illustrate the kind of cacophonic melancholia at the heart of modern "local" identity, in which a desire for wholeness and completion becomes associated with a desire for recognition and acknowledgment by the very same corporate and state mechanisms that render local bodies divided and incomplete. The local body, in this context, can be seen as not unlike the fragmented girl of Yamanaka's poem in their desires for a wholeness that is imagined to be achievable only through recognition by the author of their dismemberment.

Patriotic, masculine bodies such as Obama's and Johnson's seamlessly suture these divides in their illustration of a multicultural subjectivity that is both recognized by and recuperated through their alignment with the national body. Wounded and fragmented bodies like the ones that appear in "Parts," however, stubbornly refuse such healing. As Lee notes, the ambivalence of the poem's conclusion gestures toward an alternative mode of relationality that is expressed "not in the closed loop between two putative whole (humanist) 'Asian American' subjects—the parent and daughter—but in the distribution of affects and effects that the cutting generates."⁵⁶ In this sense, the dispersed and dismembered—though still viscerally embodied—parts of the local body circulate as fragments that call attention to the affects of "pain" and "blame" that have conditioned their *relationship* to one another, rather than requiring *restoration* to a sense of a cohesive and complete subjectivity that never existed in the first place. It is this critical attention to, and interest in, the possibilities of a local community built around a constellation of affects that draw on different and often painful or unpleasant forms of relation that makes much of Yamanaka's work both compelling and a difficult fit for both Asian American and Pacific Island studies. While her works' refusals of normative subjectivity reject assimilative (and masculinist) Asian Americanist racial justice frameworks based on "claiming America," her articulations of the persistent and lingering, if ultimately unfulfilled and unfulfillable, *desires* for recognition have also been critiqued for eliding and overlooking the other Asian American and particularly Indigenous Pacific communities and constituencies that such desires continue to render absent or abject.⁵⁷ Indeed, the "ugly feelings" (to borrow a phrase from Sianne Ngai) expressed in Yamanaka's work can be seen as indexing a form of "suspended agency . . . that points to a *specific history* of systemic political and economic disenfranchisement" that comes to represent the totality of "authentic" local experience in Hawai'i.⁵⁸

Yamanaka's conceptualization of a local identity built around a sense of suspended agency—rather than a fully recuperated one—calls attention to the historical and ongoing damages enacted on the (non-Native) local body by its circulation through capitalist and state structures and addresses how its component parts are united through the shared affective experiences of this damage. At the same time, it also holds out the promise or hope for recognition that is persistently deferred to a future date. Just as the girl subject of "Parts" longs for her mother's love and affection, the melancholic local characters that figure in Yamanaka's other works strive toward a reconfigured subjectivity that will allow them to thrive within the contours of a world shaped by Western liberal modernity. Caught up in the promises of what Lauren Berlant has termed "cruel optimism," a set of relations that emerge "when something you desire is actually an obstacle to your flourishing,"[59] the cyclical trajectories of Yamanaka's fictional characters—particularly the Ogatas of *Blu's Hanging*, the Yagyuus in *Heads by Harry*, and the Kurisus in *Father of the Four Passages*—parallel how the novels themselves ambivalently reject and embrace progressive narratives of loss and healing.

Yamanaka's depictions of the local body illustrate a suspended form of agency that is useful for charting the cacophonous dynamics of multicultural settler colonialism in Hawai'i. On the one hand, depictions of visceral fragmentation in poems such as "Parts" refuse aspirational narratives that get attached to multicultural local bodies by revealing the rhetorical and physical violence to which they are subjected, as well as the cruelty of the optimism that keeps them in circulation. Yet on the other hand, we also can see how—especially in longer narrative works such as *Blu's Hanging* and *Father of the Four Passages*—the impasses that get opened up through these moments of violent disruption are not escaped but reaffirmed through a narrative drive for resolution that parallels the local subject's persistent attachment to the promises of liberation through settler colonial subjectification. For example, while *Blu's Hanging* spends most of its time exploring how the generational violence of plantation-era racism continues to write itself onto the "local" body, the book concludes with its main character, Ivah, flying to Honolulu to complete her education, placing her on a (literally) upwardly mobile trajectory that seeks to transform her community's abjection by *transcending* the conditions that continue to render them lesser or other.[60] Moving in the opposite direction, Yamanaka's *Father of the Four Passages* (2001) concludes with its protagonists affirming and consecrating a non-normative, queer local identity on the sacred space of Mauna Kea—an act that, while grounding this local identity in a specific, meaningful site, nevertheless overlooks or elides how Mauna Kea was and continues to be contested ground in the Native Hawaiian sovereignty movement.[61] In both cases, while Yamanaka's characters exhibit creative agency in forging an affective understanding of local identity that is forthright about the many contingencies and traumatic ruptures that have created and been created by the conditions of its emergence, the overwhelming desire to ultimately *heal* those ruptures without explicitly engaging the dispossession of Native people serves to overwrite Native presence, which, ironically, upholds the structures of the very settler systems that set them on the move to begin with.

Yamanaka's abjected and fragmented local bodies certainly do not enjoy the same levels of global notoriety of the patriotic, multicultural masculinity projected by figures such as Obama and Johnson. However, her novels have nevertheless circulated widely as representations of "local" life in Hawai'i, particularly in U.S. literary circles. She has been described, in mainstream U.S. publications such as *The Atlantic* and the *New York Times*, as a "Hawaiian" writer in ways that gloss over the distinctions between Asian locals and Kānaka Maoli, allowing her specific vision of local life to stand in for a wide range of local and Indigenous experience.[62] Even the controversy over *Blu's Hanging*, which attempted to critique this particular tendency, served to secure her place in academic, as well as literary, discourse, as that text continues to be written about and taught in a number of college literature courses focusing on Asian American literature.[63] In this context, Yamanaka's local bodies and their aspirations to transcendence through spirituality circulate as figures that represent modern "Hawaiian" culture as a subset of Asian American experience, in spite (or perhaps *because*) of their disavowal or suspension of normative U.S. subjectivity. If the image of the "Hawaiian" as refracted through bodies such as Obama's and Johnson's speaks to the appealing fantasy of the fully nationalized local subject, Yamanaka's characters illustrate the incompletion and woundedness that attend a more postmodern form of subjectivity. Yet both modes of reading the "local" in this way depend on the recognition of a kind of subjecthood that continues to be leveraged through normative models of subject formation. Such models largely exclude considerations of collective or intersubjective identities that attempt to expand the default assumptions of liberal individualism through an explicit incorporation of transhuman affinities for environment and place. How might these local bodies be further transformed if they pursued the more radical forms of intersubjectivity opened up through the vectors created by *movement* (as in Obama's bodysurfing stroke, connecting body and swell) or the recognition and rejection of the settler colonial *impasse* that places the healing of Native and non-Native communities in conflict with one another? How might these opportunities allow the local body politic to acknowledge and assume responsibility for how it finds itself indebted to and entangled with the Native peoples, cultures, and environments of Hawai'i?

From Gesture to Practice: Decolonizing Local Motions

The poems collected in Brandy Nālani McDougall's *The Salt-Wind: Ka Makani Pa'akai* (2008) draw from and elegantly combine her training in both Western and Kanaka Maoli poetics, often using Western lyric forms (such as the sonnet and the sestina) as a medium for conveying imagery and narratives rooted in Kanaka Maoli aesthetics. The poems' poetic hybridity is paralleled by their linguistic hybridity, a practice that McDougall emphasizes both formally, by incorporating untranslated 'Ōlelo Hawai'i into the English verses, and thematically, in poems such as "Tiny Rebellions" and "Ka 'Ōlelo." The latter poem highlights how U.S. territorial law not only served to render Kanaka Maoli claims to the land extinct; it also instated a series of English-only policies in the schools and other public systems that were used to stamp out the very words, concepts, and genealogies that Kānaka Maoli had used to connect to and locate themselves on and within that land. Losing these words meant that "there are winds and rains / who have lost their names, descending the slopes / of every mountain, each lush valley's mouth, / and the songs of birds and mo'o, that cope / with our years of unknowing, somehow," as "English could never replace / the land's unfolding song, nor the ocean's / ancient oli, giving us use again."[64] "Ka 'Ōlelo" narrates how the severance of Kānaka Maoli from their words, language, and modes of expression directly parallels their dispossession from the environments, histories, and epistemologies that are their inheritance—a violation that carries with it the trauma and visceral pain of bodily dismemberment.

Yet McDougall's hybridized poems attest to the Native body's ability not only to survive this dismemberment, but to reconnect, heal, and push back against ongoing settler narratives that frame Kānaka Maoli as a body that is always already in fragments, a "*dying race.*"[65] Significantly, this healing takes place in terms of a return and reconnection to 'Ōlelo Hawai'i and the relationships to the land that 'Ōlelo Hawai'i is uniquely equipped to name. McDougall's deployment of Kanaka Maoli aesthetics thus operates not only as a literary technique but also as a mode of healing that seeks to reconnect these languages, histories, and relationships that have been pulled apart, isolated, and commodified under U.S. occupation and colonial rule. These aesthetic devices—which ku'ualoha ho'omanawanui translates as "meiwi moʻokalelo"—include *moʻokūʻauhau* (genealogy), *kaona* (metaphor/ intertextual allusion), and *wahi pana* (sacred/storied place).⁶⁶ McDougall's strategic deployment of these and other techniques in her work illustrates how language and literary/rhetorical aesthetics can be used to powerfully reclaim and reimagine the Native body as a unified whole rather than a body in parts.

While McDougall incorporates these and other *meiwi* in her work, for this argument I want to attend particularly to how *moʻokūʻauhau* (genealogy) and *kaona* (metaphor/intertextual allusion) serve as framing aesthetics in McDougall's volume. Similar to Māori practices of *whakapapa* (discussed in Chapter 1) and drawing from the dynamic interrelationality expressed by the concept of *vā* in Tonga and Sāmoa (discussed in Chapter 3), *moʻokūʻauhau* work to establish both relationships to place and a sense of kinship/community *across* space and time.⁶⁷ The deployment of *kaona* likewise requires a deep familiarity with these histories and genealogies; it is a literary technique that requires an ongoing engagement with these ancestral knowledges. McDougall notes that the practice of understanding and deploying *kaona* in Kanaka Maoli composition "allows [Kānaka Maoli] to actively co-construct meaning with our ancestors, to intimately connect with them," in this context operating as a process that seeks to suture and reconnect old and new generations across more than a century's worth of epistemic violence.⁶⁸

These ancestral histories, knowledges, and practices are simultaneously local and global in scope. In his study of Kanaka Maoli *moʻolelo* (stories/ histories) about exploration and migration, David Chang notes that Kānaka Maoli knew "that the islands and their people were connected to global geography by *genealogy*, by the gods and other powerful beings, and by the movement of people, birds, and other living things." Indeed, these global genealogies were used as the frame that contextualized the long history of Kanaka Maoli communities on the land.⁶⁹ Likewise, in *The Salt-Wind* McDougall uses *moʻokūʻauhau* and *kaona* to name and narrate the contours of the speakers' relationships to specific land and ocean sites and spaces both within the Hawaiian Islands *and* this broader network of Pacific Islands and communities. Such Indigenous-centered transpacific relationships are established not through the shared "universal" assumptions of settler colonial capitalism but, rather, through an understanding of the long history and complexity of these trans-Oceanic genealogical relationships, as well as a shared modern history of colonization and dispossession. In "Tehura," the poem's speaker describes the sense of recognition and genealogical connection across time and space that she feels while viewing Paul Gauguin's famous painting *Manaʻo Tupapau (Spirit of the Dead Watching)*. The painting features a young Maohi (Tahitian) girl positioned naked and fearful on a bed, a stance that the painter interprets as "waiting for love."[70] Against this narrative of rape as seduction, the speaker pushes back against Gauguin's interpretation—presented in the poem as interpolated excerpts from the painter's autobiography—of the scene as an erotic encounter. In contrast to Gauguin's characterization of the girl's nudity as an "Indecent!" invitation,[71] the speaker tenderly names and describes the component parts of Tehura's exposed body, not to further alienate or objectify her subject as a "girl in parts," but instead to revisit and reconnect these parts, reinvesting Tehura with a historical and genealogical identity that has been stripped away by the artist's gaze. Identifying with the exposed subject of the painting, rather than with the artist's gaze, the speaker calls out to the Maohi girl Tehura as "my pōki'i" (younger sibling/dear child), concluding,

> in your face I see my own,
> the same curves and shadow twisting
> into a sad silence. I know
> this is not who we are, not Why or How—
>
> only smoke from flailing ghosts, tricks
> of fading light, only the wash of gold paint over
>   this rotting wood frame.[72]

The "we" of the poem, connecting the speaker to the subject, not only asserts a sense of empathy for Tehura, the subject of the painting's eroticized gaze. It also gestures toward a more explicitly Indigenous or Oceanic mapping of the region, in which Tehura can be reimagined not only as a subject in her own right but also as "pōki'i"—a figure imagined in relation to the other children of a Pacific diaspora, whose longevity both predates and will exceed the French painter's "wash of gold paint over / this rotting wood frame."

While *Mana'o Tupapau* has circulated, through galleries and art history textbooks, as a celebrated example of figure painting in post-Impressionist art, "Tehura" presents us with an alternative perspective in which the poem's speaker/viewer stands apart not only from the position of the artist's dominating gaze, but also from the distanced and "objective" stance of the art scholar or connoisseur. The speaker identifies instead with the fearful gaze of the painting's subject as a way to highlight the painting's emergence from and embeddedness within the racialized and gendered discourses of Western colonization—the "rotting wood frame" of the poem's conclusion. At the same time, the speaker's act of rhetorically and conceptually *reframing* this image asserts a renewed sense of intimacy and kinship across these vast temporal and spatial divides, reclaiming Tehura as both ancestor and *pōkiʻi*. While such a shift in perception—and its concomitant reversal or refusal of the colonial gaze—is in keeping with the perspectival, "Oceanic" visions of the region as articulated by Epeli Hauʻofa, Albert Wendt, Vincente Diaz, and others, in "Tehura" McDougall foregrounds an explicitly woman-centered version of this Oceanic worldview—one that does not contradict, but complements, the more male-associated practices of voyaging and wayfaring frequently used as an analogy for transpacific travel.

While Kānaka Maoli had long conceptualized the ocean as a site of trans-Indigenous connection, by the mid-1970s this ocean-centered worldview was reassuming concrete shape and expression in the voyage of the Hōkūleʻa, a project that sought to reconstruct and navigate a double-hulled voyaging canoe based on a combination of Kanaka Maoli and Oceanic models. The successful, instrument-free navigation of the Hōkūleʻa from Hawaiʻi to Tahiti in 1976 under the guidance of Carolinian seafarer Mau Pialug pushed back against the social-science theories that Kānaka Maoli were isolated or cut off from the broader Pacific world by their geographical location, and it definitively countered Western academics' skepticism of Kanaka Maoli and other Pacific Islanders' navigational techniques and prowess. In the years since, the *conceptual* bases of Indigenous navigation and wayfinding have been taken up in a range of academic fields (such as cognitive and computer sciences, particularly via Edwin Hutchins's influential *Cognition in the Wild* [1995], which used Micronesian navigational techniques as a model for rethinking human-computer interactions). Yet while the intellectual and technical achievements of Indigenous Pacific navigation have thus been welcomed into the mainstream of academic study, less attention has been paid by (non-Indigenous) scholars to the genealogical and political implications of this mode of navigation, possibly because of how it has worked to disrupt not only academic assumptions about Indigenous epistemologies and the viability of instrument-free navigational techniques, but also the colonial assumptions and frameworks that have tethered Hawaiʻi to the United States. Upon being welcomed on their arrival in Tahiti as long-lost family members, both Maohi and Kānaka Maoli had a renewed sense of an *Oceanic* identity that asserted the voyage's place as one of the key events of the Hawaiian cultural renaissance of the 1970s and 1980s.[73] Yet such a cultural renaissance necessarily carried with it a political meaning. As Chang notes, since the Hōkūleʻa's maiden voyage, "The oceangoing canoe has been a powerful symbol of the reassertion of Hawaiʻi's place in the Pacific, demonstrating that Hawaiʻi's most fundamental connection is to ʻĀinamoana, not America."[74] Certainly, as the resurgence of interest in Indigenous navigation spreads throughout communities across the Pacific, the concepts and epistemologies that they engage can provide the groundwork not only for navigational practice but also for the establishment of long-suppressed transpacific connections among Pacific Island communities separated not only by ocean space but also by their different colonial histories. As Diaz has argued, Indigenous Pacific seafaring practices can provide both "an analytic and [a] practical way to advance the political and cultural struggles of indigenous peoples in lands heavily-settler-colonized."[75]

In this context, such feats of transpacific navigation are both conceptually and politically intertwined with trans-Oceanic genealogies that have been sustained through rhetorical, aesthetic, and poetic praxes. To return briefly to "Tehura" as an example, we can see the rhetorical piecing together of the girl's body operating not as a resubjectification of a specific individual so much as a process that metaphorically gestures to the reconnection of an Oceanic community that, through the past four centuries of Spanish, British, French, German, Japanese, and U.S. colonial rule, has been dismembered and classified into separate political, ethnographic, and linguistic regions. Yet even as the poem's speaker lyrically reincorporates Tehura's body into a broadly Oceanic context, when read in the context of the volume (and McDougall's body of work) as a whole, we might see the "I" as taking on a positional specificity that is entwined with broader genealogical relationships to Oceania while remaining specifically grounded in Kanaka Maoli epistemologies and environments. The act of renarrating connection to a broader Indigenous Pacific community exhibited in poems such as "Tehura" does not elide or override the specific situation of Kānaka Maoli, who continue to live under conditions of U.S. settler colonialism. Rather, the desire to reincorporate a Pacific body within a genealogical context *not* overdetermined by settler colonial logics emerges out of and in dialogue with these localized epistemologies and historical experiences.

While "Tehura" uses *moʻokūʻauhau* as one way to reincorporate a "transIndigenous" Oceanic community *across* the space of the sea, the poems collected in the book's first section, "Pō," emphasize the intimate specificity of the genealogies that connect Kānaka Maoli to the land and seas of the Hawaiian Islands. The first poem in the section, also titled "Pō," is a work inspired by the Kumulipo, the Hawaiian creation chant that traces the beginning of life through the creation of the earth, the birth of the gods, and the subsequent emergence of human life. As a genealogical narrative, the Kumulipo traditionally served the purpose of establishing the lines of descent of the ruling chiefs, who drew their power and sacred authority from their relationships to these human, nonhuman, and divine ancestors. Yet as a cultural archive, it also asserts the intimate/familial relationship that *all* Kānaka Maoli have to the land. In the nineteenth and early twentieth centuries, the Kumulipo was also deployed to assert Kanaka Maoli authority and sovereignty in the face of dispossession by U.S. influence and later colonization. King David Kalākaua (r. 1874–1891) commissioned research on and recitations of the Kumulipo not only to bolster his claim to the throne upon the death of the last lineal descendant of King Kamehameha, but also to assert Hawaiian sovereignty in the face of the increasing encroachment of white settler interests during his reign. His sister and heir, Queen Liliʻuokalani (r. 1891–1893), composed and published a translation of the Kumulipo into English while she was under house arrest following the planter-led coup that overthrew the Kingdom of Hawaiʻi and established an interim government that sought annexation by the United States. As Kamanamaikalani Beamer argues, this translation sought not only to convey the depth and complexity of Kanaka Maoli history, sovereignty, and knowledge to an English-speaking audience but also to "call attention to the record of hundreds of generations of native rule over the islands . . . at a strategic time when the continuity of native rule was in question."[76]

"Pō" draws from both the spiritual/cultural meaning and the explicitly decolonial politics of the Kumulipo's modern circulation. McDougall writes that the "Kumulipo has had a profound impact on how I view our history, how I view my own identity as a Native woman to Hawaiʻi, and how I view our future as people of this pae ʻāina (archipelago)." She notes that it also inspired her to write "Pō" as "an anticolonial genealogy, one that, in its recitation, undoes and challenges American colonial normativity by emphasizing the historical depth of all that came before its recent establishment—our own ʻŌiwi culture and lāhui, the ʻāina and our oceans, and Pō, the creative force from which the entire universe sprang."[77] In the poem, McDougall articulates this historical depth and creative power by having its speaker pull back through time, calling attention to that which existed

> before the land was tamed by industry,
> the oceanside resorts and pineapple plantations,
> before the cane knife's rust, the dark time of sickness,
> the coming of cannons, the bitter waters drunk,
> before the metallic salt of blood, the rain emptied
> into rivers, the winds carved valleys and mountains,
> before the earth spurted fire, birthed islands,
> her churning magma and her inner core of iron,
> before the stars dwarved, their coronas ignited,

> before the centripetal spin of galaxies,
> the unwinding gestures of time and space,
> before the light and heat—[78]

In this account, the time covered by settler colonial modernity is limited to the first four lines—upheavals that are rendered in violent terms yet ultimately are delimited as simply the most recent chapter in a history that reaches even further back to contextualize Hawai'i and its people within a vast cosmological framework centered within the churn of earth, space, and time itself. By repeatedly emphasizing that which came *before*, "Pō" critiques colonial histories that render the time "before" Western contact and modern intervention as a darkness marked by ignorance, or emptiness. Instead the poem compares it to the vivid potential energy and awesome creative power of "the entirety of a universe pressed into a shell / the size of an atomic nucleus, waiting."[79] Concluding the poem with this image of this latent power in "waiting," McDougall not only draws a metaphoric comparison between the depth of Kanaka Maoli genealogical knowledge and current scientific theories of life and the universe's beginnings. She also gestures toward the dynamic potential and unfolding manifestations of Indigenous knowledge, which—like life and the matter of the universe—are not limited to one spectacular event in the past but continue to materialize in new and unexpected ways.

The poem "Haumea," which honors the goddess of fertility, likewise draws on a genealogical framework to establish Kanaka Maoli relationships to the land and oceans of Hawai'i in intimate and embodied ways. Like "Tehura," "Haumea" emphasizes the centrality of women's perspectives and *mana wahine* (women's spiritual power) to the *mo'okū'auhau* that narrates the genealogical relationships between Indigenous bodies and environments. The speaker of "Haumea" recalls that it is "Out of her head / Out of her breast / Out of her mouth, / Out of her skin, / Out of her breath" that all life began, from "the gods who lived / off the length of her body" to the "soft green curve / of the sun falling into the ocean" to the most recent "offshoots of those long germinated seeds," the *kama'āina* (children of the land).[80] The blazon that begins the poem—describing Haumea through her component parts—does not indicate the trauma of colonial violence. Instead, it is a celebration of life: it is through her "head," "breast," "mouth," "skin," and "breath" that Haumea is said to have given birth to the gods and goddesses that, in turn, brought life to the world around us. As with "Tehura," the speaker's use of blazon does not serve to *objectify* their subject, as was often the case with the way blazon was deployed in European Renaissance poetry. Rather, McDougall's use of blazon highlights the power, dignity, and agency of each body part, as well as how each part might be narrated *against* this tradition to articulate new forms of life.

Although the poems collected in the section titled "Pō" draw on and cite these genealogical frameworks to assert both the longevity and the survivance/resilience of Kanaka Maoli epistemologies, in "Ka ʻŌlelo," "Tehura," and other poems, McDougall invokes the violence done to the body and its parts to articulate a pointed critique of settler colonial capitalism, calling attention to how impositions of not only Western colonial rule but also Western epistemologies have worked to violently dismember the local community. Read through this trope of trauma as dismemberment, particularly as visited on the female or feminized body, we can draw out some important resonances and affinities between McDougall's work and Yamanaka's. However, while Yamanaka's work primarily emphasizes the gendered and racialized traumas caused by the interpersonal and interethnic divisions that emerge from the specific dynamics of U.S. settler colonial capitalism, McDougall's poems focus on how the broadly universalizing epistemology of settler colonialism itself—an epistemology that categorically denies and rejects Kanaka Maoli genealogical relationships to the land—operates as a form of embodied, physical violence that does not destroy but certainly inhibits the formation of a healthy and thriving community. In this context, McDougall's poems of protest are affiliated with both a spiritual/sacred genealogy and a genealogy of protest, two strands of historical reckoning that come together through their shared dedication to preserving the life of the land.

The genealogy of Kanaka Maoli protest extends throughout the period of U.S. colonial rule; as scholars working with Hawaiian-language sources from the nineteenth and early twentieth centuries have shown, the songs, poetry, and *moʻolelo* (stories/histories) circulated among Hawaiian-language speakers during the time of the overthrow of the kingdom and subsequent acquisition by the United States offer clear messages of resistance and outright refusals of the "sin of annexation and trading away / of Kanaka civil rights."[81] McDougall's own intellectual genealogy includes these composers and activists, as well as one of the most respected figures in the contemporary Hawaiian sovereignty movement, Haunani-Kay Trask, who in her prose, poetry, and public speaking has powerfully and explicitly articulated the damage that has been, and continues to be, done to Hawaiian land and bodies by ongoing projects of settler colonialism.[82] Trask's forthright critiques highlight how settler colonial frameworks have disproportionately affected Kanaka Maoli communities, disrupting the various narratives of (U.S.-centric) multiculturalism that have characterized Hawaiʻi in the post-statehood era. Against the aspirational, progressive multiculturalism that has been mapped onto bodies such as Obama's and Johnson's, this genealogy of protest emphasizes how settler colonial state projects, premised on the separation of land and community, leave the Indigenous body both dismembered and debilitated. This genealogy of protest also seeks to move beyond the nostalgia marking the cruel optimisms that trap the (Native and non-Native) local body by deliberately turning away from attachments to state- and market-driven constructions of "the good life." Instead, such protest poems operate, in terms of both content and aesthetic form, to combat this sense of detachment/dismemberment by actively reaffirming and rebuilding a sense of intimate familial attachment and responsibility to the land and seas around them. As Joyce Pualani Warren argues, a formal (re)turn to these "indigenous epistemologies of the body" can serve to open up new discussions about local belonging and identification that both critique and break from the dividing, racializing logics of the U.S. settler colonial state.[83]

McDougall's poem "By the Blur of My Hands" is one such example of this poetry of protest, refusing to turn away from the violence visited on the Native body by the historical and ongoing criminalization of Kanaka Maoli, but also imagining how such bodies could be valued or otherwise made whole by repositioning them in right relation to the environment. The epigraph to the poem, written as a newspaper account, tells us that after a stand-off with police, a young Hawaiian man ran into the ocean, where he committed suicide. A direct reference to the historical and ongoing process by which the criminal justice system and the practice of incarceration have operated as a disciplinary mechanisms for settler colonial rule—beginning with the imprisonment and house arrest of Queen Liliʻuokalani and continuing through the present day, when Kanaka Maoli men and women are disproportionately represented in the prison population[84]—the official account represented in the epigraph tersely summarizes the man's life in terms of his history of criminality and incarceration, noting only that "Kalahiki has spent most of his 20's in prison for burglary and assault convictions." Like the excerpts from Gauguin's autobiography in "Tehura," the epigraph to "By the Blur" serves to demonstrate how the state views men like Kalahiki as individuals whose criminal conduct and institutional histories appear to confirm a preexisting narrative about Native men as always already marked for death, a view that disavows or downplays the roles that state institutions have played in driving Kalahiki and others to such extremes.

The poem that follows the epigraph moves beyond the narrowness of this official narrative. It is posthumously narrated from the point of view of Kalahiki himself, marking both a shift in perspective and a temporal shift that pushes beyond state narratives that both assume and conclude with the finality of Native death. As the poem's speaker, Kalahiki fleshes out a picture of his own personal life and history. He also highlights the institutional violence missing from the official account of the story. In fact, while the setup of the poem is framed by tragedy, the speaker shows that the tragedy in this case was not solely in his death but in the path that led up to it. Throughout his life, Kalahiki had felt limited by his misshapen hands, and describes how

> I tried, despite their useless stuttering,
> their blur of deformed fingers, ugly stubs,
> to make myself right, no matter. Even
> drawing was too hard, colors crashed, red on
> blue, over the paper and on the desk,
> then the teacher's glare, whispers behind me.[85]

Although the poem's focus on "hands" uses that body part as a metaphor for thwarted agency, the depiction of Kalahiki's hands as something that makes him an object of scorn and pity in the classroom, alongside his use of the word "stuttering" to describe their movements, aligns his debility with the modern history of Kānaka Maoli being shamed, disciplined, and punished for speaking their language to the point at which, by the end of the twentieth century, few people were using, or had knowledge of, the Hawaiian language at all.[86] The force of this historical analogy connects Kalahiki's hands not only to his sense of personal agency but also to a broader history of Kanaka Maoli language and cultural practices. Both have been stigmatized, suppressed, and "blurred" through the operation of a settler colonial hegemony that views them as "deformed," "ugly," and capable only of clumsy or criminal acts.

Framed by this sense of helplessness, hopelessness, and shame, the hands of McDougall's poem in many ways resemble the hands that appear in Yamanaka's "What the Hands Do about These Parts." In both cases, the actions that the "hands" take are geared toward self-harm, either slowly, through a thousand tiny cuts ("Parts"), or quickly, through suicide by gun ("By the Blur"). Both actions speak to and highlight the ways in which embodied local or Kanaka Maoli difference is radically incompatible with a liberal individualism whose bio- (or, perhaps more properly, necro-) political logics result in the objectification, abjection, or fragmentation of their unruly bodies. However, while "Parts" ends with a haunting coda—the image of the girl writing her abuser's name in blood, still hurting and hoping for recognition—the final image of "By the Blur" does not invoke the tragedy of Kalahiki's death so much as the joy of reconnection and renewal. The last image he gives of his hands is not in the moment that they turn against him. It is instead a memory of them operating in harmony with both his desires and the oceanic environment, in this context rendered capable and beautiful:

> This ocean, the same I fished
> as a child, the cordage secure, for once,
> in my grip. The waves washing salt over
> rocks, the quiet glide of my hands
> guiding the net in. And the pull outward after
> each break, offering love more than mercy,
> a faint whisper, This is where you belong.[87]

In contrast to the "stuttering" unsureness of his hands in the context of the classroom, his job in the service industry, or while engaged in criminal activity, Kalahiki remembers his hands engaged in the work of fishing, where they are graceful and "secure," not cacophonous but "quiet." It is in the space of the ocean—not imagined as a space of escape, rest, or repose, but a lively, challenging, and merciless entity—that Kalahiki finally finds the belonging that has eluded him in his terrestrial life. Moreover, it is through the memory of the physically embodied and experienced *movement* that connects him to both the material environment of the ocean and the fishing practices of those who had come before him ("the quiet glide of my hands / pulling the net in") that allows him to achieve this moment of epiphany. This emergence into an interrelational subjectivity through sensual and kinesthetic experience with the oceanic environment operates as what Karin Amimoto Ingersoll has identified as a "seascape epistemology," a form of knowing that is not so much a "knowledge *of* the sea" as

> a knowledge about the ocean and wind as an interconnected system that allows for successful navigation through them. . . . Seascape epistemology organizes events and thoughts according to how they move and interact, while emphasizing the importance of knowing one's roots, one's center, and where one is located inside this constant movement.[88]

This intimately interrelational way of knowing, which combines kinesthetic experience with a long historical sense of place and perspective, parallels *The Salt-Wind*'s formal deployment of what McDougall has elsewhere called "kaona connectivity," an interactive, intertextual process of composition and critical reading that requires a similarly grounded yet flexible perspective to navigate the multiple levels of meaning presented in text, chant, song, and performance.[89] In this context, we can read *The Salt-Wind*'s complex engagement with hybrid *poetic* form—grounded in Kanaka Maoli aesthetics and methodology but branching outward to incorporate English-language poetic traditions—as a mode of navigating the sea changes created by the history of settler colonialism throughout the region. Thus, what the poems of *The Salt-Wind* both outline and demonstrate are the many ways that acts of reading, writing, and aesthetic interpretation can operate as Indigenous-centered forms of ocean passage that seek not to return fragmented bodies and environments to a sense of pre-contact "wholeness" that can be restored or recognized under the law, but to a regain a sense of balance, context, and genealogical interrelationship between the communities and currents that circulate through Hawai'i and Oceania.

While these aesthetic and kinesthetic practices are drawn from cultures and histories specific to Kānaka Maoli, they may also serve as a framework or model for non-Native locals who take seriously the political and epistemological implications of the ethics and aesthetics of the "*aloha* spirit" that allows them to feel connected to the landscape. While the first section of this chapter focused on how "local" bodies—both the fully nationalized version represented by Obama and Johnson and the partial and ambivalent version represented in the work of Yamanaka—tend to assimilate into roles predetermined for them within a settler colonial discourse, such reversions to a settler colonial or neoliberal ideology are not in any way predestined or overdetermined. In other words, the embodied, affective, and gestural elements that allow these bodies to lay claim to a local identity in the first place also provide opportunities to situate or reconstitute themselves outside of a settler colonial paradigm. To do so, however, non-Native locals must—as Rachel Lee notes of Asian Americanist criticism more broadly—learn to reconsider a settler-centric social justice framework that relies on a "*distinctive rhetorical move that putatively returns the extracted body part to the violated racialized whole—a move that naturalizes a prior state of organic intactness and individuality to that racialized body*" in order to pursue a politics that is equally focused on "relishing the fragment."[90] Such a politics would consider how the heterogeneity, hybridity, incoherence, and cacophony of both Asian American and local identity might be leaned into as a unique conceptual and theoretical strength rather than regarded as a weakness to be overcome. Indeed, non-Native local bodies might turn to Kanaka Maoli ways of engaging with the terraqueous environments of Hawai'i to develop a sense of subjective fullness, not through the attempt to *master* Hawaiian land or culture and thus "make it [their] own," but, rather, by adopting a perspectival way of seeing that locates them as an integrated part of a complex and shifting constellation of relationships among different communities, histories, and environments.[91] Such approaches have included—as Candace Fujikane and Dean Saranillio have noted—engaging in "nonstatist" organizing around the maintenance and care for the land, particularly in practices such as sustainable models of farming and fishing, and organizing and mobilizing against further environmental exploitation by the state or multinational developers.[92] These and other forms of kinesthetic engagement with Indigenous-centered and -led movements do not just allow the local body to claim or "live *aloha*," as the popular slogan goes; they also allow it to gain a stronger sense of what it might truly mean to live *with* aloha—that is, to shift one's allegiance from a vaguely nostalgic or optimistic affect to a specific commitment to a particular set of interrelated histories, communities, and sites. Rather than fleeting *gestures*, these local motions can become embedded *habits* that situate them in place. Perhaps it is in the attempt to move from identifying with the "Aloha State" to a more nuanced engagement with "Aloha 'Āina" that Hawai'i locals can detach from the cruel optimisms of neoliberal subjectivity and instead imagine a future that departs from the continuing integration of land, bodies, and oceans into global circuits of capitalism.

It is to these alternative imaginations of the future that the last chapter turns, focusing on how different stories of ocean passage can work to reshape and reimagine discourses of captialist futurity that seek to extend the scope of settler colonial hegemony not only across an increasingly expansive sense of space but also through time. Focusing on Pacific Islander and Asian diasporic texts that navigate both oceanic and virtual space, I address the different ways that these authors bring an oceanic sensibility to bear on the roles that research and communications technologies have come to play not only in mediating the present but also in shaping the future. While such technologies are often closely aligned with capitalist visions of transpacific futurities that aspire to *transcend* the limitations of space, time, and the environment, the texts that the next chapter considers highlight how the future gets created by and through the material, cultural, and political conditions that support these technologies' construction and deployment across the space of the Pacific. At the same time, these works offer a vision of how oceanic ecologies and Oceanic epistemologies offer up different ways of imagining transpacific futures, opening up a range of temporal possibilities that move beyond capitalism's focus on expanding and accumulating profit.

5

VIRTUAL PASSAGES

Pacific Futures

In the U.S. imagination, the Pacific Ocean has long served to describe not only a geographic region, but also the promises and perils of the future to come. In 1852, Senator William Seward (later to become secretary of state under Abraham Lincoln) was one of the first American statesmen to call attention to the important role the Pacific had to play in the nation's Manifest Destiny, arguing before Congress that "the Pacific Ocean, its shores, its islands, and the vast region beyond will become the chief theater of events in the world's great hereafter."[1] Seward's poetic invocation of the Pacific Ocean as a region critical to America's ambitions for securing control over not only the region but the *future itself* is a trope that would be taken up again by American statesmen, including Theodore Roosevelt in 1907, Ronald Reagan in 1984, and Hillary Clinton, who, as secretary of state, reaffirmed in 2011 that "the 21st century will be America's Pacific century."[2] Such invocations of the Pacific as a passage to an (American) future emphasize not only the region's potential for helping to secure and stabilize U.S. access to Asian markets, but also the ocean's metonymic association with a progressive, technology-driven future. While the specific contours of U.S. interventions into the Pacific have certainly shifted during the century and a half between Seward's pronouncement and Clinton's, the tendency to read the Pacific as a space metaphorically aligned with futurity and technology remains remarkably resilient. In this sense, Clinton's announcement that the coprosperity of "America's Pacific century" would be underwritten by "the free flow of communications technology and the spread of green technology, as well as the coherence of our regulatory systems and the efficiency of supply chains," might be usefully read against Walt Whitman's more poetic "Passage To India" (1864), which celebrates "the oceans to be cross'd, the distance brought near" through the efforts of "You captains, voyagers, explorers, yours / You engineers, you architects, your machinists, yours / You, not for trade or transportation only / But in God's name, and for thy sake O soul."[3] Although these excerpts are separated from each other by more than a century of U.S. history, in both it is *technology* that elevates the speaker's rhetoric from a materialist claim to the maritime infrastructures of oceanic passage ("not for trade or transportation only") to a more transcendent representation of the "American" Pacific as a gateway to a better, more friction-free, and enlightened future. This turn to a future that seeks to overcome the regional strife and divisions of the present—whether for "thy sake, O soul" or to support the neoliberal imperative for "men and women [to] work in dignity, earn a decent wage, raise healthy families, educate their children, and take hold of the opportunities to improve their own and the next generation's fortunes"— is firmly grounded in the individualized potential of the liberal subject, a construct central to modern discourses around technology and futurity that have shaped both U.S. and global perceptions of the Pacific Ocean.[4]

If the concept of *futurity* that I have invoked here offers, to follow Aimee Bahng, a way to "highlight the *construction* of the future and denaturalize its singularity, while maintaining an emphasis on how narrative constructions of the future play a significant role in materializing the present," this chapter focuses on the alternative (or "migrant") futures that depart from these hegemonic narratives around progress and technology that have dominated both "Pacific Rim" and transpacific discourse.[5] To this end, I want to start not with an ocean passage, but with an impasse on a mountain. On October 7, 2014, the groundbreaking ceremony for the Thirty Meter Telescope (TMT) on the summit of Mauna Kea was interrupted by demonstrators protesting the telescope's construction. Arguing that the proposed development had not only bypassed state protocols regarding the use of land in a designated conservation district but also promoted the desecration of a site sacred to Kānaka Maoli, activists (known as *kiaʻi mauna*, or protectors of the mountain) organized a series of peaceful protests and initiated legal actions to block the construction. Continued protests and blockades in April 2015 caused Hawaiʻi's Governor David Ige to halt construction of the project. In December 2015, the Hawaiʻi Supreme Court ruled that the building permits for the telescope were invalid, as due process had not been followed when the permit was originally issued.[6] In 2016, an alternative site for the telescope was scouted out and cleared in the Canary Islands; however, in 2017 the Hawai'i state land board approved a new conservation permit for the telescopes, and the consortium hosting the TMT decided to proceed with the original plans to build on Mauna Kea. In 2018, the Hawai'i State Supreme Court approved the new permit, and construction was once again slated to begin on July 15, 2019. Once again, *kia'i* rallied to occupy the mountain access road, and while a number of activists, including several elders, were arrested and jailed for trespassing, the number of *kia'i* has made ongoing construction impossible. As of this writing, a cohort of *kia'i*—including a number of respected Kanaka Maoli scholars, activists, and allies from around the world—continue to occupy the mountain, and construction at the site so far has been suspended.

The ongoing controversy over the construction of the TMT on Mauna Kea clearly illustrates how discourses surrounding scientific and technological progress that envision their advancements as operating "for the good of mankind" remain entangled within political structures that create the material conditions necessary for such progress to continue—conditions rooted in a long history of settler colonialism that tend to preclude alternative modes of thinking about cosmology, culture, and the concept of progress itself. As Iokepa Salazar points out, the struggle over Mauna Kea not only questions the right to construct this particular telescope; it challenges the disinterestedness of the very scientific discourse that made the production of such a telescope possible.[7] In response, some of the most outraged responses to the protests—coming from senior members of the scientific community—only reinforced extant settler discourses that frame Indigenous peoples as essentially, and fundamentally, belonging to the "past." To give one widely reported example, Professor Sandra Faber of the University of California, Berkeley, circulated an email stating that the TMT project was "in trouble, attacked by a horde of Native Hawaiians who are lying about the impact of the project on the mountain and threatening the safety of TMT personnel," while the science journalist George Johnson compared the protestors' objections to the TMT to the Catholic Church's opposition to Galileo.[8] Such rhetoric, which constructs a binary distinction contrasting an impartial, progressive scientific community against regressive, self-interested Native belief, overlooks the long history of science's complicity with the projects of discovery, settlement, and colonialism.

Just as the colonial imagination of the Pacific Ocean as *mare nullius* contributed to the scientific experimentations at Bikini Atoll and other sites in the 1950s and 1960s, the rendering of Mauna Kea as an emptied, desolate, and inanimate landscape works to reconfigure the mountain as *terra nul-*

lius, stripping the site of its meaning and positioning within Kanaka Maoli histories and genealogies.[9] In this sense, the ongoing controversy over the TMT has a long history that reaches back not only through colonial histories of appropriation and extraction in the name of the biological and social sciences and the nuclear experimentations discussed in Chapters 1 and 2, but also, and more immediately, to the foundational Native Hawaiian and local protest movements in the 1970s and 1980s. As with the Native-led protests against commercial development in the Kalama Valley and Waiāhole-Waikāne on the island of ʻOahu, and against military live-fire exercises on the island of Kahoʻolawe, the protestors' objections to development at the summit of Mauna Kea focus on the issue of land sovereignty and land use.[10] While those earlier protests were primarily local in both scope and effect, the protests against the TMT—planned and financed by an international consortium of universities and research centers, including the University of California, Cal Tech, the National Astronomical Observatory of Japan, the Chinese Academy of Sciences, the Department of Science and Technology of India, and the National Research Council of Canada—have made headlines around the globe. In this broadly transpacific context, the local specifics of Hawaiʻi's colonial history and its ongoing debates around land rights and sovereignty are subordinated within media narratives that frame the conflict as a relatively straightforward case of science versus superstition. Yet opponents of the TMT do not claim to be rejecting progress so much as demanding a reconsideration of what, exactly, that "progress" has come to mean. Speaking before the Office of Hawaiian Affairs (OHA) in April 2015, protest leader Lanakila Mangauil argued that he and other activists were seeking not a return to the past but a different way to think about the future:

> We are starting to look at our world in a different way. . . . In one generation petroleum byproducts were a beautiful new discovery; one generation later, right now, they are a great thing that we rely on and use; but . . . we're the ones who have to deal with the effects of all that. And now our oceans are toxic and our air is polluted. Those technologies, those byproducts—they're not clean. They're killing us. I look at our *keiki* [children], those even younger than us, and I wonder what the heck is going to happen to them.
>   The idea of, and the perspective on, progress is much different for many in our generation than it was for those in generations past. We've been blessed with the opportunity to learn our *ʻāina* [land], how the land actually works, and to put it first. What the generation before has called progress, I call suicide.[11]

Mangauil's emphasis on the negative environmental and social consequences that have emerged out of the technological and economic progress of the past hundred years is not a flat rejection of progress. It is a call for a critical reappraisal of where such progress may be leading. This longer view takes into account the ways that human-created effects on the environment may take generations to manifest. These sentiments reflect what the Kanaka Maoli scholars Nālani Wilson-Hokowhitu and Manulani Aluli Meyer have called "*moʻokūʻauhau* [genealogy] as method," a call to approach knowledge production and reflect on its consequences through a Kanaka Maoli framework. As discussed in Chapter 4, *moʻokūʻauhau*—which roughly approximates, yet differs from, the English term "genealogy" insofar as the latter term "prioritizes human relationships" while *moʻokūʻauhau* includes an extended concept of kinship that "extend[s] well beyond the human realm to include islands, oceans, planets, and the universe"—emphasizes modes of inquiry and innovation that look backward as well as forward and seek to frame new knowledges within extant epistemological and cultural systems.[12] As kuʻualoha hoʻomanawanui points out, using *moʻokūʻauhau* as method requires academics to confront the genealogies and histories that shape their own relationships, positionalities, and responsibilities to the subjects of their study, in this way upending Western academic claims and aspirations to objectivity precisely by drawing attention to the ways in which that objectivity and "authority" are historically and materially constructed.[13] This expansively genealogical and generational way of thinking about knowledge production is something that Kanaka Maoli academics and activists share, ironically enough, with the proposed telescope itself: as the Mauna Kea Hui leader Kealoha Pisciotta—herself a former telescope operator—noted in an interview with *The Atlantic*, while protestors have been characterized as "backward-looking extremists," in fact "backward-looking is the definition of astronomy. The larger the telescope, the farther back in time you look."[14]

The ongoing struggle over Mauna Kea highlights how settler colonial projects are premised not only on the management of *territory* and its resources, but also on the management of *time*, imagined not as a layered or populated space, as in *moʻokūʻauhau* or *whakapapa*, but as a "homogeneous, empty" field through which peoples, objects, or concepts (such as "nationhood") move in a progressive unfolding.[15] This concept of secular, settler time presents itself as a shared or universal background against which other modes of experiencing or marking time are presented as aberrational. The implicit biases of progressive thought—central to settler forms of governance, as well as to modern scientific and academic frameworks—continue to render Indigenous communities, cultures, and forms of knowledge production as perpetually belated phenomena. As Linda Tuhiwai Smith notes, research methods that adhere strictly to a "modern" teleological framework tend to inform "an approach... which still conveys a sense of innate superiority and an overabundance of desire to bring progress into the lives of indigenous peoples—spiritually, intellectually, socially, and economically."[16] In this sense, Indigenous critiques of settler colonial temporality serve to illustrate how the very *perception* of time as something that can be experienced in a uniform or universal way works to center and empower the Western humanist figure as the privileged subject of history while suppressing or marginalizing alternative modes of configuring relationships between time and space. Mark Rifkin observes that even good-faith efforts to insist on the modernity or coevalness of Native peoples can serve to reify the idea that "the potential for change remain[s] contingent on belonging to that shared, unified 'now'" whose universalizing scope "threatens to elide other ways of envisioning the multivectored dynamics of Native peoples' continuity and change that exceed a frame that centers on coparticipation with nonnatives."[17] This is largely because the very concept of modernity *itself* is premised on the inaccessibility and ahistoricity of Indigenous ways of knowing. As Smith argues:

> What has come to count as history in contemporary society is a contentious issue for many indigenous communities because it's not only the story of domination; it is also a story which assumes that there was a "point in time" which was "prehistoric." The point at which society moves from prehistoric to historic is also the point at which tradition breaks with modernism. Traditional indigenous knowledge ceased, in this view, when it came into contact with "modern" societies, that is the West. What occurred at this point of culture contact was the beginning of the end for "primitive" societies.[18]

For modernity (here, rendered as *historicity*) to exist, it must assert an epochal break between the "traditional" and the "modern." By this very definition, knowledges operating by a different temporal logic are rendered "traditional," which is precisely that which is excluded from the "modern." In this way, the very concept of settler colonial modernity is foundationally premised on the belatedness or exceptionality of Indigenous epistemologies.

Yet while "settler time" relegates Native ways of knowing to the perpetual past, it also rehearses anxieties around the historical contingency of its own emergence and expansion by simultaneously configuring the *future* as a kind of territory or property that must be secured against appropriation by foreign others.[19] In the current moment, the "others" perceived to have the greatest potential and opportunity to colonize the future are, in both popular culture and political discourse, implicitly or explicitly imagined as emerging from East Asia. David Morley and Kevin Robins argue that these "techno-oriental" tropes illustrate fears that the United States and "the West" are being replaced as the privileged subjects of modernity. In particular, Japan's emergence as a world leader in finance and technology during the 1980s and 1990s, they argue,

> call[s] into question the supposed centrality of the West as a *cultural and geographical locus* for the project of modernity. It has also confounded the assumption that modernity can only be articulated through the forms the West has constructed. Indeed, what it has made clear are the racist foundations of Western modernity.[20]

Although it shifts its focus from territory to temporality, techno-orientalism amply demonstrates what Aileen Moreton-Robinson has called the "anxiety of dispossession" that "rises to the surface when . . . a white possession is perceived to be threatened."[21] Here, it is not land or resources but *modernity itself* that is considered (1) a white possession; and (2) in danger of appropriation by the Japanese and other East Asian peoples and cultures. Such fears of dispossession expose not only the "racist foundations" of Western modernity but also its grounding in a settler colonial ontology that figures both time and territory as alienable and profitable possessions.[22] This relationship between time and territory is made explicit in science fiction texts such as Ridley Scott's *Blade Runner* (1982) and William Gibson's *Neuromancer* (1984), which make liberal use of Asiatic imagery and iconography to signal their futuristic settings. By imagining Asian technologies, communities, and cultures as forming the landscape of the future, techno-orientalist speculations render "Asianness" as a background or commodity rather than a contemporary and competitor and, in this way, recenter the West's claim to modernity.[23]

Pressed into functioning as the opposite ends of the temporal spectrum of "settler time," the nuances and complexities of both Asian and Indigenous Pacific futurities are flattened or excluded altogether in order to center the progressive narratives of modern Western subjectivity. Yet the underlying assumption that a (singular) mode of linear or progressive temporality can serve as a neutral or universal way of experiencing time has been called into question again and again—not only by the Indigenous epistemologies and ontologies that operate on alternative temporal premises, but also by scholarship in the fields of theoretical physics and quantum mechanics, which posits that time might be seen as a function of movement. Individuals do not move *through* time as a universal or absolute property but, instead, *create* new timelines through the shifts in perspective that attend the act of passage.[24] Ocean passages can thus work to illustrate how multiple modes or perceptions of temporality inform the experience of being in time; they reject the notion of a singular "settler" temporal trajectory and instead open up new possibilities that can emerge when we see time, like place and space, as a site open to multiple modes of ontological and epistemological framings.

In this chapter, I read Asian North American author Ruth Ozeki's *A Tale for the Time Being*—briefly discussed in the Introduction—alongside work by the Pacific Island poets Robert Sullivan (Aotearoa/New Zealand), Emelihter Kihleng (Pohnpei), and Craig Santos Perez (Guam) to highlight how they strategically incorporate elements of scientific discovery and inquiry within a range of imagined Pacific futures and temporalities. Sullivan, Kihleng, and Perez reject the implied disjuncture between Indigeneity and modernity assumed by teleological models of progress, explicitly foregrounding motifs of tools and technology to highlight how scientific advancements work both within and alongside Indigenous epistemologies and cultural practices. The use of these theories and technologies does not inevitably lead to the adoption of a teleological, progressive conception of time. Instead, these authors articulate how they can work to illuminate intersubjective connections between human and nonhuman ecologies and accommodate a broad range of perceptions of the past, present, and future. On the other end of the temporal spectrum, Ozeki puts pressure on the racialization of Asian Americans as figures representing a dystopian, capital-driven, and relentlessly progressive futurity. Emphasizing her transpacific protagonists' affinities with the cyclical and circular temporalities characterized by the movement of oceanic currents and the recursive, retroviral space of the Internet, Ozeki turns to Buddhist practice and quantum theory to show how a range of entangled actors—including human and nonhuman bodies—cocreate the moment of the "now." The traveling figures, objects, and peoples in all of these texts illustrate how disrupting the progressive teleology of settler colonial capitalism by unsettling hegemonic views of *time* might provide ways to fundamentally revise, rather than simply mitigate, the dystopian scenarios of climate change, scarcity, and extinction that underlie current projections of our global future.[25] In so doing, their work articulates new visions of transpacific futurities that provide critiques of and alternatives to an overdetermined settler future currently mapped out by the scientific developments, military relocations, and trade infrastructures that have come to dominate the political and imaginative discourses of the contemporary Pacific.

Indigenous Technologies and Oceanic Time: Robert Sullivan's *Star Waka*

> sepia
> paint
> text
> video
> dat
> email
> html
> doc files
> water
> cd rom
> cd photo
> waka
>
> —ROBERT SULLIVAN, "xxiii Formats (1)"

In 1999, Māori poet Robert Sullivan published *Star Waka*, his third collection of poems. The collection makes frequent references to both contemporary and imagined future technologies by drawing connections between Māori *waka* (canoes) and a range of modern vehicles, including rockets ("iv 2140AD"), cars ("v Honda Waka"), and submarines ("49 [environment 1]"). Sullivan also extends the metaphor of the *waka* to include contemporary communications technologies, connecting it to online discussion boards ("39 A wave"), computers ("54 waka rorohiko"), a power cable ("xxviii Hooked"), and the whole range of media forms listed in "xxiii Formats (1)." As Chadwick Allen has observed, Sullivan uses this juxtaposition of new and old technologies to "emphasize waka . . . as Indigenous technologies" that "assert the ability of [Sullivan's] indigenous ancestors to embrace change and create complex civilizations . . . to not only recreate themselves as individuals and communities but also to re-create their symbolic and physical worlds."[26] In this broader context, *waka* serve not only as the material vehicles and vessels that transport peoples, cultures, and ideas from one place to another, but also as epistemological structures capable of projecting alternative modes of futurity that build on a concept of progress rooted in a spiralic, rather than a linear or eschatological, understanding of time. As a result, Sullivan's poems not only represent but also operate *as* Indigenous technologies that position their readers as witnesses to this alternative timeline and narrative of Māori cultural survival and futurity.[27]

While other critics have already explored the global and broadly trans-Indigenous dimensions of Sullivan's work,[28] in this section I limit myself to focusing on the more specifically transpacific—or, rather, trans-Oceanic—futurities that this collection of poems invoke. Written and published at the turn of the twenty-first century, between the Asian financial crisis (which peaked in 1997) and the bursting of the dot-com bubble (in 2000), *Star Waka* articulates a range of Pacific futurities, from the idyllic to the dystopian, in the context of a geopolitical region that was—and is—being shaped to adapt to the shifting needs of neoliberal capital and commerce. The multiple and often conflicting visions expressed in each of the numbered poems not only articulate the plurality of Indigenous Pacific futures, but also unpack how these futurities interact with, borrow from, and are appropriated by capital-driven transpacific projects that, instead of acknowledging their role in shaping the present and future of the Pacific, often ignore or dismiss the survival of Indigenous cultures and practices by relegating them to the past. Sullivan's volume gives us a way to think about how Epeli Hau'ofa's transformational framing of the Pacific not as "islands in a far sea" but a "sea of islands" might appear as it moves into the new millennium.

The first numbered poem in the *Star Waka* cycle, "i," resonates powerfully with Hau'ofa's vision of globalization viewed from the perspective of Pacific peoples, history, and culture. Introducing the Star Waka—the conceptual vessel and primary motif connecting the different poems in the volume—as a "knife through time," connecting past migrations with present-day travels, Sullivan writes:

> In ancient days navigators sent waka between.
> Now, our speakers send us on waka. Their memories,
> Memory of people in us, invite, spirit,
> Compel us aboard, to home government, to centre:
> Savai'i, Avaiki, Havaiki, Hawaiiki, from where we peopled
> Kiwa's Great Sea.[29]

Just as Hau'ofa's concept of a sea of islands worked to *spatially* reconfigure the region in the context of a long history of Pacific cultural exchange, the parallelism that the poem draws between past "navigators" and present "speakers" emphasizes the *temporal* dimensions of contemporary transpacific networks and organizations. Sullivan also gets at this temporal complexity by concluding with a moment of transhistorical connection that serves as both destination and a starting point. While the poem ends at the moment of landfall, it also introduces questions that could apply equally to the speaker's ancestors and his contemporaries:

> Let us regroup. We have never travelled further—
> just one star stays familiar in the sky. How will we ever settle
> this cold place? Makariri. Will our high magic work here?[30]

While the event described—the arrival of the first *waka* navigators in Aotearoa—is a feat of technological and navigational prowess, the ambivalence of the poem's conclusion nevertheless resists a triumphant narrative of discovery, gesturing instead toward an uncertain future whose outcome is still very much in question. From the perspective of the present day, the final lines of the poem invoke a history whose results are already known: the speaker's ancestors did, in fact, succeed in making "this cold place" their own, so a teleological narrative of successful settlement is implied, even if it is not stated outright. However, by portraying the moment of landing in the present tense and voicing doubts that may have entered the minds of the first settlers, the poem's speaker focuses on the contingency of that success. The speaker reminds us that, for the first groups who landed in Aotearoa/New Zealand, the success of settlement was not a known or a given. Their new homeland was something that was created over the span of many generations. Similarly, *Star Waka* and its readers exist in a moment in which the future of this culture was (and is) still unknown. By invoking the parallel between the first generation of Māori and the current generation, the poem's conclusion invites its readers to consider how their own actions and activities will shape, and be remembered by, future generations.

In *Star Waka*, the recognition of one's present connection to the past is only the first step. The next is to use this relational perspective to reimagine the future. These present-day struggles for the Pacific future are dramatized in the poems "iv" and "46," which posit two different future scenarios in which Māori have entered outer space. The poem "iv 2140AD" imagines a Māori-helmed rocket ship setting off to "consult with the top boss / to ask for sovereignty and how to get this / from policy into action back home" before running "out of fuel—we didn't have enough cash for a full tank."[31] In the end, the speakers end up owing the government money for a tow out of orbit, and the rocket ship is repossessed, leaving the *iwi* (tribe) with nothing. The future, in this scenario, operates as a satirical repetition of both the colonial past and the colonized present: here the *iwi* must be cleared by an outside, centralized "mission control" to petition the "top boss" and "*ask* for sovereignty." In the end, the *iwi* is left hopelessly indebted to an outside power, in an amount that is "the equivalent of the fiscal envelope / signed a hundred and fifty years ago,"[32] a reference to the fiscal limit that the New Zealand government proposed in 1994 on the amount of money that could be paid out to Māori tribes seeking reparations under the terms of the Treaty of Waitangi.[33] From the poem's title, which announces its adherence to Western temporal conventions, to the acknowledgment of economic debt as having come to replace the direct burden of colonialism, "iv 2140AD" imagines a Pacific future that is ironically stuck in the present. While it may be dressed up in the trappings of technological progress, it nevertheless rehearses the same colonial dynamics of the present and near-past.

By contrast, "46" depicts an alternative future freed from the presentist political constraints of "iv 2140AD." In this version, the "spacecraft *waka*" are setting out on a voyage of discovery rather than entreaty: they seek out not only new planets, but also "new forms of verse" and new forms of beauty.[34] In this poem, Sullivan returns to the image of orbital drift, this time framing it not as a predicament to be overcome but as a space of freedom, peace, and creation. While "46," like "iv 2140AD," combines signifiers of both Māori and Western cultures and technologies, here the weightlessness of orbit allows them to coexist peacefully and in balance rather than setting them on a collision course. Similarly, this poem's focus on the rotational movement of "orbit" operates as a metaphor for a future envisioned in spiralic, rather than linear or teleological, time. While "iv 2140AD" presents the act of orbital rotation as a space of empty repetition from which one must be rescued, "46" recasts it as a place where objects, images, and ideas can be revisited and reflected on "until it is absorbed / through layers of skin,"[35] where there is time enough to come to a considered and meaningful, rather than superficial or partial, understanding of a concept or technology. It is this reimagining of the relationship of time to technology that Sullivan forwards as a principled rebuttal to contemporary transpacific politics and policies that extrapolate visions of the future based on projections that seek to maintain the power dynamics of the present. Rather, Sullivan suggests, we might move away from such projections altogether and instead pay closer attention to the alternative modernities and futurities embedded in different cultural traditions:

> oh to be in that generation
> to write in freefall picking up the tools
> our culture has given us

and to let them go again
knowing they won't hit anyone
just stay up there

no longer subject to peculiarities
of climate the political economies
of powers and powerless

a space waka
rocketing to another orb
singing waiata to the spheres[36]

While the speaker's reference to the "tools / our culture has given us" broadly encompasses a range of knowledges, practices, and philosophies, it can also refer to specific types of tools and technologies, including the communications technologies addressed in the "xxiii, Formats (1)," which uses a list form to show the analogies among a range of "new" media technologies and storage systems, ultimately culminating in "waka." The poem's juxtaposition of these multiple media formats highlights not only the continuities among these different modes and models of communications technologies, but also some critical differences. In particular, the insertion of "water," listed on the ninth line, invites speculation as to how water has operated as a medium for communication and connectivity, as well as how it can also damage or destroy the other types of media forms listed here—a danger about which Sullivan, trained as a university librarian, would be well aware.

The water that appears in "xxiii Formats (1)" gestures toward the *physical* limits of modern media technologies and their role in preserving and communicating culture for future generations. Sullivan addresses their *conceptual* limitations in "54, waka rorohiko." In this poem, the speaker notes that they have heard recently about plans for a computerized database containing *whakapapa* (genealogies), which is "tapu information, not for publication." The remainder of the poem outlines the speaker's ambivalence toward this project:

A dilemma for the library culture
of access for all, no matter who, how,
why. A big Western principle stressing
egalitarianism. My respects.
However, Maori knowledge brings many

together to share their passed down wisdom
in person to verify their inheritance;
without this unity our collective knowledge
dissipates into cults of personality.[37]

Sullivan's poem highlights the conflict between the stated ideals and principles of cyberspatial discourse and its execution. Here, while the "Western principle stressing / egalitarianism" is received with genuine "respect," the speaker also stresses how the concomitant principle of "unity" does not necessarily follow from making such "tapu" knowledge available online. Instead, the speaker argues that certain types of Māori knowledge—requiring all members to come "in person to verify their inheritance"—cannot be reduced to binary code and stored in a database. Instead, this genealogical knowledge is presented as a regular practice that must be engaged in order to strengthen community ties. Without this type of embodied interaction, community knowledges may be reduced to mere information that is isolated, abstracted, and manipulated for a variety of reasons, creating the "cults of personality" that the speaker warns against at the end of the poem.

While postcolonial theory has long held that the elision of *information* and *knowledge* is something that was, and continues to be, central to Western colonial and settler colonial praxes, in our present, digital moment, the ability to swiftly gain access to this kind of abstracted and decontextualized information—which can be easily confused with "knowledge"—is increasingly enabled by digital communications technology.[38] Indeed, as Kate Hayles points out, the development of information technologies itself emerged out of projects by the early cybernetic scientists Claude Shannon and Norbert Wiener. They deliberately sought to abstract information as "an entity distinct from the substrates carrying it," thus reconceptualizing it as "kind of bodiless fluid that could flow between different substrates without loss of meaning or form."[39] In the context of postcolonial and settler colonial states, however, the "fluidity" of this disembodied, decontextualized information can threaten Indigenous cultures that continue to demand the importance of embodied, local, and place-based knowledges. As Carolyn Marvin argues, the valuation of digital information over physically or culturally context-bound practices is ideologically charged in how they tend to prioritize an "ethnocentric and historically provincial notion of information . . . in which it becomes a self-contained series of autonomous products without context," often at the cost of other types of knowledges that are passed on through oral or interpersonal communication.[40]

Although *Star Waka* was written before the boom in social media changed much of the political and social landscape, Sullivan's meditations on the promises and pitfalls of new technologies for Māori cultural transmission provides a timely, and still relevant, commentary on the importance of balancing digital content with community context. In this sense, the use of "modern" technologies and techniques by Indigenous artists and activists has never been a concession to the tools made available by globalization so much as a *negotiation* with them. The use of modern technology does not flatten or invalidate Indigenous culture. Rather, when it is wielded thoughtfully and critically, it speaks to its ongoing dynamism. The work of Emelihter Kihleng and Craig Santos Perez navigates this dynamic in the era of social media, articulating these poets' visions of Pacific futurity within and against an increasingly decentralized and deconstructed media landscape. While Kihleng's poetry, like Sullivan's, remains ambivalent about the double-edged nature of contemporary communications technologies, Perez's poems deliberately use social media and online forums as tools to raise awareness about the ongoing colonial history of the region and to coordinate anticolonial resistance movements. Both deploy their voices and their platforms as published poets to resist constructions of neoliberal and militarized Pacific futurities that ignore or erase the dynamic present—and future—of a Native Pacific. By mixing personal histories with documentary sources, pop culture, legends, and cultural practices, Kihleng's and Perez's poetry articulates visions of Pacific postmodernity that do *not* lose their political and cultural force in the face of contemporary cultural fragmentation. Instead, they traverse these new media currents in interesting and innovative ways.

Pacific Islands Postmodernity and the Poetic Uses of Social Media

Writing in 2001, Rob Wilson noted that while avant-garde, postmodern poetics were often viewed as "mainland U.S., metropolitan, or 'New York-centric'" productions that remained separate from or relatively indifferent to the more immediate "indigenous claims to place" invoked to assert cultural and ontological priority in the face of U.S. and multiethnic settler colonialism,[41] a number of poets from the Pacific region were creating work that brought together commitments to poetic experimentation *and* decolonial politics. Specifically addressing the work of Daniel Featherston, Kathy Dee

Kaleo-kealoha Kaloloahilani Banggo, Bill Luoma, Joseph Balaz, Juliana Spahr, Albert Saijo, Carolyn Lei-Lanilau, John Tranter, and John Kinsella, Wilson argues that these authors created work where postmodernist linguistic experimentation and postcolonial politics were explicitly and inextricably intertwined. This irreverent, deconstructive work becomes particularly important in a period in which even oppositional articulations of Native cultural authenticity can be adapted and appropriated in the name of capitalist place making. Decontexualized figures of Native Pacific "authenticity" can become an attractive commodity within broader discourses of neoliberal multiculturalism in ways that ironically work against Indigenous political actions in the present. To return briefly to the case of Mauna Kea, for example, Salazar notes that the 'Imiloa Astronomy Center of Hawai'i (operated by the University of Hawai'i, Hilo)—whose stated mission is to mediate among Native Hawaiian, local, and scientific communities[42]—"emphasizes Hawaiian culture and language throughout its exhibits, educational programs, architecture and gardens, special events, and regular guest speakers," all of which ultimately serve to "legitimate Western science in Hawai'i, and ... rationalize Mauna Kea astronomy."[43] In this way, even as educational institutions such as 'Imiloa—as well as more explicitly commercial actors such as the tourist industry and the Disney Corporation—draw attention and pay homage to the cultures and proud cultural history of the Native Pacific, they gloss over or ignore the historical role of Western contact and colonization and implicitly present the choices available to contemporary Native Hawaiian cultural practitioners as one of accommodation or assimilation rather than resistance to or resilience in the face of imposed colonial norms.[44]

Kihleng's and Perez's activist poetry draws attention to the experiences of Indigenous Pacific peoples who have been shaped by the hybrid, global, and increasingly virtual/digital culture of the late twentieth and early twenty-first century yet remain displaced or dispossessed by the deconstruction, decontextualization, and commodification of the places they call home. Rather than simply submit to the paradox of displacement created out of colonial histories and sustained through contemporary politics and policies, Kihleng's and Perez's work sharply critiques the ironies of capitalist place making by interrogating and "reterritorializ[ing]" the region and giving voice to Pacific Islanders living under conditions of postmodernity.[45] Such work necessarily foregrounds questions of representation and the role that such representations play in the process of de- and reterritorialization. In particular, Perez's and Kihleng's poems scrutinize the cultural and political networks privileged by contemporary popular culture and social media representations, then juxtapose them with personal narrative and documentary forms to think through alternative ways of constructing a sense of place that may invoke alternative visions of Pacific futurity.

Kihleng's poetry reflects her transpacific heritage and history. Born to a Pohnpeian father and American mother, she has lived in Guam, Pohnpei, Hawaiʻi, and New Zealand. The poems in Kihleng's first collection, *My Urohs* (2010), foreground many of the colonial and neocolonial histories that continue to render certain sites more or less "marginal," even within the Pacific itself. Pohnpei, the place Kihleng calls home, is part of the Federated States of Micronesia (FSM), a group of four Micronesian island states that also include Chuuk, Yap, and Kosrae. The FSM, like the Marshall Islands, were formerly a trust territory of the United States; they are now a sovereign nation with a constitutional government, linked to the United States through a Compact of Free Association (COFA) signed in 1986. Thus, unlike the state of Hawaiʻi—and even current U.S. territories such as Guam and American Sāmoa—the FSM possesses an ambiguous relationship to American empire as a Pacific nation that is considered neither a direct "part" of the United States nor entirely independent of it. For while the FSM is a self-governing entity free to enter into trade negotiations with other nations, the provisions of the compact nevertheless allow the U.S. government to appropriate any "necessary" lands and resources for U.S. military operations, as well as for other U.S. programs and services operating within the FSM (including the National Weather Service, Federal Emergency Management Agency, Federal Aviation Administration, and U.S. Postal Service).[46] In addition, citizens of the FSM are eligible to serve in the U.S. armed forces, and while the United States is not able to conscript recruits from Micronesia, large numbers of Micronesians do voluntarily enlist as a means to a stable career—as is the case in current and former U.S. territories in the region, particularly Guam, American Sāmoa, the Philippines, and the Marshall Islands.[47] In consequence, Pohnpei's status—a sovereign state that is still economically, culturally, and socially linked to the ongoing development of U.S. empire—is itself part of the many postmodern juxtapositions that make up the fabric of daily life for Kihleng and others living in the not entirely postcolonial Pacific.

These juxtapositions and contradictions are foregrounded in Kihleng's satirical narrative poem "Pohnpei Outer Space," which addresses the role of social networking in the construction of modern Micronesian diaspora. The poem immediately locates the speaker in the early years of the twenty-first century, with its reference to the first-generation social networking site MySpace ("Nahn! I saw you on the MySpace"), then continues with the inevitable friend request: "I requested you to be my friend / you have so many friends / 100 plus! And all mehn Pohnpei / in GA, SC, Kansas City, Hilo, Honolulu."[48] In just the first few lines of the poem, Kihleng invokes a digitized version of Hauʻofa's "sea of islands"—that is, she conceptualizes "mehn Pohnpei" as located within a diasporic network tied to different sites across the continental (and extracontinental) United States. The cities that the poem's faux-naïf speaker lists as places her Pohnpeian friends live are all sites where there are sizeable communities of Pohnpeians who emigrated for primarily economic or educational reasons (Kansas City, Hilo, Honolulu), while the listed states (GA, SC) are home to basic training camps for the U.S. military, in which Pohnpeians, as well as other Micronesians and Pacific Islanders, enlist in large numbers.

Yet while the very title of the piece frames these sites as being part of the literal "outer space" of Pohnpei—a move that works to recenter Pohnpei within this militarized global diaspora—the speaker also critiques the insularity of these apparently cosmopolitan communities, pointing out that while her friends "write like they're Black / posting 'holla back' / 'I'm out' / 'peace out,'" they "never even met a real Black person in their life," since "when they get to the States they only hang around with other Pohnpeians / other Pohnpeians from the same part of Pohnpei too!"[49] If this is the case, the speaker continues, "I'd rather have them write me in Pohnpeian / than in broken, fake Ebonics English / I pahn kohwei pirapw mwangas nan sapwomwen / is better than wassup homie, where you at?" Here Kihleng—like Albert Wendt and Konai Helu Thaman before her—addresses the paradox of immigrant communities' cultural insularity existing alongside aspirations to Western cultural and material capital. However, in this particular case, the kind of cultural capital that is most highly prized is not necessarily the ability to appear more "white" or Western. It is, instead, the ability to look "cool" by appropriating the language of Black American culture. The speaker's shrewd observations note that while many of her Pohnpeian friends may feel a genuine affinity with Black culture due to their shared status as racialized minorities in the United States, their understanding of blackness has been mediated not through interpersonal interaction but through a commercialized American popular culture that separates Black art, language, and style from its historical and cultural contexts so that they, too, can circulate as abstract signifiers of "cool."

Kihleng's focus on the widespread influence of American popular culture sets up the poem's ambivalent stance on Internet connection and social networking as a tool for extending one's community. The final stanza of the poem shifts from the speaker's critique of her friends' profiles to a wry reflection on her own self-presentation:

I know, I gotta work on my profile
it's so boring
I gotta add more pictures
pictures of me and my friends
holding Tequila shots
drinking straight from the pwotol en sakau
eyes half closed from intoxication
so that I look popular, cool
but then if I make it too nice
with all the moving photo albums
and graphics
it'll look like I have no life
and spend all my time
pimping my space
and not doing my homework.[50]

Here the speaker confesses to her own form of digital posturing: her desire to post pictures to look "popular, cool" is mitigated by the fact that doing so would suggest to others that she has "no life" and spends all of her time curating her online profile. (This may have seemed a quaint concern for readers just a few years later, as the emergence of other, more popular social networking sites such as Facebook in 2004, Twitter in 2006, and particularly Instagram in 2010 helped to drive much of contemporary social life online.) Yet beneath the poem's gently ironic humor, Kihleng sounds an early note of caution about the negative effects of social networking. For the speaker, the intoxicant of choice is not "Tequila" or "sakau" but MySpace itself, a digital environment that allows the speaker and her friends to reinvent themselves using both computer code ("moving photo albums / and graphics") as well as abstracted cultural codes ("holla back"). The poem's juxtaposition between the "outer space" of the title—referring to a broadly diasporic community—and the inward turn to "MySpace" further emphasizes how social networking is not only about building or maintaining a community but is centrally focused on curating one's self-image for social consumption. These curated self-images, in turn, are equally shaped *by* consumer culture: specifically, the consumption of alcohol, popular culture, and digital media itself.

The ambivalence toward social networking that Kihleng's speaker describes in "Pohnpei Outer Space" illustrates contradictions not unlike those that have rendered the broader plight of Indigenous diasporic communities instructively complex. For example, if Epeli Hau'ofa and Thaman—as discussed in Chapter 3—decried the materialism they saw motivating and infiltrating diasporic communities across the region, they also saw in this large-scale Native diaspora the potential for powerful transpacific activism. "Pohnpei Outer Space" takes a similar approach to social media. While it expresses skepticism about how it is embedded in consumer culture, it nevertheless *does* create a space for new types of transnational Native communities to emerge. In this sense, many of the tensions and contradictions created by twentieth-century globalization in the Pacific both anticipate and shape questions surrounding the efficacy and benefit of technology to Indigenous communities in the twenty-first century. Read in this context, Kihleng's poem parallels the work of social media theorists who reject the exceptionalist claims made by both boosters and critics of Internet culture, digital networks, and social media, seeking to connect them instead to already existing frameworks, architectures, and infrastructures developed in the service of global capital. José van Dijck points out that, as we now well know, while "social media can be seen as online enhancers of *human* networks—webs of people that promote connectedness as a social value," they are also "*automated systems* that engineer and manipulate connections."[51] As a result, the very concept of one's network or community comes to comprise "both (human) connectedness and (automated) connectivity"—that is, something that emerges not only from individual desires for connection, affinity, and self-expression, but *also* from algorithms that have been designed and engineered with a profitable business model in mind.[52] Indeed, many critics have argued that to ignore the political economy at work behind the apparently "democratic" or leveling tendencies of the Internet is to miss opportunities for informed activism that moves beyond the rhetorical celebration or condemnation of the technology.[53]

The interconnections and multiply layered dynamics of colonization, neoliberalism, militarization, and digital technologies that have shaped and continue to shape the region are not lost on the Chamorro poet Craig Santos Perez, whose long poem cycle *from unincorporated territory*, which to date comprises four volumes—*[hacha]* (2008), *[saina]* (2010), *[guma']* (2014), and *[lukao]* (2017)—addresses this palimpsestic nature of the contemporary Pacific, focusing critically on how dominant mappings work to obscure or erase the many contradictions inherent in the celebratory or progressive narratives of American expansion and globalization. The cycle's title refers to one of these contradictions—namely, how Perez's native Guam (Guåhan) currently exists as an "unincorporated territory" of the United States. While the FSM is a sovereign state that has elected to be in "free association" with the United States, the paradoxical political status of the unincorporated territory of Guam is one of effective disenfranchisement within the confines of a supposedly democratic nation-state. As citizens of an unincorporated territory, residents of Guam—like the residents of the United States' other territories in the Caribbean and the Pacific, including Puerto Rico, American Sāmoa, and Guantánamo Bay—are in possession of the "natural" rights granted to U.S. citizens by the Constitution. However, they enjoy neither the sovereignty granted to independent states nor the right to representation in federal governing bodies.[54]

The ambivalent status of these unincorporated territories was determined by the "Insular Cases" that came before the U.S. Supreme Court from 1901 to 1922. As one of the first cases, *Downes v. Bidwell* (1901), put it, the territories were to be considered "foreign to the United States in a domestic sense," both "belonging to" but "not a part of" the nation.[55] The outcome of the Insular Cases, which was strongly influenced by racial and cultural prejudice, effectively created a legal precedent whereby the United States could keep inhabitants of its colonial territories in a state of perpetual disenfranchisement. As Amy Kaplan observes, the "designation of territory as neither quite foreign nor domestic was inseparable from a view of its inhabitants as neither capable of self-government nor civilized enough for U.S. citizenship."[56] Yet this liminal state also has its potential advantages. As Perez indicates in the preface to *from unincorporated territory [hacha]*, full enfranchisement comes at a cost. Unlike unincorporation, full incorporation is a "permanent condition—an incorporated territory can't be de-incorporated."[57] By contrast, unincorporation remains open-ended, a place of still-emergent possibilities.

In this context, "unincorporated" refers not only to Guam's ambiguous political and legal status but also to Perez's innovative poetic praxis, which seeks to "establish an 'excerpted space' via the transient, processional, and migratory allowances of the page."[58] Yet Perez situates this act of literary unincorporation by prefacing it with the preposition *from*, a term that indicates not only "a particular time or place as a starting point . . . a source, a cause, an agent, or an instrument," but also "*forward movement, advancement—evolving in to the sense of 'movement away.'*"[59] As both source and "*forward movement*," *from unincorporated territory* reconfigures a transpacific politics based on a model of neoliberal futurity into what Hsuan L. Hsu has described as a "*poetics of emergence* that is at once rooted in Chamorro needs and practices and nomadic in its capacity to affiliate with—and transform—existing movements."[60] Like Sullivan's *Star Waka* and Kihleng's "Pohnpei Outer Space," the emergent, transformational energy of Perez's work emphasizes how Indigenous Pacific cultures are literally in transit as they continue to seek out and develop frameworks for transnational, transpacific, and trans-Indigenous alliances that run alongside, beneath, and sometimes counter to the hegemonic discourses that use the Pacific as a metaphor to naturalize the ideologies of political democracy and free-market capitalism.[61]

Each volume of *from unincorporated territory* carries a bracketed subtitle in Chamorro that indicates the book's organizing principle. For example, *[hacha]*, which translates as "one," indicates the first volume's interest in origins and sourcings—that is, the sites and situations *from* which the project emerges. The second volume's subtitle, *[saina]*, translates as "parents elders spirits ancestors." It is also the name that was given to the *sakman* (voyaging canoe) constructed in Guam in 2007, the first craft of its kind that had been built since they were banned and burned by Spanish colonists in the seventeenth and eighteenth centuries.[62] With a subtitle that connects ancestry and travel, the second volume brings together the recollections of Perez's grandmother, as well as reflections on navigation, the erasures and gaps in knowledge created out of the experience of colonialism, and Perez's personal experience of diaspora. The third volume, whose subtitle, *[guma']*, translates as "home" or "house," addresses how the concept of home itself gets deconstructed and reconstructed across a number of diasporic sites. The subtitle of the fourth volume, *[lukao]*, is Chamoru for "procession" and refers to movement across both space and (generational) time.

The first two volumes of *from unincorporated territory* indicate section or chapter breaks with numbers—roman numerals in *[hacha]* and the names of numbers written out in romanized Chamorro, Spanish, Japanese, and English in *[saina]*. The section breaks in *[guma']* and *[lukao]* are not numbered at all. Instead, they are grouped into sections under subheadings. In *[guma']*, each subheading is named for a different tool: *mattiyu* (hammer stone), *guaddukon* (adzes), *asuela* (chisel), and *kannai* (hand). Along with the visual and thematic omnipresence of the *latte*, or stone pillars that served as the structural foundations for ancient Chamorro "homes, schools, canoe shelters, food sheds, and communal spaces,"[63] *[guma']*'s focus on tools, structure, and construction works to critique the cultural and environmental destruction caused by more than three centuries of colonialism. It also emphasizes how language and literature operate as tools that can be used to help rebuild and reconstruct a sense of home "*from*" which Chamorro histories and culture can continue to unfold into the future. Perez's strategic deployment of Chamorro (Chamoru) language is one way of emphasizing how language operates as a tool for both promoting and resisting colonial rule. As he notes in the introduction to *[hacha]*,

The colonial school system on Guam, when I grew up there, did not teach written Chamorro in the schools, a consequence of Americanization and a sustained desire to eradicate the native language. In the ocean of English words, the Chamorro words in this collection remain insular, struggling to emerge within their own "excerpted space." These poems are an attempt to begin re-territorializing the Chamorro language in relation to my own body, by way of the page.[64]

This project of "reterritorializing" Chamorro language through its fragmented dispersal throughout the poem cycle parallels how Perez works to recenter and reclaim narrative representations of Chamorro history, people, and culture by excerpting and repurposing texts taken from a range of other legal, scholarly, and popular writings about Guam.[65] Many of these repurposed texts are either sourced from the Internet or refer directly to web-based sources—for example, the series of poems bearing the title "*from* all with ocean views," which appear in [saina], are constructed out of text taken from travel magazines, juxtaposed with text taken and "remixed" from www.kuam.com, "the online site of a guam news network."[66] Significantly, in these poems and others in the collection, digital texts and sources are directly linked with Native voices of resistance. As Hsu notes about "*from* all with ocean views," Perez prints the excerpts from www.kuam.com in a "lightened font to indicate its shadowy status vis-à-vis mainstream print outlets," with the implication that the secondary status of digital text parallels the "shadowy status of Chamorro testimony" reflected throughout the long poem cycle.[67]

In this context we can see Perez using the Internet as another type of "tool" (or perhaps more accurately, an infrastructure) for the project of "reterritorializing" Guam and its representations in the twenty-first century. Throughout the cycle, Perez's poems include references to websites and hashtags as a way to connect his poetry, which materially manifests as a literary work in a printed volume, to broader digital networks and the activist communities they support. For example, "*from* lisiensan ga'lago" (collected in [hacha]) juxtaposes a concrete poem consisting of a box enclosing a grid of nine words, eight of them crossed out, with the superimposed, boldfaced number "**8000?***" and a polite request to "please visit" three URLs, which link to two activist blogs and a petition to the United Nations regarding concerns about the proposed military buildup in Guam, which was estimated to include the relocation of more than eight thousand U.S. troops to the island.[68] In this context, the reference "out" to the activist sites becomes an important part of the poem itself, connecting the relative per-

manence of the printed text to the swiftly moving nature of digital space—
the printed "islands" to the digital "ocean," as it were.[69] The connections to
digital archival and activist sites continue in the acknowledgments section
of *[saina]*, where Perez cites the web sources from which he drew his material. In addition to the Kuam site, he refers readers to www.TraditionalSea
farers.com and UOG.edu, as well as to the archived full texts of the Organic Act of 1950 and the Immigration and Nationality Act of 1952.[70]

In *[guma']*, Perez extends this interconnection between literary form
and digital media by including sources from, and references to, social
media. The dedication page—which appears at the beginning of the volume,
before the table of contents—intersperses the Chamorro word *hanom*
(water) with a partial reference to the website www.SavePaganIslands.org
("*hanom www.save hanom pagan.org hanom*"), while the closing page, at the
end of the book, uses the same technique to embed a hashtag ("*hanom #our
islands hanom aresacred hanom*") used in a number of posts from social
media accounts on Facebook, Twitter, and Tumblr protesting the expansion
of military presence and testing in the Mariana Islands. This shift from
hypertext to hashtags—from activist sites to activist apps—reflects how
technology changes to accommodate new types of organizing (and vice
versa). Published in the wake of movements such as the Arab Spring and
roughly concurrently with #BlackLivesMatter, the poems in *[guma']* were
written during a different era of online activism from Sullivan's *Star Waka*
and Kihleng's "Pohnpei Outer Space," and even from the first two volumes
of *from unincorporated territory*. However, Perez also gestures to how such
technologies work to reshape perceptions of time and space in ways that are
not always beneficial to community-based activism. The poem sequence
"*ginen* fatal impact statements" illustrates both of these tendencies when,
around halfway through the sequence, it self-referentially comments on its
own formal construction:

>DEIS Public Comment: "I am totally against the military
>taking over the land at the Race Track located in Pågat"
>
>—*Craig, Is this an experimental translation project?*
>
>—*I read Volume Ten of the Final Environmental
>Impact Statement, which contains nearly all the 10,000
>comments that people submitted in response to the DEIS
>during the official 90-day comment period*

> —*I copy and paste phrases, sentences, words, passages from the comments of the people*
>
> —*I post these comments as my Facebook status*
>
> —*Sometimes others comment on the comment*
>
> —*Sometimes I*[71]

The citations of the Draft Environmental Impact Statement (DEIS) and its final ("fatal") version refers to a document released by the U.S. Defense Department in November 2009 that outlined the plans for and potential impact of the proposed military buildup on the island—the infrastructural groundwork for the operation intended to transfer the "**8000?***" U.S. troops from Okinawa to Guam by 2016. The released document was several thousand pages long, and the public was given forty-five days—extended to ninety days after local groups registered their protest—to comment on these plans. As a result, the excerpted comments that appear in "*ginen fatal impact statements*" range from outrage to approval to satire to dismay, while many of the "*comment[s] on the comment[s]*" elicited from Facebook posts provide a running, often humorous metacommentary on form. One such exchange notes:

> —*The revolution will not be on Facebook*
>
> —*If it isn't on Facebook, it probably wasn't very successful*
>
> —*Or it was so successful that there is no more Facebook*[72]

This back and forth neatly outlines different attitudes toward online activism, beginning with an initial position of skepticism about mediated activism, moving to a rebuttal noting how movements thrive and expand through engagement and visibility—which, in this case, means using social media platforms—and concluding with the observation that Facebook, and other social media applications like it, are inextricably intertwined with the very systems that have created the oppressive conditions giving rise to the need for "revolution." (As if to underscore this point, the very first "poemap" that opens Perez's next volume, *[lukao]*, is an adaptation of a "Telegeography cable network map, 2009," taken from Nicole Starosielski's study of Guam's cable infrastructure, a striking visual image that shows how many undersea communication cables, which "carry almost all transpacific Internet traffic," pass through the island of Guam. Indeed, as the explanatory note continues, "More cables have landed on Guam than in either Hawai'i or California, two other major hubs for signal exchange.")[73]

In this context, the approach that Perez takes in *[guma']*, particularly in "*ginen* fatal impact statements," balances the immediacy of online activism with the longevity of print: the excerpted comments are distributed to Perez's online community of readers in real time, as well as to the community of readers who belatedly encounter this testimony in the printed book. This double archive also works as a way to amplify and publicize the concerns about and opposition to the buildup that would otherwise remain effectively buried in a relatively obscure government document that runs into the thousands of pages. Indeed, the first poem in the cycle concludes with a reprinted comment that wonders, "Where are the comments to these issues sent? Who sees them? Will the public see any of these comments?"[74] As with Perez's earlier poems, which excerpted from and linked out to activist websites as a way to give space to voices and narratives that remain unheard or obscured in mainstream discourses, "*ginen* fatal impact statements" illustrates a strategic incorporation of contemporary technologies and platforms as tools to navigate the modern global media landscape. As with Sullivan's *Star Waka*, Perez shows how this practice of adopting and adapting tools to one's purposes is not at odds with more "traditional" cultural elements. Rather, it becomes a necessary practice of survival to keep a sense of culture and community going. Indeed, the speakers featured in Sullivan's, Kihleng's, and Perez's poetry become navigators of a new terrain, attempting to keep the lines of communication open for a dynamic culture while navigating platforms and technologies that, like the ocean itself, hold out both the threat of drowning and the promise of survival. As the concluding comment in Perez's "*ginen* fatal impact statements" notes, "I feel like the ko'ko' bird [Guam rail]. My nest was on the ground. I was a flash in the forest. I took to the water."[75]

The comparison of digital media to the watery expanse of the ocean emphasizes the active, adaptive perspective that is required to actively navigate both fields. The ocean and digital media shape and skew our understandings of time and space and encompass a wide range of different times and temporalities. Just as the Internet is a space where older or "dated" material—like the activist websites linked in Perez's poetry or the MySpace profiles mentioned in "Pohnpei Outer Space"—can continue to circulate (buoyed by viral popularity) or stagnate (becalmed by broken links), the ocean's currents and gyres can operate as phenomena that mark time in similarly recursive, nonlinear, and sometimes unexpected ways. To address these connections between the complex temporalities and materialities of oceanic and digital space, I turn now to Ruth Ozeki's *A Tale for the Time Being* (2012), a novel that engages with these concepts from the different perspectives of Buddhist practice and quantum theory. Both perspectives allow Ozeki to think through how time is experienced through processes of interaction and entanglement, challenging the concept of a singular, homogeneous experience of time from the point of view of two Japanese women who—much like the speakers in Sullivan's, Kihleng's, and Perez's poetry—use their virtual travels to assert and establish their position within the space of the "now." While Sullivan, Kihleng, and Perez challenged how the monolithic structure of settler colonial time figured Indigenous cultures, practices, and peoples as fixed in the historical past, Ozeki identifies and interrogates the way these discourses simultaneously project racialized futurities that position Asian peoples and cultures as dystopian figures of mechanistic, capitalist progress. In this way, *A Tale for the Time Being* also attempts to find ways to think outside or beyond a future whose progress has been overdetermined by the trajectory of settler colonial capitalism.

Transpacific Technologies and Temporalities

A Tale for the Time Being opens with a journal entry written by Nao, a young Japanese girl sitting in a "French maid café" in "Akiba Electricity Town" (Akihabara), a setting that invokes the image of the postmodern, consumption-driven landscape of modern Tokyo. Directly referencing the district that produced many of the gadgets and home electronics associated with the rise of Japan to the status of an economic world power in the late twentieth century—and that would, by the 1980s and 1990s, become known as the center of *otaku* culture, drawing computer hobbyists and anime fans alike—Ozeki begins her story in a techno-orientalist, hypercapitalist dystopia. In this space, Nao fantasizes about consuming and being consumed; as the novel continues, she discusses her growing sense of alienation from her friends, her family, and even her own body. Her diary reveals that she feels lost within a society that treats her as just another gadget or commodity, the waste product of an industrial modernity that has set her and her family adrift. While Nao's great-grandmother, a Buddhist nun, attempts to teach Nao how to navigate the ebb and flow of her modern life by focusing on the present moment rather than the demands of a modern society that abjects those who do not follow its progressive orientation, Nao feels overcome and overwhelmed. Her struggle throughout the novel lies in how to understand her different relationship with time as a source of strength rather than a cause for shame and rejection.

While *A Tale for the Time Being* thus begins in a typically techno-orientalist setting, the association of Asian bodies with capitalist technologies long prefigured the "Japan panic" that Morley and Robins cite as the impetus for the emergence of this particular aesthetic in modern media and popular culture. As discussed in Chapter 3, Iyko Day notes that there is a form of "romantic anticapitalism" at work in discursive productions of Asianness in North America from the late nineteenth and early twentieth centuries, where Asian bodies and communities become aligned with the abstract financial and technological dimensions of capitalist production that are figured as alien forces threatening the "authentic," concrete labor performed by an indigenized (white) working class.[76] Day argues that the disavowal of the former, and the celebration of the latter, emerges from a commodity fetishism that posits an opposition between concrete and abstract forms of value—an opposition that is subsequently mapped onto "racial signifiers" that "animate the work of the fetish to misrepresent the relations between people as the relations between things."[77] By associating Asianness with the alienating abstractions of capital, settler populations seek to appropriate and align themselves with signifiers of Indigeneity—most notably, by laying claim to a more "natural" or "authentic" relationship to the land while eliding and erasing the violence and inequities of North American colonial history.

A Tale for the Time Being revisits, critiques, and revises these racialized discourses around transpacific futurities and their connections to settler colonial capitalism by aligning Asian North American racial formation with two fluid environments that are also understood in simultaneously concrete and abstract terms: the Pacific Ocean and the digital space of the Internet. Just as Asian bodies have come to stand in, through the mystifications of commodity fetishism, for the "abstract circuits of capitalism,"[78] the Pacific Ocean and the Internet have likewise come to stand as metaphorical spaces for the promises and perils of capitalist enterprise. Writing about the emergence of "Pacific Rim discourse" in the 1980s and 1990s, Chris Connery notes that this "new spatial mythology" proved to be particularly compelling to a global capitalist imaginary, since

> water is capital's element. . . . [T]he bourgeois idealization of sea power and ocean-borne commerce has been central to the mythology of capital, which has struggled to free itself from the earth just

as the bourgeoisie struggled to free itself from tilling the soil. Movable capital is liquid capital, and without movement, capital is a mere Oriental hoard.[79]

Here, Connery points out how the ocean's perceived mobility and dynamism make it an ideal vehicle for an equally flexible and free-flowing idea of capitalism. In a parallel vein, Wendy Hui Kyong Chun notes that early boosters of the commercial Internet before the 2000 dot-com bust touted its potential as a *"marketplace* of ideas" and a space for, as Bill Gates famously noted, "friction-free capitalism." Like the Pacific Ocean before it, the Internet at its best can be seen as a dynamic and fluid space, promising increased interconnectivity, exchange, and profit.[80] Yet this fluidity—both in terms of the ocean environment and the unseen and unsecured operations that allow the Internet to be an accessible, "free" space—would also prove to be deeply suspect, as its expansiveness also threatens to overrun both conceptual and physical borders and boundaries separating the local and the global, the public and private. If, as I argue in previous chapters, the openness and inappropriability of the high seas continue to haunt transpacific projections of neoliberal futurity, requiring constant vigilance against the human and nonhuman forces that regularly threaten to disrupt the shipping lanes, ports, and communication lines that allow for the "free" flow of transnational capital, Chun notes that the apparent freedom of the Internet has likewise been perceived as being unsafe precisely because it is seen as being *too* free. From campaigns against Internet pornography to cyberbullying epidemics, she points out how politicians and private companies have sought to better control and secure how people access and use cyberspace—leading to the operation of the Internet as a "gated community writ large" rather than as a public utility or global public commons.[81]

These dual representations of the Pacific Ocean and the Internet—as mediums for mobilizing capital *and* as threats that must be channeled and contained—flatten and objectify these complex ecosystems in ways that project the possessive logics of settler colonial capitalism into a militarized neoliberal futurity. Both are conceptualized as alienable properties that *must be secured*, whether through network protocol or military action, to accommodate the teleology of capitalist progress. Yet with *A Tale for the Time Being*, Ozeki rejects this logic of security and securitization and instead explores how these systems—and the Asian/North American characters who travel through them—introduce alternatives to the progressive temporality of settler colonial capitalism. Like the orbital astronauts of Sullivan's *Star Waka*, the belated social networkers of Kihleng's "Pohnpei Outer

Space," and the blended on- and offline activism of Perez's *from unincorporated territory*, the floating objects and cyber-travelers that feature prominently in Ozeki's novel question both the necessity and the inevitability of a future that is built on the logic of settler colonial time.

In *A Tale for the Time Being*, the ocean emerges as a space that possesses its own distinct modes of agency and temporality, as expressed by its various current speeds and other weather-related phenomena. In his attempt to explain how Nao's diary could have traveled all the way from Japan to British Columbia, Ruth's partner, Oliver, tells her about how objects cast into the sea circulate through the ocean via a series of gyres, a large system of interconnected currents. Noting that there are "eleven great planetary gyres," he goes on to explain:

> Each gyre orbits at its own speed. . . . The longest orbital period is thirteen years, which establishes the fundamental tone. The Turtle Gyre has a half tone of six and a half years. The Aleut Gyre, a quarter tone of three. The flotsam that rides the gyres is called drift. Drift that stays in the orbit of the gyre is considered to be part of the gyre memory. The rate of escape from the gyre determines the half-life of drift.[82]

Here, the ocean operates as a medium of connection or communication, but one that has its own internal, cyclical timeline. The pace of the oceanic gyre (and gyre memory) does not work at the accelerated pace of modern capitalism. Its speed is affected by a whole assemblage of factors, of which human intervention is only one. While the ocean-mediated correspondence between Ruth and Nao is already belated and discontinuous—we know, from the very beginning of the story, that Nao's diary recounts events that take place around 2004 or 2005, while Ruth receives the diary sometime after the Tōhoku earthquake in 2011—the intensity of their connection is such that Ruth herself forgets that Nao's diary is an artifact of the past and not the real-time musings of a contemporary. In this sense, the diary's passage through the oceanic gyres seems to have warped and altered its (and Ruth's) sense of temporality. In reading Nao's words, Ruth finds herself entering into a different time.

Using this conceit of the gyre, Ozeki draws another direct parallel between the belated temporalities of the ocean environment and the cyclical, recursive timelines that characterize the production and dissemination of information and interaction on the Internet. While one of the most appealing elements of Internet connectivity is its ability to provide a platform for "real-time" encounter and exchange, the Internet—much like the debris-crowded ocean environment—also retains information that continues to circulate asynchronously, operating as retroviruses that can extend a moment of crisis from the past into the present. The result, as Chun notes, is the creation of a virtual temporality that seems to trap us in a "never-advancing present":

> The belief in memory as storage, combined with the belief in "real time" as indexical, is a form of cruel optimism: memory, which once promised to save users from time, makes them out of time by making them respond constantly to information they have already responded to, to things that will not disappear. Information is curiously undead, constantly regenerating, and users save things, if they do, by making the ephemeral endure.[83]

Like the ocean and the debris collected in its "gyre memory," the Internet has the ability to hold on to and then later recirculate information that may no longer remain current, giving rise to the popular conception that nothing is ever lost on the Internet. "Does the half-life of information correlate with the decay of our attention?" Ruth wonders. "Is the Internet a kind of temporal gyre, sucking up stories, like geodrift, into its orbit? What is its gyre memory? How do we measure the half-life of its drift?"[84] Yet despite the disorienting nature of Internet time, the seemingly endless circularity and the cyclicality of its "never-advancing present" gets recast and reconfigured in Ozeki's novel as a way to try to enter into, and fully experience, the ephemeral moment of "now," an idea that the novel explores through its engagements with the concepts of Buddhist practice and quantum physics but that could also be read as a complement to the Indigenous Pacific temporalities addressed by Sullivan, Kihleng, and Perez.

Like Sullivan's free-floating astronauts from the *Star Waka* poem "46," the virtual travelers in *A Tale tor the Time Being* show how the cyclical, recursive timelines that characterize both oceanic and networked systems are not necessarily a trap from which we must be liberated to continue a progressive, future-oriented trajectory so much as a space where we might reflect on how the waste products and obsolete information jettisoned by this progressive narrative of history can become part of a broader cultural "gyre memory." In the novel, Ruth ultimately gains access to this gyre memory and travels back in time to communicate with Nao and her father, Haruki, stopping Haruki from committing suicide and altering the trajectory of Nao's life. Both Haruki—who lost a lucrative job as a Silicon Valley programmer because he refused to create an interface that would "gamify" weapons design for the U.S. military—and Nao are figures who feel left behind and out of place in modern society. Unable to find employment, Haruki explicitly refers to himself as trash or "*gomi* . . . garbage, the kind to throw away and not even to recycle," while Nao is sexually exploited by her classmates and an acquaintance from a local café.[85] Haruki's and Nao's understanding of themselves as human "garbage" resonates with the novel's repeated references to the Great Pacific Garbage Patch, a floating mass of waste that gets pulled into the oceanic gyres and circulates endlessly in the middle of the Pacific Ocean. Oliver points out that this would have been the fate of Nao's journal if it had gotten stuck in the gyre: "sucked up and becalmed, slowly eddying around. The plastic ground into particles for the fish and zooplankton to eat. The diary and letter disintegrating, unread."[86] Yet— much like the links, hashtags, and comment pages reprinted in Perez's poetry—the unexpected appearance of Nao's diary on the beach in British Columbia operates as an archive that *resists* erasure, that calls directly out to its reader ("Who are you and what are you doing?") and invites a response.[87] While Ruth's small intervention into Nao's and Haruki's lives does not *rescue* them from invisibility and obscurity, it helps them to *reframe* their unwillingness to conform to the demands of neoliberal modernity as a powerful and meaningful alternative. During her meeting with Haruki, Ruth seeds the idea for his next project, "MechaMu," an application that targets search engines and "eats your name to keep them from finding you."[88] Using this technology, Haruki scrubs traces of himself and his family from the Internet, returning them to a kind of anonymity that allows "true freedom" to come from "being unknown."[89] While this would seem to consign the Yasutanis back to the anonymity with which they would have existed had Nao's lunchbox never exited the Pacific gyres, their interaction with Ruth works to cocreate a situation whereby Ruth's story and theirs have become profoundly entangled, even in the absence of further information about their lives. Ruth's experience shows that it is less important for individual histories, stories, or tales to be recuperated into a historical temporality than it is to understand how those forgotten histories and memories reverberate, and remain entangled, with us all.

By embracing this ethics of relation, *A Tale for the Time Being* attempts to reimagine an Asian North American identity—exemplified by the fictionalized Ruth Ozeki—that gets aligned not with the abstract circuits of capital but with the materiality of media and the act of mediation. In this sense, Ruth's work "bridges" the transpacific divide between herself and Nao in a way similar to Ken Liu's "Charlie," Maxine Hong Kingston's China Men, and the speakers of Konai Helu Thaman's poetry (see Chapter 3). Ruth, like the Pacific Ocean itself, serves as a medium for Nao's story, and as she soon comes to realize, Nao's survival is intimately bound up with her own. When Nao's story ends prematurely, Oliver speculates that it illustrates the contingency of their very existence: if Nao is able to "fall off the page," then so are they. "If she stops writing to us, then maybe we stop being, too," Oliver posits.[90] In this reading, it is not *Ruth* who operates as the primary agentive figure in this context, but the journal itself: by finding "Ruth Ozeki" and using her words to communicate the importance of "Nao"/"now," the journal and its associated artifacts bring into being a world in which Ruth's and Nao's stories are able to exist as a new, intersubjective system. In the aftermath of her atemporal encounter with Haruki, Ruth is left wondering: "Was she the dream? Was Nao the one writing her into being? *Agency is a tricky business.* . . . Her empirical experience of herself, as a fully embodied being who persisted in a real world of her remembering, seemed trustworthy enough, but now in the dark, at four in the morning, she wasn't so sure."[91] Yet it is precisely in this ambivalence over the relationship of agency to embodiment that Ozeki locates her alignment of Asian (North) American identity with the practice of *mediation* rather than a subjectivity based on a progressive, possessive individualism. Ruth does not disavow her identity as a "fully embodied" and raced citizen subject. Indeed, she notes that her very presence in British Columbia is contingent on the genocide of the Indigenous peoples who came before her.[92] At the same time, the novel's close and detailed attention to such non-character-driven phenomena as ocean currents and quantum physics is in line with the "oceanic" or new materialist turn in Asian Americanist criticism that moves through the embodied subject to note its engagements and entanglements within a broader, complex ecosystem.[93] Agency, in this context, is considered a property not of Ruth as subject but, rather, of Ruth *in relation*: Ruth experiences and exerts a form of agency by acting, and interacting, as a literal medium for the story.

Against some of the cultural, theoretical, and political impasses that emerge between Asian settler and Indigenous populations addressed in the previous chapter, *A Tale for the Time Being*'s reconfigured racialization of Asian Americanness as media or an act of mediation provides a new strategy for approaching these moments of coalition and conflict. However, as Sullivan's "xxiii Formats (1)" suggests, media has the potential to both preserve and destroy. Without a sense of or affinity for the conflicting histories and intimate entanglements that confound and complicate the unfolding of progressive social or economic agendas within a capitalist teleology, the work of mediation can also submerge, erode, or erase the contradictory perspectives and points of view that bring these points of friction to the forefront. Without placing their own positionality under erasure, transpacific Asian/American artists and authors can perhaps best engage with Indigenous epistemologies and temporalities attempting to understand the ways in they are intimately *related* to one another—that is, how projects of Indigenous survivance are directly and materially linked with their own ability to survive within progressive systems based on the profound alienability of land, temporality, and culture. Like the intersubjective relationship that develops between Ruth and Nao over the course of Ozeki's novel, the relationship between Asian American and Indigenous Pacific cultures might thus be able to emerge as a critically entangled one. Mediating or working between settler and Indigenous logics in this way can develop new forms and new relationships that bring into being different temporalities or timelines that do *not* end with the inevitable disappearance or destruction of all who do not or cannot fit into the relentlessly progressive trajectory of transpacific capitalism. Rather, they can help to work toward a sense of cross-cultural community that can expand and thrive in the "now."

A Mighty Wave

A focus on the many "stories of ocean passage" in the literatures of the Pacific necessarily involves the excavation of—and engagement with—past histories, hidden genealogies, and forgotten or eclipsed cultural practices. In this context, a turn to the histories and patterns of the past is not only necessary for contextualizing and understanding the currents of the contemporary Pacific. It is also inextricably linked to visions of futurity that imagine the survivance and resurgence of Indigenous practices and cultures. Such imaginings encompass a wide range of potential futures—from arguments for accommodations within currently existing government structures to demands for the creation of independent states with full political sovereignty and calls for alternatives to the concept of state governmentality altogether.[94] Yet despite their political differences, these concepts of futurity are all built on the idea—central to the importance of genealogy in the process of cultural connection and transmission—that one must look back to the past in order to face the future.[95] And as Sullivan's, Kihleng's, Perez's, and Ozeki's texts illustrate, looking to the past is not the same as returning to it. Just as the oceanic travelers of the past navigated the currents and tides of their day, today's travelers and migrants negotiate contemporary global networks—using the tools and technologies they have on hand—to rebuild and reconstruct a sense of community and culture in the twenty-first century.

As a final example, I want to return to the Thirty Meter Telescope protests that opened this chapter. While the visibility of this local conflict has been amplified by the protestors' opposition to a development planned by an international scientific consortium, their tactics have engaged and mobilized equally global networks in response. Using Twitter, Instagram, and other social media platforms, activists have publicized their objections to the planned development and circulated messages of support that, in turn, have brought more national and international media attention to the protests themselves. The protestors' deployment of social media technologies to publicize their efforts did not, as Bryan Kuwada notes, mark them out as "hypocrites" or at odds with their desire to do justice to the sacred status of the mountain. Rather, it is the hegemonic discourse that casts Indigenous peoples as "living fossils" rather than "modern, innovative, future-looking" individuals that creates this sense of cognitive dissonance. While protestors are, again, accused of wanting to retreat to the past or work against scientific "progress," Kuwada argues that the

> short-sighted model of "progress"—that we seem to be standing in the way of—hinges upon all of us, all of Hawai'i's people, all of the Pacific's people, all of the world's people losing connection to land, to sea, to other human beings. The less you feel these connections, the easier it is for you to be convinced that unrestricted development is the highest and best use of land.... All of [the] things done in the name of rootless progress show (un)surprisingly little care for trying to truly progress and create a future that we all want for the coming generations.[96]

This concept of "connection"—not only among different groups of people, but also between people and their environments—again emerges from, and is a motivating force for, the many ocean passages that this book has explored. Contemporary experiences of transpacific passage do not emerge only through the currents of the air and the oceans, or the circuits of trade and capital that help to distribute material goods, print culture, and migrant populations. They also emerge through the virtual (and material) pathways created by new visual technologies and digital networks, negotiating and interrogating both disembodied and embodied forms of protest, cultural connection, and aesthetic experimentation. Reading, sharing, and learning from these diverse stories of ocean passage allows their different imaginations of the future to assert relevant and necessary alternatives in the face of a monolithic, even apocalyptic, interpretation of "progress." It is by approaching these ocean passages not in terms of establishing their paradigmatic singularity but to openly and honestly address their entanglement, their points of conflict, and their potential for connection and coalition that we may contribute to a new Oceania and decolonial Pacific future that will rise—in the powerful words of Kumu Pualani Case as she closes the daily ceremonies for the community of *kia'i* at Mauna Kea—"like a mighty wave."[97]

CONCLUSION

I began writing this book in my childhood home, in the Honolulu suburb of Salt Lake. The area takes its name from a shallow volcanic crater lake known to Kānaka Maoli as *ālia pa'akai* (salt bed, salt lake), said to have been created by the goddess Pele during her first passage through the Hawaiian islands.[1] Since the nineteenth century, the lake has been mined for its "exceptionally fine" salt, silted by plantation runoff, and finally filled in with concrete, thus creating the only version of Salt Lake that I ever knew: a middle-class neighborhood marked by single-family homes on one side, high-rise condos on the other, and a private golf course at its center. What remains of the lake is used as a water feature on the golf course, and I only ever saw glimpses of it through a chain-link fence that formed the boundary of the district park.

I have often thought of this lake as I researched and read and wrote the words that would eventually take the shape of this book. On one hand, it is a vivid reminder of the violent history of extraction and development that created the conditions that made it possible for me—a non-Native, fourth-generation Japanese American—to grow up on Hawaiian land. On the other, it serves as an invitation to reconsider my surroundings along a different historical and affective axis. To locate oneself on *ālia pa'akai* encourages a different way of seeing and thinking about the land and one's relationship to it in a way that day-to-day living in Salt Lake generally does not. *Ālia pa'akai* reminds me to respect the limitations that the environment can place on the desire to make oneself at home. According to some *moʻolelo* (stories/histories), Pele did not stay in this place because the land was not hospitable to her design. When she dug down, the salt water rose up and flooded her crater.[2] By contrast, Salt Lake is a post-statehood residential development whose creation flies in the face of that wisdom. The concrete that reshaped the topography of this land supported the postwar prosperity of families like mine, but it also made it possible to go about daily life in Salt Lake without giving a thought to the contingency of the ground beneath one's feet.[3] Yet *ālia paʻakai* still exists, and even in attenuated form it reminds us that the land will have its due. Although it cannot always be seen, at some times it can certainly be smelled, particularly after sediment, trash, and runoff have accumulated in its basin. Such smells confront the neighborhood's current residents, drawing attention to both the lingering presence of the lake itself and the ongoing effects of dumping and pollution on the land. In this sense, the past and its meanings can linger—quite literally—in ways that index histories that lack an official monument or archive.[4]

As I bring this book to a close, returning to this space also helps me to situate this project itself in terms of the specific ocean passages (and impasses) that have contributed to its emergence. My experiences of growing up in Hawaiʻi during the 1980s and 1990s, a time when narratives of multicultural harmony and local Asian American ascendance were beginning to be explicitly complicated and interrogated by Kanaka Maoli decolonization and sovereignty movements, have necessarily informed my interests and investments in thinking through the many ways that transpacific discourses have been intimately entangled with transnational dynamics of settler colonialism in Hawaiʻi and other sites in and across the Pacific. The texts addressed in this volume not only uncover or emphasize the palimpsestic histories of transpacific travel and exchange that have been occluded by settler narratives informing practices of colonial extraction, militarized securitization, capitalist expansion, and racial and gendered forms of hierarchy. They also articulate ways of thinking critically and creatively about the Pacific as space networked by relationships that foster intimacy and abundance, rather than alienation and scarcity.

Writing and reflecting about these overlapping ocean passages allow Pacific and Asian diasporic authors and artists not only to critique the contemporary demands of a globalizing economy, but also to ground that critique in a sense of human and nonhuman relationality that exceeds the market logics of contemporary discussions of the term and label "transpacific."[5] If, as Keith Camacho and Setsu Shigematsu have argued, the need to foster "cross-regional and cross-disciplinary" coalitions by "demonstrating how currents of militarization and demilitarization [in the Pacific] connect and divide people with potentially common interests" remains critical to establishing a truly "decolonial genealogy of the transpacific,"[6] reading for the diversity of transpacific ocean passages may allow us to understand our own relationships to these various constituencies, rediscovering important connections to the past and highlighting potential sites of coalition in the present.

While encouraging us to see the complex ways that these transoceanic trajectories have become entangled and interconnected, these works also draw attention to the unevenness and incommensurabilities that continue to shape different passages through, and impasses on, the contemporary Pacific. By refusing to render these differing positionalities into equivalent or exchangeable sites, these ocean passages can help us to map not only relationships between but also responsibilities to the human (and nonhuman) entities whose circulations are often left out of hegemonic renderings of the region. Indeed, this book suggests that it is precisely by attending to these "other(ed)" histories, experiences, and circulations that we might be able to arrive at an understanding of transpacific partnership that is better suited to responding to the contemporary challenges of economic inequality, militarized violence, and climate change that have emerged from more than a century of colonial rule.

By way of conclusion, I want to reflect on the connections between these region-spanning stories of ocean passage and the subversive histories that accumulate in the intimacy of other kinds of watery spaces—rivers, lakes, ponds, and marshes—as a way to open up to other sites that lie outside the purview of this book. I began this conclusion with the story of one specific lake, *ālia pa'akai*, but its history of land development/extraction and the subsequent pollution of waterways and watersheds rehearses a dynamic that resonates across a number of sites, not only in the Hawaiian Islands and across the Pacific Ocean, but in decolonial and environmental struggles around the world. From the blockades set up at Mauna Kea and Standing Rock to the protests and lawsuits filed on behalf of communities disproportionately affected by water shortages or polluted water in the United States, Latin America, Africa, and the Indian subcontinent, water rights constitute an important site of struggle for the future not only of these local communities but for the health of the planet as a whole.

Discourses around oceanic phenomena such as warming, acidification, and sea level rise often impart a generalized sense of global crisis or threat, even if—as I argued in Chapter 2—such threats may seem distant or abstract to people whose lives and livelihoods are not directly affected by oceanic phenomena. By contrast, struggles over water sources are more easily dismissed as localized affairs, as a problem that affects only the residents of, say, Flint, Michigan, or Newark, New Jersey, or the Standing Rock reservation of North and South Dakota. Yet contemporary struggles over waterways and water sources operate as a site of intersectional activism that draws together antiracist, decolonial, and environmental work.[7] Activists engaged in fighting for clean water and unpolluted waterways insist on the need for large-scale structural changes and the importance of working toward futures that push beyond the limited scope of the solutions offered by the settler state. While state-based solutions have focused primarily on short-term mitigative strategies to defer impending environmental and social crises, activists have called for long-term reconsiderations of the settler logics that continue to impose limitations on environmental and social forms of redress.

Despite the fact that long-term activism must often grapple with these seemingly intractable settler structures and systems, what it can offer regarding water protection that panic about anticipated water "crises" cannot are (1) historical context and (2) a direct course of action. Both run directly counter to the production of apathy or helplessness that can emerge in response to the more apocalyptic or crisis-based prognostications projected from information provided by scientific studies and surveys.[8] Putting a water crisis—such as pollution, drought, or flood—into a broader historical framework does not deny its severity or the necessity of responding to an individual crisis event. Rather, it draws attention to how such events have been shaped by structural, historical, and political, as well as natural, conditions. Such a framework likewise demands more thoughtful and long-term approaches to "solving" crises that result in meaningful changes that do not end at infrastructural or technological fixes but extend to perhaps altering the habits of everyday life. To this end, water advocates have not only been putting their bodies on the line in protests and in blockades, as many did at Standing Rock; they also monitor and care for riverbeds, bays, and harbors; maintain fisheries and estuarine environments; and show up to courtrooms and legislatures to fight for water rights and water sovereignty. Caring for water sources requires an awareness of the complex interconnectedness of local ecosystems, yet like other forms of grassroots activism, it can be at its most powerful when such knowledge and awareness is expressed through everyday practice. It is also intensely community-focused work in the sense that it is not a project that can be undertaken by an individual alone. Just as Epeli Hau'ofa's call to reconceptualize Oceania as "a sea of islands" rather than "islands in a far sea" helped to articulate an important paradigm shift in Oceanic and transpacific studies, so have activist movements around water foregrounded the need for communities to radically reconceptualize themselves as part of and connected to the ecosystem, rather than simply living off of it.

Indeed, it is in this conceptual shift that organized activism around water protection expresses its radical decolonial potential. While practices of ecological repair can be—and certainly have been—undertaken without fully confronting the dynamics of settler colonialism and racialized dispossession that have contributed to a site's overall environmental degradation, to be effective in the long term, the practices of water source protection and restoration must grapple with questions regarding *who* is doing the "protecting" and "restoring," how such goals are being defined, and the end to which the efforts are being put. Who exerts sovereignty over a particular waterway or water source, and how is that sovereignty negotiated with developments or dumping that may happen upstream or on a piece of land that falls under a different jurisdiction? Does the project of restoration frame land and seas as passive or victimized figures in need of human protection, or are they framed as acts of *responsibility to* an ecology and environment that has sustained and nourished them? Will the emphasis of the project lie in restoring the site to the way it was "before," or will it focus on remediating the site to better sustain the life that exists on it today, and for generations to come?

Like the stories of ocean passage outlined in this book, the sedimented histories that have accumulated in and around watersheds and waterways can unsettle extant understandings of water as an abstract, alienable, and alternately limitless or endangered resource. Attention to the ways that water sources have shaped and been shaped historically by different human and nonhuman communities can not only work to critique modern modes of water management; it can also articulate venues for resistance and resilience. Returning to Hawai'i, for example, a number of Kanaka Maoli–led initiatives to restore *lo'i kalo* (taro beds in terraced irrigation systems) and *loko i'a* (fishponds in estuarine environments) have combined local cultural revitalization with ecological remediation.[9] In contrast to the industrial-scale plantation agriculture that denuded the islands' upland forests and forcibly diverted water for irrigation, Kanaka Maoli practices of crop and fish cultivation were designed around the natural flow of water from the mountains to the sea. These agricultural and aquacultural practices were developed in ways that support and promote the overall health of the local watershed, streambeds, and oceans. Over time, it is hoped, these revitalized sites will have demonstrated a modest improvement in local environmental conditions.

While these projects—like other initiatives supporting water remediation and water sovereignty elsewhere in the United States and around the world—illustrate the resilience of the land and the peoples who cultivate it, they cannot be expected to do all the work of remediating the damage created by the emissions and effluents of industrial capitalism. This is particularly true for the Indigenous, impoverished, and minoritized communities who often bear a disproportionate burden of the world's environmental pollution. Yet as the global environmental consequences of modern industrial capitalism—particularly around the *excess* (flooding/sea level rise) or *absence* (drought/pollution) of water—become increasingly difficult for even the settler state to isolate or ignore, these different stories of ocean passage, waterways, and watersheds that have circulated outside of, or have been buried under, settler colonial networks and infrastructures can help to move us toward a future beyond apocalypse.

To think with stories of ocean passage is to adopt a framework for transpacific study that not only analyzes and critiques how the contemporary Pacific has been both conceptually and materially structured by settler colonial logics of securitization, alienation, and extraction. It also engages the encounters, alliances, and impasses that have emerged from human and nonhuman passages through and across the Pacific to focus on the networks that exist outside or in the interstices of militarized and capital-driven models of transpacific partnership. Similarly, sedimented stories around watersheds and waterways help us to consider how settler colonial infrastructures have directly affected and reshaped the environment and the communities that live on them and offer up these spaces as important sites of direct action and redress. The liveliness and potential resilience of these oceans, rivers, lakes, and bays emphasize how the damage manifested in these sites are not mere *symptoms* of a future global crisis but are sites for action in the present: like the communities that live in and around them, they are not already too far "gone" for repair but require immediate forms of remediation that can often run counter to the structural capacities of the settler state. Against the presumptive fixity of settler colonial networks and infrastructures, the fluidity and porosity of oceanic and riparian environments materialize the complex connections among different human and nonhuman communities, offering different ways to be and live together in the world. It is up to us to attend to the stories they have to tell.

NOTES

INTRODUCTION

1. George (2006), 164, 383.
2. Hauʻofa, "Our Sea of Islands" (1994), 152. From here on, I capitalize "Oceanic" when referring specifically to the regional formation "Oceania"—as used by Sāmoan writer Albert Wendt in "Towards a New Oceania" (1976), and later by Tongan author and academic Epeli Hauʻofa in "Our Sea of Islands" (1994)—to indicate the deep historical and ongoing cultural connections between different Pacific communities and cultures. These communities are not limited to those who identify as Native or Indigenous peoples, but they imply a deep cultural and political commitment to Indigenous Pacific communities, epistemologies, and environments (Hauʻofa [1998], 401–402).
3. Hauʻofa (1998), 408.
4. See, e.g., Crocombe (1976); Diaz and Kauanui (2001); Hau'ofa ("Our Sea of Islands" 1994; 1998); Teaiwa (1995); Wendt (1976), to name just a few well-known examples.
5. Works by Wilson (2000), Wilson and Dirlik (1995), and Najita (2006) are early exceptions that address both Asian American and Indigenous Pacific work in an explicitly transnational frame.
6. See T. Chen (2020).
7. See Wendt (1976); Yoneyama (2017). I discuss these (as well as the formations of the "Asia-Pacific" and "Pacific Rim" mentioned earlier) in greater detail in the next section of this chapter.
8. Suzuki and Bahng (2020).
9. Medak-Saltzman (2015), 18.
10. Ong (1999, 4), Cruz (2012, 8), and Allen (2012, xiv–xv) have each observed that the prefix "trans-," when applied to the terms "transnational," "transpacific," and "transindigenous," respectively, can simultaneously imply movement *across*, passage *through*, and "states of transition and change."

11. In addition to work by Indigenous Pacific scholars, other recent ocean-centered work in the field of history and cultural studies has begun pushing back on this erasure. See, e.g., Igler (2013); Matsuda (2012); Okihiro (2008); Starosielski (2015).

12. Blum (2010, 640). See also Braudel (1972); Gilroy (1993).

13. Blum (2013, 152–153).

14. See Jackson (2012); Te Punga Somerville (2017); T. Teaiwa, "For or Before an Asian Pacific Studies Agenda?" (2010); Weaver, *The Red Atlantic* (2017).

15. See Allen (2002, 2012); DeLoughrey (2007); Keown (2004, 2007); Najita (2006); Te Punga Somerville (2012).

16. For an extended analysis of the divergence of Asian American and Pacific Islander studies both inside (Kauanui, Hall) and outside (Hall) U.S.-centered contexts, see Hall (2015); Kauanui (2005).

17. See, e.g., Lowe (1996); Palumbo-Liu (1999); Wilson and Dirlik (1995); Y. Huang (2008). Naoki Sakai and Hyon-Joo Yoo (2012, ix) explicitly note that their conception of the transpacific "marks the realpolitik and metaphoric territorialization of *Asia* in an *American*-centered global capital and military-political systems" (emphasis added), while Viet Nguyen and Janet Hoskins (2014) acknowledge and regret that "the complexities of the Pacific Islands are not represented in the coverage that is present, and the voices of Pacific Islanders are not represented" in their field-spanning volume of *Transpacific Studies* (Sakai and Yoo [2012], 33).

18. See Kauanui (2005); Diaz (2004); Hall (2015).

19. Fujikane and Okamura (2008); Saranillio (2020). See also Labrador and Wright (2011), which uses a Hawai'i-based case study as a basis for a broader argument for engaging in comparative critical race studies in the field.

20. Y. Espiritu (2014, 2017); Gonzalez (2013); Perez (2015); Shigematsu and Camacho (2010); Yoneyama (2017).

21. Tuck and Yang (2012, 17).

22. See, e.g., Espiritu, Lowe, and Yoneyama (2017); Gonzalez (2013); Man (2018); Shigematsu and Camacho (2010).

23. Asian Americanist critics Lisa Lowe (2015), Lisa Yoneyama (2016), Anne Anlin Cheng (2018), and Kandice Chuh (2019) have invoked queer and feminist invocations of relationality in their recent work. Mel Chen (2012), Rachel Lee (2014), and Michelle Huang (2017) have evoked science studies frameworks as a way to engage these discussions of human/nonhuman relationality in terms of embodiment, affect, and environmental critique.

24. Articulating and analyzing these Indigenous Pacific epistemologies of relation and entanglement have been a part of Pacific scholarship from the 1970s through the present day, as illustrated in the literary and critical work of scholars/activists/artists such as Epeli Hau'ofa, Konai Helu Thaman, Albert Wendt, Vilsoni Hereniko, Haunani-Kay Trask, Teresia Teaiwa, Selina Tusitala Marsh, Linda Tuhiwai Smith, Alice Te Punga Somerville, Manulani Meyer, ku'ualoha ho'omanawanui, Brandy Nālani McDougall, Craig Santos Perez, and more. In the chapters to come, I will further outline these and many other Indigenous scholars' analyses of relationality as articulated from within a Pacific/Oceania-centered discourse.

25. DeLoughrey (2007, 2).

26. Here I borrow and slightly adapt the concept of "disjuncture and difference" in Appadurai (1996) to emphasize his point that such differentiation is a *process*, not a fixed quality.

27. See Māhina (1990); Matsuda (2012); Petersen (2000); Taonui (2007).

28. See Te Punga Somerville (2017, 25); Matsuda (2012, 3). Igler (2013, 11) likewise notes the tendency of "European and American outsiders [to rationalize] the ocean—as *one* Pacific Ocean—in a vain attempt to simplify its tremendous social and natural complexity."
29. Vaʻai (1999, 32–33).
30. Hauʻofa, "Our Sea of Islands" (1994), 152.
31. Ibid.
32. Ibid., 153.
33. Wendt (1976), 49.
34. Wilson and Dirlik (1995, 2).
35. Connery (1994, 32).
36. Sharrad (1990, 597).
37. T. Teaiwa (1999), 251.
38. For a brief overview of the emergence of the term "transpacific" in critical scholarship, see Suzuki (2014).
39. Nguyen and Hoskins (2014, 2–3).
40. Wilson and Dirlik (1995, 5).
41. Wilson (2015, 228–229).
42. Palumbo-Liu (2012, 1).
43. Kandice Chuh (2019) argues that we might similarly turn to the "aesthetic" as an important space for decoupling the idea of the "human" from received notions of liberal subjecthood.
44. See Byrd (2011); Day (2016); Moreton-Robinson (2015).
45. Chuh (2003, 8–9).
46. Y. Huang (2008, 10).
47. Ibid., 2, 9.
48. Ibid., 10.
49. Moreton-Robinson, qtd. in Byrd (2011, 211).
50. Byrd (2011, 211).
51. For example, Mel Chen (2012) and Rachel Lee (2014) have combined Asian Americanist critique with new materialist theories that think through what it means to de-center the traditional human(ist) subject by focusing instead on the relationships between (and within) human and nonhuman entities, the vital materiality of human and nonhuman bodies, and how these changing relationships and shifting boundaries give rise to circulation of affects and feelings that inform or sustain certain social constructions.
52. The concept and central importance of a "spiralic," non-linear understanding of time appears in several artistic manifestoes, critical texts, and articulations of Indigenous epistemologies from scholars around the Pacific Islands. For examples, see Diaz (2011); Kameʻeleihiwa (1992); Māhina (2010); Marsh (1999); T. Teaiwa, "What Remains to be Seen" (2010). The central importance of genealogy to Indigenous narrative is discussed at length as *moʻokuʻauhau* in a Kanaka Maoli context in hoʻomanawanui (2015); McDougall (2016); Silva (2004); Trask (1993); Wilson-Hokowhitu (2019). It is discussed as *whakapapa* in a Māori context in Te Rito (2007); Te Punga Somerville (2012); Walker (1990). On Kānaka Maoli *kaona*, see, e.g., Arista (2010); McDougall (2016); Pukui (1949). On Tongan *heliaki*, see Kaeppler (1993); Māhina (1993). Allen (2012), Hereniko (1995), Marsh (1999), and Sinavaiana and Kauanui (2007) address the process of weaving as both an aesthetic process and metaphor for scholarly methodology.
53. Ingersoll (2016, 6).
54. Ibid.

55. See, e.g., Diaz (2011), Te Punga Somerville (2017), and Vaka'uta et al. (2018), who discuss the role of the ocean in these terms in, respectively, Carolinian, Māori, and Sāmoan/Tongan contexts.

56. Hau'ofa (1998), 409.

57. See, e.g., Silva (2004, 2017), McDougall (2016), and ho'omanawanui (2014), who have written about the extensive body of Indigenous language literatures in 'Ōlelo Hawai'i, particularly published in periodical form, from the nineteenth century to the present. Sudo (2010) has also engaged a study of "Nanyo-Orientalism," or representations of the South Pacific by Japanese writers.

58. See Suzuki (2010, 2012, 2018).

59. Writings from Papua New Guinea and the Solomon Islands were, in fact, some of the earliest published Pacific writing in English, and these sites, along with Fiji, were key players in the decolonization movements of the 1960s and 1970s. For more on the postcolonial dynamics of West Pacific literatures, cultures, and politics, see Banivanua Mar (2016); Subramani (1985); K. Teaiwa (2014); Va'ai (1999); Winduo (1990).

60. Connery (1994, 40).

61. See Diaz and Kauanui (2001, 317).

CHAPTER 1

1. For discussions of how Cold War militarization has served to occlude and extend colonialism in Asia, see Fujitani et al. (2001); Jodi Kim (2010); Man (2018); Yoneyama (2016). For analyses of how U.S. militarized infrastructures have worked to erase/elide critical analyses of colonialism in the Pacific, see Wilson and Dirlik (1995); DeLoughrey (2007); Shigematsu and Camacho (2010); T. Teaiwa (1994).

2. Yoneyama (2016, 21).

3. Man (2018, 8).

4. Following Buzan et al. (1998, 25), I define "securitization" as the range of responses taken to "existential threats that legitimize the breaking of rules"—a process that, in the case of the postwar Pacific, included the ability of the United States to abrogate other states' sovereignty in the course of Cold War militarization.

5. DeLoughrey (2007, 33).

6. Ibid., 31.

7. Truman (1945).

8. Ibid.

9. Ibid.

10. Byrd (2011, xxi–xxii).

11. T. Teaiwa (1994, 87).

12. Sandra Pannell notes that in this context Indigenous island and coastal communities are *doubly* dispossessed, as their rights to traditional ocean resources and fisheries have been appropriated through a corresponding doctrine of *mare nullius*. Indeed, Pannell (1996, 22) argues that the discrepancies between official legal discourses around Indigenous rights and the actual exercise of Indigenous sovereignties are "particularly noticeable when it comes to things of a marine nature."

13. Mulrennan and Scott (2000, 685–693).

14. Pannell (1996, 26).

15. Grotius (1916, 28).

16. R. P. Anand (1983, 5) notes that, prior to European arrival, Asian and Pacific states had their own "rules of inter-state conduct," which "differed from ... European state prac-

tice, but there can be no doubt about their widespread acceptance among Asian states." Indeed, Anand further posits that, "thanks to [Asian states'] liberal traditions of freedoms of peaceful navigation and trade, and permission to foreign merchants to establish themselves by their own laws, the Europeans got an easy foothold in Asia."

17. Mawani (2018, 61).
18. Schmitt ([1942] 2015), emphasis added.
19. Chun (2009, 8).
20. For more on the potential of EEZs to expand the economic and political influence of island and coastal nation-states, see Anand (1983). Tamatoa Bambridge and Stéphanie Leyronas (2018, 133–141) have also argued that island states can take a leading role in environmental and climate change by developing locally determined *rahui* (restrictions on resource use) within the boundaries of their EEZs.
21. Foreshore and Seabed Act (2004, 4[b], 4[c:i]).
22. Bargh (2006, 15–16).
23. Epeli Hauʻofa's essays "Our Sea of Islands" (1994) and "The Ocean in Us" (1998) clearly articulate the outlines of an ocean-centered approach that is shared across several Pacific groups. Alice Te Punga Somerville (2012) uses this oceanic worldview as an analytic for a comparative study of Māori and Oceanic/Pasifika literatures and cultural productions, while David Chang (2016) and Karin Amimoto Ingersoll (2016) analyze Kanaka Maoli-specific ways of understanding and relating to the ocean that see it as being coextensive from and continuous with land.
24. DeLoughrey (2007, 20).
25. Helmreich (2009, xi).
26. Ibid., 16.
27. Alaimo (2012, 184).
28. Jodi Kim (2010) and Man (2018) address the Asian American body as a site of potential subversion or subversiveness in Cold War transpacific military projects, while Diaz (2001), Bevacqua (2010), and Camacho (2011) discuss the ways that the Pacific Islander (here, specifically the Chamorro/Micronesian) body is rendered as a site of *sacrifice* through military enlistment.
29. Connery (1994, 31).
30. Fujitani et al. (2001), Klein (2003), and Jodi Kim (2010) have discussed (in a transpacific/Asian American context) how Asian bodies are made alternately invisible or hypervisible, depending on the extent to which their appearance or existence draws attention to the imperialist structure of Cold War militarization. Similarly, Davis (2015), DeLoughrey (2007), Gonzalez (2013), and Teaiwa (1994) observe that the wholesale erasure of the Pacific *Islands* during Cold War mappings and discourses of the "Pacific" has likewise operated to conceal the imperialism of U.S. militarization.
31. Klein (2003, 150).
32. Atomic Energy Commission (1956).
33. Yoneyama (1999, 15).
34. Klein (2003).
35. Arvin (2019, 3).
36. Ibid.
37. Kauanui, *Hawaiian Blood* (2008, 1–36).
38. See Hall (2015).
39. See Arvin (2019, 1–13).
40. See ibid., 17–18; Kauanui (2007); Lyons (2006, 166–167).
41. See Klein (2003, 11–12, 19).

42. Hayes (1984, 66).
43. Michener (1947, 121).
44. Ibid., 97.
45. Ibid., 102.
46. Ibid., 103.
47. Ibid., 203.
48. Arvin (2019, 4).
49. Michener (1947, 169).
50. Kauanui, "Colonialism in Equality" (2008); Moreton-Robinson (2015, xxi). While Aileen Moreton-Robinson refers to how "white possession" of Indigenous land operates through a discourse of "security" as refracted through the twenty-first century's war on terror, these dynamics, I argue, are equally at play during the World War II and Cold War eras.
51. Michener (1947, 304–305).
52. Ibid., 12, 82.
53. Klein (2003, 166–167).
54. Peattie (1992, 44).
55. United Nations Security Council (1947), Resolution 21, emphasis added.
56. Ibid.
57. See T. Teaiwa (1994).
58. Wilson (2000, 165); Lyons (2006, 21); Gonzalez (2013, 162–163).
59. Akin (2013, 257).
60. See DeLoughrey (2012).
61. Ibid. For more on the ethical violations in Project SUNSHINE's tissue sampling methods, see Roff (2002).
62. See Revelle and Suess (1957).
63. George (2006, 59).
64. Klein (2003) notes how *South Pacific*, as well as Rodgers and Hammerstein's *The King and I*, served to promote these particular visions of transpacific domesticity as part of a larger project of "Cold War Orientalism."
65. Te Punga Somerville (2018, 71).
66. Vizenor (2008, 1).
67. George (2006, 20–21).
68. Ibid., 27.
69. Ryan (2012, 12), italics added.
70. Steinberg and Peters (2015, 255).
71. See Chakrabarty (2009).
72. See, e.g., Davis and Todd (2017); Whyte (2016).
73. DeLoughrey (2019, 2).
74. Shewry (2015, 16–22).
75. George (2006, 52).
76. Ibid., 26.
77. Ibid., 115, 198.
78. Ibid., 361.
79. Ibid., 232.
80. Ibid., 297.
81. Virilio (1994, 69).
82. Chow (2006, 26–27).
83. Ibid., 32.

84. DeLoughrey (2009, 469). This concept is also foregrounded in B. Smith (1960); T. Teaiwa (1994).
85. For more on the circulation of the images of Indigenous Pacific masculinities in colonial/neocolonial contexts, see Hokowhitu (2003, 2004); B. Smith (1960, 317–332); Tengan (2008).
86. Sontag (1977, 3).
87. George (2006, 3).
88. Ibid.
89. Ingersoll (2016).
90. Saranillio (2018, 9–10).

CHAPTER 2

1. See, e.g., Farbotko (2010); Hartmann (2010); Pickering (2001, 173).
2. Arendt (qtd. in Agamben [1995, 116]) notes that "the concept of the Rights of Man . . . collapsed as soon as those who professed it found themselves for the first time before men who had truly lost every other specific quality and connection except for the mere fact of being humans," a state that Agamben terms "bare life."
3. Agamben (1995, 116; 1998, 126–136).
4. In *The Intimacies of the Four Continents* (2015, 7), Lisa Lowe draws the explicit connection between the genealogy of liberalism and histories of race, observing, "Race as a mark of colonial difference is an enduring remainder of the processes through which the human is universalized and freed by liberal forms, while the peoples who created the conditions of possibility for that freedom are assimilated or forgotten. The genealogy of modern liberalism is thus also a genealogy of modern race; racial differences and distinctions designate the boundaries of the human and endure as remainders attesting to the violence of liberal universality."
5. Sharpe (2016, 3, 14).
6. Ibid., 8.
7. Agamben (1995, 117). In *Homo Sacer* (1998, 131), Agamben again notes the way that refugees productively and critically disrupt the naturalized relationship between the nation-state and its claims to "nativity" through occupation, observing that "by breaking the continuity between man and citizen, *nativity* and *nationality*, they put the originary fiction of modern sovereignty in crisis."
8. E. Espiritu (2018, 9).
9. On the "whiteness" of the security state, see Moreton-Robinson (2015, 137–152).
10. For critiques of the ways that refugee populations have entered a domestic narrative of "immigration" and settlement that upholds the settler colonial state, see E. Espiritu (2018); Le (2018).
11. Mimi Thi Nguyen (2012, 52) defines "refugee condition" as a "discursive, medico-juridical disposition" that posits refugees as suffering from "arrested affect or potentiality." Marguerite Nguyen and Catherine Fung (2016) critique the ways that comparative refugee studies have inadvertently reified this universalized "condition." Carol Farbotko and Heather Lazrus (2012) argue that emergent discourses around "climate change refugees" in the Pacific likewise serve to erase local histories, practices, and particularities by attempting to fit them into the models designed for the resettlement of war/political refugees.
12. Y. Espiritu (2014, 11).
13. Malkki (1995, 497–498).
14. United Nations General Assembly (1951, I.1.A.2), emphasis added.

15. Y. Espiritu (2014); M. T. Nguyen (2012).
16. Y. Espiritu (2014).
17. M. T. Nguyen (2012, 25).
18. Y. Espiritu (2014, 86).
19. V. Nguyen (2012, 930).
20. See Farbotko and Lazrus (2012, 1).
21. El-Hinnawi (1985, 4).
22. See, e.g., Bates (2002, 465–466); Williams (2008, 506–507).
23. See, e.g., Davis and Todd (2017); Whyte (2017).
24. See Watts (2013).
25. See Espiritu and Duong (2018, 588). Yến Lê Espiritu and Lan Duong identify this definition of "refugee epistemology" as explicitly "feminist," focused on questions of intimacy and the domestic practices of everyday life
26. See Lowe (2015, esp. 17–18).
27. On rethinking "climate change" refugee flight in terms of a longer history of Indigenous Pacific migration, see Farbotko and Lazrus (2012, 3). For more on Indigenous Pacific concepts of "sustainability," including *tapu/taboo* (spiritual/sacred) and *rahui* (governmental) designations and prohibitions, see, e.g., Bambridge and Leyronas (2018); Tuwere (2002); Vakaʻuta et al. (2018).
28. See Jetñil-Kijiner, "'Butterfly Thief' and Complex Narratives of Disappearing Islands" (2017).
29. Many Pacific scholars/activists have addressed the ways that European and Pacific forms of land tenure were/are based on different cultural and epistemological premises. On the "Great Mahele" in Hawaiʻi, see, e.g., Kameʻeleihiwa (1992). On land rights and the Treaty of Waitangi in Aotearoa/New Zealand, see Awatere (1984).
30. For more on the dangers of universalizing a "refugee" narrative or "refugee" discourse, see Nguyen and Fung (2016).
31. My use of the term "affinity" here follows Grace Hong and Roderick Ferguson's (2011, 19) articulation of the "strange affinities" that outline a mode of comparative study of racial/ethnic difference focused around a "*relational* comparative analytic," as opposed to a more "empiricist" mode that posits comparison as a process that takes place between two discrete (rather than entangled/overlapping) entities.
32. Intergovernmental Panel on Climate Change (2018).
33. See de Agueda Corneloup and Mol (2014).
34. Nixon (2011, 2).
35. Such local cultural productions include the Water Is Rising tour of 2011, where performers from the nations of Tuvalu, Tokelau, and Kiribati toured the United States to call attention to the impact of climate change through dance and cultural exchange, as well as the 2014–2016 Malama Honua (Care for the Earth) voyage of the Hōkūleʻa, a Hawaiian voyaging canoe whose navigational techniques were revived and inspired by Micronesian seafaring practices. For more on local artistic, political, and cultural responses to climate change, see Cox et al. (2018); Hermann and Kempf (2017); Steiner (2015).
36. de Agueda Corneloup and Mol (2014, 287).
37. Ibid.
38. Paragraph 21 of the Paris Agreement (UNFCCC [2015, Decision 1/CP.21]) explicitly "*invites* the Intergovernmental Panel on Climate Change to provide a special report in 2018 on the impacts of global warming of 1.5 degrees C above preindustrial levels and related global greenhouse gas emissions pathways."
39. See Jaeger and Jaeger (2011).

40. Some recent examples of Pacific Islands leadership on climate issues are the Majuro Declaration of 2013, which committed the nations of the Pacific Islands Forum to a program of "ambitious greenhouse gas emissions reductions and a regional transition to renewable and clean energy sources" (Mulalap [2015, 211]) and Fiji's chairmanship of the United Nations Climate Change Conference (COP23) in Bonn, marking the first time in the body's history that a small island state was placed in charge of the conference negotiations and proceedings (Maclellan [2018, 462]).
41. Maclellan (2011; 2018, 466–467).
42. Borchers and Phillips (2017).
43. Webber (2013, 2729).
44. Farbotko and Lazrus (2012).
45. On the way European depictions of both "romantic" and "ignoble" savages from the eighteenth and nineteenth centuries were grounded in the idea that they were examples of "primitive" forms of culture, see, e.g., B. Smith (1960, 317–333). For more on the ways that the "disappearing Native" myth persists in the Pacific through, for example, contemporary debates over "blood quantum" in Hawai'i, see Kauanui (2007, *Hawaiian Blood* [2008]). For discussions of how the global perceptions of island "smallness" negatively affect the economic and political prospects of Pacific Island nations, see Hau'ofa, "Our Sea of Islands" (1994).
46. Farbotko and Lazrus (2012, 8). For more on the island as laboratory, see DeLoughrey (2012); Farbotko (2010).
47. On contemporary attitudes toward Pacific Islander migrants as inhabiting a temporally "backward" space, see Farbotko (2010). For attitudes toward Micronesian immigrants in the United States (particularly Hawai'i), see Blair (2015); Hofschneider (2018).
48. See de Agueda Corneloup and Mol (2014); Webber (2013).
49. See Hau'ofa, "Our Sea of Islands" (1994); Diaz and Kauanui (2001); T. Teaiwa (1995).
50. Jolly (2018, 26).
51. Bambridge and Leyronas (2018, 133).
52. L. T. Smith (1999).
53. Vaka'uta et al. (2018, 127).
54. Vaioleti (2006, 24).
55. UNFCC, "2018 Talanoa Dialogue Platform," https://unfccc.int/topics/2018-talanoa-dialogue-platform.
56. Jetñil-Kijiner, "'Butterfly Thief' and Complex Narratives of Disappearing Islands" (2017).
57. Ibid.
58. Ibid.
59. Ibid.
60. Ibid.
61. See Jetñil-Kijiner, *Iep Jāltok* (2017), esp. "The Letter B Is For," "History Lessons," and "Fishbone Hair."
62. This phrasing is borrowed/inspired by Saranillio (2018, xix), which addresses the ways that imperial projects continue to depend upon the prevention of "an awareness of the process of settler accumulation by Native dispossession, thus opposing a system set by white supremacy that, while *differently*, comes at the expense of *all of us*."
63. Steiner (2015, 150–154).
64. Barad (2009).
65. Webber (2013, 2730).

66. Anderson (1983, 22–37).
67. Tang (2015, 50).
68. P. Nguyên (2017, 96).
69. For example, Renisa Mawani (2018) focuses on the 1914 journey of the *Komagata Maru*, a Japanese ship chartered by South Asian emigrants whose legal status, upon the ship's arrival in Vancouver, became a contested international incident. While providing an example from a different context, the legal liminality of the *Komagata Maru* emigrants anticipates the vulnerability and "stateless" status of the Vietnamese emigrants at the century's end.
70. Y. Espiritu (2014, 55).
71. Ibid., 100.
72. Ibid., 106.
73. I borrow the term "absent presence" from Sturken (2001, 34), who uses it to address how the event of the Japanese American internment "speaks its presence through its absent representation."
74. As M. T. Nguyen (2012, 17), emphasis added, notes, "The gift [of freedom] is among other things a gift of time: time for the subject of freedom to resemble or 'catch up to' the modern observer, to accomplish what can be anticipated in a preordained future, whether technological progress, productive capacity, or rational government. But the invitation to coevality *also imposes violence*—including a politics of comparison, homogenous time, and other commensurabilities—through the intervention (a war, or development) that rescues history for those peoples stalled or suspended in time."
75. Y. Espiritu (2006, 421). For refugees reinterpreted as "immigrants," see E. Espiritu (2018); Q. Le (2018); V. Nguyen (2012, 930).
76. Lipman (2012, 2) and Y. Espiritu (2014) have addressed the way that refugee resettlement did not unfold along linear/progressive trajectory but was more often guided by what Lipman identifies as a "politics of contingency."
77. Caruth (1996) addresses trauma as "unclaimed experience" that disrupts linear/progressive models of narrative and temporality. David Eng and David Kazanjian (2002) focus on "melancholia" as a way to navigate the wake of historical trauma in the present, particularly for populations whose trauma remains unrecognized. And Jinah Kim (2018) focuses on the ways that unredressed "grief" around the Asia-Pacific and Cold Wars has played an important role in shaping contemporary diasporic Asian subjectivities.
78. Hirsch (2008, 103).
79. A number of scholars working in Southeast Asian American studies have focused on this archive of "everyday life" and "memory work," including Bui (2018), Schlund-Vials (2012), and Tang (2015), as well as contributors to special editions of *Positions: East Asia Critique* on Southeast Asian American studies in 2012 and of *MELUS* on refugee cultures forty years after the war in 2015.
80. Here I follow the definition of debility in Puar (2017, 65) as a condition that is not aligned with "disability" but, rather, illustrates the conditions under which certain populations are rendered (more) "available for injury" than others, their bodies and communities shaped by "exploitative labor conditions, racist incarceration and policing practices, militarization, and other modes of community disenfranchisement."
81. lê (2003, 87).
82. Ibid., 4
83. Ibid.
84. The Kingdom of Hawai'i was illegally overthrown in 1893 by a coup aided by U.S. military forces and was later annexed by the United States—due, in no small part, to

Pearl Harbor, which provided a strategic military base in the central Pacific. U.S. military forces invaded Okinawa, itself a colony of Japan, during World War II and subsequently have maintained military bases on that territory. A large number of U.S. Marines were stationed in American Sāmoa (a U.S. territory) during World War II. Today, American Sāmoa has the highest rate of military enlistment in any U.S. state or territory.

85. lê (2003, 29).
86. Ibid.
87. Ibid.
88. While other critics (e.g., Gsoels-Lorensen [2006]; V. Nguyen [2006]) have addressed the ways that the circulation of the physical photograph itself serves to draw out transpacific connections and dynamics, my focus here is on how the *occasion*, or the taking/making/framing, of the photograph serves to unsettle assumptions around individual subjectivity.
89. In the novel's afterword, lê (2003, 160) writes that, although her given name at birth was Trang, she had an older sister named Thúy who—like the narrator's brother—died by drowning in a Malaysian refugee camp. When lê arrived in the United States, her father accidentally listed her name as Thúy, an error that her mother saw as "propitious" because, lê writes, "it allowed a part of my older sister to come to this country with us." She saw herself as occupying her sister's name like a "borrowed garment." Only when lê "[broke] the name down" and restyled it as lê thi diem thúy (all in lowercase) did she feel like she had "finally managed to . . . reclaim it as [her] own." I mention this story in this book's conclusion because it seems to emphasize the way that the novel as a whole similarly remakes and reworks—and thereby reclaims—lê's family trauma and history, again as a way to contribute to a more nuanced understanding of "refugee" experience.
90. lê (2003, 130).
91. Ibid., 157–158.
92. Ibid.
93. Huýnh (1998, vii).
94. lê (2003, 158).
95. For a reading of the ways that Asian Americans have been interpellated into these progressive narratives through the mode of "expectation," see Song (2013, 29–58). For an articulation of the ways that these progressive "expectations" have been both shaped and deformed by the demands of capitalism, see Ninh (2011).
96. Hau'ofa, "Our Sea of Islands" (1994, 67); Ingersoll (2016, 103); Ryan (2012).
97. While the work of comparison, as Allen (2012, xii) points out, can often problematically render an equivalence or "sameness" between the positions being compared, a shift in focus to working *across* ("trans-") rather than working *between* ("and") can seek to juxtapose experiences without flattening out or denying these sorts of major historical and positional differences—working *against* a comparativist logic of commensurabilty that, as M. T. Nguyen (2012, 17) points out, "also imposes violence."
98. For more on the logic of erasure/extinction and its historical deployment against and around Pacific populations, see Arvin (2019); Hall (2005); Hau'ofa, "Our Sea of Islands" (1994); Kauanui (2007); Trask (1993); Wendt (1976). For the binary logics of alienation/assimilation as they circulated through and beyond the Cold War, see Jodi Kim (2010); Klein (2003); Man (2018); Josephine Park (2016).
99. Q. Le (2018) and E. Espiritu (2018) address sites of refugee complicity (as well as possible points of refusal) in settler colonial projects in the United States and in Palestine, respectively. Rajaram (2003) has written about how Australia used political and economic

pressure, as well as its neocolonial status as regional hegemon, to use Nauru as a site to detain refugees in what came to be known as the "Pacific Solution."

100. Moreton-Robinson (2015, 21) expands on the ways that the "possessive logics" of the settler colonial nation-state operate to dispossess both Indigenous and racialized (and feminized) populations within their purview; she argues that by "selectively demonizing migrants, Indigenous people, and later, refugees, [Australian Prime Minister John] Howard effectively recuperated national identity and white possession" under his government in the late 1990s and early 2000s.

101. See, e.g., W. H., "Why Climate Migrants Do Not Have Refugee Status," *The Economist*, March 6, 2018, https://www.economist.com/the-economist-explains/2018/03/06/why-climate-migrants-do-not-have-refugee-status.

CHAPTER 3

1. Liu (2016, 352, 356).
2. Ibid., 362.
3. Hu-DeHart (1999, 9).
4. Ibid., 19.
5. Ibid. In addition, while Hu-DeHart's account focuses primarily on the ways that Chinese and Japanese Americans have been incorporated into the discourse of transpacific trade, this pattern has continued through later-arriving Asian American groups, including Vietnamese Americans: see Parsons and Vézina (2018).
6. Hu-DeHart (1999), Lye (2005), Kang (2012), and Day (2016) have analyzed how the figure of the "Asian" has come to be associated with the negative excesses of capitalism in the broader U.S. and global imagination. I address these arguments in greater detail later in this chapter.
7. Connery (1994) dates the emergence of "Pacific Rim" discourse to "the mid-1970s." While arguments have been made for considering the emergence of Pacific Rim discourse as early as 1972 (Nixon's trip to China) or 1973 (the Organization of Petroleum Exporting Countries [OPEC] oil crisis), for the sake of my argument I characterize it as beginning in 1975—the formal end of the Vietnam War—to mark the shift between direct military aggression to the more "abstract," yet still military-supported, violence of finance capital. I regard this period of "Pacific Rim" discourse as continuing through 1997–1999, when the "Asian" financial crisis required a significant reconsideration and revision of Pacific Rim discourse.
8. Ong (2006, 16).
9. Bahng (2017, 120).
10. Hardt and Negri (2000, xii), emphasis added.
11. Ibid.
12. Lee and LiPuma (2002, 19). On the way that refugee narratives challenge the foundational logics of nation-state formation, see also Chapter 2 in this volume.
13. Ibid., 24.
14. Ibid., 19.
15. Ibid., 26.
16. Ibid.
17. For more on the way that capitalist exchange occludes military force in the region, see DeLoughrey (2007); Dirlik (1998); T. Teaiwa (1994); Wilson (2000).
18. Bender and Lipman (2015, 15).
19. Lye (2005, 7).

20. Ibid., 9.
21. Day (2016, 15).
22. Ibid., 19.
23. Langley (1980) coins this term in his discussions of U.S. interventions in a different oceanic space—the Caribbean—during this time period.
24. Lowe (2015).
25. For more on popular/capitalist appropriations of Indigenous Pacific myths, art forms, and epistemologies, see Imada (2012); McDougall and Nordstrom (2014); Teves (2015). A number of substantive critiques of the film *Moana* and other mainstream Hollywood appropriations of Pacific cultural texts and practices have emerged in interviews, online, and on social media. They are currently archived in the Facebook group Mana Moana: We Are Moana, We Are Maui (facebook.com/manamoanawearemoanawearem aui), accessed May 2, 2019.
26. Hau'ofa, *Tales of the Tikongs* (1994, 83).
27. Ibid., 85.
28. Ibid., 92.
29. Ibid.
30. Ibid., 93.
31. Hau'ofa (2008, 17).
32. Ibid., 29.
33. Ibid., 30.
34. Ibid., 31.
35. Ibid., 39.
36. Ibid., 31.
37. See Broad (1988).
38. Ibid., 195.
39. Rodriguez (2010, x). For more on the ways that remittance labor was linked to neoliberal reform and debt restructuring, see ibid., 12–17.
40. In particular, Robyn Rodriguez cites a brochure advertising Filipino marine labor by describing *his* "affinity to the sea" that comes from "living in an archipelago of more than 7,100 islands with a vast coastline" and having ancestors who worked as marine labor in the Spanish Galleon trade and on U.S. trading ships. Rodriguez notes that "colonialism is represented . . . as having helped hone the skills of Filipino seafarers," even as it erases imperial violence to naturalize the image of Filipinos as experienced migrant laborers: ibid., 63.
41. Lye (2005, 9).
42. Ibid., 5.
43. T. Teaiwa, "For or Before an Asia Pacific Studies Agenda?" (2010, 119).
44. Lye (2005, 2015); Day (2016).
45. Day (2016).
46. Eng (2001, 61).
47. Li (1990, 490).
48. Lee (1995, 152).
49. For more detailed critiques of the ways that Asian American settlers have used "labor" as a vector to claim land, see Fujikane and Okamura (2008); Saranillio (2013, 2018); Trask (2000).
50. Kingston ([1980] 2011, 132–133).
51. Day (2016, 51).
52. Kingston ([1980] 2011, 144).

53. Ibid.
54. Cheung (1993, 119).
55. Marx (2004, 164, 186–187).
56. Kingston ([1980] 2011, 107).
57. Connery (1994, 40).
58. Kingston ([1980] 2011, 107).
59. Ibid., 118.
60. Yang (2010, 76).
61. Lee and LiPuma (2002, 200–203).
62. Between 1962 and 1994, a number of Pacific states—particularly in the southern and southwestern Pacific—gained formal political independence from Britain, Australia, New Zealand, Germany, and the United States, including Sāmoa, Nauru, Fiji, Papua New Guinea, the Solomon Islands, Tuvalu, Kiribati, Vanuatu, the Marshall Islands, the Federated States of Micronesia, the Cook Islands, Palau, and Niue.
63. World Bank, "Personal Remittances, Received (% of GDP), 1970–2017," accessed April 21, 2019, https://data.worldbank.org/indicator/BX.TRF.PWKR.DT.GD.ZS.
64. Chapman (1979, 112).
65. Hauʻofa, "Our Sea of Islands" (1994, 157).
66. Petersen (2000, 9–10).
67. ʻOkusitino Māhina (1993, 117) cites the "murder of the 15th Tuʻi Tonga, Takalua, around 1450 AD" as the beginning of this decline.
68. Salesa (2014) has discussed vā (also known as wa or vahaʻa) in the context of other localized Pacific Island cultural formations, particularly in Fiji and Sāmoa. Similarities in terms and conceptualization across these sites is likewise indicative of the ancestral connections among the island nations.
69. Thaman (2008, 464).
70. Kaʻili (2005, 89–92). See also Māhina (2010, 169–172).
71. Ibid., 93–94.
72. Hau'ofa, "Our Sea of Islands" (1994, 157).
73. See Besnier (2011); Small (1997); Thaman (2003).
74. The significance of Thaman's work has been addressed, analyzed, or highlighted in several studies of regional Pacific Islands literature, including Keown (2007); Marsh (1999); Subramani (1985); Vaʻai (1999).
75. Vaʻai (1999, 144) writes that as a young girl, Thaman was raised by her great-aunts, who instructed her in "proper Tongan etiquette" and "important women's activities like tapa-making and mat-weaving." Yet her mother's insistence on a Western education led to Thaman's eventual path as a scholar, poet, and academic.
76. Ibid., 149.
77. Marsh (1999, 341).
78. See Marsh (1999); Vaʻai (1999); B. Wood (1998).
79. Thaman (2003, 3).
80. Ibid.
81. Thaman (1974, 1).
82. In *Routes and Roots* (2007, 138), DeLoughrey points out the way that celebratory narratives of Indigenous migrations tend to cast these voyages as an "adventurous masculine endeavor" while women tend to be aligned with the fertile and welcoming new lands.
83. Harvey (2005, 1).
84. Hauʻofa, "Our Sea of Islands" (1994, 36).
85. Thaman (1974, 1).

86. Ibid.
87. This point is taken up in Besnier (2009); Gershon (2007); Hauʻofa "Our Sea of Islands" (1994); Kaʻili (2005); Small (1997).
88. Thaman (1974, 3).
89. See B. Wood (1998, 14–15).
90. Thaman (1981, 13).
91. B. Wood (1998, 15).
92. See Māhina (2008).
93. Thaman (1981, 13).
94. Ibid.
95. Ibid., 15.
96. Helu (1978, 24).
97. Thaman (1981, 16).
98. Hauʻofa, "Our Sea of Islands" (1994, 31).
99. Thaman (2003, 12).
100. Ibid., 7.
101. Fujikane (2012) contrasts this Indigenous "economy of abundance" to capitalist constructions of scarcity. See also the essays collected in Yamashiro and Goodyear-Kaʻōpua (2014).
102. Kingston, ([1980] 2011, 116).

CHAPTER 4

1. Teves (2015, 706).
2. The Indigenous people of Hawaiʻi have been referred to in most scholarship as "Hawaiians," "Native Hawaiians," "Kānaka ʻŌiwi," "Kānaka Hawaiʻi," and "Kānaka Maoli." In this chapter (and throughout), I primarily use the term "Kānaka Maoli" to refer to these communities and cultural practices; however, I occasionally use the term "Native" or "Native Hawaiian" as a descriptor to contrast with non-Native residents of Hawaiʻi. I also use the term "Hawaiian" (always in scare quotes) to denote the hegemonic *fictions* of Hawaiianness as an appropriable, exchangeable commodity.
3. See, e.g., Fujikane and Okamura (2008); Hall (2005); Trask (2000).
4. In this vein, Trask (2000, 3) points out how "the attainment of full American citizenship actually heightens prejudice against Natives. Because the ideology of the United States as a mosaic of races is reproduced in Hawaiʻi through the celebration of the fact that no single 'immigrant group' constitutes a numerical majority, the post-statehood euphoria stigmatizes Hawaiians as a failed indigenous people whose conditions, including out-migration, actually worsen after statehood."
5. Examples of this kind of reportage included articles in *Time* magazine (Newton-Small [2008]) and the *New York Times* (Falcone [2008]).
6. Newton-Small (2008).
7. Saranillio (2018, 133) notes that Hawaiʻi's formal entrance into statehood sought to demonstrate how the U.S. incorporation of Hawaiʻi's racial and cultural diversity illustrated "above all other American achievements . . . what only American democracy could accomplish." In this context, Hawaiʻi statehood—which further ignored and suppressed Kanaka Maoli claims for redress and sovereignty—was reframed as a celebration of liberal multiculturalism that also operated as an effective piece of Cold War propaganda.
8. George Rhodes (PA), "Hawaii Statehood," *Congressional Record* 311 (1959): 3920.
9. Byrd (2011, xiii).

10. For Hawai'i's multiculturalism reimagined as a Cold War strategy, see Klein (2003, chap. 6). For how "local" style gets deployed and remixed as an object of consumption, see Wilson (2000, preface).

11. H. Wood (1999, 50–51).

12. Sharma (2011, 46) writes about the complex contours of blackness in a local context, noting that "Blacks in Hawai'i are reversely racialized from their experiences on the mainland: rather than viewing Blacks as the primary native-born minority, islanders consider Blacks to be sojourners and cultural outsiders."

13. Obama (1995, 72–91).

14. Yamanaka (2009).

15. For more on the Massie Trial and its role in defining the local body, see Rosa (2000); Stannard (2005). For an analysis of the importance of organized labor in shaping modern local identity, see Takaki (1983).

16. Okamura (2008, 121).

17. Choy (2000, 110).

18. Trask (1999, 67) cites the Kalama Valley protest and the concomitant rise of Kōkua Hawaii as the foundation of the modern movement for Native Hawaiian cultural and political sovereignty.

19. Choy (2000, 110).

20. See Goodyear-Ka'ōpua et al. (2014).

21. This is one of the central themes, for example, of Ronald Takaki's *Pau Hana: Plantation Life and Labor in Hawai'i* (1983), as well as a recurring figure in Maxine Hong Kingston's "Great-Grandfather of the Sandalwood Mountains," in *China Men* ([1980] 2011), discussed in Chapter 3.

22. See, e.g., Ho'omanawanui (2008, 124); Kame'eleihiwa (1992, chap. 1); Trask (1993, esp. 37–38, 141).

23. I draw here on the interpretation in Moreton-Robinson (2015) of settler colonialism operating as the foundation of the concept of "white possession" by which the (usually) white, Western subject takes "possession" of Indigenous land and defends it against a differently racialized "foreign" threat, thus implicating the neoliberal capitalism built on this concept of possessive individualism in these colonial and racializing discourses.

24. Wilson (2000, viii).

25. Okamura (2008, 38).

26. Ibid., 40.

27. Ibid., 11.

28. Hall (2005, 407–408).

29. Kauanui (2007, 151), emphasis added.

30. Teves (2015, 705–706).

31. Kauanui (2007, 151).

32. See Hall (2015).

33. Pratt (1992, 59).

34. DeLoughrey (2009, 475–484).

35. Chow (2006).

36. Healani Sonoda-Pale, qtd. in Omerod (2018).

37. Johnson, qtd. in Okita (2012).

38. See Arvin (2019); Kauanui (2007); Okamura (2008).

39. Michener (1959, 891).

40. Sumida (1991, 84).

41. Kauanui (2007, 150).

42. hooks (1992, 25).
43. Ibid.
44. Tengan (2008, 8–13).
45. Pomerantz (2013).
46. Weaver (2017).
47. Hokowhitu (2008, 116).
48. Lin-Manuel Miranda, "You're Welcome," *Moana Soundtrack*, Walt Disney Records, Los Angeles, 2016.
49. Seth Gordon, dir., *Baywatch*, film, Paramount Pictures, Los Angeles, 2017.
50. Yamanaka (1993, 65, 69, 71).
51. Ibid., 73–74.
52. Ibid.
53. Ibid., 76.
54. R. Lee (2014, 2).
55. This controversy came to a head at the 1998 Association for Asian American Studies (AAAS) conference in Hawai'i, when an award given to *Blu's Hanging* was revoked due to objections by the membership. This controversy, and its implications for Asian American studies as a field, is notably outlined in Chiang (2009); Chuh (2003); Fujikane (2000); V. Nguyen (2002).
56. R. Lee (2014, 4).
57. For more on the masculinity and "masculine language" that shaped Asian American cultural politics in the 1970s and 1980s, see Cheung (1993, 7–9). For analyses of how melancholic desire connects Yamanaka's protagonists in *Blu's Hanging* (1997) and *Father of the Four Passages* (2001) to the settler colonial state, see Parikh (2002); Suzuki (2006, 2010).
58. Ngai (2005, 12), emphasis added.
59. Berlant (2011, 1).
60. See Fujikane (2000, 164); Suzuki (2006, 50).
61. See Suzuki (2010, 175–176).
62. James (1999).
63. Discussions of *Blu's Hanging* and its controversy appear in several field-framing monographs in Asian American literature, including Chiang (2009); Chuh (2003); V. Nguyen (2002); Tsou (2015).
64. McDougall (2008, 66).
65. Ibid.
66. hoʻomanawanui (2015, 247). For more on the deployment of *moʻokūʻauhau* as an aesthetic, historical, and political practice, see Wilson-Hokowhitu (2019). On *kaona* as a literary practice, see McDougall (2016). And for more on *wahi pana*, see Bacchilega (2007); hoʻomanawanui (2008).
67. See Wilson-Hokowhitu (2019).
68. McDougall (2016, 6).
69. See Chang (2016, 8).
70. McDougall (2008, 48).
71. Ibid.
72. Ibid., 49.
73. Finney (1994, 74–75).
74. Chang (2016, 256).
75. Diaz (2011, 21).
76. Beamer (2014, 2).

77. McDougall (2016, 52–53).
78. McDougall (2008, 3).
79. Ibid.
80. Ibid., 8.
81. These lines are a translation of lines taken from the third verse of "Kaulana Nā Pua" (Famous Are the Children), a song written by Mary Wright Prendergast in 1893 as a protest against the overthrow of Queen Lili'uokalani. The song is still performed today by artists in solidarity with the song's call for sovereignty. For more on nineteenth- and early twentieth-century refusals of U.S. annexation and statehood, see Saranillio (2018); Silva (2004).
82. Trask's body of work has consistently sought to decolonize not only the academy but also, first and foremost, Hawaiian land. In addition to articulating a clear and unapologetic outline for Hawaiian decolonization (1990, 1993, 2001), her scholarly work has taken a critical stance toward the "invention of culture" debates in anthropology (1991, 1993), as well as toward the assumptions underlying the practices of Western feminist scholarship (1984, 1992, 1993, 1996). Her work decrying the Asian settler state has also served as the impetus and inspiration for Asian settler colonial scholarship in Hawai'i (1984, 1993, 2000). Her poetic work (1999, 2002) likewise emphasizes these themes, particularly as it incorporates and hybridizes Kanaka Maoli aesthetic practices and Western lyric forms. For more analyses of Trask's literary work and aesthetic innovation, see ho'omanawanui (2014); McDougall (2016).
83. Warren (2015, 940).
84. For statistics on Native Hawaiian incarceration rates, see Kana'iaupuni et al. (2005, 80–87). For an analysis of how settler colonial structures in the majority-minority state of Hawai'i have served to "carry on the American legacy of incarceration along racial and class lines within the framework of local systems of power that subjugate Hawai'i's indigenous peoples," see Sonoda (2008, 103).
85. McDougall (2008, 22).
86. McDougall references this history in a number of other poems included in *The Salt-Wind* (2008), including "Tiny Rebellions," "Ku'ulei, 1960," and "Kalena, 1945."
87. Ibid., 23.
88. Ingersoll (2016, 6), emphasis added.
89. McDougall (2016, 5).
90. R. Lee (2014, 7).
91. Yamanaka (2009).
92. Fujikane (2016, 62); Saranillio (2014).

CHAPTER 5

1. Qtd. in Foord (1900, 578).
2. In his State of the Union address, Roosevelt noted, "We have acquired Hawaii, the Philippines, and lesser islands in the Pacific. . . . To a greater extent than seemed probable even a dozen years ago, we may look to an *American future* on the sea worthy of the traditions of our past": Roosevelt (1917, 7108), emphasis added. In a presidential debate with Walter Mondale, Ronald Reagan argued that the United States "has a great interest in the Pacific Basin. That is where I think the future of the world lies": see "The Candidates Debate" (1984). See also Clinton (2011).
3. Clinton (2011); Whitman (2004, 430).
4. Clinton (2011).

5. Bahng (2017, 2).
6. See Overbye (2015).
7. For a thorough exploration of the conflict between settler and Indigenous epistemologies, and the way that it becomes embedded in the political debates around science studies, see Salazar (2014).
8. See Johnson (2014); Stemwedel (2015).
9. Hobart (2019, 31) writes about the way that colonial "discourses of absence" have worked to "deanimat[e]" the space of Mauna Kea through the nineteenth and twentieth centuries, rendering the site into a "terra nullius," in contrast to Kanaka Maoli mo'olelo that narrate the Mauna as possessing animacy and agency.
10. See Goodyear-Ka'opua et al. (2014).
11. Mangauil (2015).
12. Wilson-Hokowhitu and Meyer (2019, 1-2).
13. ho'omanawanui (2019, 58-61).
14. Kealoha Pisciotta, qtd. in LaFrance (2015).
15. The concept of "homogeneous, empty time" and its centrality to progressive thought is introduced in Walter Benjamin's *Theses on the Philosophy of History* (2019, 205). This concept is taken up again by Benedict Anderson in *Imagined Communities* (1983) to explain the importance of this idea of progressive time to the formation of the modern nation-state.
16. L. T. Smith (1999, 56).
17. Rifkin (2017, 1, 14).
18. L. T. Smith (1999, 55).
19. Rifkin (2017, viii).
20. Morley and Robins (1995, 160), emphasis added.
21. Moreton-Robinson (2015, 138).
22. Moreton-Robinson and Jodi Byrd (2011) have noted the ways that this settler colonial discourse overlaps with extant processes of racialization in ways that create what Byrd has called a "cacophony" of competing claims that prevents the recognition of Indigenous sovereignties.
23. See Chun (2009); Jane Park (2010).
24. See, e.g., Barad (2007, 132-185).
25. For more on how dystopian futurities (particularly regarding disasters with global dimensions, such as climate change, resource scarcity, and overpopulation) have worked to shape political, economic, and military strategy in the present, see DeLoughrey (2009); Heise (2008, 82-102); Marzec (2015); Nixon (2011).
26. Allen (2012, 196).
27. In his chapter comparing the work of Sullivan and Native American poet Allison Hedge Coke (Cherokee/Huron/Creek), Allen (2012, 197) writes that both authors "actively demonstrate the efficacy of ancient, historical, and ongoing Indigenous technologies ... [by] literally embody[ing] aspects of these technologies in their contemporary poetic practice."
28. See ibid.; Prentice (2006); Riemenschneider (2000).
29. Sullivan (1999, 3).
30. Ibid., 4.
31. Ibid., 7.
32. Ibid.
33. Aroha Harris notes that the proposed "fiscal envelope," which sought to cap Māori claims under the Treaty of Waitangi at $1 billion, was developed without significant input from Māori *iwi* and was considered a unilateral move on the part of the government. The

proposal for the fiscal envelope was met with widespread protest that served to unify Māori organizations from around the country, and it was eventually dropped: Harris (2006, 124–138).

34. Sullivan (1999, 50).
35. Ibid.
36. Ibid.
37. Ibid., 59.
38. Edward Said's *Orientalism* (1978)—one of the foundational texts of postcolonial criticism—makes explicit this relationship between the collection of information and colonial projects.
39. Hayles (2008, xi).
40. Marvin (1987, 57).
41. Wilson (2001, 122–123).
42. "Loina (Guiding Principles)," *'Imiloa Hawaii,* http://www.imiloahawaii.org/104/mission-history.
43. Salazar (2014, 69).
44. For more on this appropriative dynamic in the context of the tourist and entertainment industries, see Diaz (2016); McDougall and Nordstrom (2015).
45. Perez (2008, 12).
46. U.S. Department of the Interior (1986, esp. secs. 221, 225, 312, 321, 323).
47. See Shigematsu and Camacho (2010).
48. Kihleng (2008, 8).
49. Ibid.
50. Ibid., 9.
51. Van Dijck (2013, 11–12).
52. Ibid.
53. See McChesney (2013).
54. See Burnett and Marshall (2001, 1–2).
55. *Downes v. Bidwell*, cited in Kaplan (2005, 841).
56. Kaplan (2005, 842).
57. Perez (2008, 8).
58. Ibid., 12
59. Ibid.
60. Hsu (2012, 302), emphasis added.
61. Several critics have explored Perez's critical/political poetics in *from unincorporated territory [hacha]* and *from unincorporated territory [saina]*, including Lai (2011), who focuses on the way that Perez's poetry invites us to engage in a reading practice that imagines the United States as a "discontiguous" empire. Hsu (2012), who reads the first two volumes of *from unincorporated territory* against Shawn Wong's *Homebase* to call for an Asian American studies that engages more directly and critically with the fact of U.S. empire abroad, and Woodward (2013), who reads *from unincorporated territory [hacha]* alongside Chris Perez Howard's *Mariquita: A Tragedy of Guam* to unpack dominant narratives of U.S. "liberation" and democratic exceptionalism.
62. Perez (2010, 14–15).
63. Perez (2014, 18).
64. Perez (2008, 12).
65. In *[saina]* (Perez [2010, 131–132]), repurposed texts are cited in the acknowledgments section. In *[guma']* (Perez [2014, 85–89]), they are cited in a section titled "*from sourcings.*"

66. Perez (2010, 131).
67. Hsu (2012, 298).
68. Perez (2008, 83). For close readings and a reprint of this poem, see Lai (2011, 13–14); Woodward (2013, 87–88).
69. For example, the first link from the poem—http://petitiononline.com/haleta/petition.html—has since been taken down, as the proposed realignment has continued to move forward and the hosting site itself has closed down due to "continued cost and maintenance" and its supersession by the petition site Change.org (see http://petitiononline.com).
70. Perez (2010, 132).
71. Perez (2014, 45).
72. Ibid., 64.
73. Perez (2017, 9). The cited text is drawn from Starosielski (2011, 19).
74. Perez (2014, 25).
75. Ibid., 66.
76. Day (2016, 8).
77. Ibid., 193.
78. Ibid., 8.
79. Connery (1994, 40).
80. Chun (2008, 24), emphasis added.
81. Ibid., 2.
82. Ozeki (2013, 13–14).
83. Chun (2016, 78).
84. Ozeki (2013, 114).
85. Ibid., 88.
86. Ibid., 35.
87. Ibid., 3.
88. Ibid., 383.
89. Ibid.
90. Ibid.
91. Ibid., 392.
92. Ibid., 141–142.
93. For examples of how Asian Americanist criticism has begun to participate in this oceanic "turn," see Chen (2012, 223–238); Huang (2017).
94. An approach to Indigenous cultural sovereignty that appears to be more accommodating to current government structures can be seen, for example, in support for the "Akaka Bill," a piece of federal legislation put forth by former Hawai'i State Senator Daniel Akaka that would create federal recognition for an independent Kanaka Maoli government (similar to what is currently offered to Native Americans and Alaska Natives). However, opponents of the legislation point to how the bill's provisions will block ongoing efforts to declare full political sovereignty or secession. These demands apply particularly to Indigenous Pacific groups who live in states or territories currently occupied or settled by the United States (Hawai'i, Guam) and France (French Polynesia).

Aikau (2015, 659) makes a call to move beyond concepts of "state governmentality" altogether and focus on building futures that "do not require the nation-state as the only legitimate and intelligible governing entity for the enactment of a peoples' sovereignty." Such a claim does not *preclude* political sovereignty but rather emphasizes the fact that "sovereignty" is not only a political state but a principled, ongoing practice opposed to "global capital and military oppression."

95. As Kameʻeleihiwa (1992, 23) observes, "It is interesting to note that in Hawaiian, the past is referred to as Ka wā mamua, or 'the time in front or before.' Whereas the future, when thought of at all, is Ka wā mahope, or 'the time which comes after or behind.' It is as if the Hawaiian stands firmly in the present, with his back to the future, and his eyes fixed upon the past, seeking historical answers for present-day dilemmas. Such an orientation is to the Hawaiian an eminently practical one, for the future is always unknown, whereas the past is rich in glory and knowledge."

96. Kuwada (2015).

97. See Case (2019).

CONCLUSION

1. Pukui et al. (1976, 11).

2. "Pele Finds a Home" (traditional), translated lyrics, Huapala: Hawaiian Music and Hula Archives, 1997, https://www.huapala.org/Chants/Pele_Finds_Home.html.

3. This reflection on the literal paving over of the land vividly brings home the observation by Goodyear-Kaʻōpua (2017, 187) about the how Indigenous Pacific and settler communities' relations "with lands and with each other are structured by dominant property regimes that cannot deal with the complexity of our layered and interconnected yet differential interests in the lands on which we reside." Certainly, these were the regimes that materially shaped my earliest perceptions of what it meant to live in/on Hawaiʻi.

4. Diaz (2012, 327) makes the case that smells can operate as an unofficial archive in sites that may lack official ones, in the sense that smell is often "associated with things that are meaningful and people who matter with respect to the (ongoing) past and who, for whatever reasons, are not captured or recorded in that supposedly more permanent record called written documents and the visual conventions that underwrite their various claims to authority."

5. See, e.g., Nguyen and Hoskins (2014, 3), who observe that the appropriation of the term "transpacific" by state and capitalist interest "lends urgency to the work of theorizing the transpacific." See also the call by Yoneyama (2017, 472) for a "decolonial genealogy of the transpacific" that attends to and accounts for the militarization and settler colonial history of the region.

6. Shigematsu and Camacho (2010, xv); Yoneyama (2017, 472).

7. Writing about environmental justice movements, Sze (2020, 11), emphasis added, notes that such activism is "*interconnected* . . . focused on intersectionality and power and organized around social and racial justice, whereas polluters and government agencies argue for separation (for example, health as distinct from environmental conditions or housing as unrelated to poverty). In contrast, environmental justice advocates argue precisely for these linkages and commonsense and based on lived historical experience."

8. Robinson (2020) addresses the ways that settler discourses play in the production of apathy around large-scale climate problems.

9. See, e.g., Fujikane (2016); Goodyear-Kaʻōpua (2013, 127–166); Kawelo (2014).

WORKS CITED

Agamben, Giorgio. "We Refugees." *Symposium* 49, no. 2 (Summer 1995): 114–119.
———. *Homo Sacer: Sovereign Power and Bare Life*, trans. Daniel Heller-Roazen. Palo Alto, CA: Stanford University Press, 1998.
Aikau, Hōkūlani. "Following the Alaloa Kīpapa of Our Ancestors: A Trans-Indigenous Futurity without the State (United States or Otherwise)." *American Quarterly* 67, no. 3 (2015): 653–661.
Akin, David. *Colonialism: Maasina Rule, and the Origins of Malaitan Kastom*. Honolulu: University of Hawai'i Press, 2013.
Alaimo, Stacey. "Dispersing Disaster: The Deepwater Horizon, Ocean Conservation, and the Immateriality of Aliens." In *American Environments: Climate-Cultures-Catastrophe*, ed. Christof Mauch and Sylvia Mayer, 177–193. Heidelberg: Universitätsverlag Winter, 2012.
Allen, Chadwick. *Blood Narrative: Indigenous Identity in American Indian and Maori Literary and Activist Texts*. Durham, NC: Duke University Press, 2002.
———. *Trans-Indigenous: Methodologies for Global Native Literary Studies*. Minneapolis: University of Minnesota Press, 2012.
Anand, R. P. *Origin and Development of the Law of the Sea: History of International Law Revisited*. Boston: Martinus Nijhoff, 1983.
Anderson, Benedict. *Imagined Communities: Reflections on the Origin and Spread of Nationalism*. New York: Verso, 1983.
Appadurai, Arjun. "Disjuncture and Difference in the Global Cultural Economy." In *Modernity at Large: Cultural Dimensions of Globalization*, by Arjun Appadurai, 27–47. Minneapolis: University of Minnesota Press, 1996.
Arista, Noelani. "Navigating Uncharted Oceans of Meaning: Kaona as Historical and Interpretive Narrative." *PMLA* 125, no. 3 (May 2010): 663–669.

Arvin, Maile. *Possessing Polynesians: The Science of Settler Colonial Whiteness in Hawai'i and Oceania*. Durham, NC: Duke University Press, 2019.
Atomic Energy Commission. "Minutes of the Advisory Committee on Biology and Medicine," January 13–14, 1956. AEC, New York.
Awatere, Donna. *Maori Sovereignty*. Auckland, New Zealand: Broadsheet, 1984.
Bacchilega, Cristina. *Legendary Hawai'i and the Politics of Place: Tradition, Translation, and Tourism*. Philadelphia: University of Pennsylvania Press, 2007.
Bahng, Aimee. *Migrant Futures: Decolonizing Speculation in Financial Times*. Durham, NC: Duke University Press, 2017.
Bambridge, Tamatoa, and Stéphanie Leyronas. "The Polynesian Rahui and Global Issues of Climate." In *Tidalectics: Imagining an Oceanic Worldview through Art and Science*, ed. Stefanie Hessler, 133–142. Cambridge, MA: MIT Press, 2018.
Banivanua Mar, Tracey. *Decolonisation and the Pacific: Indigenous Globalization and the Ends of Empire*. New York: Cambridge University Press, 2016.
Barad, Karen. *Meeting the Universe Halfway: Quantum Physics and the Entanglement of Matter and Meaning*. Durham, NC: Duke University Press, 2007.
———. "'Matter Feels, Converses, Suffers, Desires, Yearns, and Remembers': An Interview with Karen Barad." In *New Materialism: Interviews and Cartographies*, ed. Rick Dolphijn and Iris Van Der Tuin, 48–70. Ann Arbor, MI: Open Humanities, 2009.
Bargh, Maria. "Changing the Game Plan: The Foreshore and Seabed Act and Constitutional Change." *Kōtuitui* 1, no. 1 (2006): 13–24.
Bates, Diane C. "Environmental Refugees? Classifying Human Migrations Caused by Environmental Change." *Population and Environment* 23, no. 5 (2002): 465–477.
Beamer, Kamanamaikalani. *No mākoou ka mana: Liberating the Nation*. Honolulu: Kamehameha, 2014.
Bender, Daniel E., and Jana K. Lipman, eds. *Making the Empire Work: Labor and United States Imperialism*. New York: New York University Press, 2015.
Benjamin, Walter. *Illuminations: Essays and Reflections*. New York: Mariner, 2019.
Berlant, Lauren. *Cruel Optimism*. Durham, NC: Duke University Press, 2011.
Besnier, Niko. "Emergence of Middle Classes in Tonga." *Contemporary Pacific* 21, no. 2 (2009): 215–262.
———. *On the Edge of the Global: Modern Anxieties in a Pacific Island Nation*. Palo Alto, CA: Stanford University Press, 2011.
Bevacqua, Michael Lujan. "The Exceptional Life and Death of a Chamorro Soldier: Tracing the Militarization of Desire in Guam, USA." In *Militarized Currents*, ed. Setsu Shigematsu and Keith Camacho, 33–61. Minneapolis: University of Minnesota Press, 2010.
Blair, Chad. "An Untold Story of American Immigration." *Honolulu Civil Beat*, October 14, 2015. Accessed July 20, 2020. https://www.civilbeat.org/2015/10/an-untold-story-of-american-immigration.
Blum, Hester. "The Prospect of Oceanic Studies." *PMLA* 125, no. 3 (2010): 670–677.
———. "Introduction: Oceanic Studies." *Atlantic Studies* 10, no. 2 (2013): 151–155.
Borchers, Callum, and Amber Phillips. "Transcript: President Trump's Remarks on Leaving the Paris Climate Deal, Annotated." *Washington Post*, June 1, 2017. Accessed February 13, 2019. https://www.washingtonpost.com/news/the-fix/wp/2017/06/01/transcript-president-trumps-remarks-on-leaving-the-paris-climate-deal-annotated/?utm_term=.e34c80c6eef1.
Braudel, Fernand. *The Mediterranean and the Mediterranean World in the Age of Philip II*, trans. Siân Reynolds. New York: Harper and Row, 1972.

Broad, Robin. *Unequal Alliance: The World Bank, the International Monetary Fund, and the Philippines.* Berkeley: University of California Press, 1988.
Bui, Long. *Returns of War: South Vietnam and the Price of Refugee Memory.* New York: New York University Press, 2018.
Burnett, Christina Duffy, and Burke Marshall, eds. *Foreign in a Domestic Sense: Puerto Rico, American Expansion, and the Constitution.* Durham, NC: Duke University Press, 2001.
Buzan, Barry, Ole Waever, and Jaap de Wilde. *Security: A New Framework for Analysis.* Boulder, CO: Lynne Reiner, 1998.
Byrd, Jodi A. *The Transit of Empire: Indigenous Critiques of Colonialism.* Minneapolis: University of Minnesota Press, 2011.
Camacho, Keith. *Cultures of Commemoration: The Politics of War, Memory and History in the Marianas.* Honolulu: University of Hawai'i Press, 2011.
"The Candidates Debate: Transcript of the Reagan-Mondale Debate on Foreign Policy." *New York Times*, October 22, 1984. Accessed April 29, 2019. https://www.nytimes.com/1984/10/22/us/the-candidates-debate-transcript-of-the-reagan-mondale-debate-on-foreign-policy.html.
Caruth, Cathy. *Unclaimed Experience: Trauma, Narrative, and History.* Baltimore: Johns Hopkins University Press, 1996.
Case, Pua. "Kūkulu: Foundations for Inclusive Lāhui (Nation)-Building at Mauna Kea." Opening plenary, American Studies Association, Honolulu, November 7, 2019.
Chakrabarty, Dipesh. "The Climate of History: Four Theses." *Critical Inquiry* 35, no. 2 (Winter 2009): 197–222.
Chang, David A. *The World and All the Things upon It: Native Hawaiian Geographies of Exploration.* Minneapolis: University of Minnesota Press, 2016.
Chapman, Murray. "The Cross-Cultural Study of Circulation." *Current Anthropology* 20, no. 1 (March 1979): 111–114.
Chen, Mel. *Animacies: Biopolitics, Racial Mattering, and Queer Affect.* Durham, NC: Duke University Press, 2012.
Chen, Tina. "(The) Transpacific Turns." *Oxford Research Encyclopedia of Literature*, January 30, 2020. https://doi.org/10.1093/acrefore/9780190201098.013.782.
Cheng, Anne. *Ornamentalism.* New York: Oxford University Press, 2018.
Cheung, King-Kok. *Articulate Silences: Hisaye Yamamoto, Maxine Hong Kingston, Joy Kogawa.* Ithaca, NY: Cornell University Press, 1993.
Chiang, Mark. *The Cultural Capital of Asian American Studies: Autonomy and Representation in the University.* New York: New York University Press, 2009.
Chow, Rey. *The Age of the World Target: Self-Referentiality in War, Theory, and Comparative Work.* Durham, NC: Duke University Press, 2006.
Choy, Peggy Myo-Young. "Return the Islands Back to the People: A Legacy of Struggle and Resistance in Ka Pae'aina." In *Legacy to Liberation: Politics and Culture of Revolutionary Asian Pacific America*, ed. Fred Ho and Carolyn Antonio, 99–133. San Francisco: AK Press, 2000.
Chuh, Kandice. *Imagine Otherwise: On Asian Americanist Critique.* Durham, NC: Duke University Press, 2003.
———. *The Difference Aesthetics Makes: On the Humanities 'After Man.'* Durham, NC: Duke University Press, 2019.
Chun, Wendy Kui Hyong. *Control and Freedom: Power and Paranoia in the Age of Fiber Optics.* Cambridge, MA: MIT Press, 2008.
———. "Race and/as Technology, or How to Do Things to Race." *Camera Obscura* 24, no. 1 (2009): 6–35.

———. *Updating to Remain the Same: Habitual New Media*. Cambridge, MA: MIT Press, 2016.

Clinton, Hillary. "America's Pacific Century." *Foreign Policy*, October 11, 2011. Accessed April 29, 2019. https://foreignpolicy.com/2011/10/11/americas-pacific-century.

Connery, Chris. "Pacific Rim Discourse: The U.S. Global Imaginary in the Late Cold War Years." *boundary 2* 21, no. 1 (1994): 30–56.

Cox, John, Glen Finau, Romitesh Kant, Jope Tarai, and Jason Titifanue. "Disaster, Divine Judgment, and Original Sin: Christian Interpretations of Tropical Cyclone Winston and Climate Change in Fiji." *Contemporary Pacific* 30, no. 2 (2018): 380–410.

Crocombe, R. G. *The Pacific Way: An Emerging Identity*. Suva, Fiji: Lotu Pasifika, 1976.

Cruz, Denise. *Transpacific Femininities: The Making of the Modern Filipina*. Durham, NC: Duke University Press, 2012.

Davis, Heather, and Zoe Todd. "On the Importance of a Date, or Decolonizing the Anthropocene." *ACME* 16 no. 4 (2017): 761–780.

Davis, Sasha. *The Empire's Edge: Militarization, Resistance, and Transcending Hegemony in the Pacific*. Athens: University of Georgia Press, 2015.

Day, Iyko. *Alien Capital: Asian Racialization and the Logic of Settler Colonial Capitalism*. Durham, NC: Duke University Press, 2016.

de Agueda Corneloup, Inés, and Arthur Mol. "Small Island Developing States and International Climate Change Negotiations: The Power of Moral 'Leadership.'" *International Environmental Agreements: Politics, Law, and Economics* 14, no. 3 (2014): 281–297.

DeLoughrey, Elizabeth. *Routes and Roots: Navigating Caribbean and Pacific Island Literatures*. Honolulu: University of Hawai'i Press, 2007.

———. "Radiation Ecologies and the Wars of Light." *Modern Fiction Studies* 53, no. 3 (Fall 2009): 468–495.

———. "The Myth of Isolates: Ecosystem Ecologies in the Pacific." *Cultural Geographies* 20, no. 2 (2012): 167–184.

———. *Allegories of the Anthropocene*. Durham, NC: Duke University Press, 2019.

Diaz, Vicente M. "Deliberating 'Liberation Day': Identity, History, Memory, and War in Guam." In *Perilous Memories: The Asia-Pacific War(s)*, ed. Takashi Fujitani, Geoffrey M. White, and Lisa Yoneyama, 155–180. Durham, NC: Duke University Press, 2001.

———. "To 'P' or not to 'P'? Marking the Territory between Pacific Islander and Asian American Studies." *Journal of Asian American Studies* 7, no. 3 (2004): 183–208.

———. "Voyaging for Anti-colonial Recovery: Austronesian Seafaring, Archipelagic Rethinking, and the Re-mapping of Indigeneity." *Pacific Asia Inquiry* 2, no. 1 (2011): 21–32.

———. "Sniffing Oceania's Behind." *Contemporary Pacific* 24, no. 2 (2012): 323–344.

———. "Don't Swallow (or Be Swallowed by) Disney's 'Culturally Authenticated' Moana." *Indian Country Today*, November 13, 2016. Accessed May 24, 2019. https://newsmaven.io/indiancountrytoday/archive/don-t-swallow-or-be-swallowed-by-disney-s-culturally-authenticated-moana-9NFXz7ZqJEa9h-I3120lrQ.

Diaz, Vicente M., and J. Kēhaulani Kauanui. "Native Pacific Cultural Studies on the Edge." *Contemporary Pacific* 13, no. 2 (2001): 315–342.

Dirlik, Arif. *What Is in a Rim? Critical Perspectives on the Pacific Region Idea*. Lanham, MD: Rowman and Littlefield, 1998.

El-Hinnawi, Essam. *Environmental Refugees*. Nairobi, Kenya: United Nations Environmental Program, 1985.

Eng, David. *Racial Castration: Managing Masculinity in Asian America*. Durham, NC: Duke University Press, 2001.

Eng, David, and David Kazanjian. *Loss: The Politics of Mourning*. Berkeley: University of California Press, 2002.
Espiritu, Evyn Lê. "Vexed Solidarities: Vietnamese Israelis and the Question of Palestine." *LIT: Literature Interpretation Theory* 29, no. 1 (2018): 8–28.
Espiritu, Yến Lê. "The 'We-Win-Even-When-We-Lose' Syndrome: U.S. Press Coverage of the Twenty-Fifth Anniversary of the 'Fall of Saigon.'" *American Quarterly* 58, no. 2 (June 2006): 329–352.
———. *Body Counts: The Vietnam War and Militarized Refugees*. Berkeley: University of California Press, 2014.
———. "Critical Refugee Studies and Native Pacific Studies: A Transpacific Critique." *American Quarterly* 69, no. 3 (2017): 483–490.
Espiritu, Yến Lê, and Lan Duong. "Feminist Refugee Epistemology: Reading Displacement in Vietnamese and Syrian Refugee Art." *Signs* 43, no. 3 (2018): 587–615.
Espiritu, Yến Lê, Lisa Lowe, and Lisa Yoneyama. "Transpacific Entanglements." In *Flashpoints for Asian American Studies*, ed. Cathy Schlund-Vials, 175–189. New York: Fordham University Press, 2017.
Falcone, Michael. "Obama: At Home in the Islands." *New York Times*, August 10, 2008. Accessed June 14, 2019. https://thecaucus.blogs.nytimes.com/2008/08/10/obama-at-home-in-the-islands.
Farbotko, Carol. "Wishful Sinking: Disappearing Islands, Climate Refugees and Cosmopolitan Experimentation." *Asia Pacific Viewpoint* 51, no. 1 (2010): 47–60.
Farbotko, Carol, and Heather Lazrus. "The First Climate Refugees? Contesting Global Narratives of Climate Change in Tuvalu." *Global Environmental Change* 22, no. 2 (2012): 382–390.
Finney, Ben. *Voyage of Rediscovery: A Cultural Odyssey through Polynesia*. Berkeley: University of California Press, 1994.
Foord, John. "The Race for the Chinese Market." *Frank Leslie's Popular Monthly*, vol. 50, 1900, 578–582.
Foreshore and Seabed Act 2004. Public Act 93, November 24, 2004. Accessed May 24, 2019. http://www.legislation.govt.nz/act/public/2004/0093/latest/DLM319839.html.
Fujikane, Candace. "Sweeping Racism under the Rug of 'Censorship': The Controversy over Blu's Hanging." *Amerasia Journal* 26, no. 2 (2000): 158–194.
———. "Asian American Critique and Moana Nui 2011: Securing a Future beyond Empires, Militarized Capitalism, and APEC." *Inter-Asia Cultural Studies* 13, no. 2 (2012): 1–22.
———. "Mapping Wonder in the Māui Moʻolelo on the Moʻoʻāina: Growing Aloha 'Āina through Indigenous and Settler Affinity Activism." *Marvels and Tales* 30, no. 1 (2016): 45–69.
Fujikane, Candace, and Jonathan Okamura, eds. *Asian Settler Colonialism: From Local Governance to the Habits of Everyday Life*. Honolulu: University of Hawaiʻi Press, 2008.
Fujitani, Takashi, Geoffrey M. White, and Lisa Yoneyama, eds. *Perilous Memories: The Asia-Pacific War(s)*. Durham, NC: Duke University Press, 2001.
George, James. *Ocean Roads*. Wellington, New Zealand: Huia, 2006.
Gershon, Ilana. "Viewing Diasporas from the Pacific: What Pacific Ethnographies Offer Pacific Diaspora Studies." *Contemporary Pacific* 19, no. 2 (2007): 474–502.
Gilroy, Paul. *The Black Atlantic: Modernity and Double Consciousness*. London: Verso, 1993.
Gonzalez, Vernadette. *Securing Paradise: Tourism and Militarism in Hawaiʻi and the Philippines*. Durham, NC: Duke University Press, 2013.

Goodyear-Kaʻōpua, Noelani. *The Seeds We Planted: Portraits of a Native Hawaiian Charter School*. Minneapolis: University of Minnesota Press, 2013.
———. "Protectors of the Future, not Protestors of the Past: Indigenous Pacific Activism and Mauna a Wākea." *South Atlantic Quarterly* 116, no. 1 (January 2017): 184–194.
Goodyear-Kaʻōpua, Noelani, Ikaika Hussey, and Erin Kahunawaikaʻala Wright, eds. *A Nation Rising: Hawaiian Movements for Life, Land, and Sovereignty*. Durham, NC: Duke University Press, 2014.
Grotius, Hugo. *The Freedom of the Seas, or the Right Which Belongs to the Dutch to Take Part in the East Indian Trade*, trans. Ralph Van Deman Magoffin. New York: Oxford University Press, 1916.
Gsoels-Lorensen, Jutta. "lê thi diễm thúy's *The Gangster We Are All Looking For*: The Ekphrastic Emigration of a Photograph." *Critique: Studies in Contemporary Fiction* 48, no. 1 (2006): 3–18.
Hall, Lisa Kahaleole. "'Hawaiian at Heart' and Other Fictions." *Contemporary Pacific* 17, no. 2 (2005): 404–413.
———. "Which of These Things Is not like the Other: Hawaiians and Other Pacific Islanders Are not Asian American, and All Pacific Islanders Are not Hawaiian." *American Quarterly* 67, no. 3 (2015): 727–747.
Hardt, Joseph, and Antonio Negri. *Empire*. Cambridge, MA: Harvard University Press, 2000.
Harris, Aroha. *Hīkoi: Forty Years of Māori Protest*. Honolulu: University of Hawaiʻi Press, 2006.
Hartmann, Betsy. "Rethinking Climate Refugees and Climate Conflict: Rhetoric, Reality, and the Politics of Policy Discourse." *Journal of International Development* 22 (2010): 233–246.
Harvey, David. *A Brief History of Neoliberalism*. New York: Oxford University Press, 2005.
Hauʻofa, Epeli. "Our Sea of Islands." *Contemporary Pacific* 6, no. 1 (Spring 1994): 148–161.
———. *Tales of the Tikongs*. Honolulu: University of Hawaiʻi Press, 1994.
———. "The Ocean in Us." *Contemporary Pacific* 10, no. 2 (Fall 1998): 392–410.
———. *We Are the Ocean: Selected Works*. Honolulu: University of Hawaiʻi Press, 2008.
Hayes, John P. *James Michener: A Biography*. Indianapolis: Bobbs-Merrill, 1984.
Hayles, N. Katherine. *How We Became Posthuman: Virtual Bodies in Cybernetics, Literature, and Informatics*. Chicago: University of Chicago Press, 2008.
Helu, Futa. "Tongan Poetry I." *Faikava: A Tongan Literary Journal* 1 (1978): 21–25.
Heise, Ursula. *Sense of Place and Sense of Planet: The Environmental Imagination of the Global*. New York: Oxford University Press, 2008.
Helmreich, Stefan. *Alien Ocean: Anthropological Voyages in Microbial Seas*. Berkeley: University of California Press, 2009.
Hereniko, Vilsoni. *Woven Gods: Female Clowns and Power in Rotuma*. Honolulu: University of Hawaiʻi Press, 1995.
Hermann, Elfriede, and Wolfgang Kempf. "Climate Change and the Imagining of Migration: Emerging Discourses on Kiribati's Land Purchase in Fiji." *Contemporary Pacific* 29, no. 2 (2017): 231–263.
Hirsch, Marianne. "The Generation of Postmemory." *Poetics Today* 29, no. 1 (Spring 2008): 103–128.
Hobart, Hiʻilei Julia. "At Home on the Mauna: Ecological Violence and Fantasies of Terra Nullius on Maunakea's Summit." *Native American and Indigenous Studies* 6, no. 2 (Fall 2019): 30–50.

Hofschneider, Anita. "#BeingMicronesian in Hawai'i Means Lots of Online Hate." *Honolulu Civil Beat*, September 19, 2018. Accessed May 24, 2019. https://www.civilbeat.org/2018/09/beingmicronesian-in-hawaii-means-lots-of-online-hate.
Hokowhitu, Brendan. "'Physical Beings': Stereotypes, Sport and the 'Physical Education' of New Zealand Māori." *Culture, Sport, Society* 6, nos. 2–3 (2003): 192–218.
———. "Tackling Maori Masculinity: A Colonial Genealogy of Savagery and Sport." *Contemporary Pacific* 16, no. 2 (2004): 259–284.
———. "The Death of Koro Paka: 'Traditional' Māori Patriarchy." *Contemporary Pacific* 20, no. 1 (2008): 115–141.
Hong, Grace Kyungwon, and Roderick Ferguson. *Strange Affinities: The Gender and Sexual Politics of Comparative Racialization*. Durham, NC: Duke University Press, 2011.
hooks, bell. *Black Looks: Race and Representation*. Boston: South End, 1992.
Ho'omanawanui, Ku'ualoha. "'This Land Is Your Land, This Land Was My Land': Kanaka Maoli versus Settler Representations of 'Āina in Contemporary Literature of Hawai'i." In *Asian Settler Colonialism: From Local Governance to the Habits of Everyday Life in Hawai'i*, ed. Candace Fujikane and Jonathan Okamura, 116–154. Honolulu: University of Hawai'i Press, 2008.
———. *Voices of Fire: Reweaving the Literary Lei of Pele and Hi'iaka*. Minneapolis: University of Minnesota Press, 2014.
———. "Ka Li'u o ka Pa'akai (Well Seasoned with Salt): Recognizing Literary Devices, Rhetorical Strategies, and Aesthetics in Kanaka Maoli Literature." In *Huihui: Navigating Art and Literature in the Pacific*, ed. Jeffrey Carroll, Brandy Nālani McDougall, and Georgeanne Nordstrom, 247–265. Honolulu: University of Hawai'i Press, 2015.
———. "E Ho'i ka Piko (Returning to the Center): Theorizing Mo'okū'auhau as Methodology in an Indigenous Context." In *The Past before Us: Mo'okū'auhau as Methodology*, ed. Nālani Wilson-Hokowhitu, 50–68. Honolulu: University of Hawai'i Press, 2019.
Hsu, Hsuan L. "Guåhan (Guam), Literary Emergence, and the American Pacific in Homebase and from Unincorporated Territory." *American Literary History* 24, no. 2 (2012): 281–307.
Huang, Michelle. "Ecologies of Entanglement in the Great Pacific Garbage Patch." *Journal of Asian American Studies* 20, no. 1 (2017): 95–117.
Huang, Yunte. *Transpacific Imaginations: History, Literature, Counterpoetics*. Cambridge, MA: Harvard University Press, 2008.
Hu-DeHart, Evelyn. "Introduction: Asian American Formations in the Age of Globalization." In *Across the Pacific: Asian Americans and Globalization*, by Evelyn Hu-DeHart, 1–28. Philadelphia: Temple University Press, 1999.
Huỳnh Sang Thông. "Live by Water, Die for Water." In *Watermark: Vietnamese American Poetry and Prose*, ed. Barbara Tran, Monique T. D. Truong, and Luu Truong Khoi, vi–vii. New York: Asian American Writers' Workshop, 1998.
Igler, David. *The Great Ocean: Pacific Worlds from Captain Cook to the Gold Rush*. New York: Oxford University Press, 2013.
Imada, Adria. *Aloha America: Hula Circuits through U.S. Empire*. Durham, NC: Duke University Press, 2012.
Ingersoll, Karin Amimoto. *Waves of Knowing: A Seascape Epistemology*. Durham, NC: Duke University Press, 2016.
Intergovernmental Panel on Climate Change. "Summary for Policymakers." In *Global Warming of 1.5°C: An IPCC Special Report on the Impacts of Global Warming of 1.5°C above Pre-industrial Levels and Related Global Greenhouse Gas Emission Pathways,*

in the Context of Strengthening the Global Response to the Threat of Climate Change, Sustainable Development, and Efforts to Eradicate Poverty, ed. V. Masson-Delmotte, P. Zhai, H.-O. Pörtner, D. Roberts, J. Skea, P. R. Shukla, A. Pirani, W. Moufouma-Okia, C. Péan, R. Pidcock, S. Connors, J. B. R. Matthews, Y. Chen, X. Zhou, M. I. Gomis, E. Lonnoy, T. Maycock, M. Tignor, and T. Waterfield, n.p., October 8, 2018. Accessed July 20, 2020. https://www.ipcc.ch/sr15/chapter/spm.

Jackson, Shona. *Creole Indigeneity: Between Myth and Nation*. Minneapolis: University of Minnesota Press, 2012.

Jaeger, Carlo, and Julia Jaeger. "Three Views of Two Degrees." *Regional Environmental Change* 11, no. 1 (2011): 15–26.

James, Jamie. "This Hawaii Is not for Tourists." *The Atlantic*, vol. 283, no. 2, February 1999, 90–94.

Jetñil-Kijiner, Kathy. "'Butterfly Thief' and Complex Narratives of Disappearing Islands," April 30, 2017. Accessed January 16, 2019. https://www.kathyjetnilkijiner.com/butterfly-thief-and-complex-narratives-of-disappearing-islands.

———. *Iep Jāltok: Poems from a Marshallese Daughter*. Tucson: University of Arizona Press, 2017.

Johnson, George. "Seeking Stars, Finding Creationism." *New York Times*, October 20, 2014. Accessed July 18, 2020. https://www.nytimes.com/2014/10/21/science/seeking-stars-finding-creationism.html.

Kaeppler, Adrienne. "Poetics and Politics of Tongan Laments and Eulogies." *American Ethnologist* 20, no. 3 (August 1993): 474–501.

Kaʻili, Tēvita O. "Tauhi vā: Nurturing Tongan Sociospatial Ties in Maui and Beyond." *Contemporary Pacific* 17, no. 1 (2005): 83–114.

Kameʻeleihiwa, Lilikala. *Native Land and Foreign Desires: Pehea Lā E Pono Ai?* Honolulu: Bishop Museum, 1992.

Kanaʻiaupuni, S. K., Nolan Malone, and Koren Ishibashi. *Ka Huakaʻi: Native Hawaiian Educational Assessment*. Honolulu: Pauahi, 2005.

Kang, Laura Hyun Yi. "The Uses of Asianization: Figuring Crises, 1997–98 and 2008–?" *American Quarterly* 64, no. 3 (September 2012): 411–436.

Kaplan, Amy. "Where Is Guantánamo?" *American Quarterly* 57, no. 3 (September 2005): 831–858.

Kauanui, J. Kēhaulani. "Asian American Studies and the 'Pacific Question.'" In *Asian American Studies after Critical Mass*, ed. Kent Ono, 121–143. Malden, MA: Blackwell, 2005.

———. "Diasporic Deracination and 'Off-Island' Hawaiians." *Contemporary Pacific* 19, no. 1 (2007): 138–160.

———. "Colonialism in Equality: Hawaiian Sovereignty and the Question of U.S. Civil Rights." *South Atlantic Quarterly* 107, no. 4 (Fall 2008): 635–650.

———. *Hawaiian Blood: Colonialism and the Politics of Sovereignty and Indigeneity*. Durham, NC: Duke University Press, 2008.

Kawelo, Hiʻilei. "Fishponds, Food, and the Future in Our Past." In *The Value of Hawaiʻi 2: Ancestral Roots, Oceanic Visions*, ed. Aiko Yamashiro and Noelani Goodyear-Kaʻōpua, 163–170. Honolulu: University of Hawaiʻi Press, 2014.

Keown, Michelle. *Postcolonial Pacific Writing: Representations of the Body*. New York: Routledge, 2004.

———. *Pacific Islands Writing: The Postcolonial Literatures of Aotearoa/New Zealand and Oceania*. New York: Oxford University Press, 2007.

Kihleng, Emelihter. *My Urohs*. Honolulu: Kahuaomānoa, 2008.

Kim, Jinah. *Postcolonial Grief: The Afterlives of the Pacific Wars in the Americas*. Durham, NC: Duke University Press, 2018.
Kim, Jodi. *Ends of Empire: Asian American Critique and the Cold War*. Minneapolis: University of Minnesota Press, 2010.
Kingston, Maxine Hong. *China Men*. New York: Vintage, (1980) 2011.
Klein, Christina. *Cold War Orientalism: Asia in the Middlebrow Imagination, 1945–1961*. Berkeley: University of California Press, 2003.
Kuwada, Bryan Kamaoli. "We Live in the Future. Come Join Us." *Ke Kaupu Hehi Ale*, April 3, 2015. Accessed July 19, 2020. https://hehiale.wordpress.com/2015/04/03/we-live-in-the-future-come-join-us.
Labrador, Roderick, and Erin Kahunawaikaʻala Wright. "Engaging Indigeneity in Pacific Islander and Asian American Studies." *Amerasia Journal* 37, no. 3 (2011): 135–147.
LaFrance, Adrienne. "What Makes a Volcano Sacred?" *The Atlantic*, October 30, 2015. Accessed July 18, 2020. https://www.theatlantic.com/technology/archive/2015/10/what-makes-a-volcano-sacred/413203.
Lai, Paul. "Discontiguous States of America: The Paradox of Unincorporation in Craig Santos Perez's Poetics of Chamorro Guam." *Journal of Transnational American Studies* 3, no. 2 (2011): 1–28.
Langley, Lester. *The United States and the Caribbean, 1900–1970*. Athens: University of Georgia Press, 1980.
Le, Quynh Nhu. "The Colonial Choreographies of Refugee Resettlement in Lan Cao's *Monkey Bridge*." *Journal of Asian American Studies* 21, no. 3 (October 2018): 395–420.
lê, thi diễm thúy. *The Gangster We Are All Looking For*. New York: Anchor, 2003.
Lee, Benjamin, and Edward LiPuma. "Cultures of Circulation: The Imaginations of Modernity." *Public Culture* 14, no. 1 (Winter 2002): 191–213.
Lee, Rachel. "Claiming Land, Claiming Voice, Claiming Canon: Institutionalized Challenges in Kingston's *China Men* and *The Woman Warrior*." In *Reviewing Asian America: Locating Diversity*, ed. Wendy L. Ng, Soo-Young Chin, James S. Moy, and Gary Okihiro, 147–159. Pullman: Washington State University Press, 1995.
———. *The Exquisite Corpse of Asian America: Biopolitics, Biosociality, and Posthuman Ecologies*. New York: New York University Press, 2014.
Li, David Leiwei. "China Men: Maxine Hong Kingston and the American Canon." *American Literary History* 2, no. 3 (1990): 482–502.
Lipman, Jana. "'Give Us a Ship': The Vietnamese Repatriate Movement on Guam, 175." *American Quarterly* 64, no. 1 (2012): 1–31.
Liu, Ken. "A Brief History of the Trans-Pacific Tunnel." In *The Paper Menagerie and Other Stories*, by Ken Liu, 344–362. New York: Saga, 2016.
Lowe, Lisa. *Immigrant Acts: On Asian American Cultural Politics*. Durham, NC: Duke University Press, 1996.
———. *The Intimacies of the Four Continents*. Durham, NC: Duke University Press, 2015.
Lye, Colleen. *America's Asia: Racial Form and American Literature, 1893–1945*. Princeton, NJ: Princeton University Press, 2005.
———. "Unmarked Character and the 'Rise of Asia': Ed Park's Personal Days." *Verge: Studies in Global Asias* 1, no. 1 (2015): 230–254.
Lyons, Paul. *American Pacificism: Oceania in the U.S. Imagination*. New York: Routledge, 2006.
Maclellan, Nic. *Turning the Tide: Improving Access to Climate Financing in the Pacific Islands*. Sydney: Lowy Institute for International Policy, 2011.
———. "The Region in Review: International Issue and Events, 2017." *Contemporary Pacific* 30, no. 2 (2018): 462–481.

Māhina, 'Okusitino. "Myths and History: The Tu'i Tonga Myths." In *Tongan Culture and History: Papers from the First Tongan History Conference*, ed. Phyllis Herda, Jennifer Terrel, and Neil Gunson, 30–45. Canberra: Journal of Pacific History, 1990.

———. "The Poetics of Tongan Traditional History, Tala-E-Fonua: An Ecology-Centred Concept of Culture and History." *Journal of Pacific History* 28, no. 1 (1993): 109–121.

———. "Was Tonga's Nukuleka the Cradle of Polynesia?" *Pacific Islands Report*, January 16, 2008. Accessed July 20, 2020. http://www.pireport.org/articles/2008/01/16/was tonga%C3%A2%C2%80%C2%99s-nukuleka-cradle-polynesia.

———. "Tā, Vā, and Moana: Temporality, Spatiality, and Indigeneity." *Pacific Studies* 33, nos. 2–3 (2010): 168–202.

Malkki, Lisa. "Refugees and Exile: From 'Refugee Studies' to the National Order of Things." *Annual Review of Anthropology* 24 (1995): 495–523.

Man, Simeon. *Soldiering through Empire: Race and the Making of the Decolonizing Pacific*. Berkeley: University of California Press, 2018.

Mangauil, Lanakila. "Speech: Lanakila Mangauil on the TMT." *Hawaii Independent*, April 25, 2015. Accessed July 18, 2020. https://thehawaiiindependent.com/story/speech -lanakila-mangauil-on-the-tmt.

Marsh, Selina Tusitala. "Theory 'versus' Pacific Islands Writing: Toward a Tama'ita'i Criticism in the Works of Three Pacific Islands Woman Poets." In *Inside Out: Literature, Cultural Politics, and Identity in the New Pacific*, ed. Vilsoni Hereniko and Rob Wilson, 337–356. Boston: Rowman and Littlefield, 1999.

Marvin, Carolyn. "Information and History." In *The Ideology of the Information Age*, ed. Jennifer Daryl Slack and Fred Fejes, 49–62. New York: Ablex, 1987.

Marx, Karl. *Capital: A Critique of Political Economy*. New York: Penguin, 2004.

Marzec, Robert. *Militarizing the Environment: Climate Change and the Security State*. Minneapolis: University of Minnesota Press, 2015.

Matsuda, Matt K. *Pacific Worlds: A History of Seas, Peoples, and Cultures*. New York: Cambridge University Press, 2012.

Mawani, Renisa. *Across Oceans of Law: The Komagata Maru and Jurisdiction in the Time of Empire*. Durham, NC: Duke University Press, 2018.

McChesney, Robert W. *Digital Disconnect: How Capitalism Is Turning the Internet against Democracy*. New York: New Press, 2013.

McDougall, Brandy Nālani. *The Salt-Wind: Ka Makani Pa'akai*. Honolulu: Kuleana 'Ōiwi, 2008.

———. *Finding Meaning: Kaona and Contemporary Hawaiian Literature*. Tucson: University of Arizona Press, 2016.

McDougall, Brandy Nālani, and Georganne Nordstrom. "Stealing the Piko: (Re)placing Kānaka Maoli at Disney's Aulani Resort." In *Huihui: Navigating Art and Literature in the Pacific*, ed. Geoffrey Carroll, Brandy Nālani McDougall, and Georganne Nordstrom, 160–178. Honolulu: University of Hawai'i Press, 2014.

Medak-Saltzman, Danika. "Empire's Haunted Logics: Comparative Colonialisms and the Challenges of Incorporating Indigeneity." *Critical Ethnic Studies* 1, no. 2 (Fall 2015): 11–32.

Michener, James. *Tales from the South Pacific*. New York: Macmillan, 1947.

———. *Hawaii*. New York: Random House, 1959.

Moreton-Robinson, Aileen. *The White Possessive: Property, Power, and Indigenous Sovereignty*. Minneapolis: University of Minnesota Press, 2015.

Morley, David, and Kevin Robins. *Spaces of Identity: Global Media, Electronic Landscapes, and Cultural Boundaries*. New York: Routledge, 1995.

Mulalap, Clement. "Micronesia in Review: Issues and Events, 1 July 2013 to 30 June 2014." *Contemporary Pacific* 27, no. 1 (2015): 211–233.
Mulrennan, Monica, and Colin Scott. "Mare Nullius: Indigenous Rights in Saltwater Environments." *Development and Change* 31, no. 3 (2000): 681–708.
Najita, Susan. *Decolonizing Cultures in the Pacific: Reading History and Trauma in Contemporary Fiction*. New York: Routledge, 2006.
Newton-Small, Jay. "When Obama Goes Home to Hawaii." *Time*, August 7, 2008. Accessed June 12, 2019. http://content.time.com/time/politics/article/0,8599,1830510,00.html.
Ngai, Sienne. *Ugly Feelings*. Cambridge, MA: Harvard University Press, 2005.
Nguyen, Marguerite, and Catherine Fung. "Refugee Cultures: Forty Years after the Vietnam War." *MELUS* 41, no. 3 (Fall 2016): 1–7.
Nguyen, Mimi Thi. *The Gift of Freedom: War, Debt, and Other Refugee Passages*. Durham, NC: Duke University Press, 2012.
Nguyên, Patricia. "Salt/Water: Vietnamese Refugee Passages, Memory, and Statelessness at Sea." *Women's Studies Quarterly* 45, nos. 1–2 (2017): 94–111.
Nguyen, Viet. *Race and Resistance: Literature and Politics in Asian America*. New York: Oxford University Press, 2002.
———. "Speak of the Dead, Speak of Viet Nam: The Ethics and Aesthetics of Minority Discourse." *CR: New Centennial Review* 6, no. 2 (2006): 7–37.
———. "Refugee Memories and Asian American Critique." *Positions* 20, no. 3 (2012): 911–942.
Nguyen, Viet, and Janet Hoskins, eds. *Transpacific Studies: Framing an Emerging Field*. Honolulu: University of Hawai'i Press, 2014.
Ninh, erin Khuê. *Ingratitude: The Debt-Bound Daughter in Asian American Literature*. New York: New York University Press, 2011.
Nixon, Rob. *Slow Violence and the Environmentalism of the Poor*. Cambridge, MA: Harvard University Press, 2011.
Obama, Barack. *Dreams from My Father: A Story of Race and Inheritance*. New York: Crown, 1995.
Okamura, Jonathan. *Ethnicity and Inequality in Hawai'i*. Philadelphia: Temple University Press, 2008.
Okihiro, Gary. *Island World: A History of Hawai'i and the United States*. Berkeley: University of California Press, 2008.
Okita, Teri. "Smell What the Rock Is Cookin.'" *Hawaii News Now*, February 6, 2012. Accessed June 14, 2019. https://www.hawaiinewsnow.com/story/16682208/smell-what-the-rock-is-cookin.
Omerod, Nani. "Hawaiians Oppose Plans for Kamehamea Biopic Feat[uring] Dwayne Johnson." Intercontinentalcry.org, September 11, 2018. Accessed June 14, 2019. https://intercontinentalcry.org/hawaiians-oppose-plans-for-kamehameha-biopic-feat-dwayne-the-rock-johnson.
Ong, Aihwa. *Flexible Citizenship: The Cultural Logics of Transnationality*. Durham, NC: Duke University Press, 1999.
———. *Neoliberalism as Exception: Mutations in Citizenship and Sovereignty*. Durham, NC: Duke University Press, 2006.
Overbye, Dennis. "Hawaii Court Rescinds Permit to Build Thirty Meter Telescope." *New York Times*, December 3, 2015. Accessed July 18, 2020. https://www.nytimes.com/2015/12/04/science/space/hawaii-court-rescinds-permit-to-build-thirty-meter-telescope.html.
Ozeki, Ruth. *A Tale for the Time Being*. New York: Viking, 2013.

Palumbo-Liu, David. *Asian/American: Historical Crossings of a Racial Frontier*. Palo Alto, CA: Stanford University Press, 1999.

———. *The Deliverance of Others: Reading Literature in a Global Age*. Durham, NC: Duke University Press, 2012.

Pannell, Sandra. "Homo Nullius or 'Where Have All the People Gone'? Refiguring Marine Management and Conservation Approaches." *Australian Journal of Anthropology* 7, no. 3 (December 1996): 21–42.

Parikh, Crystal. "Blue Hawaii: Asian Hawaiian Cultural Production and Racial Melancholia." *Journal of Asian American Studies* 5, no. 3 (2002): 199–216.

Park, Jane Chi Hyun. *Yellow Future: Oriental Style in Hollywood Cinema*. Minneapolis: University of Minnesota Press, 2010.

Park, Josephine Nock-Hee. *Cold War Friendships: Korea, Vietnam, and Asian American Literature*. New York: Oxford University Press, 2016.

Parsons, Christopher, and Pierre-Louis Vézina. "Migrant Networks and Trade: The Vietnamese Boat People as a Natural Experiment." IZA Discussion Papers, no. 10112. Bonn, Germany: Institute for the Study of Labor, 2018.

Peattie, Mark R. *Nanyo: The Rise and Fall of the Japanese in Micronesia, 1885–1945*. Honolulu: University of Hawai'i Press, 1992.

Perez, Craig Santos. *from unincorporated territory [hacha]*. Honolulu: Tinfish, 2008.

———. *from unincorporated territory [saina]*. Richmond, CA: Omnidawn, 2010.

———. *from unincorporated territory [guma']*. Richmond, CA: Omnidawn, 2014.

———. "Transterritorial Currents and the Imperial Archipelago." *American Quarterly* 67, no. 3 (2015): 619–624.

———. *from unincorporated territory [lukao]*. Richmond, CA: Omnidawn, 2017.

Petersen, Glenn. "Indigenous Island Empires: Yap and Tonga Considered." *Journal of Pacific History* 35, no. 1 (2000): 5–27.

Pickering, Susan. "Common Sense and Original Deviancy: News Discourses and Asylum Seekers in Australia." *Journal of Refugee Studies* 14, no. 2 (2001): 169–186.

Pomerantz, Dorothy. "Dwayne Johnson Is the Top-Grossing Actor in 2013." Forbes.com, December 16, 2013. Accessed January 12, 2018. https://www.forbes.com/sites/dorothypomerantz/2013/12/16/dwayne-johnson-is-the-top-grossing-actor-of-2013/#4587f19e4c1d.

Pratt, Mary Louise. *Imperial Eyes: Travel Writing and Transculturation*. New York: Routledge, 1992.

Prentice, Chris. "'A Knife through Time': Robert Sullivan's *Star Waka* and the Politics and Poetics of Cultural Difference." *Ariel* 37, nos. 2–3 (2006): 111–135.

Puar, Jasbir. *The Right to Maim: Debility, Capacity, Disability*. Durham, NC: Duke University Press, 2017.

Pukui, Mary Kawena. "Songs (Meles) of Old Ka'u, Hawai'i." *Journal of American Folklore* 62, no. 245 (1949): 247–258.

Pukui, Mary Kawena, and Samuel Elbert. *Hawaiian Dictionary*. Honolulu: University of Hawai'i Press, 1986.

Pukui, Mary Kawena, Samuel H. Elbert, and Esther T. Mo'okini. *Place Names of Hawai'i*. Honolulu: University of Hawai'i Press, 1976.

Rajaram, Prem Kumar. "'Making Place': The 'Pacific Solution' and Australian Emplacement in the Pacific and on Refugee Bodies." *Singapore Journal of Tropical Geography* 24, no. 3 (2003): 290–306.

Revelle, Roger, and Hans E. Suess. "Carbon Dioxide Exchange between Atmosphere and Ocean and the Question of an Increase of Atmospheric CO_2 during the Past Decades." *Tellus* 9, no. 1 (1957): 18–27.

Riemenschneider, Dieter. "Contemporary Maori Cultural Practice: From Biculturalism towards a Glocal Culture." *Journal of New Zealand Literature* 18–19 (2000): 139–160.
Rifkin, Mark. *Beyond Settler Time: Temporal Sovereignty and Indigenous Self-Determination*. Durham, NC: Duke University Press, 2017.
Robinson, Angela L. "Of Monsters and Mothers: Affective Climates and Human-Nonhuman Sociality in Kathy Jetñil-Kijiner's 'Dear Matafele Peinam.'" *The Contemporary Pacific* 32, no. 2 (2020): 311–339.
Rodriguez, Robyn Magalit. *Migrants for Export: How the Philippine State Brokers Labor to the World*. Minneapolis: University of Minnesota Press, 2010.
Roff, Sue Rabbitt. "Project Sunshine and the Slippery Slope: The Ethics of Tissue Sampling for Strontium-90." *Medicine, Conflict and Survival* 18, no. 3 (2002): 299–310.
Roosevelt, Theodore. "Seventh Annual Message, December 3, 1907." In *A Compilation of the Messages and Papers of the Presidents*, ed. James D. Richardson, 20 vols., 16:7070–7125. New York: Bureau of National Literature, 1917.
Rosa, John P. "Local Story: The Massice Case Narrative and the Cultural Production of Local Identity in Hawai'i." *Amerasia Journal* 26, no. 2 (2000): 93–115.
Ryan, Anna. *Where Land Meets Sea: Coastal Explorations of Landscape, Representation, and Spatial Experience*. New York: Routledge, 2012.
Saïd, Edward. *Orientalism*. New York: Pantheon, 1978.
Sakai, Naoki, and Hyon Joo Yoo. *The Trans-Pacific Imagination: Rethinking Boundary, Culture and Society*. Singapore: World Scientific, 2012.
Salazar, Iokepa. "Multicultural Settler Colonialism and Indigenous Struggle in Hawai'i: The Politics of Astronomy on Mauna a Wākea." Ph.D. thesis, University of Hawai'i, Mānoa, 2014.
Salesa, Damon. "The Pacific in Indigenous Time." In *Pacific Histories: Ocean, Land, People*, ed. David Armitage and Alison Bashford, 31–52. New York: Palgrave, 2014.
Saranillio, Dean. "Why Asian Settler Colonialism Matters: A Thought Piece on Critiques, Debates, and Indigenous Difference." *Settler Colonial Studies* 3, nos. 3–4 (2013): 280–294.
———. "Alternative Futures beyond the Settler State." *Social Text* 13 (June 2014). Accessed July 20, 2020. https://socialtextjournal.org/periscope_article/alternative-futures-beyond-the-settler-state.
———. *Unsustainable Empire: Alternative Histories of Hawai'i Statehood*. Durham, NC: Duke University Press, 2018.
Schlund-Vials, Cathy. *War, Genocide, and Justice: Cambodian American Memory Work*. Minneapolis: University of Minnesota Press, 2012.
Schmitt, Carl. *Land and Sea: A World-Historical Meditation*, trans. Samuel Garrett Zeitlin. Candor, NY: Telos, [1942] 2015.
Sharma, Nitasha. "Pacific Revisions of Blackness: Blacks Address Race and Belonging in Hawai'i." *Amerasia Journal* 37, no. 3 (2011): 43–60.
Sharpe, Christina. *In the Wake: On Blackness and Being*. Durham, NC: Duke University Press, 2016.
Sharrad, Paul. "Imagining the Pacific." *Meanjin* 49, no. 4 (1990): 597–606.
Shewry, Teresa. *Hope at Sea: Possible Ecologies in Oceanic Literature*. Minneapolis: University of Minnesota Press, 2015.
Shigematsu, Setsu, and Keith Camacho, eds. *Militarized Currents: Toward a Decolonized Future in Asia and the Pacific*. Minneapolis: University of Minnesota Press, 2010.
Silva, Noenoe. *Aloha Betrayed: Native Hawaiian Resistance to American Colonialism*. Durham, NC: Duke University Press, 2004.

———. *The Power of the Steel-Tipped Pen: Reconstructing Native Hawaiian Intellectual History*. Durham, NC: Duke University Press, 2017.

Sinavaiana, Caroline, and J. Kēhaulani Kauanui. *Women Writing Oceania: Weaving the Sails of Vaka*. Laʻie, HI: Pacific Institute, 2007.

Small, Cathy. *Voyages: From Tongan Villages to American Suburbs*. New York: Cornell University Press, 1997.

Smith, Bernard. *European Vision and the South Pacific, 1768–1850*. New Haven, CT: Yale University Press, 1960.

Smith, Linda Tuhiwai. *Decolonizing Methodologies: Research and Indigenous Peoples*. Dunedin, New Zealand: University of Otago Press, 1999.

Song, Min Hyoung. *The Children of 1965: On Writing, and Not Writing, as an Asian American*. Durham, NC: Duke University Press, 2013.

Sonoda, Healani. "A Nation Incarcerated." In *Asian Settler Colonialism: From Local Governance to the Habits of Everyday Life in Hawaiʻi*, ed. Candace Fujikane and Jonathan Okamura, 99–115. Honolulu: University of Hawaiʻi Press, 2008.

Sontag, Susan. *On Photography*. New York: Farrar, Straus and Giroux, 1977.

Stannard, David E. *Honor Killing: Race, Rape, and Clarence Darrow's Spectacular Last Case*. New York: Penguin, 2005.

Starosielski, Nicole. "Critical Nodes, Cultural Networks: Remapping Guam's Cable Infrastructure." *Amerasia Journal* 37, no. 3 (2011): 18–28.

———. *The Undersea Network*. Durham, NC: Duke University Press, 2015.

Steinberg, Philip, and Kimberley Peters. "Wet Ontologies, Fluid Spaces: Giving Depth to Volume through Oceanic Thinking." *Environment and Planning D: Society and Space* 33, no. 2 (2015): 247–264.

Steiner, Candice Elanna. "A Sea of Warriors: Performing an Identity of Resilience and Empowerment in the Face of Climate Change in the Pacific." *Contemporary Pacific* 27, no. 1 (2015): 147–180.

Stemwedel, Janet D. "The Thirty Meter Telescope Reveals Ethical Challenges for the Astronomy Community." *Forbes*, June 12, 2015. Accessed July 17, 2020. https://www.forbes.com/sites/janetstemwedel/2015/06/12/the-thirty-meter-telescope-reveals-ethical-challenges-for-the-astronomy-community/#d1dc1f969028.

Sturken, Marita. "Absent Images of Memory: Remembering and Reenacting the Japnese Internment." In *Perilous Memories: The Asia/Pacific War(s)*, ed. Takashi Fujitani, Geoffrey M. White, and Lisa Yoneyama, 33–50. Durham, NC: Duke University Press, 2001.

Subramani. *South Pacific Literature: From Myth to Fabulation*. Suva, Fiji: University of the South Pacific Press, 1985.

Sudo, Naoto. *Nanyo-Orientalism: Japanese Representations of the Pacific*. New York: Cambria, 2010.

Sullivan, Robert. *Star Waka*. Auckland, New Zealand: Auckland University Press, 1999.

Sumida, Stephen. *And the View from the Shore: Literary Traditions of Hawaiʻi*. Seattle: University of Washington Press, 1991.

Suzuki, Erin. "Consuming Desires: Melancholia and Consumption in *Blu's Hanging*." *MELUS* 31, no. 3 (2006): 35–52.

———. "Haunted Homelands: Negotiating Locality in Father of the Four Passages." *Modern Fiction Studies* 58, no. 1 (2010): 160–182.

———. "Genealogy and Geography in Patricia Grace's *Tu*." *Modern Fiction Studies* 58, no. 1 (2012): 112–127.

———. "Transpacific." In *Routledge Companion to Asian American Literature*, ed. Rachel Lee, 352–364. New York: Routledge, 2014.

———. "And the View from the Ship: Setting Asian American Studies Asail." *Verge* 4, no. 2 (2018): 44–52.
Suzuki, Erin, and Aimee Bahng. "The Transpacific Subject in Asian American Literature." In *Oxford Research Encyclopedia of Literature*, January 30, 2020. https://doi.org/10.1093/acrefore/9780190201098.013.877.
Sze, Julie. *Environmental Justice in a Moment of Danger*. Berkeley: University of California Press, 2020.
Takaki, Ronald. *Pau Hana: Plantation Life and Labor in Hawaiʻi*. Honolulu: University of Hawaiʻi Press, 1983.
Tang, Eric. *Unsettled: Cambodian Refugees in the New York City Hyperghetto*. Philadelphia: Temple University Press, 2015.
Taonui, Rawiri. "Polynesian Oral Traditions." In *Vaka Moana: Voyages of the Ancestors*, ed. K. R. Howe, 22–53. Honolulu: University of Hawaiʻi Press, 2007.
Teaiwa, Katerina. *Consuming Ocean Island: Stories of People and Phosphate from Banaba*. Bloomington: Indiana University Press, 2014.
Teaiwa, Teresia. "Bikinis and Other S/pacific N/oceans." *Contemporary Pacific* 6, no. 1 (Spring 1994): 87–109.
———. *Searching for Nei Nimʻanoa*. Suva, Fiji: Mana, 1995.
———. "Reading Paul Gauguin's *Noa Noa* with Epeli Hauʻofa's *Kisses in the Nederends*: Militourism, Feminism, and the 'Polynesian' Body." In *Inside Out: Literature, Cultural Politics and Identity in the New Pacific*, ed. Vilsoni Hereniko and Rob Wilson, 249–263. Oxford: Rowman and Littlefield, 1999.
———. "For or Before an Asia Pacific Studies Agenda? Specifying Pacific Studies." In *Remaking Area Studies: Teaching and Learning across Asia and the Pacific*, ed. Jon Goss, 110–124. Honolulu: University of Hawaiʻi Press, 2010.
———. "What Remains to Be Seen: Reclaiming the Visual Roots of Pacific Literature." *PMLA* 125, no. 3 (2010): 730–736.
Tengan, Ty Kāwika. *Native Men Remade: Gender and Nation in Contemporary Hawaiʻi*. Durham, NC: Duke University Press, 2008.
Te Punga Somerville, Alice. *Once Were Pacific: Māori Connections to Oceania*. Minneapolis: University of Minnesota Press, 2012.
———. "Where Oceans Come From." *Comparative Literature* 69, no. 1 (2017): 25–31.
———. "Inside Us the Unborn: Genealogies, Futures, Metaphors, and the Opposite of Zombies." In *Pacific Futures*, ed. Warwick Anderson, Miranda Johnson, and Barbara Brookes, 69–80. Honolulu: University of Hawaiʻi Press, 2018.
Te Rito, Joseph Selwyn. "Whakapapa: A Framework for Understanding Identity." *MAI Review* 1, no. 3 (2007): art. 2.
Teves, Stephanie Nohelani. "Aloha State Apparatuses." *American Quarterly* 67, no. 3 (2015): 705–726.
Thaman, Konai Helu. *You, The Choice of My Parents*. Suva, Fiji: South Pacific Creative Arts Society, 1974.
———. *Langakali*. Suva, Fiji: South Pacific Creative Arts Society, 1981.
———. "Decolonizing Pacific Studies: Indigenous Perspectives, Knowledge, and Wisdom in Higher Education." *Contemporary Pacific* 15, no. 1 (2003): 1–17.
———. "Nurturing relationships and honouring responsibilities: A Pacific perspective." *Living Together: Education and Intercultural Dialogue*, ed. Suzanne Majhanovich, Christine Fox, and Adila Pašalić Kreso, 173–187. Dordrecht: Springer, 2008.
Trask, Haunani-Kay. "Hawaiians, American Colonization, and the Quest for Independence." *Social Process in Hawaii* 31 (1984): 1–35.

———. "Politics in the Pacific Islands: Imperialism and Native Self-Determination." *Amerasia Journal* 16, no. 1 (1990): 1–19.

———. "Natives and Anthropologists: The Colonial Struggle." *Contemporary Pacific* 3, no. 1 (1991): 159–167.

———. "Lovely Hula Lands: Corporate Tourism and the Prostitution of Hawaiian Culture." *Border/Lines* 23 (1992): 22–34.

———. *From a Native Daughter: Colonialism and Sovereignty in Hawai'i*. Honolulu: University of Hawai'i Press, 1993.

———. "Feminism and Indigenous Hawaiian Nationalism." *Signs* 21, no. 4 (1996): 906–916.

———. *Light in the Crevice Never Seen*. Corvallis, OR: Calyx, 1999.

———. "Settlers of Color and 'Immigrant' Hegemony: 'Locals' in Hawai'i." *Amerasia* 26, no. 2 (2000): 1–24.

———. "Native Social Capital: The Case of Hawaiian Sovereignty and Ka Lahui Hawai'i." In *Social Capital as a Policy Resource*, ed. John D. Montgomery and Alex Inkeles, 149–159. Boston: Springer, 2001.

———. *Night Is a Sharkskin Drum*. Honolulu: University of Hawai'i Press, 2002.

Truman, Harry S. "Executive Order 9633, Reserving and Placing Certain Resources of the Continental Shelf under the Control and Jurisdiction of the Secretary of the Interior," September 28, 1945. Harry S. Truman Presidential Library and Museum. Accessed May 23, 2019. https://www.trumanlibrary.org/executiveorders/index.php?pid=789.

Tsou, Elda. *Unquiet Tropes: Form, Race, and Asian American Literature*. Philadelphia: Temple University Press, 2015.

Tuck, Eve, and K. Wayne Yang. "Decolonization Is not a Metaphor." *Decolonization, Indigeneity, and Society* 1, no. 1 (2012): 1–40.

Tuwere, Ilaitia S. *Vanua: Toward a Fijian Theology of Place*. Suva, Fiji: Institute of Pacific Studies, 2002.

United Nations Framework on Climate Change. "Adoption of the Paris Agreement." January 29, 2016. Accessed July 12, 2020. https://unfccc.int/documents/9097.

United Nations General Assembly. "Convention Relating to the Status of Refugees," July 28, 1951. Accessed May 24, 2019. https://www.unhcr.org/en-us/3b66c2aa10.

United Nations Security Council. "Security Council Resolution 21," S/318, April 2, 1947. Accessed May 24, 2019. http://unscr.com/en/resolutions/21.

U.S. Department of the Interior. "Compact of Free Association Act of 1985." U.S. Public Law 99-239, 99th Cong, January 14, 1986. https://www.doi.gov/oia/about/compact.

Va'ai, Sina. *Literary Representations in Western Polynesia: Colonialism and Indigeneity*. Apia: National University of Sāmoa, 1999.

Vaioleti, Timote. "Talanoa Research Methodology: A Developing Position on Pacific Research." *Waikato Journal of Education* 12 (2006): 21–34.

Vaka'uta, Cresantia, Frances Koya, Lingikoni Vaka'uta, and Rosiana Lagi. "Reflections from Oceania on Indigenous Epistemology, the Ocean, and Sustainability." In *Tidalectics: Imagining an Oceanic Worldview through Art and Science*, ed. Stefanie Hessler, 126–131. Cambridge, MA: MIT Press, 2018.

Van Dijck, Jose. *The Culture of Connectivity: A Critical History of Social Media*. New York, NY: Oxford University Press, 2013.

Virilio, Paul. *The Vision Machine*. Bloomington: Indiana University Press, 1994.

Vizenor, Gerald. *Survivance: Narratives of Native Presence*. Lincoln: University of Nebraska Press, 2008.

Walker, Ranginui. *Ka Whawhai Tonu Matou: Struggle without End*. Auckland, New Zealand: Penguin, 1990.

Warren, Joyce Pualani. "Embodied Cosmogony: Genealogy and the Racial Production of the State in Victoria Nalani Kneubuhl's 'Hoʻolu Lāhui.'" *American Quarterly* 67, no. 3 (2015): 937–958.
Watts, Vanessa. "Indigenous Place-Thought and Agency amongst Humans and Non-humans (First Woman and Sky Woman Go on a European World Tour!)" *Decolonization: Indigeneity, Education, and Society* 2, no. 1 (2013): 20–34.
Weaver, Caity. "Dwayne Johnson for President!" *GQ*, May 10, 2017. Accessed June 14, 2019. https://www.gq.com/story/dwayne-johnson-for-president-cover.
Weaver, Jace. *The Red Atlantic: American Indigenes and the Making of the Modern World, 1000–1927*. Chapel Hill: University of North Carolina Press, 2017.
Webber, Sophie. "Performative Vulnerability: Climate Change Adaptation Policies and Financing in Kiribati." *Environment and Planning A* 45 (2013): 2717–2733.
Wendt, Albert. "Towards a New Oceania." *Mana Review* 1, no. 1 (1976): 49–60.
Whitman, Walt. *The Complete Poems*, ed. Francis Murphy. New York, NY: Penguin, 2004.
Whyte, Kyle Powys. "Our Ancestors' Dystopia Now: Indigenous Conservation and the Anthropocene." In *Routledge Companion to the Environmental Humanities*, September 8, 2016. https://ssrn.com/abstract=2770047.
———. "Indigenous Climate Change Studies: Indigenizing Futures, Decolonizing the Anthropocene." *English Language Notes* 55, nos. 1–2 (2017): 153–162.
Williams, Angela. "Turning the Tide: Recognizing Climate Change Refugees in International Law." *Law and Policy* 30, no. 3 (October 2008): 502–529.
Wilson, Rob. *Reimagining the American Pacific: From South Pacific to Bamboo Ridge and Beyond*. Durham, NC: Duke University Press, 2000.
———. "From the Sublime to the Devious: Writing the Experimental/Local Pacific." *boundary 2* 28, no. 1 (2001): 121–151.
———. "Toward an Ecopoetics of Oceania: Worlding the Asia-Pacific Region as Space-Time Ecumene." In *American Studies as Transnational Practice: Turning Toward the Transpacific*, ed. Yuan Shu and Donald E. Pease, 213–236. Hanover, NH: Dartmouth College Press, 2015.
Wilson, Rob, and Arif Dirlik, eds. *Asia/Pacific as Space of Cultural Production*. Durham, NC: Duke University Press, 1995.
Wilson-Hokowhitu, Nālani, ed. *The Past before Us: Moʻokūʻauhau as Methodology*. Honolulu: University of Hawaiʻi Press, 2019.
Wilson-Hokowhitu, Nālani, and Manulani Aluli Meyer. "Introduction: I Ka Wā Mamua, The Past Before Us." In *The Past Before Us: Moʻokūʻauhau as Methodology*, ed. Nālani Wilson-Hokowhitu, 1–8. Honolulu: University of Hawaiʻi Press, 2019.
Winduo, Steven. "Papua New Guinean Writing Today: The Growth of a Literary Culture." *Manoa* 2, no. 1 (1990): 37–41.
Wood, Briar. "Heka He Vaʻa Mei Popo: Sitting on a Rotten Branch of the Breadfruit Tree: Reading the Poetry of Konai Helu Thaman." *Women's Studies Journal* 14, no. 2 (1998): 7–29.
Wood, Houston. *Displacing Natives: The Rhetorical Production of Hawaiʻi*. New York: Rowman and Littlefield, 1999.
Woodward, Valerie. "'I Guess They Didn't Want Us Asking Too Many Questions': Reading American Empire in Guam." *Contemporary Pacific* 25, no. 1 (2013): 67–91.
Yamanaka, Lois-Ann. *Saturday Night at the Pahala Theater*. Honolulu: Bamboo Ridge, 1993.
———. *Blu's Hanging*. New York: Farrar, Straus and Giroux, 1997.
———. *Father of the Four Passages*. New York: Farrar, Straus, and Giroux, 2001.

———. "This Man Is an Island." *New York Times*, January 17, 2009. Accessed June 12, 2019. http://www.nytimes.com/2009/01/18/opinion/18yamanaka.html.

Yamashiro, Aiko, and Noelani Goodyear-Kaʻōpua, eds. *The Value of Hawaiʻi 2: Ancestral Roots, Oceanic Visions*. Honolulu: University of Hawaiʻi Press, 2014.

Yang, Caroline. "Indispensable Labor: The Worker as a Category of Critique in China Men." *MFS: Modern Fiction Studies* 56, no. 1 (Spring 2010), 63–89.

Yoneyama, Lisa. *Hiroshima Traces: Time, Space, and the Dialectics of Memory*. Berkeley: University of California Press, 1999.

———. *Cold War Ruins: Transpacific Critique of American Justice and Japanese War Crimes*. Durham, NC: Duke University Press, 2016.

———. "Toward a Decolonial Genealogy of the Transpacific." *American Quarterly* 69, no. 3 (2017): 471–482.

INDEX

Page numbers in italics refer to illustrations.

activism, 68, 210n35; decolonial, 198, 199; against dispossession, 102; environmental, 68, 200–202, 210n35, 224n7; Kanaka Maoli, 133–134, 201–202; "local," 133–134, 218n18; of ocean passage, 128; online, 184–186; settler colonialism and, 201; sovereignty, 44; water protection, 200–202
aesthetics: Indigenous, 98; Kanaka Maoli, 128, 148–149, 159; *kaona*, 149; ocean, 21, 26, 57, 65; of ocean passage, 14, 128
affinity, 65–66, 88, 210n31
Agamben, Giorgio, 57, 58, 64, 209n2, 209n7
agency: capitalism and, 119; in *China Men*, 113; in "Parts," 143–144; performance and, 76–77; of refugees, 65; in *The Salt-Wind*, 157; in *Tale for the Time Being*, 190, 193; in Yamanaka, 143–144, 146–147
Aikau, Hōkūlani, 223n94
Akaka Bill, 223n94
Alaimo, Stacey, 32
Allen, Chadwick, 221n27
aloha, 128; aloha spirit, 128, 137, 159; appropriation of, 127
alterity, 14–15; in Asian American literary studies, 16, 18; decolonization and, 18; in Indigenous Pacific scholarship, 18; in Oceanic discourse, 17–18

Anand, R. P., 206n16
Anderson, Benedict, 78, 221n15
Anthropocene, 49–50, 87
anticolonialism: U.S. militarization and, 24
appropriation: of aloha, 127; of blackness, 178; of Indigenous culture and thought, 98–99, 215n25; of the transpacific, 224n5
Arendt, Hannah, 57, 58, 209n2
Arvin, Maile, 35
Asian American literary studies: alterity in, 16, 18; Pacific Island literatures in, 6. *See also* Asian American studies
Asian Americans: "Asian American" as term, 16–17; as bridge builders, 92, 104–105, 110; hybrid identity of, 159; labor and, 106; racialization of, 168, 193; subject formation of, 15–16; subjectivity of, 3; transnational trade and, 92, 214n5
Asian American studies, 159; American studies, relationship to, 7; Association for Asian American Studies (AAAS), 219n55; diaspora in, 7; feminist studies and, 8, 17, 204n23; Indigenous Pacific in, 6–9; migration in, 7; new materialist turn in, 17, 193, 205n51; queer studies and, 8, 204n23; science studies and, 8, 204n23; transnational, 3; transpacific, 8, 204n23. *See also* Asian American literary studies

Asianness: authenticity and, 188; capitalism and, 188; techno-orientalism and, 167
Asians: assimilability of, 35; as bridge builders, 92–93; global capitalism and, 214n6; proximity to whiteness, 39, 51; racialization of, 15–16, 97–98, 104; racism against, 15–16, 104; stereotyping of, 3, 104; visibility of, 41, 207n30
"Asia Pacific": origin of concept, 12
assimilability: of Asians, 35; of Melanesians, 38; of Polynesians, 35; of refugees, 61–62, 83
assimilation, 14–15; discourse of progress, 58; incorporation and, 125; of refugees, 56, 70, 78, 80–81, 85–88
Association for Asian American Studies (AAAS), 219n55
authenticity: Asianness and, 188; capitalism and, 141; local identity and, 137–138, 148; Native Pacific, 98, 176; settler colonialism and, 96, 137

Bahng, Aimee, 93, 162
Bambridge, Tamatoa, 207n20
Barad, Karen, 76
Benjamin, Walter, 78, 221n15
Bevacqua, Michael Lujan, 207n28
Black Atlantic, 5
blackness: appropriation of, 178; in Hawai'i, 218n12; Melanesians and, 38; Obama and, 132; Pacific Islander proximity to, 39; slavery and, 58
blood quantum, 18
Blum, Hester, 5
Braudel, Fernand, 5
Byrd, Jodi, 15–17, 26–28, 131, 221n22; on *homo nullius*, 29; on paradigmatic Indian, 31

Camacho, Keith, 198–199, 207n28
capitalism: agency and, 119; Asianness and, 188; discourse of, 89–90; erasure of colonialism, 94–95; global, 107–108, 214n6; multiculturalism and, 127; the "Pacific" and, 15; Pacific Islanders and, 96; settler colonialism and, 4, 107; speculative, 94–95; universalism of, 97, 101–103
Caruth, Cathy, 212n77
Case, Pualani, 196
Chamorro language, 183
Chamorros, 10, 207n28. See also *from unincorporated territory* (Perez)
Chang, David, 149, 151, 207n23
Chapman, Murray, 114
Chen, Mel, 204n23, 205n51
Cheng, Anne Anlin, 204n23

Cheung, King-Kok, 110
China Men (Kingston), 96, 107–114, 192; agency in, 113; Americanness in, 109; Asian migrant labor in, 107, 124–125; devaluing of Hawaiians in, 112–113; global capitalism in, 107–108, 112; masculinity in, 109; ocean in, 111–112, 113; silencing in, 112; time in, 108–109
Chow, Rey, 52–53, 138
Choy, Peggy Myo-Young, 133
Chuh, Kandice, 204n23, 205n43; on "Asian American," 16–17; on subjectless discourse, 16–17
citizenship, 18; bare life and, 57; in Hawai'i, 217n4; modernity and, 63; race and, 57–58; refugee, 59; in unincorporated territories, 180
climate change, 20, 45; activism, 68, 210n35; decolonization and, 65; deterritorialization and, 89; discourse of, 49–50; in Marshall Islands, 89; Pacific Islanders and, 60, 65, 210n35, 211n40; slow violence of, 67–68
climate change policy: Alliance of Small Island States (AOSIS), 68; Intergovernmental Panel on Climate Change (IPCC), 66–67; Majuro Declaration, 211n40; Paris Agreement, 69, 210n35; United Nations Framework on Climate Change (UNFCC), 68
Clinton, Hillary, 130, 161–162
Cold War: containment strategy, 32, 44, 93; Orientalism and, 34–35, 208n64; securitization and, 43, 54; sovereignty and, 206n4; U.S. militarization and, 19, 25, 43, 206n1, 206n4, 207n28, 207n30
colonialism, 9; debt and, 171–172; displacement and, 176; gender and, 13; language and, 182–183; neocolonialism, 13, 103, 114; Pacific cultures and, 10; Philippines and, 215n40; photography and, 53; race and, 35–36; science and, 163; U.S. militarism, 23, 35; whiteness and, 35. See also settler colonialism
commensurability, 213n97
commodification: of dispossession, 176; of epistemology, 102; of Hawaiian culture, 137; of Indigenous peoples, 176; of native bodies, 142; of Pacific Island cultures, 98, 100
Connery, Chris, 12, 20, 111, 188–189
containment, 32, 44, 93
Cousins, Norman, 33
critical refugee studies, 59; deterritorialization in, 64

Day, Iyko, 15–16, 97, 106, 188
de Agueda Corneloup, Inés, 70
decolonization, 7; alterity and, 18; climate change and, 65; commodity fetishism and, 123; environment and, 63; feminism and, 3, 117–119; of Korea, 24; militarization and, 43; of the Pacific, 10–11, 25; in Pacific Islands studies, 7; relationality and, 8; of Vietnam, 24; Western theory and, 118
DeLoughrey, Elizabeth, 24, 31, 50, 138, 207n30; on migration, 216n82; on oceanic turn, 5, 9
deterritorialization: climate change and, 89; in critical refugee studies, 64; of the Pacific, 20, 94, 96; refugees and, 58–59
development, 11, 13, 25, 29; environment and, 121; in "Glorious Pacific Way," 100–101; Hawai'i, 133, 162, 164, 195, 197–199; overdevelopment, 25, 121; of Pacific Islands, 37, 42, 95, 99–103, 116; of Salt Lake, 197–199
diaspora: in Asian American studies, 7; epistemology, 167–168; Micronesian, 177–178; survival/survivance of, 60
Diaz, Vicente, 9, 70, 152, 207n28, 224n4; *etak*, 9
Dirlik, Arif, 12
dispossession: activism against, 102; colonial, 176; commodification of, 176; of Indigenous islanders, 28, 147, 148, 206n12; of Indigenous peoples, 69, 176, 196; of Kānaka Maoli, 147, 148; modernity and, 60; in *Ocean Roads*, 46; of ocean space, 30; of Pacific Islands, 56; of refugees, 60; settler colonialism and, 211n62, 214n100; war and, 77–78, 81–83
Duong, Lan: on refugee epistemology, 64, 210n25

ecocriticism, 6
ecopoetics, 15
empire, 93; neocolonialism and, 114
Eng, David, 106, 212n77
epistemology: commodification of, 102; Pacific, 102; of passage, 4–5; place-based, 17; refugee, 64, 78, 210n25; the sea and, 1–2; seascape, 87, 188
epistemology, Indigenous, 4, 16, 65; appropriation of, 98–99, 215n25; the body in, 156; climate refugee discourse and, 70–71; commodification of, 98; diasporic, 167–168; Indigenous Pacific, 4, 65; navigation, 151–152
epistemology, Kanaka Maoli, 87, 152; erasure of, 127–128, 135–136; in *The Salt-Wind*, 155

Espiritu, Evyn Lê, 58–59
Espiritu, Yến Lê, 61, 79; on critical refugee studies, 59; on refugee epistemology, 64, 210n25; on refugee resettlement, 212n76
etak, 9
exclusive economic zones (EEZ), 24, 25, 30, 207n20

Faber, Sandra, 163
fakatangi, 122
Farbotko, Carol, 64, 209n11
Federated States of Micronesia (FSM), 10, 24, 68, 177; diaspora, 177–178; relationship to United States, 180–181; U.S. claiming of, 33
feminist criticism: Asian American studies and, 8, 17, 204n23; decolonial, 3; *mana tama'ita'i*, 117; *mana wahine*, 154; transpacific, 17
Ferguson, Roderick, 210n31
Fiji, 9–10, 99; climate leadership of, 68, 72, 211n40; Pacific Way rhetoric and, 10; "Sea of Islands" and, 110; Tu'i Tonga and, 114–115; *vā* and, 216n68
from unincorporated territory (Perez): digital media in, 183–186, 192, 223n69; online activism in, 184–186; the past in, 194; repurposed texts in, 183; social media in, 184
Fujikane, Candace, 160, 217n101
Fujitani, Takashi, 207n30
Fung, Catherine, 209n11
futurity: capitalist, 160; Indigenous, 194; Māori, 170–171; neoliberal, 189; the Pacific and, 161, 220n2; in Pacific Rim discourse, 162; of *Star Waka*, 170; technology and, 162; transpacific, 21, 160, 162, 168–170, 188–189

The Gangster We Are All Looking For (lê), 22, 77, 81–87, 213n88; cyclical temporality of, 85–86; photography in, 83–85, 213n88; refugee temporality of, 85, 87; subjectivity in, 84; trauma in, 85; Vietnamese refugees in, 82–87; war in, 82–83; water imagery in, 85–86
Gauguin, Paul, 149–150, 156
gender: in *China Men*, 109; colonialism and, 13; and "Hiroshima Maidens," 33; masculinity, 139–143, 147; migration and, 216n82; in *The Salt-Wind*, 150–151, 152; in Thaman, 118–119
gender studies, 3, 17. *See also* feminist criticism
genealogy: in Indigenous narrative, 205n52; Kānaka Maoli and, 149, 152–154, 164; as praxis, 17; in *The Salt-Wind*, 153–155

George, James, 55; *Ocean Roads*, 1–3, 19, 26, 46–55
Gilroy, Paul, 5
globalization: of Asian labor, 97; in Indigenous Pacific studies, 3; "Pacific Rim" and, 12; transnational capital, 15
"The Glorious Pacific Way" (Hauʻofa short story), 100–103; capitalist development in, 100; Pacific Way rhetoric in, 100–101
Gonzalez, Vernadette, 42
Goodyear-Kaʻōpua, Noelani, 224n3
Grotius, Hugo, 28
Guam: relationship to United States, 180–181; sovereignty of, 181

Hall, Lisa Kahaleole, 7, 35–36; on consumption, 135, 137; *etak*, 9
Hardt, Michael, 93–95
Harris, Aroha, 221n33
Harvey, David, 119
Hauʻofa, Epeli, 1, 5, 18, 70, 204n24; critique of Pacific Way, 11, 100–101; on globalization, 170; "The Glorious Pacific Way," 100–103; labor in, 20; on Oceanic trade, 114; "Our Sea of Islands" (essay), 99, 101, 114, 203n2, 207n23; on reciprocity, 116; "sea of islands" (concept), 2, 3, 11, 95, 105, 122, 170, 200–201, 207n23; on seascape epistemology, 87. *See also* "sea of islands"
Hawaiʻi: Asian settler colonialism and, 7; citizenship in, 217n4; development in, 133, 162, 164, 195, 197–199; independence movement, 133; labor in, 134; local activism, 133–134, 218n18; "local" identity in, 128–129, 132–139, 145, 148, 159; masculinity in, 139; as multicultural state, 129, 130–132, 139, 140, 155; plantation economy of, 144; settler colonialism in, 126, 128, 131, 198; state multiculturalism in, 20, 126; tourist economy of, 128; U.S. intervention in, 212n84
Hawaiianness, 217n2; performance of, 135–137
Hawaiians: in *China Men*, 111–113; "Hawaiian" identity, 129. *See also* Kānaka Maoli
Hayles, Kate, 174
Hedge Coke, Allison, 221n27
Heidegger, Martin, 29
Helmreich, Stefan, 31
Helu, Futa, 122
Hereniko, Vilsoni, 204n24
Hirsch, Marianne, 81
Hobart, Hiʻilei Julia, 221n9

Hokowhitu, Brendan, 141
Hōkūleʻa voyage, 151–152
Hong, Grace, 210n31
hooks, bell, 140
hoʻomanawanui, kuʻualoha, 148, 165, 204n24, 206n57; on *moʻokūʻauhau*, 165
Hoskins, Janet, 204n17, 224n5
Hsu, Hsuan L., 181, 183, 222n61
Huang, Yunte, 16
Hu-DeHart, Evelyn, 92, 214n5
Hutchins, Edwin, 151
Huỳnh Sang Thông, 86

Ige, David, 162
Igler, David, 205n28
imperialism: erasure of, 34; Japanese, 23, 91; transpacific, 8; U.S., 33, 207n30; violence of, 62, 83
incommensurability, 15
Indianness, 26–27
indigeneity, 9; Asianness and, 188; modernity and, 166, 168; race and, 39–40; settler colonialism and, 39, 97, 137, 188
Indigenous critical theory, 25
Indigenous Pacific studies, 3
Indigenous peoples: dispossession of, 28, 66, 147, 148, 176, 196, 206n12; as *homo nullius*, 26–28, 29; linked to past, 41, 163
Indigenous rights, 7
Ingersoll, Karin Amimoto, 17–18, 207n23; on seascape epistemology, 87, 158
Internet, 185–186, 188–189; in "Pohnpei Outer Space," 177–180; in *Star Waka*, 183, 186; in *Tale for the Time Being*, 168, 190–192
invisibility: of labor, 105–106; of the Pacific, 27; of Pacific Islanders, 33; of slow violence, 68. *See also* visibility

Jackson, Shona, 6
Japanese: as paradigmatic victims, 34
Jetñil-Kijiner, Kathy, 19–20, 60, 72–76, 77, 80; "The Butterfly Thief," 66, 73–76, 89; "Dear Matafele Peinem," 72, 75; on Indigenous Pacific epistemologies, 65
Johnson, Dwayne "The Rock," 129, 138–139, 159; multicultural masculinity and, 141–143, 147; progressive multiculturalism of, 155–156
Johnson, George, 163
Jolly, Margaret, 70

Kaʻili, Tēvita, 115
Kalākaua, David, 153
Kamanamaikalani, Beamer, 153

Kameʻeleihiwa, Lilikala, 224n95
Kamehameha, 138, 153
Kānaka Maoli, 10, 217n2; blood quantum and, 35; decolonial activism, 198, 199; dispossession of, 147, 148; genealogy and, 149, 152–154, 164; poetics of, 148–149, 159; recognition of, 129–130, 223n94; relationship to land, 134, 153, 154; sovereignty of, 21, 128, 133, 153, 164, 198, 217n7, 218n18; water activism, 201–202
Kaplan, Amy, 181
Kauanui, J. Kēhaulani, 7, 70; on consumption of local identity, 137; *etak*, 9; on settler colonialism, 135
Kazanjian, David, 212n77
Kihleng, Emelihter, 168, 176–180, 186–187, 191; the past in, 194; "Pohnpei Outer Space," 177–180, 181
Kim, Jodi, 207n28, 207n30
Kingston, Maxine Hong, 20, 105. See also *China Men* (Kingston)
Kiribati: climate leadership of, 68, 71
Klein, Christina, 33, 41, 207n30
knowledge production, Indigenous, 14. See also epistemology, Indigenous
Kōkua Hawaiʻi, 133
Korea: decolonization of, 24
Kumulipo, 150–151
Kuwada, Bryan, 195

labor: in Hawaiʻi, 134; migration and, 20; of oceanic passage, 96; racialization of, 106; settler colonialism and, 106–107; time and, 108–109
labor, Asian: in *China Men*, 107, 124–125; commodification of, 105; globalization of, 97; invisibility of, 105–106; maritime, 109–110; migrant, 113–114
labor, migrant, 20; Asian, 107, 113–114; in *China Men*, 107, 124–125; commodification of, 105; erasure of, 95–96; Tongan, 114
Lagi, Rosiana, 71
Lai, Paul, 222n61
Lazrus, Heather, 64, 209n11
Le, Quynh Nhu, 64
Lee, Benjamin, 94–95
Lee, Rachel, 144, 145, 204n23, 205n51; on Asian American criticism, 159
lê thi diễm thúy, 22, 60, 213n9. See also *The Gangster We Are All Looking For* (lê)
Leyronas, Stéphanie, 207n20
Liliʻuokalani, 153, 156, 220n81
Lipman, Jana, 212n76
LiPuma, Edward, 94–95

Liu, Ken, 20; "A Brief History of the Trans-Pacific Tunnel," 91–93, 97, 109, 125, 192
local identity (Hawaiʻi), 128–129, 134–138, 139; authenticity and, 137–138, 148; consumption and, 135; hybridity of, 159; melancholia of, 145; Obama and, 132–133, 135–138, 159; performance of, 135–137; Yamanaka on, 129, 135, 137, 145–147, 159
Lowe, Lisa, 204n23, 209n4; on racialization, 98
Lye, Colleen, 97, 104, 106
Lyons, Paul, 43

Magellan, Ferdinand, 10
Māhina, ʻOkusitino, 115
Man, Simeon, 24, 207n28
Manaʻo Tupapau (Spirit of the Dead Watching), 149–150
mana tamaʻitaʻi, 117
mana wahine, 154
Mangauil, Lanakila, 164
Māʻohi, 10
Māori, 10; fiscal envelope of, 172, 221n33; futurity of, 170–171; sovereignty of, 30. See also *Star Waka* (Sullivan)
Mara, Kamisese, 10
Marcos, Ferdinand, 103
mare liberum, 27–29, 33
Mars, Bruno, 139
Marsh, Selina Tusitala, 117–118, 204n24
Marshall Islands: climate change, 89; nuclear testing, effects of, 33–34, 51, 69, 72; U.S. claiming of, 33
Marvin, Carolyn, 174
Marx, Karl: on commodity fetishism, 110–111
masculinity: "Golden Men," 139–141; in Hawaiʻi, 139; multicultural, 139, 141–143, 147; violence and, 142
Massie Trial, 133, 140
Matsuda, Matt, 10
Mauna Kea: telescope protests, 162–165, 176, 195; as *terra nullius*, 163–164, 221n9
Mawani, Renisa, 28, 212n69
McDougall, Brandy Nālani, 20–21, 126, 204n24, 206n57; agency in, 157; gender in, 150–151, 152; on Kanaka Maoli aesthetics, 149; Kanaka Maoli poetics of, 148–149, 159; Native body in, 129. See also *The Salt-Wind: Ka Makani Paʻakai* (McDougall)
Medak-Saltzman, Danika, 4
Meyer, Manulani Aluli, 165, 204n24
Michener, James, 19, 139; "Golden Men," 139–140. See also *Tales of the South Pacific* (Michener)

Micronesia. *See* Federated States of Micronesia (FSM)
migration, 216n82; in Asian American studies, 7; gender and, 216n82; Tongan, 114. *See also* labor, migrant
militarism, 9; Cold War, 206n4; colonialism and, 23, 35; interventionism, 161, 212n84; transpacific, 8
militarization: during Cold War, 19, 25, 43, 206n1, 206n4, 207n28, 207n30; decolonization and, 43; of the Pacific, 23–26, 33–36, 199; Pacific Islanders and, 33; photography and, 52; sovereignty and, 206n4; trauma and, 45; whiteness and, 45
Moana, 98, 142, 215n25
modernity: citizenship and, 63; dispossession and, 60; indigeneity and, 166, 168; technology and, 187; as white possession, 167
Mol, Arthur, 70
moʻokuʻauhau, 134, 149–155; as method, 165
Moreton-Robinson, Aileen, 15–17, 214n100, 221n22; on white possession, 167, 208n50, 218n23
Morley, David, 167, 188
multiculturalism: in Hawaiʻi, 20, 126, 129–132, 139, 140, 155; intermarriage and, 36; Obama and, 130, 132, 147, 155–156; racism and, 36; settler colonialism and, 127; state, 20; transnational capitalism and, 127

nationalism: settler colonial, 20–21
Native Hawaiians: displacement of, 130; dispossession of, 147; sovereignty of, 139, 146. *See also* Kānaka Maoli
navigation, Indigenous Pacific, 151–152
Negri, Antonio, 93–95
neocolonialism, 13, 103, 114
neoliberalism: defined, 119; futurity and, 189; neocolonialism and, 13; the "Pacific" and, 15; possessive individualism and, 218n23; Trans-Pacific Partnership, 132; women's lib and, 119
new materialism: in Asian American studies, 17, 193, 205n51
New Zealand: whiteness and, 45
Ngai, Sianne, 145
Nguyen, Marguerite, 209n11
Nguyen, Mimi Thi, 61, 209n11, 212n74
Nguyên, Patricia, 79–80
Nguyen, Viet, 14, 61–62, 204n17, 224n5
Nixon, Rob, 67–68
nuclear tests, 42–43, 163; environmental science and, 44–45; in *Ocean Roads*, 47, 50

Obama, Barack, 129, 131–139, *136*, 159; blackness and, 132; multicultural masculinity of, 130, 132, 147; progressive multiculturalism of, 155–156
ocean: aesthetics of, 21, 25–26; in *China Men*, 111–112, 113; as metaphor, 4; Pacific, 1–3; race and, 25
Oceania, 11–12, 203n2; interdependence of, 114–115, 117; in Pacific studies discourse, 12; relationality and, 12; as sea of islands, 101–102, 105
ocean passage: activism, 128; aesthetics of, 14, 128; labor migration, 96
Ocean Roads (George), 1–3, 19, 26, 46–55; Asian female body in, 50–51; choreography in, 51–52, 54; circular structure of, 54–55; displacement in, 46; nuclear testing in, 47, 50; Pacific Wars in, 2; photography in, 52–54; time in, 39, 49–50; war trauma in, 46–47
ocean space: as alien, 32; dispossession of, 30; territorialization of, 26, 28–31, 54
Odum, Eugene, 44
Odum, Howard, 44
Okamura, Jonathan, 133, 135
Orientalism: Cold War, 34–35, 208n64; as racializing technology, 25–26; reterritorialization and, 94; techno-orientalism, 167, 187–188
Ozeki, Ruth, 1. *See also A Tale for the Time Being* (Ozeki)

Pacific, the: decolonization of, 10–11, 25; deterritorialization of, 20, 94, 96; futurity and, 161, 220n2; as invisible, 27; militarization of, 23–26, 33–36, 199; U.S. interventionism in, 161, 212n84
"Pacific" (term): capitalism and, 15; discourses of, 207n30; as European concept, 10. *See also* Pacific Rim discourse
Pacific Islanders: as "almost white," 36; capitalism and, 96; climate change activism, 68, 210n35; as climate refugees, 60; dispossession of, 28; invisibility of, 33; land, relation to, 38; militarization and, 33; proximity to blackness, 39; racism against, 36; use of term, 6; visibility of, 35–36
Pacific Island literatures, 6, 206n59
Pacific Islands: climate change discourse and, 80; development in, 37, 42, 95, 99–103, 116; dispossession of, 56; erasure of, 207n30; independence of, 216n62; Pacific Rim discourse, exclusion from, 13–14, 93; U.S. claim to, 24–27, 33, 45

Pacific Islands studies: decolonization in, 7
Pacific Ocean: in *Ocean Roads*, 1–2; in *A Tale for the Time Being*, 1; visibility of, 3
Pacific Rim: as geopolitical formation, 4; globalization and, 12
Pacific Rim discourse, 12–14, 33, 188; emergence of, 93–94, 214n6; exclusion of Pacific Islands, 13–14, 93; racialization of, 96–97; transpacific turn in, 13–14
Pacific studies: Oceania in, 12; refugees in, 64
Pacific Way rhetoric, 10–11; in "The Glorious Pacific Way," 100–101
Palumbo-Liu, David, 15
Pannell, Sandra, 27, 206n12
passage: epistemology of, 4–5; impasse and, 9, 14, 96, 128
patriarchy: settler colonialism and, 109
Perez, Craig Santos, 168, 176–177, 191, 204n24. See also *from unincorporated territory* (Perez)
performance: agency and, 76–77; of Hawaiianness, 135–137
Philippines: colonialism and, 215n40; debt of, 103–104; neocolonialism and, 103; U.S. colonization of, 103
photography: colonialism and, 53; in *Gangster We Are All Looking For*, 83–85, 213n88; militarization and, 52; in *Ocean Roads*, 52–54; popular culture and, 138
Pialug, Mau, 151
Pisciotta, Kealoha, 165
poetics, Kanaka Maoli, 148–149, 159
"Pohnpei Outer Space" (Kihleng), 177–180, 181; the past in, 194; social networking in, 177–180, 186
Polynesians: as "almost white," 35; assimilability of, 35; bodies, 13, 45; racialization of, 35, 38–39; in *South Pacific*, 41; in *Tales of the South Pacific*, 38–39
postcolonial theory, 174
postmemory, 81
Pratt, Mary Louise, 138
Prendergast, Mary Wright, 220n81
progress: discourse of, 195–196; settler colonial discourse of, 163, 165–166; TMT protests and, 164–165
Puar, Jasbir, 212n80

race: citizenship and, 57–58; colonialism and, 35–36; indigeneity and, 39–40; liberalism and, 209n4; ocean aesthetics and, 25; settler colonialism and, 94; in *South Pacific*, 41; as

technology, 29; universalism and, 209n4; visibility and, 33
racialization: appropriation and incorporation, 98; Asian American, 168, 193; of Asians, 15–16, 97–98, 104; elimination and exclusion, 97–98, 106; of labor, 106; of Pacific Rim discourse, 96–97; settler colonialism and, 16, 25–26, 221n22
racism: against Asians and Pacific Islanders, 36; multiculturalism and, 36; stereotyping, 125; Western modernity and, 167
reciprocity, 116; in Thaman, 120
recognition: Kanaka Maoli, 129–130, 223n94
refugee epistemology, 64, 78, 210n25
refugees, 20; agency of, 65; assimilability of, 61–62; assimilation of, 56, 70, 80–81; citizenship of, 59; dehumanization of, 57; deterritorialization and, 58–59; displacement of, 60; dispossession of, 60; environmental, 62–63, 69–70; as figures of bare life, 58; Geneva Conventions, 61, 63; "good refugee" narrative, 61–62; as immigrants, 61–62; oceanic metaphors and, 57, 65; in Pacific studies, 64; refugee temporality, 78, 86–87; resettlement of, 64, 79, 81, 212n76; settler colonialism and, 58–59; Southeast Asian, 60–61, 80–81; sovereignty and, 209n7; statelessness of, 79, 88–89; survival/survivance of, 66; trauma of, 81; universalism and, 209n11; as victims, 63–64, 69
refugees, climate, 60, 61; displacement of, 69; environmental refugees, 62–63, 69–70; erasure of, 88; as victims, 69
refugees, Vietnamese: in *Gangster We Are All Looking For*, 82–87; "gift of freedom," 79, 212n74; subject formation, 78
refugees, war, 60; displacement of, 60–61; erasure of, 88
relationality, 8; Indigenous Pacific, 8
resources management, 71
reterritorialization: Orientalism and, 94; post–World War II, 59; of the sea, 29
Revelle, Roger, 45
Rifkin, Mark, 166
Robins, Kevin, 167, 188
Rodriguez, Robyn, 104, 215n40
Roosevelt, Theodore, 161, 220n2
Ryan, Anna, 49

Said, Edward, 138, 222n38
Sakai, Naoki, 204n17
Salazar, Iokepa, 163, 176
Salesa, Damon, 216n68

Salt Lake (ālia pa'akai), 197–199
The Salt-Wind: Ka Makani Pa'akai (McDougall), 148–151; gender in, 150–151, 152; genealogy in, 153–155; Kanaka Maoli epistemologies in, 155; kaona in, 149, 158–159; mo'okū'auhau in, 149, 152; settler colonial violence in, 153; women's perspectives in, 154. Poems: "By the Blur of My Hands," 156–158; "Ka 'Ōlelo," 148, 155; "Pō," 152–154; "Tehura," 149–151, 152, 154–156; "Tiny Rebellions," 148
Sāmoa, 9; vā and, 149, 219n68
Saranillio, Dean, 55, 211n62, 217n7
Schmitt, Carl, 28–29
science studies, 3, 8, 17, 204n23
"sea of islands," 2, 3, 11; as counterculture of circulation, 102–103, 105, 117; Oceania as, 101–102, 105. See also Hau'ofa, Epeli
securitization, 54–55, 59, 202, 206n4; liberation through, 24; logic of, 25–26; self-determination and, 44; in Tale for the Time Being, 189; in Tales of the South Pacific, 54; territorial logic of, 43
settler colonialism: activism and, 201; antiblackness and, 39; Asian, 3, 7; capitalism and, 4, 107; dispossession and, 211n62, 214n100; in Hawai'i, 126–128, 131, 135, 198; indigeneity and, 39, 97, 137, 188; Indigenous, erasure of, 7, 125; labor and, 106–107; land-sea binary and, 30–31; multiculturalism and, 127; nation and, 4; nationalism and, 20–21; patriarchy and, 109; progress, discourse of, 163, 165–166; race and, 94; as racialization, 16, 25–26, 221n22; recognition, politics of, 130; refugees and, 58–59; temporality of, 165–168, 189–190; territorialization and, 78; violence of, 153, 155; white supremacy and, 211n62. See also colonialism
Shannon, Claude, 174
Sharma, Nitasha, 218n12
Sharpe, Christina, 58
Sharrad, Paul, 13
Shigematsu, Setsu, 198–199
Smith, Andrea, 15–16
Smith, Linda Tuhiwai, 71, 166, 204n24
social media: in from unincorporated territory, 184; political organizing and, 185–186, 195
Sontag, Susan, 53
Sopoanga, Enele, 71–72
Southeast Asians: as war refugees, 60, 61
South Pacific (Rodgers and Hammerstein), 43, 208n64; race in, 41; racial prejudice in, 41; securitization and, 54

sovereignty: activism, 49; Cold War militarization and, 206n4; of Guam, 181; Indigenous, 17, 55, 223n94; Kanaka Maoli, 21, 128, 133, 153, 164, 198, 217n7, 218n18; land-sea binary and, 30–31; Māori, 30; refugees and, 209n7; over sea space, 27–28; territory and, 58
Standing Rock, 199–200
Starosielski, Nicole, 185–186
Star Waka (Sullivan), 181, 186–187, 189, 191, 193; indigenous technology in, 169, 173; media technology in, 173–175; the past in, 194; spiralic time in, 169–170, 172; technology in, 169, 173–175; transpacific futurity of, 170, 171; water in, 173; whakapapa in, 173–174
Sturken, Marita, 212n73
subject formation: Asian American, 15–16; Vietnamese refugee, 78
subjectivity: Asian American, 3; in Gangster We Are All Looking For, 84; Indigenous, 16–17; Indigenous Pacific, 3; liberal, 15, 162; oceanic, 79–80; Vietnamese, 78, 79–80, 84
Sudo, Naoto, 206n57
Suess, Hans, 45
Sullivan, Robert, 168, 221n27. See also Star Waka (Sullivan)
Sumida, Stephen, 140
survivance, 47, 60, 66, 73–74, 194

A Tale for the Time Being (Ozeki), 1, 2–3, 21, 187–194; agency in, 190, 193; circular temporality of, 168, 191–192; Internet in, 190–192; the past in, 194; "Ruth Ozeki" in, 192–193; securitization in, 189; temporality in, 190–191; time in, 167
Tales of the South Pacific (Michener), 19, 25–26; Asian female body in, 51; "Fo' Dolla," 36–37, 38; interracial intimacy in, 37, 43, 45, 54; Melanesians in, 38–39, 40; as military propaganda, 36; racial liberalism of, 36–37, 38–39, 40, 42; securitization and, 54; "Those Who Fraternize," 37, 39–40
Tang, Eric, 78
Teaiwa, Teresia, 6, 70, 204n24; on Asian prosperity, 104; militourism, 13, 43; on Pacific as empty space, 27
technology: futurity and, 162; indigenous, 169, 173; modernity and, 187; political organizing and, 184–186; progress and, 163, 168; race as, 29; sea, 44; in Star Waka, 169, 173–175; temporality and, 168; territorialization and, 29; time and, 21, 172–173

techno-orientalism, 167; dystopic, 187
temporality, 59; cyclical, 85; in *Gangster We Are All Looking For*, 85; Indigenous, 191; oceanic, 58, 190; progressive, 109, 166-168; refugee, 78, 86-87; settler colonial, 165-168, 189-190; in *Tale for the Time Being*, 190; technology and, 168; of trauma, 81. *See also* time
Tengan, Ty Kāwika, 141
Tepania, Waata, 30
Te Punga Somerville, Alice, 6, 10, 204n24; oceanic world view, 207n23; on *whakapapa*, 47
terra nullius, 27; Mauna Kea as, 163-164, 221n9
territoriality, 59
territorialization: deterritorialization, 20, 58-59, 64, 89, 94, 96; of ocean space, 26, 28-31, 54; reterritorialization, 29, 59, 94; settler colonialism and, 78; technology and, 29
Thaman, Konai Helu, 20, 114-115, 178, 193, 204n24, 216n75; environment in, 120-122; gender in, 118-119; on Indigenous knowledge, 123-125; reciprocity in, 120; *vā* in, 117, 122-123. Poems: "Langakali," 120-122, 124; "They Won't Leave," 119-120; "Women's Lib," 118-119, 121; "A Working Relative," 119, 120
Thirty Meter Telescope (TMT) protests, 162-165, 176, 195
time: in *China Men*, 108-109; labor time, 108-109; oceanic, 21, 49-50; in *Ocean Roads*, 39, 49-50; progress and, 49, 221n15; settler time, 165-168; spiralic, 17, 169-170, 172, 205n52; in *Tale for the Time Being*, 167; technology and, 21, 172-173
Tong, Anote, 71-72
Tonga: political independence of, 10, 99; remittance economy of, 114, 116, 120; Tu'i Tonga, 114-115; *vā* and, 117, 122-123
Tongans: circular migration of, 114; remittances, 114, 120
trans-, 4-5, 203n10
transnationalism, 2; in Asian American studies, 3
transnational studies: settler colonialism and, 4
transpacific: appropriation of, 224n5; decolonial genealogy of, 199; futurity, 21, 160, 162, 168-170, 188-189; origins of term, 13-14; use of term, 4
transpacific discourse: liberal turn in, 35
transpacific studies: Indigenous Pacific in, 6-9; oceanic turn in, 3

Trask, Haunani-Kay, 155, 204n24, 218n18, 220n82; on citizenship, 217n4; on settler colonialism, 135
trauma: in *Gangster We Are All Looking For*, 85; melancholia and, 212n77; militarization and, 45; in *Ocean Roads*, 46-47; refugee, 88; temporality of, 81
Truman Proclamation, 29, 30, 32-33, 55
Trust Territory of the Pacific Islands (TTPI), 24-25, 41-42
Tuck, Eve, 8
Tu'i Tonga, 114-115
Tuvalu, 69; climate leadership of, 68, 71

unincorporated territories, U.S., 180-181
United Nations Climate Change Conference, 72
United Nations Convention on the Laws of the Sea (UNCLOS), 24-25, 55
universalism: of capitalism, 97, 101-103; of "Pacific Rim," 12; race and, 209n4; refugees and, 209n11

vā, 115-116, 149, 216n68; in Thaman, 117, 122-123
Va'ai, Sina, 118
Vaka'uta, Lingikoni, 71
van Dijck, José, 180
Vang, Ma, 64
Vietnam: decolonization of, 24
Vietnam War: as "good war," 80; periodization of, 81
violence: abstract symbolic, 94-95; of climate change, 67-68; colonial, 34, 39, 43, 53, 154; gendered, 43; imperialist, 62, 83; masculinity and, 142; militarized, 19, 53; of plantation system, 129; racialized, 43, 129, 133; settler colonial, 153, 155
visibility: of Asians, 41, 207n30; of Pacific Islanders, 35-36; of Pacific Ocean, 5; of race, 33
Vizenor, Gerald, 47

wardship, 41-42
Warren, Joyce Pualani, 156
Weaver, Jace, 6
weaving: as praxis, 205n52; trope of, 17
Webber, Sophie, 70, 77
Wendt, Albert, 21, 178, 203n2
whakapapa, 47, 149, 165; in *Star Waka*, 173-174
whiteness: Asian proximity to, 39, 51; in Australia, 40-41, 43, 45; colonialism and, 35; hybridization of, 35; militarization and, 45; in New Zealand, 45

white possession, 39–40, 208n50, 214n100, 218n23; American expansionism and, 40–41; modernity as, 167
Whitman, Walt, 162
Wiener, Norbert, 174
Wilson, Rob, 12, 15, 43, 134; on Pacific poets, 175–176
Wilson-Hokowhitu, Nālani, 165
Wood, Briar, 118, 121
Wood, Houston, 132
Woodward, Valerie, 222n61
World War II (Pacific War): as "good war," 23

Yamanaka, Lois-Ann, 20–21, 126; agency in, 143–144, 146–147; female body in, 143; Filipino men in, 144–145; local bodies in, 129; on Obama, 132–133; "ugly feelings" in, 145. Works: *Blu's Hanging*, 144, 146–147, 219n55, 219n63; *Father of the Four Passages*, 146–147; "Parts," 143–146, 157
Yang, K. Wayne, 8
Yoneyama, Lisa, 204n23, 224n5
Yoo, Hyon-Joo, 204n17

ERIN SUZUKI is an Assistant Professor of Literature at the University of California, San Diego.

www.ingramcontent.com/pod-product-compliance
Lightning Source LLC
Chambersburg PA
CBHW022011300426
44117CB00005B/127